ENERGY AND SECURITY

A REPORT OF HARVARD'S ENERGY AND SECURITY RESEARCH PROJECT

Written under the auspices of the Center for Science and International Affairs, the Energy and Environmental Policy Center, and the Center for International Affairs, Harvard University.

ENERGY AND SECURITY

Edited by

DAVID A. DEESE
JOSEPH S. NYE

BALLINGER PUBLISHING COMPANY
Cambridge, Massachusetts
A Subsidiary of Harper & Row, Publishers, Inc.

Copyright © 1981 by Ballinger Publishing Company. All rights reserved. No part of this publication may be reproduced, stored in a retrieval system, or transmitted in any form or by any means, electronic, mechanical, photocopy, recording or otherwise, without the prior written consent of the publisher.

International Standard Book Number: ISBN 0-88410-640-3

Library of Congress Catalog Card Number: 80-19922

Printed in the United States of America

Library of Congress Cataloging in Publication Data

Main entry under title:

Energy and security.

"A report of Harvard's Energy and Security Research Project, John F. Kennedy School of Government."
Includes index
1. Energy policy—United States—Congresses. 2. Energy policy—Congresses. I. Deese, David A. II. Nye, Joseph S.
HD9502.U52E454   333.79'0973   80-19922
ISBN 0-88410-640-3

CONTENTS

LIST OF FIGURES

LIST OF TABLES

FOREWORD

The vulnerability of industrialized nations to oil supply interruptions has never been more clear. The Iranian revolution and the armed conflict between Iraq and Iran underscore the strategic implications of depending too much on others for energy supplies.

The relationships between energy, economic growth, and national security are complex. Energy issues are necessarily intertwined with other domestic and international policy concerns, making both the problem and the potential solutions often difficult to define and assess.

But the energy problem did not arrive overnight. Our dependence, and that of our allies, on oil grew rapidly following World War II because oil was inexpensive, relatively abundant, easily accessible, and reliable. Our economies were geared to it. That affected our capital stock, which became increasingly less energy efficient; our patterns of residential and industrial location, which became more sprawling; and the evolution of our transportation system, which grew to meet individual and not necessarily society's needs.

The post World War II path of development is changing, brought about by new energy realities. The nations in the Organization of Petroleum Exporting Countries (OPEC) have emerged as the supreme powers in setting oil production policies, and thus prices. At the same time, the ability of the consuming nations to influence the course of events in the vital Middle East, particularly the Persian Gulf, has waned. As a result, major oil consumers have lost market power to OPEC and exposed themselves to the potentially disastrous consequences of major supply disruptions. For those reasons, industrialized nations now place excessive oil import dependence at the top of the list of major concerns and issues.

The problem is not insoluble, but it is complex and requires the commitment of many nations acting together and on their own to achieve three fundamental goals. First, oil imports must be reduced through aggressive conservation efforts and realistic energy prices. Second, domestic energy resources must be developed and used to the fullest extent possible consistent with other national goals. And third, national and international contingency plans, including stockpiles of oil, must be developed to assure an adequate individual and collective response to unreasonable market pressures and supply interruptions.

The benefits of collective actions are large, but the mechanisms to bring them about are difficult. And we cannot expect significant progress in the absence of common understanding of our vulnerability and the consequences of failing to act.

Energy and Security makes a major contribution toward achieving that critical understanding. It is a thought-provoking guide on how industrialized nations can reduce their vulnerability and, by doing so, contribute to a more energy secure world.

John C. Sawhill
Deputy Secretary
U.S. Department of Energy
October 1, 1980

PREFACE

There has always been talk about energy as a national security issue, but little effective action. In the United States, Western Europe, and Japan, energy policies have frequently been justified with vague references to national security. Security analysts have long acknowledged the importance of energy, but current concerns have focused almost exclusively on resource distribution as an element of a nation's power. The problem of energy and security has remained undefined and misunderstood, and nations continue to stand almost blindly hostage to a threat of major proportions.

The war between Iran and Iraq starkly confirms this threat. As of this writing, no one can be sure of the depth or duration of this conflict. Even if this war does not cut off the 40 percent of Western oil consumption that comes from the Persian Gulf, it again highlights the serious possibility of such a disruption in the 1980s. The recommendations in the chapters that follow are all the more urgent in light of this possibility.

A year and a half ago, senior faculty and researchers at Harvard University decided to address this issue by drawing together experts from the energy, security, and foreign policy fields. First we convened a small group to consider the most likely sources of oil supply interruptions and the list of urgent U.S. preparations. These intensive sessions included Alvin Alm, Francis Bator, Albert Carnesale, David Deese, William Hogan, Henry Lee, Michael Nacht, Joseph Nye, and

Thomas Schelling. At the same time, Deese and Nye launched the research project, including a series of seminars that helped to map the central issues. Presentations were made by Alvin Alm, John Deutch, Marshall Goldman, William Griffith, William Hogan, Munemichi Inoue, Henry Jacoby, Geoffrey Kemp, Kunisada Kume, Linda Miller, Ted Moran, Daniel Poneman, Gary Samore, Herbert Sawyer, Thomas Teisberg, Ernest Wilson, and Agatha Wong. Many others participated in the seminar series.

On the basis of these sessions and ongoing research, the book design was completed and detailed research papers were commissioned. Authors presented early drafts to a group of outside reviewers in May 1980 for in-depth critique. This workshop developed a wealth of material from a number of important contributors to our efforts: Francis Bator, Robert Bowie, Albert Carnesale, Loren Cox, John Deutch, Paul Doty, Charles Ebinger, Henry Jacoby, Richard Kessler, Henry Lee, Ted Marmor, Ted Moran, A. J. Meyer, Barry Posen, Henry Rowen, Herbert Sawyer, Thomas Schelling, John Stewart, Raymond Vernon, Ernest Wilson, David Wood, and Daniel Yergin. The draft chapters were then revised several more times, building on comments by the editors and additional reviewers.

We benefited from parallel studies conducted at MIT and Stanford University. The work of Henry Jacoby, Thomas Neff and others at MIT provided strong background in the world oil markets. Henry Rowen, John Weyant, Susan Missner, and others at Stanford contributed through their work on many similar and complementary questions.

We relied on important support from three unique centers at Harvard University. The Center for Science and International Affairs in the John F. Kennedy School of Government, directed by Paul Doty, and its associate director Albert Carnesale were central to our efforts. We worked closely with William Hogan's Energy and Environmental Policy Center (EEPC), also in the Kennedy School. We also benefited greatly from the support of Henry Lee, Executive Director of the EEPC, and Samuel Huntington, Director of the Center for International Affairs.

Our study was facilitated by a grant from the U.S. Department of Energy and the support of many of its offices and officials. We are in debt to the continuous assistance of John Stewart and William Taylor.

The project could not have been completed without the enthusiastic and professional efforts of Barbara Kates-Garnick, the principal research assistant, and additional research assistance from E. Michael Schafer, Carol Thorn, Allen Jebson, Mark Spitz, Mark Brown, and Bishara Bahbah. Our editorial team included Richard Bertelson, who offered invaluable advice and met an extremely tight schedule; Sylvia Seiferman; and Carol Franco at Ballinger, who provided amazingly consistent and professional support over several months.

Valerie Grasso did a highly professional job of coordinating a wide range of administrative tasks from the smooth running of the seminar series to the preparation of several drafts of this volume. Michelle Marcouiller also contributed administrative and editorial support at key points during the project.

October 15, 1980   David A. Deese
Cambridge, Massachusetts   Joseph S. Nye

ENERGY AS A SECURITY PROBLEM

1 ENERGY AND SECURITY

Joseph S. Nye

When the seventies began, Americans imported 3.5 million barrels of oil a day, about one quarter of our needs. The price was about $2 per barrel and we were the largest oil producer in the world. Three years earlier, we had easily foiled an attempted oil embargo triggered by the June War. But by the end of that distressing decade, we were importing 8.5 million barrels per day—nearly half our needs—at fifteen times the price charged only a few years before, and domestic oil production was in decline. The painful 1973 Arab oil embargo seemed to have taught us nothing when the Iranian Revolution curtailed production in 1979. President Carter did not exaggerate when he called the situation "a clear and present danger to our national security."

Today, nearly two-fifths of the oil consumed by the free world's economy is vulnerable to terrorism, accident, warfare, and extortion. The sudden loss of Persian Gulf oil for a year could stagger the world's economy, disrupt it, devastate it, like no event since the Great Depression of the 1930s. The Congressional Budget Office estimates that the loss of Saudi Arabian oil for a year would cost the United States $272 billion, increase the unemployment rate 2 percent, and boost the already worrisome inflation rate by 20 percentage points. And costs to our allies would be even greater. According to another estimate, a 9 million barrel per day cutback of Saudi oil for a year would slash our GNP 5 percent, the European GNP 7 percent, and the Japanese GNP 8 percent. The loss of *all* Persian Gulf oil would cut our GNP 13 percent; Europe's, 22 percent; and Japan's, 25 percent (Congressional Budget Office 1980; Rowen 1980; see also Department of Energy 1980). Of course, these estimates are only approximations, and they could be overstated. But even if they are twice as high as they should be, the potential economic costs of major supply interruptions are clearly terrifying.

So is the threat to our foreign policy. Since the end of World War II, American strategy has focused on the defense of Europe and Japan, the two greatest concentrations of economic power outside the United States and the Soviet Union. The prosperity and strength of the democratic alliance has been central to the postwar balance of power. But today this balance could be upset by the stress and strain that energy security problems pose to Western prosperity and the solidarity of our alliances. The vulnerable and volatile Middle East is outside the scope of our formal alliance frameworks. Moreover, coordination of domestic economic and energy policies among democracies with different interests is bound to be particularly difficult.

In fact, differences in our allies' vulnerability to energy disruptions present the Soviets—and others—with better opportunities to disrupt Western alliances than direct military threats. Europeans and Japanese, for example, might respond positively to Soviet offers to guarantee energy supplies, even though we would argue that such steps would legitimize Soviet influence over these regions' economic lifeline. Western policy toward Israel shows a similar tendency to reflect different degrees of economic exposure to Arab wrath. Other foreign policy costs include the temptation to trade sensitive nuclear technology for oil supplies—witness Italy's relations with Iraq—and the problems of managing the world economy as well as preserving stability in crucial but economically fragile allies such as Turkey when oil prices rise precipitously. These foreign policy costs are not susceptible to numerical statement, but their magnitude can be judged by speculating about the resources that we would spend to avoid them.

Our concern about military security leads us to spend $150 billion yearly on military forces, the largest part of which is devoted to strengthening the North Atlantic Treaty Organization (NATO). Important as these expenditures are, the probability of Soviet tanks rolling across the North German plain is much lower than the likelihood of an interruption of oil supplies stemming from various conflicts in the Middle East. Yet our energy plans and our diplomatic strategy do not reflect those probabilities. We are far less prepared for an energy emergency than for a military attack.

In the face of our growing exposure to these economic, political, and military dangers, we Americans have not yet risen to the challenge. "Consider this anomaly," noted *The Washington Post* early in 1980, "The president and a great many more Americans are prepared to talk openly of war to secure the oil routes out of the Gulf. But neither the president nor many others are ready to impose a tax on gasoline to diminish imports that, everyone agrees, constitute a clear and present danger to the national security" (*The Washington Post* 1980). Yes, the president did propose a modest import fee, but it was rejected by the Congress. The sad truth is that many government actions taken after 1973 — domestic price controls for instance — have actually made our situation worse. Unwilling to allow rising prices to benefit some Americans while penalizing others, we have squabbled among ourselves and followed policies that have let our society's burden grow. Our dependence on oil imports increased 25 percent between 1973 and 1979, and our overall energy security diminished. We *talked* the high rhetoric of energy security but our policies belied our words.

Why have we not done better? Our policy performance reflected public attitudes and misunderstandings. For one thing, the public has persistently refused to believe in an oil shortage. In 1979, "as gasoline lines grew longer, the belief that the energy crisis is contrived became more prevalent." In February 1980, 41 percent of Gallup poll respondents believed the United States was self-sufficient in energy, and other polls showed the public expecting solar and nuclear energy to replace oil as the principal sources of energy in six to ten years (Schneider 1980: 153–156).

These attitudes reflect reality in an odd, distorted way. It is true that the energy problem is not one of absolute shortage. Even conservative estimates maintain that Saudi Arabia and Kuwait have reserve-to-production ratios of fifty to seventy-five years. And domestic alternative energy sources can be developed well within that time. Thus, in July 1973, the London *Economist* labeled the problem a "phony oil crisis" (*The Economist* 1973). Many eminent economists argued that the 1973 oil price rises would solve themselves by constraining demand and calling forth additional supply that would lead to the collapse of OPEC. A Nobel Laureate predicted that the cartel could not last at prices above $10 per barrel. If the world had no friction or politics, all might be right.

These unrealistic views infected our policy in the mid-seventies. Our diplomacy focused on negotiating a $7 per barrel price *floor* to protect alternative energy sources against falling oil prices. We pressed Saudi Arabia to moderate prices by holding auctions and increasing its productive capacity toward 20 million barrels per day, even though this would make us more dependent on the Persian Gulf. And we did little to increase our military posture. Instead, we began talks on Indian Ocean arms control. American political-military policy and energy policy were poorly related. The "Vietnam Syndrome" had its effect, but we also listened too much to economists who told us that international energy policy would take care of itself.

It didn't. So today—nearly a decade after the first warning signals—we still need a coherent policy for energy security. But devising a strategy and thinking about energy as a security problem is not as simple as it first seems; any judgment about security is necessarily complex. Security is a matter of degree, and how much insurance one needs in order to feel secure is a function of the probability of the threatening event and the magnitude of the potential damage. Damages can be defined narrowly, in terms of survival, or broadly, in terms of a whole range of values including welfare, independence, status, and power. We generally speak of national security as the absence of threat to a broad range of values in addition to survival. Indeed, some national security policies, such as our possession of nuclear weapons, may increase the risk to simple survival in order to deter threats to our other values. Similarly, energy security is only part of national security; in some circumstances we would risk energy supplies for other values we consider part of our national security.

Looking back at American policies for energy security in the 1970s, we are struck by two strong ironies. First, we talked about energy security, but some of the policies that followed the talk actually made us more insecure. Second, we acted as though government controls at home and market forces abroad would solve our energy security problems when the opposite was closer to the truth. We failed to recognize the changing realities of world politics that eroded the international regime that once governed oil transactions. In the 1970s, our energy security policies reflected an under-reliance on economic remedies domestically and an over-reliance on them internationally. The first step toward sound policies for the 1980s must be a better understanding of the international political context.

THE DECLINE OF THE INTERNATIONAL OIL REGIME

In 1970, world oil was still generally governed by a loose international regime which might be described as "guided laissez-faire." It had two essential characteristics. First, price and production decisions were made largely by major international oil companies for their own commercial reasons. Second, the major powers — particularly the United States and Britain — occasionally intervened diplomatically to guarantee these companies access to oil. Thus, for example, the United States pressed diplomatically in 1943 to ensure access to Middle East oil; again in 1950, to ensure the companies' position in Saudi Arabia; and in 1954, to assume broadened access to the Iranian oil that had been boycotted by the companies during nationalization by Mossadegh. With few exceptions, these governing arrangements were stable and accepted. There seemed to be no real alternative.

As a result of this regime, oil prices and production levels tended to reflect supply and demand conditions in major consumer countries rather than oil's expected long-term scarcity value or the political interests of producing countries. As low-cost Middle East oil became more plentiful in the postwar period, most of the difference in value between its low production cost and the high price of alternative energy sources went to consumers in the form of low and declining oil prices.

Under these favorable conditions, the United States and other major consuming nations devoted little time or attention to developing a coherent energy security policy. Even Europeans and Japanese, with a longer tradition of thinking about oil as a security problem, were lulled into increasing their dependence on Middle East oil. Supply seemed assured by a Pax Americana that was enforced by occasional diplomatic assurances and by antitrust measures promoting a modicum of effective competition.

But dramatic changes were in the offing. By the end of the 1970s, prices and production levels were being set by producer governments rather than by the international oil companies, and for political as well as commercial motives. These decisions were difficult to predict because they did not follow stable or recognizable rules. Now, producers rather than consumers were capturing a large part of the difference between the low costs of production and the higher costs of possible replacements for Middle East oil. Increasingly constrained international oil companies found that their assured access to crude oil under predictable long-term contracts had diminished. Moreover, guarantees of access and oversight of price and production decisions had become widely regarded as absolute sovereign prerogatives of producer governments.

Why did such a remarkable change occur over the course of a decade? Basically, because of longer term trends in the underlying structure of power. In 1960, six of the thirteen present OPEC members were colonies or protectorates, and the key straits of Hormuz, Aden, and Malacca were under European control. As decolonization proceeded, Western dominance of the producing countries diminished. The rise of nationalism in the producer countries also made Western intervention more controversial and costly—witness events in Iran in 1953 and 1979.

In military terms, the British withdrawal from the Persian Gulf in 1971 was a major turning point. America's reaction to the Vietnam War made it certain that the United States would neither replace the British, as it had in the Eastern Mediterranean in 1947, nor fully counter increasing Soviet military capabilities in the area. Instead, the United States sought to fill the power vacuum in the Gulf by building up the Shah of Iran as the local leviathan. This policy allowed policing of the Gulf "without any American resources" (Kissinger 1979: 1265). At least in terms of annual budgets, it seemed we were buying energy security on the cheap; but the fall of the Shah eventually revealed the true costs to America's energy security policy.

In addition to these general political and military changes, were changes in the structure of power in the oil issue. A turning point came with the loss of the American oil surplus after 1971. U.S. production peaked, and America's dependence on imports began to increase. The power to balance the market in a time of crisis passed from the United States to OPEC, particularly Saudi Arabia. No longer did America have the spare capacity to supply its allies when oil flows were interrupted for political reasons, as it had at the time of the Suez Crisis in 1956 and the June War in 1967.

The relative power of the oil companies and of the producer governments also shifted radically. Consistent with longer standing patterns in the relations between multinational corporations and less developed countries, original bargains became obsolete and contracts "renegotiable" as the host countries gradually developed their indigenous capabilities. This trend was accelerated by the entry of new independent oil firms into the world oil markets in the fifties and sixties. Eager to gain access to crude oil, their competition with the established majors increased the options and enhanced the bargaining power of the producer country governments.

Initially, the increased production by the new entrants forced the price of oil down, and producer governments tried to maintain revenue levels by increasing production. Ironically, in 1959, the United States reacted to the falling prices by imposing protectionist quotas that exacerbated the problem of glut in world markets, increased the resentment of producer governments, and contributed to the creation of OPEC. But it was not until the oil market tightened for other reasons that OPEC proved effective in raising prices.

The developments of the 1970s occurred in three major steps, with political events acting as catalysts in the political-economy education of the producer countries. At the beginning of the seventies, the closing of the Suez Canal and the destruction of a pipeline allowed the new revolutionary regime in Libya to capitalize on its geographical location and the weak position of the independent companies by extracting a price increase. Libya's success in turn triggered a similar demand upon the major oil companies by Persian Gulf producers. Eager for political harmony, the U.S. government did not support the companies (Sampson 1975). In this first halting step toward today's energy market, the Middle East producers learned that they could threaten the major oil companies with nationalization and shutdown without incurring serious penalties from the Western powers.

The second step was larger. Resentful of America's resupply of Israel during the October 1973 Arab–Israeli war, Arab producers cut production 25 percent. Although OPEC had planned to increase prices 70 percent to reflect the tightening markets caused by increased U.S. imports, the embargo and cutback had unexpected success. It created a scarcity and panic in world markets which drove prices for marginal quantities to extraordinary levels and allowed Iran to lead the other OPEC states in a 400 percent increase over prewar prices (Penrose 1975: 50). Essentially, the political catalyst of war taught oil producers the value of cutbacks and indicated that the long-run price of oil might be much higher than they had believed.

This lesson was reinforced by the third step—the Iranian Revolution in 1979—which curtailed oil production and showed that even uncoordinated cutbacks can have large effects on price. In addition, some producers concluded that exceedingly high oil revenues had helped erode the Shah's regime and that production cutbacks might make domestic political as well as economic sense.

The result is that control over prices, production, and, to an increasing extent, distribution channels, has largely passed to OPEC countries. Historically, OPEC price increases have generally reflected market tightness more than the accompanying political rhetoric suggests, but economic motives are hardly the only considerations that influence OPEC behavior. Although economics can tell us a lot about demand in energy markets, it tells us only part of the story about supply in a world of sovereign states. Production decisions are made on a national basis and often reflect domestic political conflicts and decisions about matters as diverse as development plans, desirable social trends, and external events. For example, following the Camp David Agreement of 1979, Saudi Arabia's political decision to reduce production to 8.5 million barrels per day contributed greatly to the market's turbulence. Earlier, the Saudi's had helped replace Iranian oil in the market so their reversal shook assumptions about future production levels. A panic buildup of stocks in a tight market resulted, driving prices to record levels (see Stobaugh and Yergin 1980 and Nissen 1980).

Production decisions are also affected by prior investments in capacity that may reflect earlier domestic political considerations. It appears that Saudi slowness in developing capacity a few years ago may have been designed to avoid U.S. pressure for higher production, which would have been embarrassing in intra-Arab politics. Current reported Saudi efforts to increase capacity toward 12 million barrels per day might be interpreted as an effort to regain pre-eminence in oil markets. But we do not fully know the determinants of Saudi behavior. Revenue needs and foreign policy positions provide clues, but it may be that oil production decisions really reflect shifts in coalitions within the royal family or efforts to minimize the family's sense of domestic and international political pressure.

Nor can we be certain about the domestic politics of other producing states. Reserves and revenue needs are only part of the political story. Mexican production, for example, should probably increase on the basis of economic needs, but rates of increase reflect internal politics. In fact, Mexicans worry that too rapid growth of oil exports will create inflation and a high-priced industrial structure unable to export other goods and unable to ease their massive unemployment problem. Similar political arguments over economically and socially desirable production levels occur in such developed allies as Norway and Britain.

A few years ago it was widely assumed that OPEC production would climb toward 40 million barrels per day in the 1980s, and that tight markets would not be a problem until the latter half of the decade. Current conventional wisdom, expressed in the International Energy Agency (IEA) and elsewhere, says otherwise: that OPEC production will not rise much above the late 1970s level of 30 million barrels per day and that it may even be lower. The IEA sees growing demand encountering lowered OPEC production with a notional gap of 2 million barrels per day in 1985 and 5 million barrels per day in 1990 (International Energy Agency 1980). Even if these predictions of a tightening market prove wrong, a softer market would not remove the danger of production cutbacks due to revolutions, accidents, or sabotage beyond the producer's control.[1] If we again ignore the political fact that production decisions are controlled by the producer governments, we may be condemned to repeating the costly cycle of disruption raising prices; high prices causing reduced consumption; prices softening; crisis; and severely disruptive price increases again. Faced with risk and uncertainty about production decisions, we should be skeptical about all projections and carry plenty of insurance!

In summary, the loose regime that once governed the oil market broke down in the 1970s under the influence of catalytic political

---

1. William Brown and Herman Kahn, for example, predict soft markets "barring wars, insurrections, or replays of the Iran debacle . . ." (1980: 67–68).

events and long-term shifts of power, not because of OPEC's formation or because of market forces alone. The chances of our creating a regime that is more satisfactory to us will be very low so long as we consumers remain politically divided, militarily weak, and economically dependent on unstable oil-producing states. For the foreseeable future, our world is one of political uncertainty with unpredictable prices, renegotiable contracts, and the lurking threat of disruptive interruptions.

PITFALLS

There are at least five important pitfalls to avoid in designing an energy security policy. Many of our past policy and analytic efforts have fallen into one or another of them.

Thinking of the United States in Isolation.   Even if we reduce our own vulnerability to oil imports, we will remain at risk to supply interruptions because of our interdependence with allies who are less able to reduce their dependence on imports. Nixon's "Project Independence," which aimed at eliminating our imports by 1980, was doomed to ultimate failure because it diverted our attention from the broader dimension of the problem. Nor will this situation change quickly. If Japan's ambitious energy program is successful, that nation will still depend on oil imports for half its energy needs in 1990.

Turning to Western Hemisphere sources of oil to reduce our dependence on the Middle East will not solve our energy security problem either. We are committed under an IEA agreement to share all available oil in times of emergency. And if there were no oil-sharing agreement, or if it failed to work, Japan and Germany would still be forced to bid even higher prices for whatever oil was available on the world market. The net effect of failing to cooperate would be higher costs to all: higher oil prices, foreign policy costs, and disarray within our alliances. Clearly, we cannot think of the United States in isolation.

Equating Imports and Vulnerability.   All too often the American energy policy debate has focused on import reduction to the exclusion of all other necessary measures. But the extent of our energy security cannot be measured only in terms of imports. Although imports are an important factor in the security equation, the cost and effectiveness of measures to reduce consumption, increase domestic production, exploit alternative sources, and build stockpiles are essential to any sound evaluation and solution of our predicament.[2]

In the case of most commodities, we tolerate some dependence while insuring ourselves against supply interruptions by maintaining multiple sources and stockpiles. Our degree of vulnerability in these cases depends not only on the level of imports but also upon the other instruments and policies available. So it is with oil. Reducing our energy vulnerability requires reducing our extremely high level of imports while also putting other remedies in place. These remedies, once established, will allow us a certain amount of import dependence without leaving us vulnerable. The larger the insurance policy, the larger the tolerable level of imports.

Confusing the Time Scale. Too often over the past decade, disputes about energy policy have been unnecessary and unfruitful because participants confuse different time horizons. It helps to sort energy security problems into short-term issues (inside two years), intermediate-term problems (two to ten years), and long-term considerations (beyond a decade) as Table 1–1 illustrates. These categories are rough and the remedies overlap. But they show us that oil will remain at the heart of the energy security problem for the next decade. Synthetic, nuclear, and solar programs have long lead times and can only offer us secondary help in the short and intermediate terms.

Table 1–1. Time horizons and energy security problems.

	Time	*Dominant Problem*	*Major Solutions*
Short term	2 years	How to cope with potential oil supply interruptions	Stockpiles, demand restraint
Intermediate term	2 to 10 years	How to reduce dependence on Persian Gulf oil	Conservation, coal, gas, non–OPEC oil
Long term	10 years or more	How to adjust to higher priced alternatives	As above, plus synthetic fuels and energy from nuclear and solar power

2. For a detailed discussion, see Robert Keohane and Joseph Nye (1977).

Even if the U.S. and Japanese nuclear programs proceed as now planned, they will provide only about 10 percent of total primary energy in each country by 1990. Only the French have a nuclear program with any immediate promise; it could increase its contribution to the national energy supply from a current level of 5 percent to 20 percent by 1985 (Harsch 1980). Of course, our current nuclear plants can produce some extra electrical capacity in the short run. But such programs should not be confused with the major measures such as stockpiles which do the most to solve the short-run problems.

Similarly, it is estimated that the ambitious U.S. synthetic fuels program may produce around 1 million barrels per day (6 percent of current oil consumption) by 1990. This projection does not mean that efforts to create alternatives are irrelevant to energy security; on the contrary, it indicates eventual limits to oil price increases, which in fact in turn has some moderating effect on current prices by reducing the value of oil still in the ground. But whatever the long-term values, a dollar invested in synthetics is worth much less in the short run than a dollar invested in stockpiles.

Neglecting Security of Supply. Over the last ten years, our energy policy has focused on preventing price rises and has ignored the influence of price on security of supply. In our effort to protect consumers from world prices, we encouraged consumption and actually increased our dependence on imports. Similarly, our diplomatic efforts in the late 1970s were designed to get Persian Gulf states to produce more and moderate OPEC prices. But this made us more dependent on Persian Gulf oil, as we discovered to our regret in 1979. Price and security considerations sometimes work in opposite directions; we sometimes have to accept higher prices for security purposes. Some actions that raise prices—filling the strategic reserve for instance—also increase our security. And moreover, as prices rise, conservation increases.

This is not to say that high oil prices are unimportant. Quite clearly they are, and efforts to moderate the price of oil are important because they can prevent instability in the international banking system and mitigate national financial problems like those now being suffered by Turkey and Jamaica. A Department of Energy study estimates that the annual cost to the U.S. economy of high and uncertain world oil prices runs in the range of $20 to $30 billion (Department of Energy 1980). But large as these price effects are, they would have to continue for ten years before they equalled the costs of a major interruption. And in fact, the largest price increases have been precipitated by the 1973 and 1979 supply crises. A sensible policy would be to seek price moderation, but not at the cost of forgetting the primary dangers and costs of major interruptions.

Dreaming of Quick Fixes and Single Solutions.   A final pitfall in thinking about energy security is imagining that there is some easy way to solve our problems. Unfortunately, the broad issue of energy security will be with us well into the coming decade or longer. During the past ten years, proposals have been made to invade the oil fields, "break" OPEC, nationalize the oil companies, set up a new international organization, produce synthetic fuels, and so forth. None of these proposals is a complete and realistic solution. Although some could be vital elements of a long-term strategy, others merely divert our attention.

DRAMATIC POLITICAL ALTERNATIVES

Attractive though they might at first appear, the quick fixes and dramatic political solutions all suffer from flaws.

Political-Military Coercion.   Given the political limits of the international market, some analysts have urged that we take over the Persian Gulf oilfields (see, for example, Tucker 1975). They argue that the global (and national) costs of continued acquiescence to cartel price rises are so high that they merit a change in our frame of reference — that they justify military intervention, or "internationalization."

The political and economic costs of such a remedy, however, are likely to be extremely high. First, the risk of destroying the oil infrastructure through fighting or sabotage could *create* one of the major costly disruptions that good energy security policy is supposed to avert. Second, there is little prospect for establishing the international legitimacy of what would inevitably be characterized as a new colonial occupation. Our foreign policy could be severely disrupted. Third, unless the situation approaches what Kissinger termed "strangulation," it is uncertain how long the American public would support any occupation, particularly if less questionable alternatives had not been attempted first. How many lives are worth a few minutes saved in a gasoline line?

Nevertheless, an enhanced defense posture in the Middle East is certainly a good energy investment. The ability to deter Soviet intervention and to protect quickly those who ask for our assistance are important assets in the complex diplomacy of oil. But force alone is not a sufficient strategy.

"Break OPEC."   Some analysts believe that efforts to break OPEC are appropriate, given the enormous gap between the cost of producing Persian Gulf oil and what they consider its artificially maintained cartel price. A variety of cartel-busting schemes have been suggested, ranging from food-export embargoes to governmental purchasing in sealed-bid auctions (House of Representatives 1979).

There are several problems with this "solution." Today, OPEC is not the basic cause of high prices. OPEC as an organization has never succeeded in controlling production rates; that is in the sovereign control of producer states. The fundamental problem is that cheap oil is scarce and concentrated within the borders of a very few states while alternatives to oil are expensive and take time to exploit. Producers have learned the benefits of oligopolist pricing and limiting production; successful oligopoly behavior does not require organization. It is unlikely that producers would forget this lesson even if OPEC disappeared tomorrow.

According to some estimates, at current high prices key Persian Gulf countries could cut production by some 40 percent without bringing their revenues below the value of their current imports. Saudi Arabia is the key country because it can by itself *increase* its revenues by *reducing* production. Yet in 1979, Saudi Arabia produced more than its stated target and sold its oil for less than its OPEC partners. It is an odd cartel whose members produce more than their revenue needs in order to dampen their partners' price rises.

In a tight market, a sealed-bid auction is unlikely to result in lower prices. On the contrary, if such producers as Saudi Arabia retaliated by refusing to bid, such a device might result in *higher* prices. Similarly, efforts to embargo or to limit food shipments would fail in the face of alternative sources of food supplies. And they might well trigger expensive retaliation.

Efforts to "break OPEC" are likely to be costly in the other ways as well. They would almost certainly cause friction with our European allies and Japan, who feel too vulnerable to engage in such economic brinksmanship. In particular, exacerbating the already burdened U.S.–Saudi relationship would be costly to our foreign policy as well as to our energy security.

Government Control of Purchasing. While efforts to "break OPEC" may not work, it is sometimes argued that consumers could at least organize to reduce the producers' ability to use the multinational oil companies as their "tax collectors." According to this line of reasoning, government control of oil purchasing would make it more difficult for producer countries to play off one company against another to bid up prices, and would bring the full bargaining power of our government to bear directly on oil price decisions. After all, government-to-government dealings are increasing in oil markets; even our allies have government corporations. We must follow suit to keep our position of power in the game.

One could postulate stronger and milder variants of this approach. A sole government purchasing corporation would strengthen the buyer's power, but it would mean the creation of another large government bureaucracy subject to various domestic political pressures. A competing government import corporation without exclusive import powers could serve as a yardstick for the performance of other importers, and it would provide an instrument in countries where we wish to bring a U.S. government presence to the bargaining table. A still milder variant would leave purchasing in the hands of existing companies but would require them to receive approval from the secretary of energy before they paid more than a designated price.

None of these approaches would appear to have much effect on price when markets are tight, nor would they enhance security of supply. France, for example, did not obtain significantly more or cheaper oil in 1979 as a result of its government-to-government purchasing deals. In a tight market, why should the bargaining power of a consumer government be much greater than that of a private corporation when producer governments have such enormous leeway to control price by altering production? Suppose the corporation or the secretary of energy declared that no oil should be purchased above a given price, and some key producers "conserve" production rather than sell at that price. Faced with greater domestic political concern about supply than price, would consumer governments cut back demand accordingly? More likely they would raise the designated price to ensure supply.

It is true that a government corporation could bring nonoil considerations to bear in a manner that private corporations cannot, but such linkages are a two-way street. We might find that producers would link sensitive political issues, such as the Middle East peace process, to the details of oil negotiations in a manner that reduced our diplomatic flexibility and bargaining power—hardly a gain for energy security, broadly defined. The burden of proof must rest with those who believe that the marginal price benefits that might result from governmental negotiations with weak producers would be greater than the potential foreign policy costs of angering stronger producer states willing to cut back production. Moreover, whatever price benefits we stood to gain from across-the-board government purchasing might as easily be made without the same risks by selective diplomatic jawboning.

We should also be cautious about following the example of other nations in this regard. As home base for the largest number of international oil companies, we have more influence and information than any other consumer country. And although it may be true that the proportion of oil sold through the thirty-four companies that support the IEA emergency oil-sharing plan has diminished from 90 to 60 percent of the total markets, it does not follow that we should encourage the trend toward government-to-government purchases. It is not clear how much oil must flow through the companies to ensure enough market flexibility to defeat selective embargoes and make the IEA sharing system work, but it would not help to weaken such an important buffer. Consumer country coordination in a crisis is important, but it does not require government purchasing.

In sum, it is easier to identify significant potential costs than it is to find significant gains to energy security through government control of purchasing.

International Collective Bargaining.   One can imagine a smooth, long-term transition from cheap oil to more expensive energy alternatives that would benefit both consumers and producers. Given the long lead times for alternatives and the opportunities for price gouging during periods of political uncertainty, the real price of oil during the eighties may be pushed higher than the long-term price. This development could reduce the long-term revenues of producer states; create uncertainty for their development planning; and, by destabilizing the world economy, threaten the value of their new investments. Politically, a stable world economy enhances the security of producers who depend on an unprovoked and reliable West. It also reduces the economic sources of political instability in the oil-importing developing countries. A consumer-producer dialogue might well help nations concentrate on issues of long-term mutual interest.[3]

Such a dialogue might seek two- or three-year intergovernmental agreements to stabilize the oil market. For example, OPEC and IEA countries would agree on production targets and consumption limits (at first separately, and then in joint bargaining) which would allow for modest real price rises over the decade. A band of prices might be established for the duration of the agreement. OPEC countries would agree to maintain sufficient spare capacity to keep prices within the agreed range. They would cut production (or permit consumers to increase demand) if prices threatened to fall below a designated minimum. If additional inducements were needed to ensure adequate production levels, consumers might index assets, offer assurances of assistance, and allow new OPEC industries access to their home markets. Special credit or aid provisions might be established for oil-importing developing countries. In fact, representatives of such countries might participate in the bargaining sessions.

The number of problems and questions that have to be solved should make us cautious about embarking on such a course: *Could we keep the agenda focused on energy?* Given the politics of the Middle East and the strong bargaining position of the producers, we might find ourselves unable to keep certain awkward political issues off the table. If developing countries were to participate, we might find ourselves reenacting sterile North–South debates, but with much higher stakes than in the United Nations. We need to be sure we can control the Pandora's Box effect before we start down the path to serious international collective bargaining.

Is a reasonable bargain likely? At modest prices, the economic interests of OPEC's surplus producers who lean toward conservation diverge from those of producers who are interested in maximizing

3. For a recent proposal, see Ian Smart (1980: 22–29); also *North–South*, the report of the Brandt Commission (Brandt et al. 1980).

revenues. Large price increases, which maximize revenues and allow painless production cutbacks, tend to reconcile that division. Would OPEC countries be able to agree to a bargain that meant higher production and lower prices than the market would otherwise allow? Or would the process of collective bargaining help OPEC members act again in concert—but at a higher price? Given the weak bargaining position of the consumers, they would have a poor chance of negotiating that price down.

Is OPEC cohesive enough to keep any bargain it makes? Thus far, OPEC countries have been unwilling to limit their separate sovereign control over production decisions because it is their major source of power. They compete for power within the oil arena, and they reserve the right to use oil as a weapon in wider political games. Considering the politics of oil and the domestic instability of many OPEC governments, how credible would an OPEC promise to increase production be if political advantage could be gained from a shortfall?

Would the benefits exceed the costs? International collective bargaining would give consumers a formal framework for debating production and price decisions that are now almost entirely in OPEC hands. What is such a framework worth? If collective bargaining were achieved only at the cost of OPEC solidarity on higher prices, the risks of the new framework could be greater than the benefits. Special instruments such as indexing could prove very costly, particularly if the precedent were to spread.

This is not to argue that conversations with producer states are not useful, or that restoration of an international regime is not a worthy long-term goal. Various bilateral and multilateral discussions are essential. But the time is not ripe for fruitful collective bargaining. The balance of power is too imbalanced. Efforts to reconstruct a satisfactory regime under current circumstances are unlikely to be fruitful unless they are part of a larger strategy to enhance energy security discussed in the rest of this volume.

STEPS IN THE RIGHT DIRECTION

Painful though it was, we learned some important lessons from the interruption of the Iranian oil supply. In April 1979, we began the gradual decontrol of domestic oil prices that will end the subsidization of imports. We also finally seem to have learned the folly of excessive dependence on the Persian Gulf, for at the Tokyo Summit of June 1979 we began work on government agreements to set ceilings on imports. And the double shock of the Shah's fall and the Soviet invasion of Afghanistan led to steps to repair our military posture in the area.

There is still a long way to go. Even with decontrol, oil industry sources project declines in domestic oil production during the 1980s, and we will be hard pressed to meet our goal of cutting imports in half by 1990 (Exxon Company 1979; Duncan 1980). At the current rate, our Strategic Petroleum Reserve will not be filled for *two decades*. Moreover, even if we are successful in reducing our own dependence, our allies will remain vulnerable to interruptions of supply.

A successful energy security strategy will have to focus on preventing interruptions and alleviating their damage in the short term while reducing Western vulnerability over the course of the eighties. To execute this strategy will require better integration of political-military policy, domestic energy policy, and international energy policy than we have achieved in the past. Only when all the major oil-consuming countries have taken the hard steps described in this book will we be able to look forward to collective energy security.

REFERENCES

Brandt, Willy, et al. 1980. *North–South*. Report of the Brandt Commission. Cambridge, Mass.: MIT Press.

Brown, William, and Herman Kahn. 1980. "Why OPEC is Vulnerable." *Fortune* (July 14): 67–68.

Congressional Budget Office. 1980. "The World Oil Market in the 1980s: Implications for the United States." Washington: Government Printing Office.

Department of Energy. 1980. "The Energy Problem: Costs and Policy Options." Policy and Evaluation Staff Working Paper, Draft, March 12.

Duncan, Charles. 1980. "Posture Statement before Committee on Science and Technology, House of Representatives." Washington, January 31.

The Economist. 1973. "The Phony Oil Crisis: A Survey." (July 7): Supplement, pp. 1–42.

Exxon Company, U.S.A. 1979. *Energy Outlook, 1980–2000*. December.

Harsch, Jonathan. 1980. "France Maps an Independent Course on Nuclear, Afghanistan." *Christian Science Monitor*. (February 12): 1.

House of Representatives. 1979. "Alternatives to Dealing with OPEC." Hearings before a Subcommittee of the Committee on Government Operations, June 20. Washington: Government Printing Office.

International Energy Agency. 1980. (80) 9 Paris, June 9. Mimeographed press release.

Keohane, Robert, and Joseph Nye. 1977. *Power and Interdependence*. Boston: Little, Brown.

Kissinger, Henry. 1979. *The White House Years*. Boston: Little, Brown.

Nissen, David. 1980. "OPEC Oil Pricing." Chase Manhattan Bank. Mimeo.

Penrose, Edith. 1975. "The Development of Crisis." *Daedalus* 104 (Fall).

Rowen, Henry. 1980. "Western Economies and the Gulf War." *Wall Street Journal* (October 2).

Sampson, Anthony. 1975. *The Seven Sisters*. New York: Viking Press.

Schneider, William. 1980. "Public Opinion and the Energy Crisis." In *The Dependence Dilemma*, edited by Daniel Yergin. Cambridge, Mass: Harvard Center for International Affairs.

Smart, Ian. 1980. "Communicating with the Oil Exporters: The Old Dialogue and the New." *Trialogue* 22 (Winter).

Stobaugh, Robert, and Daniel Yergin. 1980. "Energy: An Emergency Telescoped." *Foreign Affairs* 58, no. 3.

Tucker, Robert. 1975. "Oil: The Issue of American Intervention." *Commentary* 59 (January): 21–31.

The Washington Post. 1980. Editorial. January 28.

2 THE CHANGING WORLD OIL MARKET

Thomas L. Neff

Since late 1978, structural changes in the world oil market have taken place at an accelerating rate. The roles of the major international oil companies in producing and distributing oil internationally have been restricted. Producers have taken greater control of these activities, while also experimenting with refining, transportation and other new roles. On the consumer side, independents, trading companies, national oil companies and governments are increasingly involved in procuring oil directly. These changes raise questions about the future evolution of the world's oil supply system, about its behavior under normal and stressed conditions, and about the nature and predictability of pricing decisions. For most oil-importing nations, these oil market changes have far-reaching domestic and foreign policy implications.

STRUCTURAL CHANGES

Changes in oil market structure have been especially evident since 1973–74, when OPEC producers assumed much greater control over crude oil prices and revenues. Producer governments gradually reduced the amounts of crude output automatically allocated to the foreign companies that produced the oil within their borders and

I wish to thank M. Adelman, L. Cox, N. Sharif, and R. Toohey for sharing with me their views of world oil market changes, and H. Jacoby for his insightful comments and criticisms. I am also grateful to V. Faust, M. Lynch, and S. Sieferman for their assistance in research and in the preparation of this chapter. The research on which this chapter is based was supported by the Center for Energy Policy Research of the MIT Energy Laboratory.

23

began to intervene in production decisions. In 1978, for example, Saudi Arabia began to restrict production of its highest quality oil, requiring that a fraction of output consist of less desirable heavy crude. But the real catalyst for change was the revolution in Iran. The loss of supply, and the ensuing disruptions of normal patterns of oil trade, created opportunities for other producers to act—independently and according to national interests—to take greater control of their own oil. Rapid price increases during this time also enhanced the producers' freedom of action by lowering the output required to meet revenue needs.

Prior to 1973–74, the seven international majors and other participating companies[1] not only produced OPEC's oil but also handled the distribution of more than 90 percent of it. The companies received some of the oil through direct "equity" agreements, and obtained the rest through "buyback," the purchase of oil produced by the companies on behalf of the host country. This volume exceeded the refining and product marketing systems of the companies, making it possible for them to sell nearly 7 million barrels per day to third-party customers. The companies also had sharing arrangements among themselves, to deal with quality differences in crudes and to distribute the oil efficiently. Less than 10 percent of OPEC oil flowed outside the supply channels of the majors. This system was resilient and flexible: the majors could act as a buffer between producers and consumers and allocate oil throughout the world market. This role was most effective when the volumes they handled surpassed their own needs, providing flexibility to adapt to disruptions or other changes in the market, and at least some ability to separate producers and consumers politically.

The initial loss of 5.5 million barrels per day in Iranian exports cut the daily supply to the seven majors by about 3.3 million barrels. Because of this loss and the ensuing logistic disruptions, the majors reduced third-party sales (which had amounted to about 4.5 million

---

1. The seven international majors are: British Petroleum, Royal Dutch/Shell, and five U.S.–based companies: Exxon, Mobil, Standard Oil of California, Texaco (the four partners in Aramco, the producer of Saudi Arabia's oil) and Gulf. These companies are vertically integrated, with refining and distribution systems in many countries. Other large companies, such as France's Elf Aquitaine and U.S.–based Occidental Petroleum, participate in producing oil but have refining and distribution systems that are more restricted geographically, often to the home country market. Finally, there are companies and agents that do not participate directly in producing oil but act as traders, refiners, or distributors of oil and oil products.

barrels per day just prior to the crisis) and sharing arrangements began to break down. When Iranian production resumed, the majors regained less than 1 million barrels per day of supply. Instead, Iran began to sell directly to consumers, some of whom had been cut by the majors and most of whom were motivated by extreme security concerns. The consumer scramble for oil—both for near-term needs and for increased inventories—then spread, allowing other producers to take greater control of their oil. Kuwait, Iraq, Venezuela, and other producers cut equity and buyback volumes for many companies and Nigeria nationalized British Petroleum.

Producers are now selling the oil taken away from the majors and other participating companies directly to nonparticipating oil companies, to consumer governments or their agents, or on the spot market. Direct sales have increased to nearly 45 percent of the producers' total volume and have resulted in significant structural changes in the world oil market, as shown in Figure 2−1. Producers are using direct sales to advance their economic and political interests and to extend their control over international markets for crude oil and its products. They have taken a variety of measures oriented toward such ends, including:

- *Direct premium*: sales of longer-term contract oil at higher-than-official prices. Such high-priced oil is often sold as part of a package with oil at lower official prices—usually as a condition for its sale or as a "supplementary" volume.

- *Exploration fees or requirements*: additions to the price of crude oil intended to increase and finance exploration in the producer country.

- *Incentive crude*: access to crude oil (as in Saudi Arabia) offered in return for foreign investments in petrochemical or other facilities.

- *Signature bonuses*: fees charged simply for the opportunity to write a supply contract.

- *Government-to-government term sales*: sales involving participation by consumer government officials.

- *Destination restrictions*: for example, boycotts of Israel or South Africa or refusal to allow shipment through the Suez Canal.

- *System restrictions*: requirements that oil be used only in the refining and distribution or home market of the purchaser.

Figure 2-1. Oil market structure.

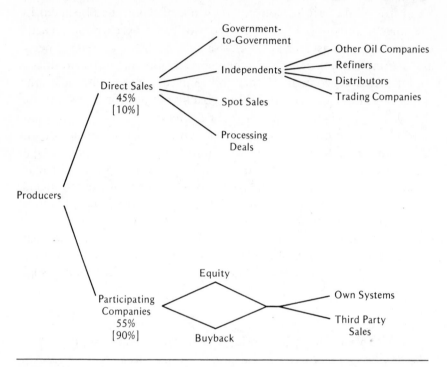

Note: Percentages shown are estimates for early 1980; percentages in brackets are for 1973.

- *Resale restrictions*: limits on third-party sales and exchanges between companies.

- *Anticompetition clauses*: requirements that buyers of crude not compete with the primary producer's direct sales. Such clauses further restrict third-party sales and the activities of traders and other intermediaries.

- *Direct spot crude sales at high prices*: sometimes a condition for term oil.

- *Mandatory purchases*: requirements that a purchaser buy petroleum products or lower quality crude, often at high prices, to ensure access to its usual crude supply.

- *Transportation restrictions*: requirements that crude be transported in tankers owned by producer interests.

- *Processing requirements*: efforts by producers to increase involvement in refining, petrochemical, or other downstream activities.

Two important trends are evident here: producers are taking greater physical control over their crude oil and its uses, and they are extracting higher economic and political prices for that oil. It is notable both that there are significant differences among OPEC producers in the extent to which these trends are manifest and that some non-OPEC producers (for example, Mexico, Peru, and even Norway and the United Kingdom) are taking actions very similar to those taken by some OPEC producers.

With these market changes, the roles of the international majors have been altered significantly. Many are now short of crude, with activities increasingly restricted to their own refining and distribution systems. Third party sales have been reduced drastically and most remaining agreements are scheduled to be eliminated by 1981 or 1982. The exchange mechanisms that contributed to logistic and other efficiencies have largely broken down.

Producer Control

Today, about 13 million barrels per day of internationally traded oil (OPEC and non-OPEC) are being sold directly by producers. About 40 percent of this oil is being sold in transactions between producer and consumer governments. Many of these transactions are with developing country consumers, though the volumes involved are usually small (typically around 20,000 barrels per day); they are sometimes financed with low- or no-interest loans. Government-to-government deals with industrialized countries often result from high-level governmental discussions, though they may be channeled by the consumer through a national company. Prices are usually at official government selling price, well below the price for other direct deals, which have included a per-barrel premium of as much as $11 per barrel. In many government-to-government deals, however, the buyer agrees to provide technological or other assistance. In other cases, the "premium" is less explicit—typically, political concessions that rarely extend beyond "goodwill."[2] But the establishment of any political context for oil transactions is very important.

A similar volume of crude is being sold directly to nonparticipating companies: independent oil companies, traders, trading companies, refiners and distributors, and the national oil companies of consumer countries.[3] Many of these sales result from the reduction in third party sales by the majors. For example, the large-scale increase in direct purchases (spot and long-term contracts) by Japanese trading companies in 1979 resulted largely from crisis-induced reductions in crude supply by the majors. Thus the independent companies, with their new and expanded roles, may be extremely important to the functioning of the international oil market under both normal and abnormal conditions.

Many government-to-government and other direct deals are subject to important new restrictions. System restrictions require that the crude be used in the refineries of the purchaser, and destination restrictions mandate that the oil and its products be used in the home market of the purchaser. The penalty for violation is often contract termination. For example, crude oil under India's contract with Libya involved expensive transportation over long distances, and the product mix after refining was not well-suited to India's needs. Following practices that were previously nearly universal, India in 1979 sought to trade its Libyan crude for more suitable oil. But Libya threatened cancellation, and India was forced to refine the Libyan crude first and then trade some of the products, a more expensive and logistically difficult procedure.

These and other new restrictions reduce the flexibility of the international system. In normal times, the principal result is a loss of economic efficiency. In a crisis, however, the problem is potentially much more serious. Such restrictions inhibit the ability of the international market to respond to disruptions by redirecting oil flows.

---

2. An exception is the recent contract between Denmark and Saudi Arabia that allows Saudi Arabia to cancel the arrangement if Denmark takes action or expresses sentiments contrary to Saudi interests. A similar provision in Belgium's contract with Saudi Arabia has recently been reported. Note also that Libya has threatened to cut off deliveries to the United States and the United Kingdom because of the expulsion of Libyan nationals from these countries.

3. Included here are transactions in which there is no explicit consumer government involvement. As is evident, the distinction between government-to-government deals and direct producer sales to national oil companies is more one of degree than of kind.

They also limit the ability of traders and other independent intermediaries to contribute to new market flexibilities; thus they bias market evolution in directions unfavorable to consumers.

Producers have also used their new crude supply leverage to force acceptance of their participation in transportation, refining, and other downstream operations, though the extent to which they will pursue these activities remains uncertain. Some are building refineries or petrochemical plants at home or abroad, often in joint venture with foreign oil companies, for whom such investments are a condition for access to crude supply. Others are asking for a share of downstream profits. And at least one producer, Kuwait, is asking for the right to refine a quantity of its own crude in the purchaser's facility for its own account, rather than to the benefit of the purchaser. The motives for these steps seem to include downstream experience, products for home markets, control over or information about oil companies, or simply capturing downstream profits.

There has also been a shift away from long-term crude contract sales. In the scramble to rearrange oil supply following the disruptions caused by events in Iran, producers found that they were able to sell large volumes of oil on a spot cargo basis at high prices. By the middle of 1979, OPEC producers appeared to be selling more than 3 million barrels per day in this way. Previously, the spot crude market had involved relatively small quantities of oil sold by middlemen in Rotterdam, Singapore or elsewhere; spot sales were basically a mechanism for detailed balancing of supply and demand. Producers created an essentially new spot market in 1979, a market of greater size and with a different role in the oil market system. Spot crude volumes have receded since then, but not yet to previous levels.

Price Structure

Changes in the price structure for oil have paralleled the increasing complexity in the market structure. In the past, oil was sold almost exclusively at official government selling prices. Price variations were due largely to quality and transportation differentials, and price unity among the members of the OPEC cartel was readily maintained. With the events in Iran, producers were suddenly able to act independently to alter pricing practices. As Figure 2−2 shows, oil is now sold in three primary categories: long-term contracts at official price, term

Figure 2-2.   Price structure.

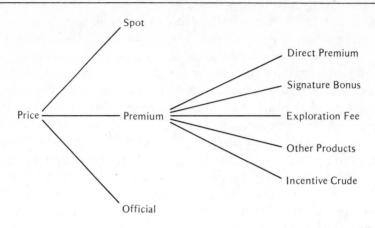

contracts at official price plus a premium, and single cargoes or short-term sales at spot prices. Today, official prices vary more than would be justified by quality or transportation differentials, the most evident example being the comparatively low price of Saudi light crude. Official prices are generally charged for the equity oil due participating companies and for many government-to-government transactions.

The price of oil in other term contracts, which total perhaps 30 percent of OPEC sales, is generally set at the official price plus a premium. The premium may take many different forms. In early 1980, for example, Kuwait simply charged a $5.50 per barrel premium on quantities in excess of a basic volume for each purchaser; Iran required that purchasers of crude also buy fuel oil; Mexico required that buyers take heavy as well as light crude; and Algeria collected a $3 per barrel fee to finance exploration. Variations in such premia were greater than official price differentials; that the market could sustain such differences was a measure of the disturbed state of the international oil system. While premia were declining due to excess supply in mid–1980, there is little doubt that they will increase when the supply/demand balance tightens again.

Spot sales are an even more sensitive measure of market instability. Over the past year, volumes and prices for such sales have fluctuated with the precise state of the market and with consumer perceptions. In mid–1979, spot prices were as much as double official prices on a volume of several million barrels per day. More recently they have declined, approaching premium prices for term oil on a volume of less than a million barrels per day.

Efforts to restore unity to cartel pricing have thus far failed. Whether individual producers continue to have the freedom to act independently will depend largely on supply and demand balances and on the presence or absence of new stresses. But the new richness of price structure will almost certainly increase the volatility of crude oil prices, and the large volume of term contract sales at premium prices will put continued upward pressure on official prices. Because equity crude is sold at lower official prices, producers may withhold more of this oil from participating companies in order to earn premia in direct sales or concessions in government-to-government deals.

The effects of the structural rigidities and inflexibilities identified above have been aggravated by diverging supply and demand trends with regard to oil quality differences. The average barrel produced is becoming increasingly heavy and high in sulfur content while the average barrel demanded is shifting toward the light, low-sulfur type. As a result of this—and the limited capabilities of current refining capacity—the efficiency of the world system in matching crude supplies to final product demand is reduced further and its capability for substituting and reallocating oil in a crisis is further compromised.

PATTERNS OF CHANGE

The changes underway in the world oil market will inevitably alter how we think about the problems of oil and security, and how we deal with them. But the difficulty of our present situation is that we cannot yet see the full extent and implications of these changes. Producers clearly have greater influence over the economic and noneconomic terms of trade, and the traditional majors have lost much of their capacity to provide flexibility to the international system. The increasing number of government-to-government deals, destination restrictions, and system requirements also inhibit the efficient flow of oil under normal conditions and militate against the ability of the international system to readjust to disruptions or other crises. But it is not evident how far these trends will go, or whether there may be compensating changes occurring in the world market.

Consider two extreme scenarios for the possible evolution of the market. In the first, producers would establish complete control through destination restrictions, government-to-government agreements, downstream involvements, and tight leashes on the majors and other market participants. Such a market would have few degrees of freedom left; instead, both producer and consumer sides of the market would be fragmented and oil flows would follow paths linking the specific interests of particular producers with those of particular consumers. Such a system would be highly politicized and economically inefficient under normal circumstances; in a crisis, it would be inflexible, prices would be volatile, and readjustment costs would be great.

In the second scenario, producers would also succeed in removing much of the flexibility of the old system, greatly restricting the logistic efficiencies (and economic opportunities) of the majors, but new actors and market mechanisms would restore flexibility and efficiency to the system. These might include independent oil companies, refiners, trading companies, and expanded and elaborated oil product markets. In such a system, intermediaries (whether companies or market devices) would separate the interests of producers and consumers, and would also provide logistic and economic efficiencies. In a crisis they would help reallocate oil much as the majors appear to have done in the 1973–74 crisis.

Of course, the world oil supply system is not presently in either of these extreme states, nor is it likely to come to resemble either one completely in the near future. Flexible and inflexible elements will coexist, their nature and relative importance altering with time. To understand the system and its potential evolution, consider the analogy of a pond that is close to the freezing point. When water freezes, many degrees of freedom are lost; fluidity is replaced by rigid relationships between the parts. Ice cleaves along the dimension it is struck or it shatters. A liquid has many more degrees of freedom: a pressure applied to any part is distributed over the whole fluid system and disturbances die rapidly away in ripples.

For the world oil market, the frozen state is analogous to the first of the extreme evolutionary possibilities. In this situation, stresses, such as an embargo or cutback or revolution in a producer country, could be directionally effective against particular consumers (as in a targeted embargo) or cause a major disruption in the entire system. But such a rigid system might also have certain strengths. For example, producers might be constrained in individual actions or in their ability to act together in a cartel—by government-to-government agreements or by investments in downstream activities or in consumer economies. A fluid market has more evident advantages; its primary disadvantage is just the lack of political constraints on producer behavior.

The current world oil market is clearly in a mixed state: there is evidence of both freezing and thawing, both ice and open water. Some degrees of freedom, formerly provided primarily by the majors, are now frozen out by supply reductions and by a plethora of direct deals and special restrictions; but other sources of flexibility may be emerging. This circumstance is complicated by rapid variations in the market as surpluses create price softness and greater flexibility, only to be countered by new disruptions, output changes, or new consumer fears.

The difficulties of our situation are, first, that we cannot yet determine the basic direction of the system—whether it is spring or fall—and, second, that many of our previous understandings of the world oil market do not apply to a system in flux.[4] But is is important to identify the forces at work and trace their implications, since, unlike the climate in the analogous physical system, the policies and actions of the participants in the world oil market can be reshaped to alter the evolution of that market.

DIRECTIONS AND IMPLICATIONS

The expansion of government-to-government agreements and the wide range of other arrangements in which the particular interests of individual producers and consumers are expressed tends not only to reduce flexibility but also to reduce cohesion among producers and among consumers. The tightness of the market, the high level of supply-security concerns among consumers, and the rise of producer revenues well above expenditures enables producers to act more independently in setting prices, production levels, and other terms. There is thus little need for explicit cartelization; indeed, OPEC as an institution—to the extent that it functions—may now be a force for

4. Models based on a single assumption—whether atomistic free markets, cartel behavior, economically efficient resource allocation, or the parallels in political theory—are likely to prove of minimal use in the current circumstance. This situation is analogous to that in the physical parallel: the analytic treatments of liquids and of solids are generally much simpler than those for phase transitions or mixed states.

moderation, encouraging the reconciliation of economic and political interests among producers. But cartel leadership — traditionally Saudi Arabia — appears weakened. Instead, decisions and events in many producer countries can result in major short-term perturbations in the system and affect its long-run evolution.

This new volatility on the producer side is likely to lead to an unpredictable variance in market behavior, including prices. When there are many sources of initiative and producers can act independently, even small market changes or disruptions can release forces leading to a ratcheting up of oil prices everywhere. As a result, power over price is dispersed; even relatively small producers are able to bump prices upward. This problem is aggravated by the new multitier pricing system. While official price increases may be retarded by political constraints, premium and spot prices affecting large volumes of oil can move rather freely. But these higher prices put upward pressure on official prices, making increases more likely.[5]

Fragmentation and volatility also afflict consumers. Government-to-government transactions, for example, may induce a consumer nation to sacrifice nonoil domestic and foreign policy goals in the belief that this will ensure supply security or more acceptable prices. Each nation generally perceives a different set of such goals, and weighs tradeoffs accordingly. The United States, whose foreign policy agenda is broader than that of most other consumers, faces special problems in this regard. Other nations may more easily accept the compromises demanded for "secure" access to oil. This diversity of perspectives, however, hinders consumers' ability to cooperate in dealing with oil problems; it also increases the potential for significant conflict among them.

Consumer reactions to perceived insecurity have also contributed to the problem. Events in Iran catalyzed market changes not so much because of a decrease in total supply (which was small[6]) but because

5. On three recent occasions the Saudis increased the official price for their light crude in an effort to restore price unity to the cartel. Unfortunately for consumers, Saudi Arabia appears to be leading from below since their actions simply triggered increases in the official prices charged by other producers, prices that were already above those of Saudi Arabia.

6. Total world output (excluding centrally planned economies) in 1979 was below third-quarter 1978 levels only in January (down 1.3 million barrels per day or less than 3 percent of 1978 output levels) and February (down 0.2 million barrels per day). By the end of March, output was a million barrels per day above the 1978 level and by June, two million. See Henry D. Jacoby and James L. Paddock, "Supply Instability and Oil Market Behavior," in *Energy Systems and Policy* 3, no. 4 (1980), p. 407.

of the panic induced by uncertainty and by the need to rearrange supplies. This problem was particularly severe because the loss did not affect all companies and consumers equally but rather affected a few quite deeply. This meant that some market actors were especially desperate and that very large readjustments between parts of the system were necessary. Panic also created widespread desires for larger inventories and so demand increased as the crisis evolved. Thus, consumer and company responses enhanced volatility and tightening of the market, which in turn set the stage for other producer actions. It is evident that measures to restrain or reduce the effects of such consumer responses would help inhibit similar market changes in the future. However, given the changes in the market that have already occurred, it is not clear that consumers can achieve the coordination and sharing required to implement such measures.

Not all of the trends toward structural rigidity and fragmentation necessarily work to the disadvantage of consumers. The government-to-government ties that restrict consumer action may also restrict producers: the chains bind at both ends. And since producers have disparate interests, the growing web of bilateral relationships may make it more difficult for producers to act in concert. In addition, the existence of a particular bilateral relationship may reduce the likelihood of disruption of the corresponding supply channel, or at least this is the hope of the consumers involved. But if there are many such agreements and one disruption occurs, that consumer may find its ability to arrange new supplies limited by the government-to-government deals of others.

Downstream producer involvements, another source of reduced flexibility, may also benefit consumers. If producers become extensively involved in refining or product markets abroad, they will have a stake in the efficient and undisrupted functioning of these markets. Such involvement may also help moderate prices. If crude and product prices rise too much and demand slackens, the downward pressure on prices is first felt in product markets. If producers are not involved in product markets, they can hold crude prices up longer, letting the intermediary companies suffer the erosion of profit margins. But if producers are involved, they will feel the demand effects more directly. In addition, producers involved in refining and product sales may find themselves in competition with each other, reducing the commonality of their interests. Of course, these are all good reasons for producers to avoid extensive downstream commitments.

Producers will have to weigh them against their desire to recapture the profits being made by others when markets are tight.

While some consolation may be found in these market trends toward rigidity, it would be more encouraging to find indications of changes that help restore lost flexibilities. There are indications of such changes, but their significance is not yet clear. As discussed earlier, some of the oil taken from the majors and other participating companies is being sold to independent oil companies, traders, and trading companies. While a number of these entities have strong ties to particular consumer countries and thus tend only to facilitate bilateral trade, others have begun to carry out the international transactions that provide increased flexibility. But the volume traded internationally in this manner is still far from comparable to that previously handled by the majors as exchanges or third-party sales, and producers will probably resist the replacement of the majors with an even less controllable group. Indeed, several producers are now putting restrictions on the sizes and types of companies to whom crude is sold and putting lower limits on sales volumes.

COPING WITH CRISIS

The implications of these changes in the world oil market are troublesome under "normal" market conditions (if today's market is regarded as the new norm), especially with regard to price and efficiency. Even small perturbations during periods of calm may result in upward price movements. Any restrictions on where and how oil may flow generally increase transportation distances; restrictions also exacerbate problems in matching crude types to refinery capabilities and product demand that vary geographically and temporally. Solutions to these problems include upgrading refineries, maintaining larger inventories of crude and products, and increasing trade in products. All of these are expensive and add to the already large strains on industrial economies. But these are not the most worrisome problems.

Of even greater concern are interruptions of oil flows that result in social, economic, or political disruptions potentially far larger than those caused by more gradual changes in prices or supply patterns. We have experienced two such crises in the past decade: the embargo and associated events of 1973−74 and the Iranian revolution in 1978–79. The prospects for further crises seem only to be increasing.

Disruptions of oil flows may be distinguished according to two classes of events: intentional interruptions (such as an embargo) and accidental or undirected disruptions. An intentional interruption is likely to be politically motivated and targeted against particular consumers. Under earlier market conditions (as in 1974), it was difficult for producers to carry out an embargo successfully since the majors and other intermediaries could reallocate supplies. Even an embargo accompanied by a cut in total output could be handled, with what would otherwise be a large shortfall for one consumer country distributed over the system as small shortages for many consumers. In today's altered market, however, it is not clear that the international system can cope with intentional interruptions. Producers bent on targeting a supply interruption could control not only the oil moving directly to the country in question, but could also use government-to-government transactions and contracts explicit in restrictions on third-party sales or system limitations to restrain the reallocation of other oil supplies to the targeted country. It is thus possible that, when used intentionally, rigorous control over relatively small volumes of crude can have a disproportionate effect.

But market changes may also be working to decrease the likelihood of such intentional interruptions. Not only do individual producers now have other sources of leverage, but their ability to act in concert has been reduced by the very market changes that otherwise would increase the effectiveness of an embargo. Producers can now use both price and access as tools to advance political and other goals, and each producer can act independently to achieve its goals. But an embargo desired by any one producer would require that other producers stand firm on their destination and other restrictions and resist pressures to increase output. If the embargo were targeted against a consumer that had government-to-government agreements with other producers, these producers would have to abrogate these agreements in order to make the embargo successful.

Future crises are therefore more likely to result from accidental disruptions than from embargoes. War, revolution, natural disaster, or other causes may reduce total world supply and initiate new scrambles to reallocate what is available. Such a cut may be relatively small—say, the loss of a few million barrels a day—or large—as with the loss of Saudi Arabia or several smaller producers simultaneously.

For large disruptions there is little hope of avoiding very serious political and economic costs. Even the impact of smaller disruptions may prove large. Increased structural rigidities inhibit the nearly automatic reallocation of oil that took place in the past, and this inhibition may be greater than any new fluidities introduced by other market changes.

If the market's ability to readjust to smaller disruptions is reduced, or if the costs of such readjustment become too great, governments will increasingly feel the need to respond. Should a disruption occur that had no overt political motive, some producers might be willing to increase total supply enough to overcome logistic tangles, meet new demand for inventories, and put a lid on prices; some might even relax destination and other restrictions temporarily. But producers are likely to exact economic and political concessions in return for such favors. Moreover, it is not obvious that adequate logistic infrastructure for rapid large-scale reallocation, or for the handling of additional quantities from other producers, would be maintained simply as a contingency.

On the consumer side, governments could reallocate oil, restrict demand, and distribute economic costs. Particular attention has been given to sharing agreements as a way for consumers to deal with disruptions. These agreements may be multilateral, as in the International Energy Agency (IEA) system, or bilateral. The difficulty of implementing such agreements has been increased by recent changes: new efforts and commitments will be necessary if sharing agreements are to be of value in a crisis. In many cases, reallocation of one consumer's supply to another consumer might violate (or appear to violate) producer/consumer government agreements or destination restrictions, and consumers might well fear that such violations would compromise future access to crude. This problem is obviously greater in the case of politically motivated interruptions. But restrictions may also serve as an excuse for unaffected consumers not to participate in oil sharing even during accidental disruptions. Finally, the efficacy of such sharing arrangements depends on consumers' ability to reallocate oil. In the past, the international majors would have done the reallocating; now, governments may have difficulty reallocating oil quickly and without large economic costs, even if the political will can be marshalled.

TOWARD IMPROVEMENT

The evolution of the world oil market can be affected, for good or ill, by a number of consumer policies and actions. At a minimum, consumers should avoid measures that reduce system flexibility (such as emergency allocation systems that mis-distribute oil or products). We can distinguish three classes of constructive measures: those that increase flexibility directly; those that augment supply, especially in times of crisis; and those that reduce demand. The last two operate primarily by enhancing opportunities to exploit existing flexibilities.

Increase Flexibility

Some new flexibilities may emerge automatically, as in the expanding role of new actors in the market. Some of the oil taken from the majors that is now being handled by other companies may be less vulnerable to control by producers. Producer attempts to dictate the behavior of one small buyer may merely result in the appearance of another. By this argument, consumer policies that encourage the active participation of such entities in the international market will help increase flexibility. Some current policies encourage such participation; others, such as the crude allocation system that tempts smaller companies to depend on larger, may discourage it.

The recent trend toward holding larger crude and product inventories may be another beneficial development. Such inventories provide a cushion of time, restrain the hoarding impulse that turns a disruption into a crisis, and provide the flexibility to redirect crude streams temporarily or to reallocate products. To do this, however, inventories must be held in ways that mesh well with domestic and international distribution systems. Since these systems are largely private, reallocation might take place more promptly and efficiently if inventories were privately held. But since the societal value of such inventories is generally greater than their value to private agents, private holders will probably maintain smaller inventories than are socially optimal, unless there is public intervention in the form of regulation or subsidy, as in Japan and some countries of Western Europe.

Product markets have expanded and should be encouraged to do so further. Products (with the exception of unleaded gasoline) are far more interchangeable than crude oil, with its many quality differences and with the variety of producer restrictions attached to its use. Although the costs of storing and transporting products are greater than those associated with crude, the ability to respond quickly and flexibly in a crisis to meet product demand could help consumer nations minimize economic disruption and panic about supply.

In addition to these trends toward flexibility, which can and should be encouraged, there are a number of positive steps consumers might take. Perhaps the most important of these is the upgrading of refinery capacity. Many refineries can handle only certain types of crude oil, usually light, low-sulfur crudes. Moreover, there are too few ways to match refinery capabilities with the crude slates that might be available in a crisis. These constraints multiply the effect of producer destination and other restrictions.

The United States has a particularly low level of refinery flexibility; it depends heavily on the cooperation of other nations. It could compensate for the loss of a supplier of light, low-sulfur crude only if other consumers agreed to accept less desirable crudes (and the associated environmental costs) in order to free high quality crude for use in U.S. refineries. Despite economic incentives for private companies to upgrade refineries, particularly if lower grade crudes are disproportionately low in price, these incentives do not completely reflect the benefits that would accrue to the nation from increased flexibility and ability to respond in a crisis.

Measures to increase other degrees of freedom would also be worth far more than their immediate costs. But such measures are sometimes difficult to achieve because they involve other public policy issues. For example, Alaskan oil is politically restricted and does not play a role in international oil trade. To a more limited extent, this is also true of Mexican oil, which comes primarily to the United States. Such restrictions may be politically justifiable and perhaps economically efficient in normal times, but failure to provide for the flexible use of non–OPEC oil in international markets probably increases the impact of OPEC constraints during crises. For example, a crisis affecting light, sweet crude supplies might be especially damaging to the United States unless heavy Mexican or North Slope crude can be sent to refining centers in the Far East or Europe to displace premium crudes for use in U.S. refineries.

Market flexibility would also be increased by further diversification of supply sources. The importance of new sources can be much greater than is indicated by the volumes involved if they contribute to increased flexibility in the system. Even small producers, or small increases in the capacities of established producers, can alter system performance. This change may not be particularly evident in normal times since such producers—whether Mexico, Norway, or Peru—often seek price and other concessions comparable to those demanded by OPEC producers. But in a crisis their behavior may be considerably more sympathetic to consumer needs.

In addition to efforts to increase flexibility directly are measures that would augment supply or reduce demand. In a crisis, such measures can reduce market tightness and enhance the effectiveness of system flexibilities. In normal times, such measures might even influence the evolution of the world market in constructive ways.

Augment Supplies

The most desirable way to augment supply would be to create additional production capacity in stable and politically neutral areas. In normal times, such new capacity would provide a moderating force. However, it is difficult to identify sources large enough to affect the prevailing supply/demand balance appreciably, especially in a world in which producers with revenue surpluses are able—indeed eager—to cut output. And for economic and political reasons, new producers would probably rather sell into a tight market than help contribute to its softening.

However, even if it is not possible to find additional sources large enough to affect market developments, some producers might be willing to install excess capacity to be used in a crisis. At present, much of this surge capacity is in Saudi Arabia. While seeking to make this source of emergency capacity more secure, consumers might also seek to convince Mexico, Norway, the United Kingdom, or other producers to create surge capacity. Obviously, agreements would be needed to protect the producer from any depressive effect on prices in normal times and to ensure that the capacity is used in a crisis: some form of consumer subsidy or other encouragement might be required. Still it would be difficult to implement the complex multilateral agreements that would be necessary to achieve a reliable surge capacity outside consumer borders. Because reliable foreign sources of surge capacity do not exist, some consumer nations with domestic oil reserves, such as the United States, might consider installing additional production capacity for use in a crisis, though this temporary use might—for technical reasons—compromise long-term production from the fields affected.

A number of consumer nations have also sought to augment crisis supplies by increasing domestically held stocks. However, the acquisition of stocks can create economic and political strains. The new demand tightens the market, leading to upward pressure on prices and perhaps even helping set the stage for the disruptions one is trying to avoid.

In order to acquire strategic stocks and use them effectively several market-related issues must be addressed. Stocks must be accumulated and distributed through the market channels that ordinarily distribute crude oil and products; a separate emergency system would be costly and unreliable. In addition, a workable plan must be devised for making and implementing decisions about stocks—how and when they are to be purchased, how they are to be priced and allocated, and when they are to be used. In the ordinary market, overall stock policy is the sum of many small decisions made by private actors. As indicated above, this may result in normal stocks that are smaller than society might find desirable on security grounds, and too much demand that stocks be increased rapidly in moments of crisis. It is thus at least possible for the market to make and implement decisions about stocks, but private decisions may not be socially optimal.

There seem then to be two alternatives for national policy: to find mechanisms to influence private stock decisions in socially beneficial directions, or to accumulate and hold stocks publicly. Several nations have taken the first course, working through regulation and subsidy; at present, the United States has chosen the second. But public stocks require that governments make and implement highly visible, politicized, and costly decisions; this is not always possible, as the United States has discovered with its strategic reserve. And although it would be desirable to develop both public and private stocks, the effort required to pursue public stocks in the United States appears to have left little political capital to devote to private initiatives.

It is also very important to realize that stocks cannot be considered solely in a domestic context. The oil market is international, and the United States and other countries act within a broad web of economic and political interdependencies. When reserves are built or used, they flow out of or into this international system. In a crisis affecting many nations, those holding stocks domestically would be under pressure—or explicit obligation, as in the IEA sharing agreement—to use them to meet as much of the total shortfall as possible. Thus from a narrow domestic perspective, the value of a strategic reserve can be diluted by the needs of allies. Ironically, consumer fragmentation and losses in market flexibility may decrease the international role of stocks and make them more a matter of domestic security alone.

Reduce Demand

Demand reduction is the other strategy proposed as a response to present market trends and to the security risks accompanying the potential for disruption. Obviously, any reduction in the dependence of a nation on particular supply sources lessens its direct vulnerability to interruptions or other producer actions. But given the interdependencies of markets and alliances, there are important indirect vulnerabilities. For example, the United States may not import oil from a particular producer, but if exports from that producer stop, efforts will be made (by the market and under sharing agreements) to reallocate other U.S. oil supplies. To minimize the potential loss to any particular consumer country, and the high economic and political costs of reallocation should an interruption occur, consumers should seek to allocate the output of risky producers widely, so that no consumer takes more than a small fraction of that country's output.

Long-term demand reduction is often proposed as a way to loosen the supply/demand balance, reduce the upward pressure on prices, and make it easier to cope with crises. If long-term demand reduction would actually accomplish these objectives, it would be extremely important. Unfortunately, it is more likely that this strategy would simply be matched by reductions in supply. The market would remain tight. Many producers, especially Saudi Arabia, are producing oil at levels above their present revenue desires, in part because reductions in output could have a catastrophic effect on Western economies (and thus on producers' investments, military security relationships, and so forth). In fact, some of these producers would have an easier time reconciling domestic political forces—which now include strong conservationist voices—if output were lower. These producers would welcome a reduction in demand—indeed several have called repeatedly for it. And if reduced output alleviates internal political stresses, there may be less likelihood of interruption of consumer supplies.

There are, however, better arguments for long-run demand reduction. It may be one way to create surge capacity and increase other market flexibilities. Convincing producers to maintain excess capacity created automatically through demand reduction would be easier than convincing them to create new capacity for use in a crisis. Indeed some producers might agree to maintain surge capacity if consumers agreed to curb demand. In addition, output reduction would come primarily from OPEC producers; demand reduction would thus decrease the relative importance of these producers in the world market. The result could be increased average flexibility in the international system.

Short-term demand reduction, usable in a crisis, might, in fact, be of greater value than long-run demand reduction. In a crisis, one must be able to restrain both consumption and the demand for additional inventories. Efforts to increase stocks *prior* to a crisis can help reduce panic buying during a crisis and thus are an important complement to measures to effect short-term reductions in consumption.[7] These measures range from an emergency tax (which, properly implemented, might also restrain crisis-induced stock building and encourage the use of inventories when appropriate) to long-term shifts in social or economic structure that would allow a more elastic demand response in times of crisis.

As with supply augmentation, the goal of short-term demand reduction is to loosen the supply/demand balance in a crisis. This loosening may be critical to the ability of the system to find and exploit

---

7. Rationing by government might also seem to suit these purposes; but it is difficult—if not impossible—to implement rationing schemes in a timely and efficient fashion. Indeed there is a danger that pursuit of such a scheme would not only distract from other more productive approaches but would actually encourage stock building in the early days of a crisis.

the flexibilities necessary to reallocate oil supplies. The creation of such flexibilities is the ultimate test of consumer policies.

PROSPECTS

Important changes in the structure of the world oil market have been occurring since early in 1979. Many of these changes reduce traditional degrees of freedom and undermine traditional mechanisms for coping with crises. However, there is also evidence that elements of the new market structure may help restore some of the flexibility to allocate supplies and to mediate between producer and consumer interests formerly provided by the major oil companies. Moreover, some of the new structural rigidities might even serve consumer interests by constraining the actions of individual producers and by making it more difficult for them to act in concert.

The eventual outcome of these market changes is still uncertain. It seems clear, however, that current trends are likely not to favor consumer nations unless they undertake major individual and collective efforts to increase flexibility, both through measures to influence the market's evolution and through crisis planning. Improvements in market flexibility will not only increase the chance that the market alone will be able to deal with at least some crises; they will also amplify the effects of emergency measures directly initiated by consuming nations.

Measures to increase flexibility and deal with crises will undoubtedly be expensive, economically and politically. But without intervention there is serious danger that the international oil system will become increasingly fragile. If it loses resiliency, conflict among consuming nations may become the new order and domestic economic and social stability will be difficult to maintain. Because of linkages through the oil market, domestic energy security has an important and often unrecognized international dimension.

National consensus and resolve, however difficult to achieve, are not the only requisites of an adequate response to the altered international oil regime. As the system has fragmented, the diversity of interests among nations—among producers as well as consumers—has become more important. The simplifications of the past are no longer adequate, whether one is talking about the cartel or about alliance structures. What is needed instead is a realistic and detailed understanding of the nations involved and of their relationships in the international system, of which the oil market is an increasingly important part. The chapters that follow seek to develop these understandings.

PROBLEMS AND POLICIES OF KEY NATIONS

3 THE PERSIAN GULF

Gary Samore

The 1970s revealed both the critical importance and precariousness of the Persian Gulf, which is the source of two-thirds of the West's oil. In the 1980s, the oil policies of the Gulf producers will largely determine whether oil supplies are available in sufficient quantities and at tolerable prices. In addition, the continuous flow of oil from the Gulf is threatened by a volatile combination of internal instability within the Gulf states, regional tensions, and superpower rivalry. Both these dimensions of Persian Gulf oil security affect the political strength and economic welfare of the West, the prospects for stability in the Third World, and the functioning of the international trading and financial systems. This chapter explores this precarious situation. First, it discusses the factors that influence the production and pricing decisions of the major Gulf producers. Then it considers the threat of supply interruptions by evaluating the danger of internal upheavals, local wars, and Soviet activities in the Middle East. Ways in which the United States could influence oil policies and prevent and react to supply interruptions follow each section.

THE DETERMINANTS OF OIL POLICY

For all of the Gulf countries, oil is the major—and in some cases, the only—asset of national power and promise. National control over

The author would like to thank Professor Nadar Safran for comments and assistance in writing this chapter.

Figure 3-1.   The Persian Gulf.

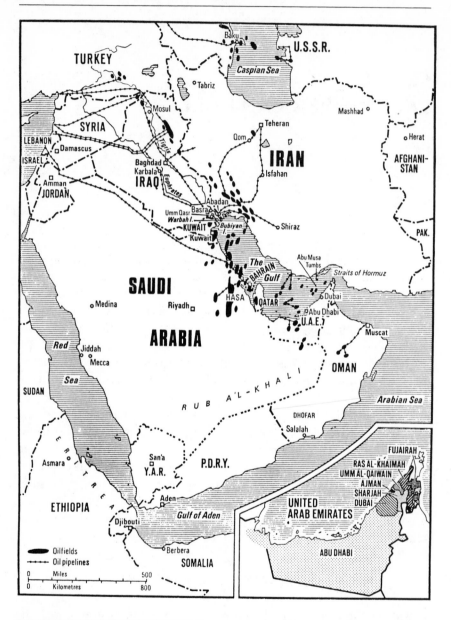

Source: The Institute for the Study of Conflict (1979).

Table 3–1. Countries of the Persian Gulf.

	Population[a] (millions)	Area (sq. miles)	Population Density (sq. mile)	1977 GNP (million $)	GNP ($ per capita, 1977)	Army Size[b]	Type of Government
Iran	35.3	636.0	55	81.2	2,301	285,000	Islamic Republic
Iraq	12.5	168.0	74	19.0	1,524	180,000	Socialist
Kuwait	1.2	6.9	174	13.9	11,545	10,500	Sheikdom
Saudi Arabia	5.5	830.0	7	48.0	8,727	35,000	Monarchy
Bahrain	0.3	0.2	1,235	0.6	2,113	2,300	Sheikdom
Qatar	0.2	4.0	40	3.2	19,753	1,800	Sheikdom
United Arab Emirates[c]	0.7	32.0	20	8.9	13,500	27,000	Sheikdom
Oman	0.6	82.0	7	1.4	2,393	14,000	Sultanate

a. Population figures are only estimates, especially for Saudi Arabia. The figures for Kuwait, Qatar, United Arab Emirates, and Saudi Arabia include large immigrant populations.

b. Excludes Naval and Air Force personnel, and paramilitary forces.

c. Includes Abu Dhabi, Dubai, Sharjah, Ajman, Umm al-Qaiwain, Ras al-Khaiman, Fujairah. Abu Dhabi is the largest, most populous, and greatest oil producer.

decisions affecting production, capacity, and prices is exercised because oil power must create more diverse and enduring sources of
national power. Internally, oil exports provide each state with revenues to satisfy raised expectations and to support vast development
projects. Externally, oil is a principal source of international influence and prestige; it can buy friends and buy off enemies. Even
so, oil power creates problems. Rapid development and sudden
wealth require curbing corruption, efficiently managing oil revenues,
and adapting to profound social change. And oil creates new international responsibilities, intensifying the demands and threats of foreign actors.

The utility of oil power and the problem it raises vary widely
for individual Gulf states. These states also have different amounts of
oil power and widely divergent prospects for transforming their oil
assets into other sources of power. For ambitious states like Iraq, oil
revenues can create such enduring and diverse forms of power as a
modern military establishment, an industrial sector not based on oil,
and a technological infrastructure. It manipulates oil power to expand its influence and prestige in foreign affairs. Other things being
equal, this use implies an expansionist oil policy of greater production and capacity. For unambitious powers such as Kuwait, however,
oil revenues are stretched out as long as possible. This nation trades
oil power for security and protection, displaying a conservationist
attitude of minimum production and capacity. Other Gulf states fall
between these extremes; their oil policies are shaped by both expansionist and conservationist pressures.[1]

Saudi Arabia

Saudi Arabia is by far the largest oil producer in the Gulf. It has the
greatest spare capacity and most extensive oil reserves in the world.
It is no wonder that Saudi oil decisions have the single most important influence on the supply and price of OPEC oil and, to a large
extent, on the world's ability to compensate for sudden shortages.

Yet the Saudis are a lopsided and threatened power in this dangerous world. With the exception of oil in the ground and money in
the bank, they lack critical industrial, political, military, and human

1. The changing role of OPEC countries in the world oil market and its implications for
oil security are discussed in Chapter 2 in this collection.

Table 3-2. Persian Gulf Oil.

	Proven Reserves[a] (billion barrels)		Average Production[b] (million barrels/day)		Sustainable Production Capacity[c] (million barrels/day)	
	1973	1979	1973	1979	1974	1979
Saudi Arabia	138.0	166.0	7.3	9.2	9.2	9.5–10.5
Kuwait	64.9	66.2	2.7	2.3	3.5	2.5
United Arab Emirates	22.8	31.3	1.5	1.8	2.3	2.4
Iraq	29.0	32.1	2.2	3.4	2.5	3.5
Iran	65.0	59.0	5.7	3.0	6.5	4.5– 5.5
Qatar	7.0	4.0	0.6	0.5	0.7	0.6
Neutral Zone[d]	16.0	6.5	0.6	0.6	0.5	0.6
Persian Gulf Total	342.7	364.8	20.6	20.7	25.2	23.6–24.6
OPEC Total	465.6	445.0	31.3	30.6	37.1	34.4–35.4
Free World Total	531.7	555.0	48.4	51.4		

Sources: (Fesharaki 1980), *OPEC Annual Statistical Review*, Central Intelligence Agency (1973; 1979), *International Energy Statistical Review* (1973; 1979), *British Petroleum Statistical Review of World Oil Industry* (1973; 1979), *Petroleum Intelligence Weekly* (1973; 1979).

a. Figures for proven reserves exclude enhanced recovery techniques and possible field discoveries which could substantially increase reserves. In addition, the quoted reserve figures for some countries are questionable. For example, Iraq's reserves are generally believed to be much larger, while the figure for Kuwait is considered to be exaggerated.

b. Actual oil exports are slightly less than production due to domestic consumption within Gulf countries. In 1979, approximately 1.2 million barrels/day of total Gulf production was reserved for domestic consumption, and this figure may nearly double by 1985.

c. Sustainable capacity indicates production that could be maintained for several months without damage to oil fields and is somewhat less than surge capacity. As for proven reserves, figures for capacity are controversial. For example, Saudi capacity is estimated to be 9.5 million barrels/day by the CIA and 10.5 by *Petroleum Intelligence Weekly*. The figure for Iran is also uncertain because it is not certain how much facilities have deteriorated since the revolution.

d. Shared by Saudi Arabia and Kuwait.

Table 3-3.   1985—Comparative forecasts of Persian Gulf oil production.

	Study[a]		Million Barrels/Day	
	(Samore 1980)	(Fesharaki 1980)	(DOE 1980)	(CRS 1977)
Saudi Arabia	8.5– 9.5	6.3	8.5–10.2	16.3
Kuwait	1.5– 2.0	1.5	1.5– 2.0	1.8
United Arab Emirates	1.8– 2.3	1.8	1.8– 2.2	2.5
Iraq	3.5– 4.0	4.0	3.0– 4.0	4.0
Iran	3.0– 4.0	3.0	3.5– 4.5	6.7
Neutral Zone	0.5	0.5	0.5	0.5
Qatar	0.5	0.5	0.5	0.5
Persian Gulf Total	19.3–22.8	17.6	19.3–23.9	32.3

a. For sources, see reference section at end of chapter. The methodologies and relative weight assigned to political, economic, and technical factors by each of these studies are widely divergent.

assets; their prospects for transforming their transient oil power into enduring, well-rounded power are not very bright. The discrepancy between Saudi Arabia's oil power and its other weaknesses make this vital nation an inviting target for demands, pressures, and threats.

Hence, the Saudis feel extremely vulnerable to a whole array of internal and external threats. Regionally, they are surrounded by stronger and potentially (or actually) hostile forces — Ethiopia, Egypt, Israel, Syria, Iraq, and Iran — and by a ring of small, weak states that have historically served stronger powers as toeholds on the Arabian Peninsula. Globally, the Saudis are open to domination, partition, or conquest by the great powers if the scramble for world oil becomes less civil. These threats, in turn, are connected to a number of potential internal threats to the Saudi royal family.

The Saudis' oil policy must reinforce the stability of the Western economic system, in which they have become increasingly interdependent, while conserving oil for the future and avoiding the strains of overly rapid development. They seek to curb Western demand for oil by encouraging conservation and alternative energy sources. At the same time they need to protect the long-term value of oil. They must balance Western demands for lower prices and higher production with OPEC's demands for higher prices and lower production.

On the political level, Saudi Arabia tries to use promises and threats about oil to move the United States toward pressuring Israel into a comprehensive settlement without undercutting American willingness and ability to defend Saudi Arabia against regional and Soviet threats. In inter-Arab politics, the Saudis try to buy friends and buy off enemies — without losing control over oil policy. Internally, oil power creates the instruments to centralize power, develop modern institutions, and satisfy raised expectations; but the corrosive effect of oil wealth, rapid social change, and economic dislocations threaten the survival of the royal family. Legendary Saudi caution, vacillation, and paranoia have good basis in fact.[2]

There are two schools of thought about appropriate production levels among the technocrats who are involved in setting oil policy. The "technocratic conservationists" advocate limiting production to the minimum level required to meet domestic revenue needs. They argue that by remaining the supplier of first resort for the West's

2. An excellent study of Saudi decisionmaking under these conflicting pressures is found in Moran (1980).

unchecked oil appetite, Saudi Arabia may deplete its oil reserves too fast for orderly development and productive investments while also depriving future generations of Saudi Arabia's only important asset. Furthermore, they point out, the return on savings and investments generated by revenue surpluses is often reduced to a loss by inflation, the dollar's depreciation, and the other factors. Therefore, oil is worth more in the ground than in the bank. Planning Minister Nazir, one of the most vehement advocates of this view, has frequently cited 5 million barrels per day as a prudent production level.

Opposing the conservationists are the "technocratic spenders" who argue that higher production and lower prices protect Saudi Arabia's stake in the stability and health of the Western economic system. They believe that the conservationists' policies will cause international inflation and recession to erode the value of Saudi overseas investment, bring a higher inflation rate to Saudi Arabia, and hinder Western exports needed for further development and consumer satisfaction. They are determined to push ahead with ambitious development plans that would increase Saudi revenue needs. The most prominent technocratic spender, Minister of Petroleum Yamani, argues: "We cannot go to extremes in our nationalistic outlook and ignore the world economic situation by producing at levels that would satisfy our strict requirements alone. Such actions would lead to world economic recession, shake governments all over the world, and generate massive unemployment—factors that would inevitably lead to war in which we would be a party and a target" (Long, 1979 page 86).[3]

Actually, the arguments of the technocrats are less important than their alliances with the senior princes of the royal family, the true decisionmakers in Saudi Arabia. Among these princes, oil policy is only one of many issues requiring resolution through frequently shifting alliances and compromises.

The question of succession is a major source of tension within the royal family. Government offices are distributed among the important princes with an eye to maintaining a balance among various factions. The central balance within the royal family is reported to be between the frequent alliance of King Khalid and Prince Abdullah,

---

3. Long presents a succinct overview of Saudi oil policy, including a discussion of bureaucratic politics in the Supremem Petroleum Council. Cogent descriptions of the "new conservationists" can be found in Levy (1978/79) and Stobaugh and Yergin (1979).

head of the National Guard on one hand and that of Crown Prince Fahd and Prince Sultan, Minister of Defense on the other. Abdullah and Sultan are said to have rival ambitions for the throne, though Abdullah is generally considered to be better positioned and both are behind Fahd. Abdullah's prominent supporters include Princes Mohammed (the influential older full brother of the King), Badr (deputy head of the National Guard), and Saud al-Feisal (Foreign Minister). Fahd and Sultan are frequently supported by their full brothers Nayef (Minister of Interior), Ahmad (Deputy Minister of Interior), and Salman (Governor of Riyadh). These alliances are by no means rigid, however, and other prominent and rising princes frequently change their allegiances on specific issues.[4]

The split between these princes frequently extends to matters of basic policy. Fahd, considered cosmopolitan and progressive, favors more rapid modernization and major development projects. Abdullah, with close ties to religious and tribal leaders, is inclined to prefer slower development and preservation of traditional ways.

In foreign affairs, Fahd is said to stress the importance of maintaining close ties with the United States and of protecting the Western political/economic system. Abdullah emphasizes the need to maintain Saudi Arabia's high standing in inter-Arab politics. These differences have a direct bearing on Saudi oil policy. Fahd's concern for American–Saudi relations and fast-paced development implies a policy of high production and low prices, while Abdullah's interest in Arab unity and slower development implies the opposite. As a result, important decisions cannot be made without first consulting, compromising, and finally — sometimes after protracted and intricate negotiations — agreeing.

At a fundamental level, the internal debate on Saudi oil policy raises basic strategic, almost philosophical, questions. Can Saudi Arabia turn back its drive to develop and modernize and slip into the reassuring envelope of traditional values and historical isolation? It seems clear that the simpler days of bedouin life and tribal society are on the road to extinction; the clock cannot be turned back. The enormous spending of the first two five-year development plans has created a momentum of its own — infrastructure projects are half-

4. Conclusions about the internal politics and policy debates within the royal family are highly speculative. Further details can be found in Kraft (1975), Kelidar (1978), Mishlawi (1979), Hottinger (1979), and Cooley (1979). A highly insightful and irreverent tour of the royal family is presented in Blandford (1976).

finished; a new crop of educated Saudis require jobs; revenue is better spent at home than depreciating abroad; and, most important, raised expectations cannot be denied when the upper crust has so visibly benefited from the oil boom.

So oil production in some large amount will continue. With expenditures estimated at $46 billion and oil revenues forecast at $91 billion in the current budget, Saudi Arabia's foreign exchange requirements could be met with less than 5 million barrels of oil per day (DOE 1980). But rising costs in the ambitious 1980–1985 development plan, world inflation, and a slower rate of increase in oil prices may boost necessary production levels as high as 7 million barrels of oil per day by the mid–1980s.[5]

Externally, the world will not leave the Saudis alone; they will remain at the center of conflicting demands. But it seems unlikely that the Saudis can abandon their stake in Western strength and retreat to a more modest position of isolation. Both fear and ambition compel them to seek a major, if not a dominant, position in OPEC, while also attempting to preserve the organization's unity through compromise. Politically, the Saudis will need to juggle oil policy between their dependence on the United States and their exposed position in Arab politics.

Given the political balance within the royal family and the real dilemmas facing Saudi Arabia, Saudi oil production will probably not shift away dramatically from the present official ceiling of 8.5 million barrels per day by 1985, except on a temporary basis. The implication of this analysis is that Saudi production is more likely to rise slightly than fall. But any projection is hostage to future developments in Saudi internal politics, regional relations, and ties with the United States, as well as to a number of economic factors.[6]

In any case, it is likely that Saudi Arabia will increase its sustainable capacity. Though increased capacity may result in greater pressures to raise production to meet Western demand, these pressures

5. The tendency for escalating development costs to absorb budget surpluses is discussed in Moran (1978) and Kanovsky (1979).

6. A pessimistic analysis by Fesharaki argues that domestic political pressures and the inability of Saudi Arabia to dominate OPEC will gradually drive Saudi production down to a "floor" of 6.3 million barrels of oil per day, the technical requirement for operating Saudi gas-gathering facilities at full capacity (Fesharaki 1980). An extremely optimistic projection of 16.6 million barrels per day in 1985 made by Congressional Research Service (1977) seems very unrealistic.

are easier to bear and less dangerous than the helplessness and declining influence of insufficient spare capacity. In 1979, constraints on Saudi capacity during the drop in Iranian production considerably reduced their ability to dictate OPEC price levels and resulted in a deterioration of their political influence and prestige in both the West and the Arab world. A restoration of Saudi influence in OPEC by increasing capacity could reverse this erosion and perhaps allow the Saudis to control the oil markets once again. On prices, the Saudis are unlikely to be as moderate as they were from 1974 to 1978. Nonetheless, they are likely to continue being more moderate than OPEC's more rapacious members.[7]

New spare capacity would also provide the Saudis with some insurance against unexpected supply interruptions, leading to chaos in world oil markets or possible military intervention. The ability to make up supply losses would also be a marvelous bargaining chip.[8] There is some evidence that the Saudis are already quietly acting to increase capacity from 10.5 million barrels per day at present and to 12 million barrels per day by the end of 1981. It is difficult to predict how much further they will go in the next decade. But both Yamani and Nazir, who rarely seem to agree on anything, announced recently that Saudi Arabi plans to reach a capacity of 14 million barrels per day between 1983 and 1985.[9]

Kuwait

Like Saudi Arabia, Kuwait enjoys considerable flexibility in setting production levels because of the vast discrepancy between its revenue needs and productive capacity. Current sustainable capacity is around 2.5 million barrels per day, but only about 40 percent of that is nec-

---

7. Whether the Saudis can actually restore their dominant position in OPEC will depend on such factors as world demand and supply of oil and the interal dynamics of OPEC. For a more complete discussion, see Moran (1980).

8. Surplus Saudi capacity is a necessary, but not sufficient, safeguard against supply disruptions since regional political pressures may constrain Saudi actions or Saudi Arabia may, itself, be the source of disruptions. For these reasons, a Western Strategic Petroleum Reserve is an absolutely essential element of oil policy. Though the Saudis have objected to the American reserve, it is unlikely to become a critical issue in Saudi-American relations.

9. Recent Saudi plans to increase capacity are discussed in *Quarterly Economic Review of Saudi Arabia* (1979 and 1980). A detailed, but overly pessimistic, study of Saudi capacity is found in United States Senate (1979).

essary to satisfy foreign exchange requirements (DOE 1980). Unlike Saudi Arabia, however, Kuwait has little incentive to raise production much above a minimal level. It has already built an extensive welfare system and has even fewer prospects than Saudi Arabia for establishing a self-sufficient non-oil-based economy or for transforming oil power into military and political strength. Hence, the conservationist ethic is strongly embedded in Kuwaiti oil strategy. Kuwait was one of the first producers to establish a ceiling on oil production and the first to inaugurate a "Fund for Future Generations," consisting of 10 percent of all government revenues. By the time that oil wells run dry, Kuwait hopes to have become a banking and financial center sustained by the revenues from foreign investments.

Kuwait's conservationist ethic tends to create its own dynamic. At higher prices, revenues are maintained by less production, and oil in the ground grows in value. There is little political incentive to break the circle, for Kuwait is even more exposed than Saudi Arabia to regional threats stemming from the Arab–Israeli conflict and inter-Arab tensions. It is therefore more inclined than Saudi Arabia to reflect the dominant trend of Arab politics and even less inclined to pursue oil policies that risk angering other Arab states.

Even if political barriers to higher oil production were removed, Kuwait would be unlikely to reward the West with greater production. Although it ultimately depends on a peaceful oil system and the economic prosperity and political stability of the West, Kuwait prefers to let Saudi Arabia bear the burdens of overproduction and isolation at OPEC meetings. About the only bright aspects of Kuwaiti oil policy to Western eyes are its inclination to moderate the demands of OPEC's most radical members and to maintain some surplus production to fund a generous foreign aid program.

Due to these factors, Kuwaiti production is likely to remain modest through the 1980s, probably nearer the low end of the range between 1.5 and 2 million barrels per day.[10] Kuwait could probably expand its present productive capacity of 2.5 million barrels per day to 3 million barrels per day within a year and up to 4 million barrels per day after that, but there is little incentive to make this investment (CIA 1979). In keeping with Kuwait's political strategy of

---

10. Kuwait has announced a new production ceiling of 1.5 million barrels per day in April 1980, but 1.8 million barrels per day may be necessary to operate its Liquefied Natural Gas plants by 1985 (DOE 1980).

avoiding controversy, low capacity prevents Western demands to expand production as world oil requirements increase. But at the same time, Kuwait has a strong interest in maintaining some capacity to cushion unexpected supply interruptions as it did during the Iranian cutoff. Hence, Kuwaiti productive capacity is likely to be in the range of 2.5 to 3 million barrels per day in 1985, but a number of political factors will determine whether Kuwait actually uses its surge capacity in the context of supply disruptions.

The United Arab Emirates[11]

The strategic situation of the Emirates is basically the same as that of Kuwait: they are too small and too rich to pursue expansionist oil policies. But UAE oil policy has typically corresponded with Saudi oil policy for several reasons: closer political ties with the Saudis, less satisfaction with the level of internal development, and somewhat less exposure to radical regional pressures.

These factors may very well change over the next decade. As the strains of development and modernization become more apparent, the conservationist ethic is likely to become more convincing. And if Iraq's influence in the Gulf grows, the Emirates may become more reluctant to follow the Saudis. Indeed, the Emirates have already pushed for higher oil prices than the Saudis. The Emirates' dependence on the economic and political well-being of the West and concern for the Arab–Israeli conflict pose somewhat conflicting imperatives, but they may imitate Kuwait and avoid Saudi Arabia's more exposed position.

Barring dramatic changes, total Emirate production is likely to fall in the range between 1.8 and 2.3 million barrels per day in the mid–1980s. With limited reserves, Dubai is likely to produce near capacity at 0.3 million barrels per day. Abu Dhabi has more flexibility; although only 1.2 million barrels per day are necessary for its foreign exchange requirements, perhaps 1.9 million barrels per day will be required to operate its liquefied natural gas plants in 1985 (DOE 1980). In addition, Abu Dhabi shares some of its oil revenues within the federal framework of the Emirates and maintains an extensive foreign aid policy. Total productive capacity is likely to be

11. Of the seven Emirates, only Abu Dhabi is an important oil producer.

between 2.5 and 3 million barrels per day. Like Kuwait and Saudi Arabia, the Emirates will probably continue to be willing to expand production temporarily in the event of some sudden supply shortages, depending on the political factors involved.

Iraq

Iraq has taken a generally rapacious approach to oil, exploiting it now, driven by its strident anti-imperialist idealogy, and generally fair prospects for achieving a self-sustaining non-oil-based economy. Unlike Saudi Arabia, which must balance its ties to the United States with its concern for Arab solidarity, Iraq supports pan–Arab unity and has taken a hard line stance toward Israel and the United States. Rather than balance development with the preservation of traditional culture and religious values, Iraq is bent on creating a secular, socialist state that will eradicate tribal loyalties, religious sectarianism, and ethnic divisions.

Although the general direction of Iraq's oil policy has been clear and consistent, there are enormous gaps in our knowledge of its oil industry and of the internal dynamic of oil policy formation. For example, estimates of Iraq's proven and probable reserves range from 32 to 95 billion barrels. Even figures of current output and the distribution of oil exports are notoriously unreliable. To a large extent, this obscurity results from restrictions on multinational oil companies, the nationalization of oil production, and the extreme secrecy of the small clique of Ba'athist party leaders who make oil policy. For lack of a better formula, it is probably best to assume that oil decisionmaking in Iraq is even more centralized than in Saudi Arabia. What Saddam Hussien wants, he generally gets.

Nonetheless, we can build a fairly strong case that Iraq will increase production and productive capacity in the next decade while remaining a price hawk. If, under certain conditions, this policy of high production and high price becomes contradictory, Iraq would probably cut production to maintain high prices, but this will also depend on the actions of other OPEC members.

The central theme of Iraq's history has been great promise contrasted with grim reality. On paper, the nation has outstanding potential: oil, an adequate population, agricultural resources, and the assets to create a self-sustaining non-oil-based economy and respectable military forces. These internal assets, combined with Iraq's strategic location at the crossroad of the Middle East and Asia, give it the possibility of becoming a substantial regional power. Thwarting'this potential, however, has been a history of ethnic and religious fragmentation, social unrest, persistent political instability, idealogical fanaticism, and severe repression. Reflecting this bloody domestic pattern, Iraq's foreign policy has swung erratically between reckless ambition and nearly complete isolation.[12]

Now, for perhaps the first time, Iraq has an opportunity to fulfill its potential. The Ba'athist regime of Saddam Hussein has achieved a degree of internal stability unparalleled in Iraq since the overthrow of the monarch in 1958. The regime is by no means indestructible or even founded on broad popular support and legitimacy, but a combination of repression and accommodation has seemed to subdue and placate major internal threats since its ascendency in 1968. If nothing else, the regime seems to be in a position to devote more attention to long-term national goals and less to immediate survival. Egypt's isolation in the Arab world following Sadat's agreements with Israel and Iran's erosion as a regional power since the fall of the Shah have also opened unprecedented opportunities for Iraqi power in the Middle East. A growing disenchantment with the Soviet Union and increasing ties with the West, especially France, have allowed Iraq greater independence and flexibility in world politics.

If these conditions persist, Iraq's domestic and foreign ambitions are likely to be accompanied by a more expansionist oil policy. The Ba'athist regime needs higher oil revenues to pursue ambitions and internal development plans and provide higher levels of prosperity, both of which are essential for consolidating Hussien's political position and for expanding Iraq's regional potential.

Iraq's future revenue needs are difficult to establish because detailed development plans are not available, but increased production seems likely. The 1980 budget forecasts a 60 percent increase in expenditures for economic development and social welfare programs and a 50 percent increase in imports (*Quarterly Economic Review of Iraq* 1980). Assuming the typical escalation of actual costs over projections and the typical dynamic of rapid development (once hooked, it's difficult to slow down) it is reasonable to assume that Iraq's for-

12. The reasons behind Iraq's stormy history are summarized in Kedourie (1974) and Kelidar (1975).

eign exchange requirements will exceed the production level of 1.5 to 2 million barrels of oil per day postulated by the Department of Energy (DOE 1980).

Even if internal requirements can be met with production below 3 million barrels per day, Iraq's foreign policy interests may nevertheless dictate higher production and higher productive capacity. First, Iraq's active regional ambitions call for a more vigorous foreign aid program as an instrument of foreign policy. Already, the subsidy program for 1979 and projected distributions for 1980 show considerable increases, particularly to Syria and Jordan. Second, increases in Iraq's production and productive capacity could make its voice critical in OPEC and OAPEC (Organization of Arab Petroleum Exporting Countries). In the past, Iraq has been generally impotent in OPEC and ostracized in OAPEC (Penrose and Penrose 1979). But the disruption of Iranian production and the waning of Saudi Arabia's power in OPEC has broken the Saudi–Iranian domination of OPEC and left Iraq the second largest OPEC producer.

Increased Iraqi influence within OPEC would encourage Saudi Arabia to cooperate with Iraq in order to bring about the price levels and market structure that it prefers to the potentially disruptive goals of revolutionary Iran. This cooperation could also take the form of Saudi–Iraqi initiatives in the Gulf to frustrate Iran's attempts to export its religious revolution. Increased influence would also obviously give Iraq more power to mold OPEC policies. Although it is difficult to predict how Iraq would exercise new power within OPEC, it is probably safe to say that Iraq would take a more moderate position than in the past but a more hawkish position than the Saudis. Barring significant changes that could dash Iraq's hopes for more power, it is possible that Iraq will advocate some basic changes in OPEC operations, possibly a switch to basket-of-currency payments or some manner of production controls to sustain higher oil prices.

Similar conclusions can be drawn about Iraq's role in OAPEC. In the past, Iraq was ostracized because of its extreme positions, such as persistent calls for nationalizing American oil companies, which other Arab oil producers feared would backfire. Now, with Egypt isolated and with Syria and Saudi Arabia casting about for allies against Israel and Iran, respectively, Iraq has assumed a more central position in Arab politics. As a consequence, Iraq is likely to seek a more active role in OAPEC by increasing its production capacity.

Doing so will give the Saudis yet another incentive for cooperation with Iraq, if only to avoid more radical demands for nationalizing American oil companies and threats to sabotage Saudi oil fields. And if Saudi Arabia vacillates in its opposition to Camp David and Egypt, or if Saudi Arabia balks at more vigorous oil sanctions against the United States in the event that negotiations collapse, then Iraq may hope to replace Saudi Arabia as the dominant force in OAPEC.

Still another reason for Iraq to expand production is that this step would allow increased government-to-government sales, the oil trans-actions most favorable to its nationalized oil establishment. Such arrangements foster special relationships with Western nations—espe-cially France, whose extensive government involvement in the oil industry and willingness to exchange arms for oil make it a perfect partner for Iraq. Government-to-government sales would also boost Iraq's prestige in the Third World, where it seeks to become a leader of the nonaligned movement. Such direct sales are also an excellent way to obtain restricted imports, such as the nuclear technology that could give Iraq the first Arab atomic bomb. Finally, in a simple but cogent sense, a 4 million barrel per day country is twice as important as a 2 million barrel per day country. International prestige, favors, and attention can be important assets for a regime that is trying, for the first time in recent history, to achieve its potential.

For all of these reasons, Iraq is likely to expand oil production by 1985 to 3.5 to 4 million barrels per day, all the while maintaining a generally hawkish stand on prices. Production will be lower only if prices take another quantum jump in the near future. But whatever the actual production levels, Iraq will seek to expand its production capacity to above 4 million barrels per day by the mid–1980s in order to increase its oil power and exploit interruptions by temporar-ily raising production after events have driven the price of oil even higher.

Iran

In Iran, the decisive effect of politics on oil policy has been clearly visible both before and after the revolution. Oil was the key to the Shah's political ambitions to create a modern nation–state and a world power overnight. High production and high prices were the result, though the Shah was occasionally willing to moderate price increases for political reasons. During the revolution, control over oil production became a symbol of the political struggle between the Shah and his opponents. In the end, the ability of religious and leftist forces to keep oil workers on strike helped to bring the collapse of the Shah's political supremacy.

Today, the Khomeini regime sees oil as the symbol of Western exploitation of Iran and the source of Western decadence in Iranian society. The new regime has pursued an extremely hawkish policy on oil prices while abandoning the Shah's emphasis on high production and expanded capacity. Although production ceilings were set at 4 million barrels per day in early 1979 and then lowered to between 3 and 3.5 million barrels per day for 1980, actual production has been reduced to 1.5 to 2 million barrels per day for most of 1980.

Indeed, short of destroying its oil fields, Iran has done nearly everything possible to cut its oil production and limit exports. The expulsion of Western technicians, the purge of Iranian experts, and political disruptions of administration have left the state oil bureaucracy in shambles. A crackdown on leftist elements in labor unions and general mismanagement of government–labor relations has produced considerable resentment and agitation among oil workers. Khomeini's provocation of Iraq, combined with harsh repression of the Arab minority in Khuzistan, has resulted in the sabotage of pipelines and pumping stations. Iran's demands for unrealistic prices and its holding of American hostages have threatened to isolate Iranian oil from traditional markets in Europe and Japan. Even within OPEC, Iran's extreme positions have antagonized other producers, especially those in the Gulf.

Future Iranian oil policy depends on the restoration of political stability and of a sensible foreign policy. In the meantime, the West should not count on much more than the present level of oil production, which the threat of further turmoil or civil war makes precarious enough. Even if political stability and economic order are restored, estimates of future production depend on the political orientation and economic aspirations of the future regime. At present, the combination of sharp budget cuts, a drop in imports, and the doubling of oil prices has considerably lowered the production levels necessary for internal fuel and foreign exchange requirements, perhaps to the level of 2.3 million barrels per day (DOE 1980). However, any stable regime will probably require higher production just to survive. For example, Bani Sadr's program for economic self-sufficiency and agricultural revival is estimated to require production between 3 and 4 million barrels per day (*Quarterly Economic Review of Iran* 1980). This level is probably the best estimate we can make for Iranian production by 1985. If Iran's oil production does increase, incidentally, other OPEC countries may cut production in order to maintain prices and conserve resources.[13]

It seems very likely that any future Iranian government will advocate price increases. Similarly, Iranian capacity can only go down. Even before the revolution, capacity was expected to drop from 6.6 million barrels per day in 1978 to 6 million barrels per day in 1985, and this decline would have occurred despite a massive petroleum development plan that has since been shelved. One report estimates an annual loss of at least 10 percent of all capacity for as long as facilities are not kept up (CIA 1979). Productive capacity is likely to be between 4 and 5 million barrels per day, but this is a very tentative estimate.

Policy Conclusions

The extent to which American policy can influence the oil policies of Gulf producers varies widely. For Iraq and Iran, it is nearly nonexistent. Even where fairly substantial, as for Saudi Arabia, American influence operates on a discrete and delicate level. Neither American intimidation of Saudi Arabia nor subservience to Saudi wishes is likely to succeed. Instead, cooperation depends on implicit understandings based on the overall quality of American–Saudi relations and the success in pursuing mutual interests.

A "special relationship" developed between the United States and Saudi Arabia from 1974 through 1978. Favorable Saudi oil policies were implicitly exchanged for favorable American security policies; there was a growing congruence of interests. Moderate oil policies protected Western economic and political stability for the Saudis, while the United States could protect Saudi oil from regional radicals and the Soviet Union. A range of secondary economic ties bolstered the relationship.

---

13. Whether this will be an ad hoc reduction or the beginning of coordinated production policies in OPEC is a critical question. The implications of "true" cartel behavior in OPEC for Western energy policy is discussed in Chapter 9 in this collection.

Stresses and strains began appearing in 1977, when the Saudis began to believe that the United States was not successfully containing Soviet influence. What looked to Washington like ad hoc Soviet opportunism on the periphery of the Middle East (Ethiopia, South Yemen, and Afghanistan) appeared to Riyadh as a strategy of encirclement. And American energy policy had failed to reduce demand for imported oil. In fact, American demand threatened to undercut Saudi power in OPEC by increasing faster than Saudi productive capacity. To Saudi eyes, Americans were also to blame for the erosion of Saudi productive flexibility caused by rising development costs, international and domestic inflation, and the depreciation of the dollar. It seemed as if they were being charged exorbitant rates for capital goods while being discriminated against in American investment markets.

It was in late 1978 and early 1979, however, that the Camp David agreements and the collapse of the Shah's regime brought the strain in U.S.-Saudi relations to a head. The Saudis undoubtedly felt considerable annoyance at the United States for doing too little to prevent the Shah's fall and too much to promote Sadat's peace initiative. Though they were quick to deny any similarity between Saudi Arabia and Iran, the technocratic conservationists found their arguments strengthened by the lessons of overly ambitious development and American vacillation. Egypt's pending agreement with Israel threatened to consolidate a radical coalition and provide new opportunities for Soviet and Palestinian agitation, and it also seemed to disregard the royal family's support for a comprehensive settlement.

In June 1979, Saudi oil production dropped 1 million barrels per day. From a political angle, this gesture seems to have been a way of simultaneously expressing displeasure with the United States and solidarity with the Arab cause. Economically, it supported the demands of technocratic conservationists and other OPEC members for lower production and higher prices. In short, the accumulation of events seems to have fortified an alliance between conservative "pro-Arab" princes and technocratic conservationists and to have bolstered their arguments against those of the technocratic spenders. However, within a few months the Saudis announced a temporary increase of 1 million barrels per day above the official ceiling of 8.5 million barrels per day to coincide with Ambassador Strauss's Middle East tour in search of a Palestinian solution.

The collapse of the Syrian–Iraqi unity talks and Iraq's preoccupation with internal affairs had relieved some tension in inter-Arab politics. And the collapse in 1979 of OPEC's price structure through price leap-frogging and panic bidding on the spot market seemed to have strengthened the argument for international economic stability. Though the Saudis have often seen the United States as aggravating their problem, they are nonetheless largely dependent on the United States to help resolve these problems. Hence, the Saudi's willingness to produce more than their own requirements depends, in part, on American success in containing Soviet influence in the area, restoring regional stability, resolving the Arab–Israeli conflict, and, in general, bolstering the rule of the royal family. None of these measures, however, is likely to result in an explicit quid pro quo of Saudi production increases in exchange for specific American actions; instead, the critical factors are Saudi judgments about American leadership and the overall quality of American–Saudi relations. Nor is it likely that American actions, no matter how successful, can persuade the Saudis to expand production indefinitely to satisfy an unchecked Western demand for imported oil.

CRISIS IN THE GULF

The events of the 1970s made it obvious that one of the most crucial dimensions of the energy security problem is the danger of sudden oil supply interruptions, whether accidental or intentional. Conceptually, the threats of such disruptions can be organized into three general categories: (1) internal—the dangers presented by domestic instability within oil-producing states; (2) regional—potential disruptions arising from regional conflicts and tensions; and (3) international—direct and indirect Soviet threats to oil supplies. Yet however convenient this division is for analysis, we should be aware that it neglects the situation's full complexity. A simple domestic political conflict could disrupt a nation's oil production, replace a friendly regime with an avowed enemy, aggravate regional tensions, and ultimately create opportunities for the Soviet Union. So the threats to our oil security are perversely interconnected; each tends to make the others worse. Not only is the probability of any potentially disruptive event difficult to predict, the likelihood and manner in which such an event, if it occurs, actually affects oil is uncertain.

These complications suggest that any strategy to enhance oil security will be inadequate and even dangerous if it is preoccupied with any single threat. Unfortunately, American policy has had this very tendency: to search for one simplistic formula that guarantees oil security and favorable oil policies. Solve the Arab–Israeli conflict and oil is secure. Stop the Russians and oil is secure. Reform the Saudis and oil is secure. We must learn to recognize that, in some cases, an element of policy will serve multiple purposes. In others, policies intended to check one threat may actually make others more likely. And the extent to which our policies can "solve the problem" at all is clearly greater in some instances than in others.

Internal Instability

Whether they are conservative monarchies, tribal sheikdoms, socialist one-party states, or fledgling theocracies, all of the Gulf states have deep sources of internal instability. They are beset by the dislocations of rapid development and new wealth, the presence of uneasy religious and ethnic minorities and immigrant workers, conflicting religious and political ideologies, the fragility of political legitimacy, and serious divisions within ruling elites. These internal problems are often aggravated by regional tensions, expressed by propaganda and subversion, and by superpower rivalries.

Although violent political change cannot be ruled out for any Gulf state over the next decade, the occasion and outcome of such change is exceedingly difficult to predict. Yet the case of Iran illustrates that internal upheavals can have profound effects on regional politics, superpower rivalry, and oil security.

Of the three largest Gulf states, Iran is clearly the most unstable. Minority unrest persists; the economy is faltering, and Khomeini's death is likely to unleash a struggle that will probably result in some form of dictatorship or in chaos. The Ba'athist regime in Iraq and the Al–Saud regime in Saudi Arabia may survive the decade, but it is doubtful whether either of these regimes is capable of resolving the fundamental social and ideological problems that threaten political stability. Hence, the possibility of violent political change in these countries cannot be dismissed. Of the small Gulf states, Kuwait and Bahrain seem the most vulnerable to the overthrow of their traditional political systems, but the stability of all the small Gulf states is fundamentally dependent on larger political developments in the area.

Many other countries in the Middle East are also susceptible to political disruptions that could affect the West's oil security. For example, the overthrow of Sadat by radical or fundamentalist forces could be devastating, since American strategy in the region has become quite dependent on close cooperation with Egypt. Ironically, though, our record of anticipating instability has been dismal. "Pillars of stability," such as Iraq (in 1958) and Iran (in 1979) have been toppled. Countries long written off, such as Jordan, have continued to enjoy stability. Even when the United States successfully predicted a violent change, as in Libya in 1969, it bet on the wrong conspirators. With this record in mind, we discuss the sources of internal stability and conflict likely to prove important within particular Gulf states during the next decade and over the long term.

Saudi Arabia. American views of Saudi political stability have swung from complacency before Iran's revolution to something near hysteria after the revolution. A more balanced analysis suggests that, given the differences between the social systems and political structures of Saudi Arabia and Iran, a social revolution like Iran's is not at present likely in Saudi Arabia. However, the Saudi political system is probably eventually doomed to violent convulsions and upheaval. Even if the royal family uses all of its power to delay the inevitable, its overthrow in the next decade cannot be discounted.

Oil revenues controlled by the royal family has greatly enhanced Saudi economic development and social modernization, unifying the country, raising the standard of living, and enhancing national security. But in the long run these processes tend to undermine the social base and political legitimacy of traditional political systems. In this regard, Saudi Arabia is the most prominent, and nearly the last, state of its kind; the oil-rich Kings of Iraq, Libya, and Iran have already been overthrown.

The social base of the Saudi political system is built on a feudal triangle composed of the royal family, tribal chieftans, and religious authorities. The royal family is the central pivot. In the early twentieth century, it united the various tribes and important towns of the country under the banner of Wahhabism, a puritanical branch of Islam. Its conquests were consolidated through political marriages, subsidies, and patron–client networks that connected princes of the royal family with important individuals and social groups (Philby 1952).

In principle, the monarchy is the moral center of both the tribal and religious order because the King is also the head sheik of the tribal confederation and the supreme religious leader of the Wahhabi movement. This congruence of politics and religion contrasts with the situation in prerevolutionary Iran, where the two forces were generally in conflict. In the last decade the royal family's control over an enormous cash flow has allowed it to buy friends and influence enemies while the development of national transportation, communications, welfare, and military systems has enhanced its political monopoly.

Ultimately, however, this great wealth is likely to polarize the nation's social base and undercut the monarchy's moral authority. On the one hand, urbanization and education weaken the tribal order on which the sheiks' power is based; Western ideas, technology, and secularism undermine conservative religious values and traditions. On the other hand, development creates modern classes, urban workers, and salaried professionals whose interests cannot be accommodated by the traditional political network and whose loyalty to the principle of monarchism is suspect. Though individual members of the modern classes can be absorbed into the patron–client network that leads to the royal family, their collective interests and their growing importance to the country are not secured or reflected in the traditional triangle of Saudi politics.

At best, the modern elements are neutral to the fate of the monarchy. Not willing to fight for the King, they may be the first to abandon him or to flee the country during crisis. At worst, they confront the monarchy with demands for political reforms, such as parties and parliaments, and with political ideologies that are incompatible with the institutions and principles of absolute monarchy. And modernization equips these modern elements with the tools for political pressure and violent political change.

As a result, the royal family will be increasingly torn between demands for reform and demands for revival. The more modernization, the more the family will be seen as the corruptor of traditional values. If modernization is held back, the royal family will be cast as a reactionary obstacle to progress and enlightenment. As development proceeds, elements of dubious loyalty are strengthened while the family's base of support is undermined. If development is held back, the family dashes raised expectations and weakens its centralizing power over traditional forces.[14]

Reinforced by the lavish spending of wealthy princes, growing economic disparities may also weaken the royal family's moral authority and legitimacy. This danger is amplified by considerable corruption, waste, and inefficiency in government development spending, a problem exacerbated by the extensive involvement of princes in the government bureaucracy and private sector.

Furthermore, the national independence supposedly fostered by economic development is belied by a short-term dependence on the West for skilled imported labor. The influx of Western technicians and workers opens the royal family to charges of forwarding Western imperialism and blasphemy. Also, much-needed Arab and Moslem workers—the poorly treated Yemenis, Palestinians, and Pakistanis— are a potentially subversive internal group in the context of an indigenous upheaval.

Eventually, development and modernization will deprive the royal family of a firm social base and its political legitimacy, forcing it to rely entirely on greed and fear to secure its political primacy. In this situation, it will be very vulnerable to any catalytic event that appears to undercut its control. When an oil monarchy becomes "rotten at the core," change can come from several directions—a revolutionary coalition of modern and traditional elements (as in Iran) or a military coup, either from the secular left (as in Iraq) or from the fundamentalist right (as in Libya).[15]

Despite evidence of political violence from both the left and the right, however, Saudi society does not yet seem to be polarized and disrespectful of the monarchy. Saudi society and culture remain overwhelmingly traditional; underlying values and attitudes, including fealty to the throne and Wahhabism, remain traditional.[16]

---

14. The theoretical basis for this argument is found in Huntington (1968). An application to Arab countries is presented in Hudson (1979).

15. The royal family has already been shaken by a number of political incidents, including an attempted leftist coup in 1969 and the takeover of the Mecca Mosque by Islamic dissidents in 1979. Contrasting versions of the Mecca incident are found in the *New York Times*, February 25, 1980, and *Afro-Asian Affairs Newsletter*, December 1979. A more general history of opposition to the royal family is in Halliday (1975) and Lackner (1979).

16. This pattern probably does not hold for the small Shi'ite minority in Saudi Arabia, the large population of migrant workers, or even for the more cosmopolitan inhabitants of the larger cities.

Furthermore, it is important to realize that the Saudi royal family differs from other Gulf monarchies in ways that suggest that it will be able to delay, though not avoid, massive unrest. The Saudis have begun modernization from an especially traditional base. During the period of Western expansion into the Middle East, their country remained an insulated backwater of little importance, scarcely penetrated. Unlike Iraq, Libya, and Iran, Saudi Arabia escaped colonial domination, military occupation, and the concomitant disruption of traditional orders by Western ideas and institutions. The Saudis also began their modernization at a relatively recent date and, until recently, proceeded at a more cautious pace than the Shah's Iran.

In addition, the structure and sheer size of the royal family has tended to defuse some of the inevitable strains of modernization while simultaneously strengthening the family's political position. In fact, the royal family performs some of the functions of a modern political party by "representing" different regional, tribal, and individual interests through marriages and patron–client networks. This role ensures some pluralism in the political system, expands the social base of the monarchy, and encourages a limited sense of political participation.

The extensive placement of princes in key government offices, both the central and regional, also affords the royal family more effective control over the states apparatus. Penetration of the military and security bureaucracies is particularly important because it reduces the danger of a military coup and provides the dynasty with a monopoly over the means of repression.[17] Finally, the size, dispersal, and bureaucratic distribution of the royal family make its liquidation in a coup very difficult. Some princes almost certainly would remain to rally loyalist forces or call for outside help. Similarly, the large number of qualified heirs to the throne affords some protection against the sudden death or assassination of any single prince, even the King.

Can the royal family use these advantages to defuse social tensions and prolong its power? In the past, it has successfully mixed repression and accommodation. Its repressive apparatus has been fairly effective, while remaining generally less pervasive and terrifying than that of the Shah. The royal family has also been more sensitive to

---

17. The Saudi armed forces have also been divided into rival branches as an additional check against coups, but at the cost of reducing overall military capabilities.

political grievances and more willing to make some timely accommodations than was the Shah. At the same time, it is difficult to see how the family can make basic political changes without ultimately creating more serious problems. For example, top princes have, under the pressure of regional or internal unrest, frequently called for the creation of a new consultative assembly. But they have not yet delivered on these promises, in part because it is difficult to control political reforms, even when they are the King's idea. In addition, the saturation of government and business with princes makes it difficult to curb their corruption and ineptitude.

Perhaps most important, the royal family's assets would become serious liabilities if family cohesion is not maintained. At present, political tension within the royal family stems from the questions of succession and the distribution of government offices. These political issues, in turn, are intermeshed with disagreements about the orientation of Saudi foreign policy, the pace of internal development, and oil production levels—the very issues that divide Saudi society as a whole. As modernization proceeds, these divisions might become irreconcilable. In addition, modernization may disrupt the balance of power within the family by transforming the social and institutional bases of princely power. A new generation of princes educated in the West and less tied to traditional values must somehow be integrated into the political system.

These new sources of conflict within the royal family are likely to lead to protracted debate at the expense of rapid and decisive action. But the dilemma of satisfying the modern and traditional elements of Saudi society while discharging an increasingly important and complex role in international affairs makes indecision and procrastination extremely dangerous. Divisions within the royal family could lead to a palace coup, or even a civil war, if competing princes call upon their social and bureaucratic bases for support against each other. In this sense, tensions within the royal family and Saudi society could overlap to create an upheaval.

Despite family feuds and royal opposition to the status quo, it does not appear that the family is on the verge of internal dissolution or open breaks. From all indications, the line of succession appears settled for the next one or two kings, and the balance of power within the family at present appears equal enough to deter palace coups. The princes of the royal family have a very strong interest in avoiding open breaks, and they have often managed to coalesce in crises and resolve differences without force. There is little guarantee, however, that this pattern will hold for the next decade.

These conclusions suggest several implications for Western oil security. First, there is distinct danger that the Saudi royal family will be violently overthrown and this danger increases with time. If the family resisted any effort to overthrow it, prolonged internal fighting would be nearly certain to disrupt oil production. Both royalist and antiroyalist forces would seek control over the oil fields in order to bid for external support. If the royal family were overthrown, its replacement would very likely be less accommodating to Western oil interests. For example, a good case can be made that the most powerful challenge to the royal family would come from military leaders who espouse, in the manner of Qaddafi, a combination of anti-imperialism, religious fundamentalism, and Arab socialism.

Second, social unrest also presents a threat to Saudi oil production. Arab oil workers, who include a considerable number of Palestinians, have not struck for labor rights since the 1950s, but a renewal of labor pressure—perhaps to gain the right to unionize—is possible. The oil-rich areas of Saudi Arabia also contain a small Shi'ite minority whose agitation for religious rights might result in minor oil disruptions.

Third, a palace coup from within the royal family has uncertain implications for oil security. Fighting that leads to a wider civil war is very likely to disrupt oil supplies, but quick victory by one faction of the family might actually strengthen the monarchy as an institution. Nonetheless, the implications for future Saudi oil policy will depend on the composition of the winning faction.

Finally, serious political instability in Saudi Arabia, especially the overthrow of the royal family, is likely to have destabilizing regional effects that could further undermine oil security. If the Saudi monarchy fell, the traditional political systems of the smaller Gulf states would be much more exposed to destabilizing pressures.

The Small Gulf States.   In general, the small Gulf states have social and political systems similar to Saudi Arabia's, so their prospects for political stability are similar: less immediate danger, but trouble down the road. There are, however, a number of important differences among the small Gulf states and between them and Saudi Arabia that affect their prospects for stability. For example, tensions between collateral branches of the ruling family and rival princes affect the stability of all smaller Gulf states. But in some cases, intra-family coups have tended to strengthen their traditional political systems without leading to widespread social unrest or serious economic disruptions (Anthony 1975). In addition, immigrants and minorities pose a much greater potential problem in some of these nations than in Saudi Arabia, if only because the ratio of immigrants to native citizens is so much higher. The large Palestinian presence in Kuwait and the Shi'ite majority in Bahrain, which is ruled by the Sunni al-Khalifah family, are particular sources of potential unrest.

Of all the small Gulf states, Bahrain and Kuwait have the most modern societies and political structures, and, not coincidentally, the most troubled domestic histories. Compared with other conservative Gulf states, they have highly urbanized, well-educated populations, relatively free press, labor unions, and professional organizations. Both have even experimented with constitutional assemblies, although their experiments were short-lived. They are also somewhat more exposed to potentially destabilizing regional forces than the other small Gulf states. Kuwait has tended to be especially susceptible to radical Arab influences because of its large Palestinian population, long border with Iraq, and relatively cosmopolitan citizenry. In Bahrain, radical Arab pressures are compounded by the possibility of an Islamic fundamentalist movement among the Shi'ite majority, a large population of Iranian immigrants, and Iran's historical claims on Bahrain (Cooley 1979).

By contrast, the lower Gulf states have been more insulated from regional pressures, but this may change as a result of developments in regional relations and domestic politics in the Emirates. Despite numerous dynastic, territorial, and personal rivalries among the individual Emirates, they have a strong common interest in preserving a homogenous political and ideological milieu that supports their traditional political systems.

Although it is a minor oil producer, Oman has great strategic importance; it serves as a buffer between radical South Yemen and the oil-rich Gulf shiekdoms and shares the Straits of Hormuz with revolutionary Iran. American policy depends heavily on closer relations with Sultan Qabus, but the prospects for stability in Oman are uncertain. Qabus appears more progressive and popular than his father, whom he replaced in a bloodless coup in 1970, but the latent conflict between tribal politics in the hinterlands and growing urban modernization may eventually erupt. In addition, Oman's border with the radical South Yemen was a source of trouble for the Sultan during the rebellion in Oman's Dhofar region from the late sixties to early seventies, and a large-scale renewal of subversion and rebellion is possible (Price 1975).

Despite differences among them, all of the small Gulf states have weak national defenses and heterogeneous populations. Their stability is therefore closely linked to regional politics, especially relations among Saudi Arabia, Iraq, and Iran. The sudden overthrow of any one of the traditional elites that rule the smaller Gulf states could easily accelerate the collapse of the others and multiply the chances that an internal dispute could escalate into a wider regional conflict. Hence, even if a coup in one of these countries had little immediate effect on oil policy or security, it could ultimately raise more serious consequences.

Iraq. Of all the Gulf states, Iraq has had the most violent history. Its regimes have been plagued by assassinations, coups, conspiracies, riots, revolts, and civil wars, especially since the overthrow of the monarchy in 1958. Successive regimes have frequently resorted to widespread social repression and purges to maintain their power.

In large part, the failure to develop political stability based on legitimate authority and a true political community has resulted from the historical fragmentation of Iraq's society. Carved out of the Ottoman Empire by the British and French after the First World War, Iraq is almost equally divided into Sunni Arab, Shi'ite Arab, and Kurdish strongholds. Sectarian and ethnic tensions have been aggravated by ideological fanaticism and a tendency for the military to form conspiratorial cliques and intervene in politics (Kelidar 1975).

Nevertheless, the Ba'athist regime of Saddam Hussein has managed to survive since 1968.[18] The most critical question for the future of Iraq's political stability is whether the Ba'ath party has become a true instrument of totalitarian rule or is merely a facade covering control of the country by the "Takriti Mafia," the clique of friends and relatives from the Sunni village of Takrit who occupy the most sensitive positions in the Ba'athist apparatus. If the former is true, the Iraqis would seem to have finally found a means of ruling their

---

18. The history of the Ba'athist regime is discussed in Khadduri (1978) and Batatu (1978). For more recent developments, including the cabinet shake-up and purges of 1979, see Wright (1979/80).

volatile country. If the latter is true, the regime could disappear tomorrow.

The Ba'athist regime certainly appears to have achieved many of the prerequisites for one-party totalitarian rule. The power of traditional and bourgeois elites has been severely undercut by the growing strength of the central government and party apparatus. The penetration of the Ba'ath organization into government bureaucracies, state industries, universities, the mass media, and the military establishment has facilitated central control and limited the power of modern classes. In addition, Ba'athist ideology—a jumbled combination of socialism, pan-Arabism, anti-imperialism, and anti-Zionism—seems to be a useful instrument of indoctrination. And, like all totalitarian governments, Iraq has an efficient secret police organization.

All the same, there is considerable evidence that power is actually held by an extremely narrow elite personally loyal to Hussein. Power is clearly concentrated in the hands of the "Takriti Mafia" and, beyond them, in the Sunni elite. Neither the Kurdish nor Shi'ite populations have been successfully incorporated into the power structure. Furthermore, unlike true one-party systems, the Ba'athist regime has been forced to accommodate and maneuver around independent political organizations, such as the Kurdish Democratic Party and Iraqi Communist Party. Typically, this has meant temporary alliances to consolidate power against the most immediate threats. Finally, and perhaps most important, tensions remain between the military and civilian wings of the Ba'athist Party. At present, the civilian wing appears dominant, but Saddam Hussein's relations with the professional military have never been as cordial as those of his predecessor. In addition, the officer corps remains susceptible to penetration by other political forces, as illustrated by the periodic execution of officers suspected of communist connections.

On balance, it seems unlikely that the Ba'athist regime will be overthrown by social forces outside the Ba'ath party. The very social fragmentation that makes national integration difficult makes rule by narrowly based elites possible. Periodic outbursts of Shi'ite and Kurdish violence are quite certain, but they are unlikely to destroy the well-armed central government. The regime has shown some sensitivity to the need for increasing political participation (though only symbolically) and it has used Iraq's expanding oil revenues to increase its power and create general prosperity. For the time being,

the Ba'athist apparatus appears to be an effective instrument for fulfilling increasingly complex governmental responsibilities.

The greatest danger for Saddam Hussein comes from within the
Ba'athist Party and the military. Since this threat necessarily involves
small, clandestine groups, it is difficult to predict their chances for
success. On one hand, the entrenchment of the Takriti Mafia in the
party/government bureaucracy and the formation of a well-armed
Iraqi Peoples' Militia complicate plans for a simple military coup. On
the other hand, Iraq is in many ways a one-bullet regime: without
Saddam Hussein, the Takriti Mafia could fall apart and be replaced
by another clique that would inherit the Ba'athist organization and
ideology. The chances for a successful military coup might be considerably increased if prolonged social disturbances shifted the balance
of power within the party in favor of the military wing.

If a new clique were to replace quickly the Takriti Mafia, the immediate consequences for Iraqi oil production would probably be
minimal. The longer term consequences could be major, however,
depending on the composition and stability of the new regime. In the
past, coups have brought to power more radical governments that
assumed increasingly militant positions in OPEC and OAPEC. A communist or more radical Ba'athist regime could be quite troublesome
in its effects on regional stability and Soviet opportunities in the
Gulf.

If, however, one coup leads to a new round of coup and counter-
coup, Iraq's ambitions to become a greater power would be derailed.
A collapse of the central government could also revive Kurdish ambitions for autonomy and Shi'ite demands for equality. These events
would lead to oil disruptions, since the major Iraqi oil fields are located in Kurdish and Shi'ite areas. Even under the present regime,
minor sabotage of these facilities could result from developments in
neighboring Iran.

The future influence of foreign actors on Iraq's politics is unclear,
but the country has been extremely vulnerable to subversion in the
past. Iraq's more active regional policy and increasing importance are
likely to cut both ways. In some cases, improved relations may check
external subversion, as in the case of more cordial Iraqi–Syrian relations. In other cases, Iraq's ambitions may invite subversion – Iranian
support for restive elements in Iraq's Shi'ite community being a case
in point. In addition, the Soviet Union may actively support commu-

nist conspiracies within Iraq, in line with its more aggressive policies in the Third World.

Iran. The immediate prospects for Iran's political system seem quite grim: either dictatorship or chaos. This is not a new dilemma. Conflict between supporters and opponents of the central government has persisted throughout Iran's history. Chaos and collapse have long paved the way for a charismatic leader who could subdue fractious elements, unify the country, and restore order. Any balance between decentralization and dictatorship has always been a fragile truce subject to disruption by intrigue and opportunism. Even despots have been vulnerable at times of succession or weakness, particularly if their policies created a united opposition. An extraordinary degree of foreign penetration has contributed to this internal dynamic, leaving a legacy of inflamed nationalism, xenophobia, and obsession with external conspiracies.[19]

Shah Reza Pahlevi's ambitious policies to centralize power and force modernization failed to win widespread loyalty and eventually alienated virtually every segment of Iranian society. This created the basis for a curious coalition of religious and secular opponents. Furthermore, his identification with the United States put him on the wrong side of Iranian nationalism. Once brought to life, the forces of revolution fed on each other; escalating strikes and demonstrations filled the streets with closet revolutionaries and made it unsafe for any faction to strike a separate bargain with the Shah. Perhaps this cycle of slow-motion revolution could have been broken by ruthless repression or serious liberalization, but the Shah, whose confusion was exacerbated by confusion in Washington, vacillated until it was too late for any solution.[20]

Now the cast of characters in Iranian politics has changed. The aristocracy was broken by the Shah and the monarchy destroyed by the revolution. Yet Iran seems once again suspended between chaos and dictatorship. The religious and secular elements of the unusual coalition that overthrew the Shah have utterly divergent visions of Iran's future and profound mutual suspicions. It is doubtful that

19. For a fuller discussion of Iranian politics in the twentieth century, see Upton (1960), Bill (1972), and Cottam (1964).

20. Literature on Iran's revolution is rapidly growing in quantity, but not quality. Graham (1979) and Saikal (1980) are the best works to date. For a provocative view of the American role, see Leeden and Lewis (1980).

they can reconcile their differences and cooperate to govern effectively. No single leader or faction appears to possess the power and acumen necessary to rule without resorting to force.

Iran's political fragmentation reflects fundamental disagreement on basic issues, such as the proper mixture of Western and Islamic culture in Iranian society. Fundamentalist religious leaders tend to have greater support among the working classes and peasants, while secular leaders have greater strength in the middle classes. But the broad distinction between modern secular forces and traditional religious forces represents only one aspect of current political rivalries. Secular elements encompass groups from the extreme right to the extreme left. Nor does the fragmentation end here. The left alone includes a number of organizations—Marxist Fedayeen guerrillas, the Islamic leftist Mujahaddin, and the Communist Tudeh Part, for example—that all have access to well-armed paramilitary units and even some military elements. Already coups from several quarters have been plotted and foiled. In the streets, rival mobs clash between Islamic and leftist forces. The confusion in Teheran and harsh attempts to restore central control have provoked the ethnic groups of the periphery, especially the Kurds, Arabs, Azerbaijanies, Turkomans, and Baluchis, who are themselves divided along tribal and ideological lines.

In this creeping civil war, Khomeini occupies a curious position. By virtue of his mass appeal and moral authority, he holds the political system together. But because he is an ailing old fanatic, a wily politician, or both, he has neither consistently supported any of the rival factions nor created any enduring institutional framework for his successor. His death is likely to leave a power vacuum and intensify rivalries. Perhaps, as in the past, a new strongman will emerge from this chaos with enough force and popular appeal to restore order and unify the country. If so, a dictatorship of some kind will probably be the result.

Speculatively, it appears that the religious forces may be in the best position to rule after Khomeini's death because of their moral authority, control over the largest street mobs, ties to the traditional Bazari merchant class, and dominance within the new parliament. At the same time, it is not clear that any of the religious leaders, such as the tough Ayatollah Beheshti or Ayatollah Montazeri, Khomeini's presumptive heir, have broad popular support. Nor is it clear that a theocratic dictatorship will be capable of running a modern economy, governing Iran's complex society, or conducting an intelligent foreign policy. For example, a cultural revolution that attempts to eradicate Western influences and restore Islamic purity has very dubious prospects for success.

If the Mullahs fail, a military coup appealing to middle-class nationalism and democratic aspirations may be the next most likely alternative, particularly if religious leaders reconstitute the military to deter external enemies and quell internal rebels. But although military force may be the most essential instrument for taking power and imposing order, rule based entirely on force is precarious. Hence, any military regime will probably seek to extend its legitimacy, perhaps through accommodations with moderate religious leaders and politicians.

A leftist takeover seems likely only if others have tried and failed. Recent street clashes show that left-wing groups would be the first victims in an open struggle for power. The communist Tudeh Party appears to be the weakest of the factions and might actually need Soviet help to survive if it ever came into power. At the same time, a situation of extreme confusion and general collapse may allow small and well-organized groups to seize power.

The restoration of secure and orderly oil production will be a critical objective for any stable Iranian government, but the volume and terms of sale will depend on the nature of the new regime. A theocracy would probably limit Iranian production to the bare minimum, and a leftist regime might enter into closer economic ties with the Soviet Union. Any new regime, however, is likely to boost production above the present level in order to generate the oil revenues necessary for survival.

In a broader context, either a theocracy or a leftist regime could pose serious problems for oil security in the Persian Gulf. An aggressive theocracy could promote religious upheavals in other Gulf countries, and a leftist regime, particularly one dominated by communists, would undoubtedly extend Soviet influence in the Gulf. It would be a mistake, however, to make the ideological tinge of any new regime the sole basis for predicting its policies. Any regime not based on blind fanaticism will follow a pragmatic foreign policy designed to avoid regional isolation and complete dependence on one of the superpowers.

If no faction, or combination of factions, prevails in Iran, or if the struggle for power results in a prolonged civil war, the nation could disintegrate into a swarm of autonomous ethnic regions. This development would present much more problematic and unpredictable consequences. But it is fairly certain that a serious struggle in oil-rich Khuzistan province between Arab separatists and representatives of Teheran would massively disrupt Iran's oil production. The appearance of autonomous entities within Iran might also provide Iraq with more opportunities to extend its influence, although the example of Iran's minorities might foment ethnic unrest within Iraq. The fighting within Iran could in fact prompt a war between Iraq and Iran. Other Gulf countries would view the breakup of Iran with alarm, particularly if it allowed the Soviet Union to inch closer to the Gulf.

The future of Iranian politics will be one of the most critical determinants of Persian Gulf oil security but this future is highly uncertain. Iran is a major oil producer, a pivotal regional power, and a focus of superpower rivalry. In the near term, considerable turmoil and bloodshed are likely. Order and stability may be restored by an authoritarian regime, but the danger of disintegration, however temporary, cannot be ruled out.

American Policy and Internal Threats

Many of the basic causes of the internal political instability of Persian Gulf states are beyond American control. The United States lacks the power and mandate, as well as the skills and wisdom, necessary to direct countries through the perils of development and modernization and to smooth the transition from traditional to modern political systems. The United States cannot possibly supply the values and ideas necessary to bridge an Islamic past and a Western present. Indeed, to the extent that American ideas and values filter into traditional societies, they may cause disturbances, not continuity. Nonetheless, the United States cannot entirely escape responsibility for internal political developments, both because American influence is often seen as critical by Middle Easterners themselves and because American policies and influences, whether deliberate or not, do influence to some extent the stability of all Gulf countries.

This responsibility varies for different countries. In Egypt, for example, the United States can buttress political stability through aid and assistance programs, while in Saudi Arabia it may be able to provide managerial and technical assistance to ease social dislocations. In other countries, such as Iraq and Iran, the American role in internal politics is much more limited. The dilemmas for American policy are most acute where our influence is the greatest. In Saudi Arabia, for example, hectic development and wasteful spending may boost oil production and recirculate petrodollars, but they may also hasten the destruction of the traditional regime.

On a political level, the United States shares the dilemma of rulers who must combine short-term repression with long-term reform. By pressing for liberalization, the United States may undermine the traditional political base and encourage opponents of an existing government. But by supporting repression, it may frustrate necessary reforms and feed revolutionary forces. Furthermore, if the United States is too closely identified with the status quo, any new regime is apt to be hostile; but if we distance ourselves too much from a present regime, it may become vulnerable to internal opponents who do not fear an American reaction.

There is little to suggest that the United States can resolve these dilemmas. The vacillating American reaction to the revolution in Iran tarnished the American image considerably. Even if the United States discovered the key to peaceful political development, it is not clear that local rulers could be pressed to accept it. As Middle East countries become more important and independent, they are likely to be less constrained to follow American advice on internal matters.

There will undoubtedly be strong pressures on Washington to support the status quo in countries led by pro-American regimes. It will probably appear safer to back existing rulers to the hilt than to experiment with political reforms and human rights campaigns. Even if unavoidable, this policy will raise a number of dangers. First, it is important not to identify the status quo with any one ruler in every country. In some cases, such as Sadat's Egypt, this is hard to avoid, but in others, such as Saudi Arabia, it would be foolish to pin all hopes on one prince. Second, the United States must be prepared for the possibility that present political systems, such as the monarchy in Saudi Arabia, will become too discredited to maintain power without external help. There are several alternatives in this situation, but none of them are very reassuring. To abandon a friendly but hopeless leader may lead to support for yet another lost cause or to futile attempts to woo implacably hostile leaders. Intervention to prop up shaky regimes may undercut their legitimacy further and focus regional hatred against American imperialism.

It is nearly impossible to resolve these issues in the abstract. In principle, for example, a communist coup in Saudi Arabia might require American intervention or at least support for the intervention of other local actors. But in practice the situation is likely to be confusing, obscure, and fluid. It may not be clear whether incumbents can hold their own or what the orientation of their challengers might be. Speed, rather than massive force, is the essence of any successful intervention, but it can be as dangerous to react too soon as too late.

The basis for any successful policy toward internal threats lies in sound intelligence that can anticipate upheavals and judge their outcome. In Iran, the failures of American intelligence contributed to surprises and blunders. The barriers to excellent intelligence are considerable, but some improvements can be made. Although many Middle East leaders are sensitive, with some reason, about American contacts with their political opponents or investigations of their stability, Americans could still cooperate with other intelligence services that may have more accurate insights into local politics. In addition, more attention should be paid to social, economic, and cultural variables that affect stability.

These considerations raise the delicate subject of covert operations. Washington may be tempted to resort to covert actions since the stakes in the Middle East are so high and since the politics of this region often lend themselves to subversion and intrigue. The Soviet Union is not reticent in this regard, and the United States will often be blamed for interference in any case. The covert American aid to Afghan rebels could be extended to support for a large number of groups and conspirators battling pro-Soviet regimes in Libya, Ethiopia, and South Yemen. These considerable temptations should be weighed against two facts: that covert operations are exceedingly dangerous and tricky, and that the finesse and secrecy of American actions are questionable. In many instances, difficult political and moral judgments may be avoided because a number of local groups are likely to continue subversive activities and counter-intelligence that coincides with American interests.

Although American ability to anticipate and control internal political developments is limited, American policies toward regional conflicts and Soviet ambitions can indirectly promote internal stability and limit the damage of any upheavals. For example, progress toward an Arab–Israeli settlement could reduce the danger of instability and facilitate closer cooperation between the United States and Gulf countries on security matters. In the event of turmoil, efforts to block any direct intervention by the Soviet Union or its allies could allow indigenous political forces, which are less likely to be blatantly pro-Soviet, to operate freely. These steps, however, cannot resolve the basic problem of political instability in the Gulf: violent political change, sooner or later and in one country or another, is very likely to pose serious threats to Western oil security.

Regional Conflicts

At the regional level, the greatest threats to oil security center on the Arab-Israeli conflict and conflicts among the oil-producing states of the Persian Gulf. At present, the Arab-Israeli conflict is unlikely to erupt into a major war featuring Arab use of the oil weapon. But if negotiations collapse, the danger of war and another oil crisis will become much greater. It is also possible that the collapse of negotiations will produce less favorable Gulf policies even if no war results.

The revolution in Iran has resulted in a volatile and unpredictable transformation of Gulf politics. A major clash between Iraq and Iran is the most likely and serious threat, since it could very easily go beyond an oil disruption to an American-Soviet confrontation. A number of factors restrain Iraq's action, but the critical factors of Iran's internal developments and Iraq's intentions remain unclear. The danger of an Iraqi move against Kuwait or Saudi Arabia is relatively less critical for the time being.

The Persian Gulf is also surrounded by a number of festering regional disputes in the Horn of Africa, the Southern Arabian Peninsula, the Levant, and Southwest Asia. In all of these, the prospects are for more intrigue, instability, and border clashes, perhaps leading to open warfare. Tensions between Somalia and Ethiopia and between North and South Yemen are particularly troublesome. Although these problems do not directly threaten oil security and may remain contained, the political situation in these peripheral conflicts is so confused and fragmented that we should expect some setbacks and surprises.

Finally, there are regional threats from nonnational actors: the terrorist organizations that have the means to sabotage oil facilities and disrupt the transportation of oil. The likelihood and severity of this threat varies widely but, in general, it is less catastrophic and more manageable than wars between nations.

The interconnections between regional conflicts and the internal and international situations must be kept in mind in considerating all of these threats. Even if major wars are avoided and minor clashes contained, regional tensions will often be translated into subversion, sabotage, and propaganda battles that could undermine the fragile stability of some Gulf regimes. Conversely, political instability can upset regional politics by replacing temperate leaders with reckless ones, by creating power vacuums, or by involving neighboring actors in opposite sides of internal struggles. At the international level, Soviet–American rivalry can aggravate indigenous tensions, and serious regional conflicts might escalate to the point of direct superpower confrontation.

The Arab–Israeli Conflict and the Arab Oil Weapon.   If present circumstances prevail, a concerted use of the Arab oil weapon in the context of another major Arab–Israeli war is not likely. The local military balance is heavily in Israel's favor; the front-line Arab states are badly divided; the second circle Arab states, including the major oil producers, are preoccupied with other concerns and reluctant to support a desperate military gamble; and the Soviet Union does not appear interested in pushing for a war that might raise the danger of military defeat for its allies and confrontation with the United States. But present circumstances are not tenable indefinitely, particularly if the Egyptian–Israel settlement is not extended to include other Arab countries and resolve the Palestinian problem. The Camp David agreements buy time against another Arab–Israeli war and oil crisis, but failure to achieve a comprehensive settlement is likely to renew the danger.

A prolonged diplomatic stalemate could consolidate a military alliance of Jordan, Syria, and Iraq on Israel's eastern front, persuade or pressure the oil producers to support a new Arab war, and even contribute to policy changes of political instability in Egypt. Attempting to exploit this polarization, and trying to supply enough arms to appease its Arab allies but not enough to make war possible, the Soviet Union may once again find itself on the slippery road to an unwanted and uncontrollable war. Faced with a plausible military threat in the East or with a collapse of the settlement with Egypt,

Israel may be much more inclined to take preemptive action. To make matters worse, both sides are likely to be armed with nuclear weapons in the 1980s.

A major war under these circumstances is very likely to provoke use of the oil weapon, especially since the 1973 embargo is widely regarded in the Arab world as a success. The Saudis would probably feel compelled to use their oil power in some capacity, whether because of Arab pressure and fear of domestic turmoil, as in the 1967 War, or out of a desire to lead Arab unity and break the Arab–Israeli diplomatic stalemate, as in the 1973 War.[21] In addition, another round of Arab–Israeli fighting is much more likely to involve Saudi Arabia itself and the damage of Saudi oil facilities. Even if Saudi participation in the fighting or oil sanctions were half-hearted, more militant producers such as Iraq could surface as leaders of a concerted Arab embargo.

The likelihood of Arab oil sanctions during a war depends on a number of variables, including the state of Arab politics, American and Soviet involvement, European reactions, and the origin and outcome of the war. A preemptive Israeli strike leading to a military stalemate and American resupply efforts would seem to provide the greatest pressure for Arab oil sanctions. By contrast, a swiftly defeated Arab bid to control the occupied territories is likely to splinter Arab unity, especially if the United States makes visible efforts to restrain Israeli advances and restore the antebellum lines.

How powerful would future embargoes be? In one view, Arab oil power is greater than ever, given the increased Western (and especially American) dependence on Middle East oil, the growing importance of petrodollars in the international financial and monetary markets, and the steadily eroding power of the multinational oil companies. Not only is the threat of production cuts and selective embargoes more severe, but producers can now manipulate a number of less drastic instruments, such as prices, foreign assets, and oil payments in dollars, to pressure Israel's supporters. In the opposing view, IEA sharing agreements, oil stockpiles, threats of counterembargoes and frozen assets, and growing economic interdependence between the West and the Arab oil producers have eroded Arab oil power. Further, the world oil market remains relatively flexible despite recent changes. If the Arabs pressure the United States severely, they

---

21. Past use of the Arab oil weapon is considered in Safran (1974) and Smart (1977).

will also hurt Europe; if they damage the Western economic system, they will ultimately damage themselves.[22]

Separating economic from political considerations can help resolve this debate. On a purely economic level, the oil producers appear able to inflict considerable damage on the West and to withstand Western countersanctions, at least in the short run. And the Western consumer coalition is more apt to fall apart than the Arab producer coalition, especially if the Europeans think they are being dragged into a precipitous Arab–Israeli war. From the Arab standpoint, Europe's special vulnerability to oil sanctions could be used to undermine U.S. support of Israel. Politically, however, there are clear limits to Arab oil power. At some point, massive production cuts or price increases would backfire by undercutting Western capabilities to contain the Soviet Union or by provoking an American military response. In any "strangulation" attempt, a desperate European situation would create support for drastic American responses. For these reasons, then, future oil sanctions are likely to be as rational—both discriminating and incremental—as those of 1973. Attempts to create a favorable bargaining situation are more likely than hysterical attempts to destroy the West, or the United States, at any cost. If oil stockpiles, sharing agreements, flexible oil markets, and government-to-government oil deals allow some flexibility and time for American diplomacy to arrange a truce in another Arab–Israeli war, the oil embargo may be manageable.

The extent to which Arab oil producers are willing to use oil to influence Israel's allies in situations short of war is unclear. The Saudis have frequently stated their intentions to use production and pricing to punish American failures to pressure Israel into making concessions, or to reward successful American efforts. But many economic and political factors unrelated to the Arab–Israeli conflict help determine Saudi oil policy.

Even if the Saudis do not use their oil weapon in the midst of negotiations, the failure of negotiations is likely to create a situation in which use of the oil weapon becomes a reality. A comprehensive peace or, at the very least, avoidance of a complete diplomatic collapse is important for this reason alone. A comprehensive peace would also enhance oil security by limiting other potential sources of oil disruption. A settlement would facilitate containment of the

22. For a detailed discussion, see Knorr (1976), Maull (1975), Singer (1978) and Itayim (1975).

Soviet Union by removing one barrier to closer cooperation between the United States and local countries. To the extent that a settlement accommodates the Palestinian movement, it could remove one potential source of sabotage and domestic disturbances in the conservative Gulf states.

Tensions in the Persian Gulf. The countries of the Persian Gulf have long engaged in war scares, military threats, and border clashes (to say nothing of subversion and intrigue). Nonetheless they have managed to avoid any major wars among themselves. At the same time, a seemingly endless series of negotiations has failed to produce a Gulf-wide regional security pact.[23] This pattern results from several factors.

From a strictly military standpoint, the armed forces of Persian Gulf countries are largely untested in modern, full-scale combat; the region's arms buildup has been more for political than for military reasons. Political considerations have also resulted in frequent purges and the division of the military establishments into rival branches. Therefore, political leaders probably have little confidence in their forces' capabilities against any but the most poorly armed rebels.

The preoccupation with economic development and political stability within the Gulf states has also tended to limit capabilities for serious military endeavors. Without a secure political base and dedicated population, modern warfare is difficult to carry off. This is especially true since the principal source of revenues, oil, is potentially vulnerable in wartime. All of the Gulf states have a common interest in preserving peaceful navigation in the Gulf and straits of Hormuz.

Nevertheless, political instability, restive minorities, and such supranational ideologies as pan-Arabism and pan-Islam have fed regional tensions, supplying opportunities and motivations for subversion and intrigue. The result of persistent meddling in each other's internal affairs has been mutual suspicion which obstructs any regional security pact.

On the regional level, the fluid triangle of Saudi-Iraqi-Iranian diplomacy with its shifting alliances and cross-cutting issues has also helped lower the danger of war while preventing a regional security

23. The regional politics of the Persian Gulf has received very little systematic study. Chubin (1976) and Ramazani (1979) are good introductions. In addition, the regional policies of individual Gulf states are discussed in Chubin and Zadih (1974), Ramazani (1975) and Dawisha (1980).

pact. While the Shah was in power, Iran and Saudi Arabia opposed Iraq's radical politics and Saudi Arabia worked with Iraq to frustrate the Shah's imperial ambitions. The resulting balance afforded the small Gulf states a measure of security and independence. At the same time, the crosscutting issues that reduced the danger of war also reduced the possibility of agreement on regional matters. As the strongest Gulf power, the Shah's Iran took an increasingly unilateral approach to Gulf security, much to the discomfort of Saudi Arabia and Iraq.

The role of the great powers in the Gulf has also contributed to this pattern of no wars and no pacts. In some cases, superpower support for opposing sides in local feuds tended to aggravate regional tensions. However, tacit and explicit superpower commitments have also tended to deter serious military attacks. Furthermore, the Gulf states have a common interest in avoiding conflicts that would draw the superpowers into their region. These states have only recently emerged from a long period of colonial domination and tenuous independence. If the scramble for world oil becomes military, they will be the first to suffer. At best, their independence and flexibility would be restricted; at worst, they would either be destroyed or carved into spheres of interest.

Hence, if past is prologue, Gulf politics are likely to follow the historical pattern of persistent tensions without major wars and persistent negotiations without regional security pacts. The revolution in Iran, however, may have disrupted this pattern in two ways.

First, the ultimate outcome of Iran's revolution could have destabilizing effects on regional politics. The disintegration of Iran into civil war could create new states in the Gulf and draw external actors into the conflict. Or a militant theocracy could replace the Shah's dreams of empire with an even more reckless religious imperialism under the banner of a Shi'ite revival.

Second, the collapse of the Shah's army and Iran's political hegemony in the Gulf has left Iraq the most powerful local force. We now have reason to be concerned about Iraq's military expansion against Iran and the conservative Arab states, especially Kuwait.

Iraq and the Danger of War.   A major Iraqi military thrust against Kuwait or Saudi Arabia would almost certainly disrupt oil supplies, but such an attack is not likely at present. Thus far Iraq has tried to replace Egypt as the leader of the Arab world and Iran as the dominant power in the Gulf by cooperating with the conservative Arab states of the Gulf. Military pressure or subversion would probably throw Saudi Arabia back into Egyptian and American arms, isolating Iraq in the Arab world, undercutting its regional political importance, and possibly causing a military confrontation with the United States. Furthermore, the souring of Iraqi–Soviet relations has deprived Iraq of certain great power support. In short, Iraq's good neighbor policy has been too successful to trade in for a risky policy of military expansion.

Still, the deterioration of Iran's forces has removed the most immediate military check to Iraq's military options against the conservative Arab states. Intimidation and limited aggression may result.[24] Intrigue and assassination have become a pervasive instrument of foreign policy for Iraq. Although these activities are today directed against Iran and such Soviet allies as South Yemen and Ethiopia, they could be employed against other targets. Despite the tentative rapprochement between Iraq and Saudi Arabia, the axis between secular, socialist Iraq and religious, conservative Saudi Arabia has inherent ideological and political tensions. They also have latent differences on the Arab–Israeli conflict and relations with the superpowers. On Israel, Saudi Arabi is more moderate, and, not coincidentally, more interested in restoring Egypt to the Arab fold, if only to balance Iraq's power. Despite both countries' increased neutrality in the East–West sphere, Saudi Arabia depends on the United States and Iraq on the Soviet Union in a crunch, and Iraq is much more adamantly opposed to a greater American presence in the area than is Saudi Arabia.

Of all the potential armed conflicts in the Persian Gulf, war between Iraq and Iran is the most likely and probably the most dangerous threat to oil security and peace between the superpowers. The combination of Iran's reckless foreign policy and Iraq's ambitions in the Gulf, at a time when the relative strengths of Iraq and Iran have been reversed, has created an explosive situation. Even if a major war is avoided, minor border clashes, subversion, sabotage, and assasination are nearly certain to continue for the immediate future.

---

24. Iraq's most serious challenge to Kuwaiti sovereignty came in 1961 and was an utter failure. Since then, Iraq's ambitions have focused on control of the Kuwaiti islands of Bubyan and Warba, which Iraq feels are necessary to protect its narrow waterfront and major port at the head of the Gulf.

Ever since the Iraqi monarchy was overthrown in 1958, Iraq–Iranian relations have gone from bad to worse.[25] Aggravated by domestic politics, religious and ideological tensions, the Kurdish problem, border disputes, conflicting ambitions, Arab–Iranian antagonism, and the enactment of the superpower rivalry by proxy, the problems between Iraq and Iran almost resulted in war in 1969 and 1974. In both cases, Iraq generally backed down against Iran's superior military and political resources. Since its revolution, however, Iran's military strength has diminished and its international isolation has grown. At the same time, Khomeini's ambition to spread his Islamic revolution to Iraq has clashed head on with Saddam Hussein's ambition to extend Iraqi influence in the Gulf.

Now that the tables have turned, fewer factors constrain Iraq's direct military options. On the domestic level, Iraq and Iran hold each other hostage. The Arab population in Iran's oil-producing region of Khuzistan is susceptible to Iraqi subversion (on the basis of Arab nationalism against Iran's Persian-dominated politics), while the Shi'ite population in Iraq's southern oil-producing region is susceptible to Iranian subversion (on the basis of Shi'ite militancy against Iraq's Sunni-dominated politics). The two countries share an uneasy Kurdish population, which they have tried to manipulate against each other.

Though Iraq enjoys the present advantage in subversion, it is not clear how the loyalties of its population would hold up in a major war with Iran. An appeal by Khomeini to defend the faith could stir up Shi'ite trouble behind Iraqi lines, and Iraqi Kurds might seize an opportunity to join their brethren in Iran in a bid to create a separate Kurdish state.

A major Iraqi attack on Iran could also disrupt Iraq's regional political objectives and lead to bitter, prolonged fighting. Although the conservative Gulf states are very unlikely to support Iran in a war, they might find Iraqi aggression a prudent reason to search for other sources of protection—perhaps Egypt. In addition, Syria, Iraq's traditional Ba'athist rival, has been forming a tacit alliance with Iran that could threaten the Iraqi pipelines that cross Syrian territory on the way to the Mediterranean.

---

25. The only serious attempt to mend relations came in 1975, when the Shah agreed to suspend support for Kurdish rebels in Iraq in exchange for Iraq's agreement to settle the Shatt al-Arab border dispute and give the Shah a freer hand in the Persian Gulf.

Even on a military level, Iraq cannot be sure its war would be won. Though it has air superiority, its ability to mount an amphibious operation across the Shatt al-Arab or an overland strike across the mountainous land border is limited. On the sea, the Iraqi shoreline on the Gulf is difficult to defend and Iran's navy, the military branch least affected by the revolution, is still perhaps superior to Iraq's. Iran's oil fields and refineries are extremely exposed to military attack, but so are Iraq's.

The final, and perhaps most critical, factor complicating Iraq's war option is the role of the superpowers. Historically, Iraq's regimes have tended to look toward the Soviet Union for support against Iran. The Shah sought the support of the United States. Iran generally got the better end of the deal because the United States provided complete support while the Soviets took a more ambiguous position to avoid antagonizing the Shah. The present superpower alignment in Iraqi–Iranian tensions is very hazy. More than ever, the Soviet Union is hedging its bets between Iraq and Iran; Iraq has displayed increasing independence from the Soviet Union, while the Soviets see an opportunity to court (if not install) a friendly regime in Iran. The United States is in the uncomfortable position of having unfriendly relations with both Iraq and Iran, though this situation could of course change.

From the Iraqi standpoint, the unpredictability of superpower reaction makes a risky venture even more perilous. Both the United States and the Soviet Union could call on Iraq to honor Iran's territorial integrity. Or, one or both of the superpowers could intervene, using the Iraqi–Iranian fighting as justification for a greater presence in the Gulf. Of all the Gulf countries, Iraq has perhaps the greatest interest in limiting the great power presence in the Gulf: its relations with the superpowers are ambiguous; it is vulnerable to subversion; and it aspires to become the dominant regional power.

So Iraqi–Iranian tensions have reached their highest levels since 1975 and Iraq, for the first time, has the upper hand. Khomeini's willingness to provoke Iraq at a time when Iraq believes it can press Iran for territorial and other concessions could lead to a military confrontation. If a stable government and sensible diplomacy are restored in Iran, then war will become much less likely. But if Iran disintegrates further or steps up its attacks on Iraq, the danger of war will grow. Or, Iraq may seize this opportunity to settle old scores with Iran. If the fighting is limited to punitive raids by Iraq against

Iran, then the danger of disrupting oil production could be relatively low. In full-scale war, however, damage to productive capacity in both Iraq and Iran is nearly certain, and disruption of oil tanker traffic in the Gulf is likely.

Peripheral Conflict.   In addition to these central conflicts, Gulf oil is indirectly jeopardized by a number of regional tensions and conflicts on the periphery that could influence the pattern of regional politics and the balance of superpower influence within the Gulf.

In the southern Arabian Peninsula, relations between North and South Yemen are likely to continue their historical oscillation between subversion and tentative unity talks. Prone to coups, these extremely poor and fragmented societies have ambiguous foreign policies. Although the Marxist regime in South Yemen is heavily dependent on Soviet and Cuban support, its new leader Ali Nasser Mohammed has attempted to improve relations with conservative Saudi Arabia and Oman. North Yemen, heavily dependent on Saudi subsidies, has attempted to cultivate better relations with the Soviet Union. On balance, it seems unlikely that North and South Yemen will unite and march on Riyadh or that South Yemen troops, spearheaded by Cuban advisors, will conquer North Yemen. All the same, the ability of the United States to match the Soviet Union in the shadowy game of proxies and intrigue in southern Arabia will be taken as a measure of American fortitude and skill.

The same considerations apply to tensions between Somalia and Ethiopia in the Horn of Africa. Though Ethiopia's Marxist strongman, Mengistu, has appeared to crush his rivals in Addis Ababa, he remains besieged by separatist uprisings in Eritrea and the Ogaden, which have required his dependence on the Soviet Union and the presence of Cuban forces. As long as Somalia's support for the Ogaden guerrillas continues, a renewal of serious fighting between Ethiopia and Somalia is quite possible. But it seems less likely that Ethiopia would press its advantage to the point of conquest, particularly since the United States is cautiously improving its relations with Somalia in order to obtain base rights.

American Policy and Regional Threats

The most direct and serious regional threats to Western oil security are major wars between local states. With patience and skill, the

United States ought to be able to deter such wars, or at least keep them contained. In some cases, American policies could even contribute to a lasting resolution of tensions. It can also reduce the danger of war by supporting a stable local balance of power and by committing itself, however implicitly, to protect the security of the region's weaker countries.

Seeking political solutions while maintaining a military balance is tricky. Steps taken to maintain a military balance can easily complicate diplomacy, as in the Arab–Israeli conflict, where the United States arms both sides while encouraging negotiated settlements. The debate on arms transfers to the Middle East is symptomatic of the larger political difficulties facing the United States in its attempt to maintain good relations with both Israel and the moderate Arab states.

Whether this American position continues to be a source of tension with local states or becomes an asset for American interests hinges, in large part, on whether American diplomacy can contribute to a truly comprehensive resolution of the Arab–Israeli conflict. Though prospects for a comprehensive peace in the near future are quite cloudy, ongoing negotiations aimed at a broader settlement are likely to defuse the most explosive implications of the conflict for oil security. In the meantime, the Egyptian–Israeli rapprochement supported by the United States is an effective check against the immediate danger of war. However, regional security cannot rest entirely on these two states. They are politically as well as geographically too far from the Gulf itself to assume the role Iran once played. One way or another, the shifting triangle of Saudi–Iraqi–Iranian politics will remain the critical factor in regional security.

Any American strategy to buttress the Gulf's security requires a subtle and discrete mixture of policies. An extravagant American military buildup in the Gulf would only open diplomatic opportunities for the Soviet Union in Iraq and Iran and escalate regional tensions. However, complete reliance on regional forces to ensure Gulf security is neither safe nor plausible. An enduring Gulf-wide regional security pact is unlikely, just as the strategy of supporting a regional policeman has collapsed with the Shah.

Thus, the best American strategy to deter and contain local conflicts in the Gulf area will combine several approaches. Limited proxy arrangements could be useful. Although Saudi Arabia cannot patrol the entire Gulf, its forces can deter or contain conflicts in the southern Arabian Peninsula and lower Gulf. Egypt's offer to aid smaller local states, such as Oman, North Yemen, Kuwait, and—perhaps under some circumstances—Saudi Arabia is yet another ingredient of regional security. The relative emphasis on the different elements of this multiple strategy must be sensitive to changing political circumstances in the Gulf. For example, a sudden rupture of the Saudi-Iraqi rapprochement or an escalation of tensions between Iraq and Iran may require the United States to emphasize its unilateral commitment to regional peace.[26]

The greatest political impediment to American efforts to secure regional peace will probably continue to be the tense relations between Washington and Baghdad and Teheran. Prospects for improving these relations are unclear. Diplomatic relations between Washington and Baghdad were broken in 1967. Though Iraq has since moved further away from the Soviet Union, it remains unalterably opposed to American "imperialism." Iraq has opposed Oman's recent proposal for a regional security force that would include Americans and has pressured local countries, such as Oman and Somalia, to refuse base rights to the United States. Furthermore, the differences between Baghdad and Washington on the Arab–Israeli conflict are nearly insurmountable; occasional hints of moderation in the Iraqi position seem intended only to woo Saudi Arabia. And yet American and Iraqi interests do sometimes agree: both countries oppose the Soviet invasion of Afghanistan and Khomeini's regime in Iran. If Paris and Washington could work together, perhaps French relations with Iraq could establish a basis for tacit cooperation between the United States and Iraq.

For the United States and Iran, the future is even more nebulous. Any improvement in relations hangs on a resolution of Iran's internal chaos and the hostage crisis, both of which are inextricably linked. Some Iranian politicians favor a restoration of relations with the United States, if only to reduce Iran's international isolation and balance the Soviet threat. But even if American–Iranian relations are mended, the level of cooperation promoted by the Shah is extremely unlikely.

It is in the Gulf's peripheral conflicts that American cooperation with local governments presents the most effective substitute for

---

26. From a military standpoint, the forces necessary to deter and react to local aggression must emphasize flexibility and quick reaction.

direct American involvement, particularly since vital American interests are not immediately threatened. For example, both Egypt and Saudi Arabia have strong interests in preventing the spread of radical, pro-Soviet forces in the Horn of Africa and the southern Arabian peninsula, and, with American support, they possess many of the means to pursue these interests.

The Soviet Threat

Historically, the Soviet position in the Persian Gulf has been extremely weak. Though the Soviets did manage to win influence in the Arab countries surrounding Israel and improve relations with the countries of the Northern Tier and Indian subcontinent, Soviet allies in the Persian Gulf and Arabian Peninsula itself have tended to be either geographically isolated and impotent (South Yemen) or politically isolated and erratic (Iraq). From the 1973 Arab–Israeli War until the revolution in Iran in 1979, American diplomacy and arms transfers eroded the Soviet position in the central core of the Middle East and the Gulf by gradually forming an anti-Soviet alliance stretching from Egypt to Saudi Arabia to Iran. Even Iraq and Syria became more independent and dissatisfied with Moscow.

Balancing these losses in the center, however, the Soviets pursued an aggressive policy to gain and strengthen positions on the periphery of the Middle East. They pursued closer ties with Libya, provided military support for the shaky radical regime of Ethiopia, encouraged Communist coups in South Yemen and Afghanistan, and instituted a naval buildup in the Indian Ocean. Although several of these moves produced problematic results, they gave the Soviets a chance to exploit any disturbances in the American-supported alliance.[27]

These disturbances were not long in coming. The Camp David accords, which disrupted the Egyptian–Saudi axis and polarized Arab politics, and the revolution in Iran, which opened an enormous breach in the Western *cordon sanitaire* around the Gulf, created numerous opportunities for Soviet diplomacy and expansion. The Soviet invasion of Afghanistan and the extension of the Brezhnev Doctrine to the Third World demonstrated Soviet willingness and

---

27. Soviet policy in the Gulf is discussed in Yodfat and Abir (1977), Golan (1979), and Chubin (1980).

capability to use direct military force beyond Eastern Europe and improved Soviet ability to threaten Iran and Pakistan with subversion and intimidation.

As a result, the Soviet Union has become a greater threat to Persian Gulf oil security than ever before. Supply disruptions could result from a direct Soviet thrust to control oil fields or from Soviet attempts to heat up local tensions and destabilize oil-producing countries. Soviet diplomacy and pressure could also bring about less favorable oil policies and divisions among the Western allies.

The appearance of further Soviet ascendency and American decline could cause the Gulf states to sell more oil to the Soviet Union and the Eastern block. Any confrontation between OPEC and the West, any stalemate in the Arab–Israeli peace process, any failure to restore and improve American relations with local states could open even broader opportunities for Soviet diplomacy. The mutual recriminations and diverse interests within the Western alliance offer still other possibilities.[28] For example, a Soviet proposal to exchange a neutralized Afghanistan for a formal Soviet role in creating an international peace zone in the area could easily complicate American relations with Europe. Acceptance of an equal role for the Soviet Union in the Gulf would probably be a concession of superior influence, given its proximity to the Gulf, and result in increased Soviet leverage over Europe and local countries.

At the same time, Soviet regional and global diplomacy suffers from a number of handicaps. The appeal of Soviet trade, technology, culture, and ideology is distinctly lackluster, particularly to the conservative Gulf states. The fundamental confluence of political and cultural interests between the West and the Gulf is significant; the differences separating the two blocs are probably manageable, at least in principle. Neither the shrewdness and resources of the Soviet Union nor the gullibility and divisiveness of the West should therefore be overestimated.

A direct Soviet blitzkrieg for oil seems the least likely of all possibilities. The Soviets have opportunistically exploited weakness, but they also have been extremely cautious about military confrontations with the United States. Unless this characteristic caution disappears, a blitzkrieg for oil seems too risky. The importance of the Gulf

---

28. For a discussion of energy dilemmas facing the Western alliance, see Chapter 6 in this collection.

to the United States and the American commitment to defend the area against direct Soviet moves is clear. America's stake in the Persian Gulf is clearly more vital than the Soviets', even if they do come to need imports of Gulf oil. Furthermore, heavy-handed Soviet moves are likely to create a regional and international backlash; the Islamic and Western reaction to the Soviet invasion of Afghanistan, though incomplete and fractious, has probably warned the Soviets that further expansion would be very damaging politically. All the same, Soviet military power complicates any American intervention in the region, especially in the case of Iran.

A desperate Soviet gamble or miscalculation cannot be completely ruled out. The conventional military balance is distinctly favorable to the Soviet Union right now while U.S. forces are hampered by political, logistic, and budgetary restraints.[29] Bold Soviet leaders might calculate that a successful move in the Gulf could intimidate local countries and splinter the West.

But the most likely origin of superpower confrontation would be from superpower involvement in a local or civil war. The confused and rapidly changing situation that could result can make rational calculation difficult. At present, these dangers are focused on Iran, whose turmoil and a reckless foreign policy have destroyed any mutually understood commitment of American protection and created greater opportunities for Soviet intervention. American claims on Iranian oil are challenged by the Soviet stake in secure and calm borders. Even if the Soviets did invade Iran, however, they would be unlikely to push their advantage further. The conservative Arab side of the Gulf remains under tacit American protection, and Iraq retains a relatively formidable force to defend itself. This may be little comfort, though, because any American–Soviet confrontation in Iran or attempt to partition the country is likely to spill over into the Persian Gulf.

The opportunity to affect Western oil security indirectly by encouraging and exploiting local conflicts and internal instability offers the Soviets mixed prospects. In general, indirect means reduce the risk of direct confrontation. However, they are harder to control, since indigenous factors are so important to their success. At present,

29. Steps necessary to rectify this imbalance are discussed in Chapter 12 in this collection. Clearly, the thrust of American military policy must be to deter Soviet aggression rather than actually fight a localized contest, since any superpower shootout in the Gulf is certain to disrupt oil supplies.

these factors tend to limit any bold Soviet schemes to instigate local wars, though the continuation of tensions may create more favorable opportunities in the future. The local balance of forces in the Arab-Israeli conflict does not favor the Soviets, and it would be difficult for them to exploit a failure of the peace talks without causing a dangerous war.

Lukewarm relations between Moscow and Gulf regimes, including Baghdad, also reduce the likelihood of Soviet-supported wars. Even on the periphery, Soviet endorsement of a South Yemeni drive against Oman or an Ethiopian drive against Somalia, aided by Cuban proxies, offers dubious prospects. Should local wars break out, Soviet prospects are still mixed. In some cases, opportunities would be opened but in others, the Soviets might be caught on both sides of a local conflict or their allies might be threatened by defeat.

Soviet attempts to subvert Gulf states have followed an odd pattern. Direct efforts against the conservative Gulf states have generally been avoided. The Soviet involvement in local politics and attempts to overthrow existing regimes have been most commonly directed at Soviet allies and at nonaligned nationalist leaders (Fukuyama 1979). When successful, this strategy may only produce leaders with little popular support—witness Afghanistan. When failed, it can sour Moscow's relations with nonaligned regimes as it did with Iraq. Even if Soviet gains in the periphery prove difficult to reverse, new Soviet clients and such old Soviet allies as Libya and Syria will probably continue to complicate Soviet policy in the region by experiencing persistent internal strife. At the same time, of course, any purely indigenous upheavals in pro-American regimes could benefit the Soviets, if only by weakening the American position in the area.

Iran clearly offers the best immediate prospects for Soviet subversion. Though the Soviets did not anticipate the revolution or contribute to it significantly, their opportunity to penetrate the country is now greater than at any time since the 1940s, when the Soviets supported separatist movements in Kurdish, Turkoman, and Azerbaijani areas of Iran. These historical opportunities have been reopened by the revolution, and the Soviet occupation of Afghanistan enhances opportunities to exploit unrest in Iranian Baluchistan, which borders the Indian Ocean. Ironically, there may be too many options for the Soviets. They will find it difficult to support minority unrest in the hope of picking up the pieces if Iran falls apart, to encourage and protect a leftist coup in Teheran, and to court Khomeini all at the same time. The critical political game remains among the Iranians themselves, and indiscrete Soviet meddling could backfire.

In conclusion, the Soviets are likely to play a patient and persistent game in the Persian Gulf, seeking to accumulate a political advantage over time rather than seize it in a single stroke. They will pressure existing regimes, exploit regional tensions, and carry out subversion in an attempt to expand their influence gradually while weakening that of the United States. The politics of the region, the balance of forces, and the constraints on Soviet policy are not conducive to sudden breakthroughs and irreversible changes.

The Soviet interest in the Gulf is not oil per se, but the manipulation of Western dependence on that oil. More important than disrupting the oil supply and wrecking the West, the Soviets hope to use their influence in the Gulf to gain leverage over the West, especially Europe. All the same, Soviet activities toward this end may increase the chances that regional tensions and internal disturbances will disrupt oil supplies and induce oil policies that are harmful to Western interests.

From their strong points on the periphery, the Soviets hope that the center will eventually yield openings. They believe that time is on their side. The conservative regimes in the Gulf will eventually collapse and be replaced by more approachable leaders. Regional tensions will inevitably yield openings for Soviet influence. A confrontation between the West and oil producers will eventually force the latter into the Soviet sphere. What the Soviets cannot do themselves, local conditions may do for them.

Policy Conclusions.   The American response to the Soviet threat in the Persian Gulf, as in the wider context of American–Soviet relations, requires a mixture of containment and cooperation. Though the United States must deter direct Soviet expansion and limit Soviet influence, it is unlikely that the Soviet Union can be completely excluded from the area. Hence, the possibility of reaching tacit understandings, if only to avoid a confrontation neither side desires, cannot be dismissed. To achieve its policy goals, the United States must maneuver to neutralize Soviet military advantages and maximize American advantages based on political position and economic links.

It is doubtful that the United States could ever match the Soviet military strength one for one, especially in ground forces. But a greater ability to project conventional force into the Gulf is necessary both to fortify the American deterrent and to provide some alternatives to escalation should deterrence fail. Creation of a rapid deployment force, the predisposition of supplies, prudent acquisition of base rights, and a greater naval presence in the Indian Ocean are all necessary, especially since the military burden of deterrence falls almost exclusively on the United States. Local forces may slow down a Soviet invasion, but they could never stop it. Nor can the Europeans be expected to make substantial contributions, except perhaps by increasing their share of Europe's defense.

By itself, however, a military response to the Soviet threat is inadequate. Given Soviet opportunities to exploit local conflicts and internal instability, it will be nearly impossible to disentangle Soviet machinations from those of Soviet allies who have their own reasons to cause trouble and who are only imperfectly controlled by Moscow. In many cases, a direct military response by the United States is not a plausible reaction to indigenous turmoil. Indirect threats must be answered with political and economic policies, with which the United States enjoys certain advantages over the Soviet Union. To some extent Soviet objectives can be denied by defusing or delaying local tensions and domestic turmoil.

Despite the resurgence of Islam, the American ability to woo local regimes is enhanced by the greater attractiveness of American economic assistance, trade, technology, and culture. The continuity of interests between oil producers in the Persian Gulf and oil consumers in the West could therefore serve as a barrier to Soviet influence if the differences between OECD and OPEC were moderated. To make this advantage count, the United States must talk to and cooperate with nonaligned or even nominally anti-American regimes, such as Iraq.

Finally, a number of indirect Soviet threats are best met indirectly—by American cooperation with local states prepared to use covert means and the threat of force to balance the efforts of Soviet allies. Again, the critical factor here is the political relationship between the United States and local countries. Despite recent setbacks, the American position in the heart of the Middle East remains superior to that of the Soviet Union, and prudent diplomacy by Washington may eventually restore working relations, however informal, with Baghdad and Teheran.

The United States should not insist on the creation of a formal alliance with local states, however. Under present circumstances, the effort required to enlist them would cause the neglect of more pressing problems or even aggravate other threats to oil security. For example, a formal military league including Israel, Egypt, Saudi Arabia, and Oman is likely to run afoul of domestic politics, inter-Arab relations, and Arab–Israeli tensions. American cooperation with local states will probably be best pursued on an informal and bilateral basis.

The United States cannot completely exclude the Soviet Union from the Middle East. Both superpowers are likely to remain entangled there, each with a strong interest in avoiding situations that could escalate to nuclear war. At present, the dual crisis in Afghanistan and Iran present the greatest tests for cooperation and containment. In the case of Afghanistan, both superpowers have to face difficult choices. For the Soviet Union, the military stalemate in Afghanistan and its failure to create a stable client regime presents unattractive options. A military solution requiring massive destruction of rebel villages, attempts to seal the Afghan border, and even an invasion of rebel sanctuaries in Northwest Pakistan is likely to provoke more bitter international condemnation. A political solution requiring Soviet withdrawal, on the other hand, does not seem likely to satisfy any important Soviet objectives.

Washington has predicated all of its anti-Soviet sanctions on the Soviet invasion of Afghanistan. Yet it generally concedes that Afghanistan is a lost cause and that its primary objective is to hold the line there. In the meantime, other important issues, such as arms negotiations, are stalled. What Soviet concessions are necessary before the United States resumes business as usual? And what assurances can the United States accept that Moscow intends to go no further?

In Iran, both superpowers await unpredictable developments which neither controls; meanwhile, the Soviet Union may face opportunities that appear too good to pass up. Iran's tenuous political structure may collapse before the United States has a credible deterrent to Soviet intervention and Soviet capabilities for subversion are probably greater than those of the United States.

In the best of circumstances, the Soviet Army would withdraw from Afghanistan in exchange for a nonaligned regime, and Iran would become stable under a regime balancing superpower influence. In the worst case, the Soviets would successfully impose a communist regime in Afghanistan and then manage to extend their control to Teheran. Future events in these two Middle East nations will probably be the principal determinants of the Soviet threat to Persian Gulf oil in the next decade.

CONCLUSION

This analysis of the situation in the Persian Gulf suggests at least two very important conclusions about Western oil security during the next decade. First, something is very likely to go wrong, resulting in a shortage or disruption of oil supplies. Second, it is difficult to know exactly what this damaging event will be or when it will occur. The future oil policies of Gulf producers are uncertain. The legion of threats to oil supplies is ominous. The potential for the unexpected is very great.

The United States is not completely helpless, however. There are a number of ways to check, or at least delay, threats to oil security. Further, it may be possible to limit the duration and damage of any disruptions that do occur, maximizing our political flexibility.[30] And fortunately, to a large extent, the measures needed to prevent and to prepare for oil disruptions are those that would influence favorably the oil policies of the oil producers.

For most of the 1980s, American dependence on Persian Gulf oil will remain high. Some of our most vital political and economic interests will be inextricably tied to events in this most volatile region. We therefore have no choice but to work for regional security through a combination of commitment and restraint, of subtlety and forcefulness. American cooperation with West European and Middle East countries will be essential, but a leading American role is unavoidable. In the longer run, however, the complexity of threats to the Gulf oil, the limitations on American abilities to check all of these threats, and the likelihood of declining Gulf exports suggest that the United States should pursue a strategy of "oil disengagement." There are, however, several dangers in this strategy of buying time while decreasing American dependence:

1. The search for oil security in the Gulf is likely to lead the United States deeper into the politics of the Gulf's periphery. This dynamic raises not only the now-familiar pitfalls of entanglement

---

30. The requirements for American energy policy are discussed in Part III.

in local conflicts but also the danger of wasting effort on issues that are not intrinsically important or whose importance will decline over time. The chain of defense for oil lanes, could, for example, extend down the entire east coast of Africa, complicating American policy throughout Africa.

2. The energy and attention spent building up oil security in the Gulf may hinder our incentive to make the painful and costly adjustments to reduce our dependence on imported oil from unstable regions. For example, the political base for a military commitment in the Gulf may not match the political base for a coherent energy policy of conservation and alternative energy sources.

3. Even if the United States achieves a measure of energy independence for itself, however, we will still bear some continuing responsibility for the oil security of Western Europe and Japan which are likely to remain more dependent on Gulf oil. Our allies will be unable to defend their stake in the Gulf, and any damage to their economic prosperity and political independence will inescabably injure the United States, especially since the Middle East is likely to remain a geopolitical bone of contention between the United States and the Soviet Union for some time.

Hence, the high priority assigned to reducing the importance of Persian Gulf oil for American needs will not necessarily change the critical importance of oil security for broader American interests. This may seem paradoxical, but the situation in the Persian Gulf is perhaps the profoundest paradox of our time.

REFERENCES

Anthony, John. 1975. *Arab States of the Lower Gulf: People, Politics, Petroleum.* Washington: Middle East Institute.

Batatu, Hanna. 1978. *The Old Social Classes and the Revolutionary Movements of Iraq.* Princeton, N.J.: University of Princeton Press.

Bill, James. 1972. *The Politics of Iran: Groups, Classes and Modernization.* Columbus, Ohio: Merrill.

Blandford, Linda. 1976. *Oil Sheikhs.* London: Weidenfeld and Nicolson.

Central Intelligence Agency. 1979. "The World Oil Market in the Years Ahead." Reprinted in *Petroleum Intelligence Weekly,* September 3, 1979.

Chubin, Shahram. 1976. "International Politics of the Persian Gulf." *British Journal of International Studies* 2, no. 3 (October): 216–230.

_____. 1980. "Soviet Policy Toward Iran and the Gulf." Adelphi Papers 157. London: International Institute for Strategic Studies.

Chubin, Shahram, and Sepehr Zadim. 1974. *The Foreign Relations of Iran.* Berkeley: University of California Press.

Congressional Research Service. 1977. "Project Independence: U.S. and World Energy Outlook through 1990." Prepared for the U.S. Senate, Committee on Energy and Natural Resources, November.

Cooley, John. 1979. "Iran, the Palestinians, and the Gulf." *Foreign Affairs* 57, no. 5 (Summer): 1017–1034.

Cottam, Richard. 1964. *Nationalism in Iran.* Pittsburgh: University of Pittsburgh Press.

Dawisha, Adeed. 1980. "Saudi Arabia's Search for Security." Adelphi Papers 158. London: International Institute for Strategic Studies.

Department of Energy. 1980. "Free World Dependence on Persian Gulf Oil in the 1980s." Reprinted in *Petroleum Intelligence Weekly.* March 10, 1980.

Fesharaki, Fereidun. 1980. "Petroleum Sector Policy Plans and Options of the Major Exporting Nations in the 1980s." *United Nations World Energy Balance in the 1980s.*

Fukuyama, Frank. 1979. "A New Soviet Strategy?" *Commentary* 68, no. 5. (October).

Golan, Galia. 1979. "The Dilemmas and Options for Soviet Middle East Policy Today." Research Paper 35. Jerusalem: University of Jerusalem, Soviet and East European Research Center.

Graham, Robert. 1979. *Iran: The Illusion of Power.* New York: St. Martin's Press.

Hallidy, Fred. 1975. *Arabia Without Sultans.* New York: Random House.

Hottinger, Arnold. 1979. "Does Saudi Arabia Face Revolution?" *New York Review of Books* (June 28): 14–17.

Hudson, Michael. 1979. *Arab Politics.* New Haven: Yale University Press.

Huntington, Samuel. 1968. *Political Order in Changing Societies.* New Haven: Yale University Press.

The Institute for the Study of Conflict. 1979. *The Security of Middle East Oil.* London, May.

Itayim, Fuad. 1975. "Strengths and Weaknesses of the Arab Oil Weapon." Adelphi Paper 115. London: International Institute for Strategic Studies.

Kanovsky, Eliyahu. 1979. "Deficits in Saudi Arabia: Their Meaning and Possible Implications." In *Middle East Contemporary Survey,* edited by Colin Legum, pp. 318–359. New York: Meier.

Kedourie, Elie. 1974. "Continuity and Change in Modern Iraqi History." *Asian Affairs* 61, no. 2 (June): 140–146.

Kelidar, Abbas. 1975. "Iraq: The Search for Stability." *Conflict Studies* 59 (July). London: The Council of the Institute for the Study of Conflict.

Khadduri, Majid. 1978. *Socialist Iraq: A Study in Iraq: Politics Since 1968.* Washington: Middle East Institute.

Kraft, Joseph. 1975. "Letter From Riyadh." *New Yorker* (October 20): 111– 139.

Knorr, Klaus. 1976. "The Limits of Economic and Political Power." In *Oil Crisis,* edited by Raymond Vernon. New York: Norton.

Lackner, Helen. 1979. *A House Built on Sand: The Political Economy of Saudi Arabia.* London: Ithaca Press.

Ledeen, Michael, and William Lewis. 1980. "Carter and the Fall of the Shah: The Inside Story." *Washington Quarterly* 3, no. 2 (Spring): 3–40.

Levy, Walter. 1978/79. "The Years That the Locust Hath Eaten: Oil Policy and OPEC Development Prospects." *Foreign Affairs* 57, no. 2 (Winter): 287–305.

Long, David. 1979. "Saudi Oil Policy." *The Wilson Quarterly* 3, no. 1 (Winter): 83–91.

Maull, Hans. 1975. "Oil and Influence: The Weapon Examined." Adelphi Papers 117. London: International Institute for Strategic Studies.

Mishlawi, Tewfik. 1979. "A New Direction." *The Middle East* (May): 25–31.

Moran, Ted. 1978. *Oil Prices and the Future of OPEC.* Washington: Resources for the Future.

_____ . 1980. "Modeling OPEC Behavior: A Critical Review of Economic Models and Political-Behavioral Alternatives for Saudi Decision Making." Unpublished draft. Washington: Georgetown University, International Business Diplomacy School of Foreign Service.

Philby, St. John. 1952. *Arabian Jubilee.* London: Clowes and Sons.

Price, David. 1975. "Oman: Insurgency and Development." Conflict Studies 53. London: The Council of the Institute for the Study of Conflict.

Quarterly Economic Review of Iran. 1980. London: The Economist Intelligence Unit (First and Second Quarter).

Quarterly Economic Review of Iraq. 1980. London: The Economic Review of Saudi Arabia, 1979 and 1980. London: The Economist Intelligence Unit (Second Quarter, 1979, First Quarter, 1980).

Ramazani, Rouhollah. 1975. "Emerging Patterns of Regional Relations in Iran's Foreign Policy." *Orbis* 19, no. 4 (Winter): 1043–69.

_____ . 1979. "Security in the Persian Gulf." *Foreign Affairs* 57, no. 4 (Spring): 821–835.

Safran, Nadav. 1974. "Arab Politics, Peace, and War." *Orbis* 18, no. 2 (Summer): 377–401.

Saikal, Amin. 1980. *The Rise and Fall of the Shah.* Princeton, N.J.: University of Princeton Press.

Singer, Fred. 1978. "Limits to Arab Oil Power." *Foreign Policy* 30 (Spring): 53–67.

Smart, Ian. 1977. "Oil, the Superpowers and the Middle East." *International Affairs* 53, no. 1 (January) 17–35.

Stobaugh, Robert, and Daniel Yergin. 1979. "Energy: An Emergency Telescoped." *Foreign Affairs* 58, no. 3: 563–595.

U.S. Senate. 1979. "The Future of Saudi Arabian Oil Production." Subcommittee on International Economic Policy, Committee on Foreign Relations. 96th Congress, 1st session (April).

Upton, Joseph. 1960. *The History of Modern Iran: An Interpretation.* Cambridge, Mass.: Harvard University Press.

Wright, Claudia. 1979/80. "Iraq—New Power in the Middle East." *Foreign Affairs* 58, no. 2 (Winter): 257–277.

Yodfat, A., and Mordechai Abir. 1977. *In the Direction of the Gulf: The Soviet Union and the Persian Gulf.* London: Cass.

4 THE ROLE OF COMMUNIST COUNTRIES

Marshall I. Goldman

Energy security for the communist countries must be viewed differently than it is for most of the other areas considered in this book. In part, this is because many of us view the Soviet Union as our chief antagonist in the Persian Gulf and the one most anxious to disrupt our supply patterns. Thus, our energy security depends upon restrained Soviet behavior in the area.

However, the problem is more complicated than that. To some extent we may be able to influence Soviet behavior. For example, one way to reduce pressure on the Soviet Union to move into the Gulf area might be to help the Soviet Union develop its own energy resources. This would not only increase Soviet energy security but also Western energy security. Alternatively, some have suggested a joint agreement between the United States and the Soviet Union to promote tranquility in the Middle East and thereby the continued export of petroleum.

Whatever the strategy, it is clear that communist and capitalist policies often interact in ways that may not only be perverse but unpredictable. What is good for one may be bad for the other, but not necessarily. If the East Europeans and the Soviets are able to increase their production of energy, their economic and military strength would be enhanced relative to the capitalist world. At the same time this could mean that the communist countries would be spared the need to seek petroleum in the Middle East, thereby reducing both the pressure on world oil prices and the likelihood of war.

With the issuance of the Central Intelligence Agency report on Soviet petroleum in April 1977, most observers have come to expect that the Soviet Union and its fellow members of the Council of Mutual Economic Assistance (CMEA) will find it necessary to give up their net exports of over 1 million barrels of oil per day to the hard currency world, as was the case in 1977 to 1979, and become a net importer of as much as 3.5 to 4.5 million barrels per day by 1985. Imports of anything approximating that amount would play havoc with world petroleum markets. Consequently it is impossible to evaluate energy security without considering energy prospects in the communist world.

CHINA

With 1979 production of about 2 million barrels per day of petroleum, China probably has the least cause of all the communist countries to worry about its energy security. It is one of the world's ten largest petroleum producers. But what makes Chinese energy security seem so certain is a per capita consumption that is far below average. The Chinese do not need to be told to conserve energy—they already do. In the winter, there is virtually no heat anywhere, except in hotels frequented by foreigners. Concert halls and opera houses, universities, and even trains are unheated. This miserly attitude toward energy explains why, despite the size of their population, the Chinese are able to export 10 percent of their output.

Assuming that this energy-saving behavior will not change drastically as China continues its industrialization, the Chinese appear relatively immune to the threat of any production disruption in the Middle East. Moreover, there have been some reports of major new onshore oil finds near the Daqing oilfields. (*The New York Times* 1980c: D3).

Western oil companies have also become quite enthusiastic about the likelihood of finding some significant discoveries off the Chinese coast. If disputes with its neighbors such as Vietnam, Taiwan, Korea, and Japan over the ownership of some of their fields can be resolved, the anticipated petroleum discoveries in the area could be the source of a significant increase in future Chinese output. Even so, most experts do not expect increases large enough to make China a significant factor in world energy exports. Nonetheless, these discoveries would ensure abundant supplies for Chinese domestic consumption for some time to come.[1]

EASTERN EUROPE

The situation is not nearly as promising in Eastern Europe. In fact, these countries find themselves in a particularly vulnerable position — what may be called an energy squeeze. The Soviet Union is having an increasingly difficult time meeting Eastern Europe's expanding energy needs. To compound the problem, Eastern Europe does not have the hard currency to purchase large quantities of energy from other countries.

Eastern Europe lacks adequate supplies of the three major sources of energy — coal, oil, and natural gas — and production rates are not likely to improve significantly. The only exception is Poland, the fourth largest coal producer in the world and the second largest coal exporter after the United States. There, despite the labor unrest, the prospects are good for substantially increased hard coal and maybe even a little natural gas production. Otherwise, East European countries depend heavily on the Soviet Union for their energy supplies. As a group, they imported almost 1.5 million barrels per day of crude and petroleum products in 1977, close to 90 percent of which came from the Soviet Union. (This figure excludes Rumanian imports of about 260 thousand barrels per day which came largely from Iraq and Iran).

Since 1977 the Soviets and some of the East Europeans have classified data on petroleum imports and exports, making it difficult to determine the exact dimensions of Soviet influence over the energy markets of Eastern Europe. But there is little to indicate that it has changed much since 1977. Table 4-1 shows that from 1972 through 1976, Czechoslovakia imported 93 to 95 percent of its petroleum crude and oil products from the Soviet Union. Almost as dependent

1. These are the views of most petroleum specialists who have studied Communist China (Park and Cohen 1975: 33, 40; and *The Washington Post* 1978: 13). The prediction that there will be no sudden reversal in Chinese petroleum production also happens to coincide with the views of the CIA (Central Intelligence Agency 1977b: 1, 23). In contrast, we are much more critical about the CIA analysis of the Soviet Union because, as will be argued, it projects a much more radical reversal of Soviet energy prospects.

Table 4-1.   East European petroleum imports from the Soviet Union (*as a percentage of consumption*).

	1972	1973	1974	1975	1976
Bulgaria[a]	68%	78%	75%	89%	92%
Czechoslovakia	94	93	93	94	95
East Germany	75	80	87	87	92
Hungary	82	83	85	80	87
Poland	92	87	97	81	77

Note: Figures are for crude and oil products for all countries except Bulgaria, whose figures reflect crude oil only.

Sources: Author's estimates and Sovet Ekonomicheskoi Vzaimopomoshchi, *Statisticheskii Ezhegodnik Stran Chlenov Soveta Ekonomicheskoi Vzaimopomoshchi 1977* and various years, Moscow, Statistika.

a. Crude oil only.

were Bulgaria and East Germany, which in 1976 obtained about 90 percent of their crude oil either from the Soviet Union or through Soviet barter with Middle East countries. In recent years, the percentage of petroleum imported from the Soviet Union has increased for both countries.

Similar year-to-year variations show up among other East European countries. Hungary has imported anywhere from 80 to 87 percent of its petroleum from the Soviet Union; Poland, which imported as much as 90 percent from the Soviet Union in 1972 and 1973, has managed to reduce this figure in recent years to 80 percent or less. During the last decade, therefore, we have seen Bulgaria and East Germany become more dependent on the Soviet Union while Poland has become less so. With respect to natural gas, though, the trend for the next few years may be toward even greater reliance on the Soviets. Except for some domestic production, all the natural gas imported into Eastern Europe comes from the Soviet Union. With the opening of the new Orenburg gas pipeline in 1979, even Rumania now imports Soviet natural gas.

The East European nations have had mixed emotions about relying so heavily on the Soviet Union for such a large portion of their imported energy. In the 1950s and 1960s there were complaints, some not so muted, that the Soviets had forced them into this dependency and were exploiting them by charging them higher prices than other Soviet customers. In the late 1960s and early 1970s, the focus of the debate shifted as the Soviet Union began to complain that *it* was the exploited party. In order to supply Eastern Europe, the Soviets complained, they were being forced to move operations further into Siberia where their costs were higher. After 1973, when the Soviets raised their prices to the capitalist world fourfold but did not raise their prices to Eastern Europe, the Soviets seemed to have made their point.

The price of Soviet petroleum exports to Eastern Europe remained at 1970 levels throughout 1973 and 1974. Ultimately, that proved too much for the Soviets to bear. In 1975 they unilaterally broke their contractual agreement by raising their prices. Even so, Soviet export prices to Eastern Europe since then have continued to remain below the world level and the prices charged to its hard currency customers.

While the East Europeans have some advantages in dealing with the Soviet Union (they can buy most of their petroleum with soft currency, for example), they nonetheless have much to be concerned about. How long will the Soviet Union be able to supply them? The Soviets say they will increase energy exports to Eastern Europe by 20 percent over the course of the next Five-Year plan (1981 through 1985). But what if Soviet production falls or the Soviets decide to divert their exports elsewhere? After all, the Soviets have been urging the East Europeans to look elsewhere for supplementary petroleum supplies since the mid-1960s. Clearly the Soviets would rather export their petroleum to the hard currency countries, particularly as the world price continues to rise.

Recognizing that their economies would be seriously disrupted if anything happened to affect the flow of energy from the Soviet Union, most nations in Eastern Europe began to search for alternative sources of supply in the Middle East. Rumania's success in supplementing its domestic production with Middle Eastern petroleum was much admired. Throughout the 1970s, the other East Europeans tried to work out similar arrangements, in particular with Iraq and prerevolutionary Iran.

Unfortunately, the attempt has been less than a success. Because the bulk of Rumania's 260 thousand barrels per day of crude oil imports in 1978 came from Iran, even Rumania suffered. In fact, Rumania was probably one of the countries most affected by the disruption of oil exports from Iran. So severe was the disruption that in 1979, Rumania was finally forced to import petroleum from the Soviet Union, a step it had long sought to avoid.

The situation is not much better for the other East European countries. While they were importing considerably less from the Middle East, they too depended on Iran for much of their extra oil supplies. To some extent their failure to find additional sources of petroleum will be offset by the increased flow of Soviet natural gas through the Orenburg pipeline. They will also benefit from the increased production of nuclear energy both within Eastern Europe and the Soviet Union. Moreover, the Soviet Union intends to increase its exports of electricity to Eastern Europe.

Despite these alternatives, most East Europeans will be forced to use more of their own coal and lignite, something they would prefer, for pollution reasons, to avoid. Another alternative is to increase conservation. They may not have much choice. Because of their hard currency shortages, they have few options in their dealings with the Middle East producers. Barter will only take them so far among the ever richer OPEC states who are less and less interested in bartered goods. For that reason, what happens to petroleum production in the Soviet Union directly affects the energy security not only of the Soviet Union itself, but of Eastern Europe. There is also an indirect impact, for Soviet political and economic control through Comecon is negatively affected, creating a "double dilemma."

THE SOVIET UNION

On the face of it, the Soviet Union should have little to worry about. In 1979, petroleum production reached 11.44 million barrels per day, of which about 25 percent, or 3 million barrels per day, were probably exported. About one-half of these exports went to other communist countries; most of the remainder was exported for $7 to $8 billion in hard currency. Even if production should drop, that would seem to be a comfortable cushion to fall back on for internal consumption. In fact, the Soviets have come to depend on petroleum exports to pay their import bills; petroleum accounts for over 50 percent of the Soviet Union's hard currency earnings.

Nevertheless, some analysts—including those working for the CIA —have forecast a sharp drop in Soviet petroleum production to as little as 10 million barrels per day or, in the extreme, 8 million barrels per day (Central Intelligence Agency 1977a: 1). If this drop were to occur, Soviet petroleum exports would obviously cease; Eastern Europe and the Soviet Union would find it necessary to import. At one time, the CIA predicted imports of from 3.5 to 4.5 million barrels per day, although, in a subsequent CIA report, this forecast was reduced to 2.7 million barrels per day and ultimately to 1 million barrels per day by 1985 (Central Intelligence Agency 1977c: 22; and *Petroleum Intelligence Weekly* 1980: 2). If these dire predictions turn out to be correct, then the Soviet Union *will* have to join the other industrialized countries of the world in seeking external sources of supply.

Obstacles to Increased Production and Conservation

The Soviet Union is the largest producer of oil in the world and the world's third largest exporter. What led the Central Intelligence Agency to predict such a radical reversal in its oil-producing capabilities?

Some of the reasons are technical. Based on a careful engineering analysis, the CIA discovered that the Soviets are having difficulty sustaining output in many of their older wells. To restore pressure in these wells, Soviet engineers have been injecting water into oil fields. Although this technique was successful in the Volga-Ural region, the main source of Soviet petroleum in the 1960s and early 1970s, it has not produced the same results in the newer West Siberian fields. In the Volga-Ural Basin, it took eighteen years for the water content of the extracted liquid to rise to 10 percent, but in the West Siberian fields it took only three years. Were this trend to continue very long, the Soviets would soon find themselves in the water business. Indeed, water already constitutes 50 percent of the output of some wells. On the strength of this evidence, the CIA analysts concluded that petroleum production in West Siberia would peak sooner than anticipated. Since the West Siberian fields now account for over one-half of the total Soviet production, this development would be a serious loss. These fields have been the source of Soviet production increases and are now necessary to compensate for the drop in output from an increasingly large number of the older fields.

These difficulties are compounded by the Soviets' failure to discover new producing fields as large as the ones that are now being depleted. They have also been overpumping many of their wells, failing to set production at the maximum efficient rate of recovery (MER). Although that might mean higher output in the short run, in the long run the Soviets will be unable to extract as much from their wells as they might have, had they used more conservative techniques.

Traditionally we have assumed that only capitalism leads to the wasteful production and consumption of raw materials. But adherence to Marxist idealogy is, ironically, the cause of many of the Soviet Union's energy problems. As one disillusioned party member lamented,"the advantage of Communism is that it is always seeking to solve the problems that other societies somehow never seem to have." Thus the Soviets overpump their fields—not because of uncoordinated drilling but because of the nature of the Soviet planning system. The Soviet field operator does not compete against his neighbors but rather against the plan. Since his salary depends upon his meeting or exceeding his target, he is interested in extracting as much as possible from his field to meet his one-year or five-year plan. In other words, he is concerned about this year or this five-year period even though he should be thinking in terms of a longer period to achieve the MER.

The planning system induces other inappropriate practices. The performance of Soviet geologists, for example, is measured by their achievement of quantitative targets—in this instance, by the number of meters they drill. The result is predictable. Soviet geologists have become adept at drilling the largest number of meters possible. Unfortunately, that seldom coincides with finding petroleum. Rationally enough, Soviet drillers move their equipment elsewhere the minute that drilling progress begins to slow. But petroleum is not always found near the surface. In one area of Kazakhstan, the most highly paid prospectors were those who found no petroleum. Even more bizarre, drillers for the Ministry of the Gas Industry at Vuktyl Field in the Komi Republic actually found petroleum—but did not stop to test it. To do so would have made it impossible to fulfill their "meters drilled" target. Besides, they were working for the Ministry of the Gas Industry, not the Ministry of the Petroleum Industry (*Pravda* November 10, 1978: 2; and *Sotsialisticheskaia industriia* October 5, 1979: 2).

The Soviet pricing system also contributes to inefficiency. The domestic price of Soviet petroleum relative to the world market is even more understated than it is in the United States: the wholesale price has not increased since 1967! Misallocation of resources and waste are the results. Low wholesale prices stimulate industrial consumption, exactly as if petroleum usage were subsidized, by making petroleum appear cheaper than labor. Consequently, Soviet managers strive to increase their petroleum allotments and Soviet industry tends to be very wasteful and largely unconcerned with conservation.

Aided and abetted by the planning system, unrealistically low energy prices encourage water-spraying trucks to prowl Moscow's streets in prolonged rainstorms like a herd of parading elephants. They are only meeting their mileage quotas. Wastefully, farm, tractor, and truck drivers do the same. For that matter, even central heating engineers are rewarded according to how much heat their boilers distribute. Whether or not the recipient needs it, the heat is pumped. That is why so many Muscovites open their windows on mild winter days (*Pravda* November 10, 1979: 2).

Waste is also encouraged by the "val" system, which the Soviets employ wherever they have difficulty defining performance standards in concrete, measurable terms. In this system, a planner sets the manager's targets in terms of the ruble value of the enterprise's gross output. No consideration is given to net output. To win his bonus, the manager seeks to produce the highest possible output in ruble value. Since that value is determined by the sum of all the inputs, Soviet managers know that one way to increase the value of their gross output is to use expensive inputs—another incentive to consume, not conserve, oil. This line of thinking helps explain why Soviet machinery is unusually heavy, why Soviet engines require more metal per unit of engine power than most other engines, and why the Soviets require more fuel per kilowatt hour of electricity generated or per ton of steel smelted.

Finally, understated prices have made it more difficult to attract the investment and foreign currency funds needed for adequate development of Soviet energy resources. Although capital is normally allocated on the basis of physical allocation specifications rather than by an open market governed by prices, Soviet allocation authorizations are very much influenced by the profitability of each enterprise. Profitability, in turn, is determined by prices, so the fact that the wholesale price of energy has been held constant at 1967 levels means an inevitable fall in the profitability of Soviet energy production enterprises. In several instances, these enterprises have even begun to run at a loss. Profitability will continue to fall as Soviet geologists find it necessary to push farther north and east to increasingly remote, hostile, and costly sites in their search for new energy sources.

Just how important energy prices are is dramatically reflected by the profit-to-capital ratio of the various energy-producing enterprises. In 1965, before wholesale prices were increased, the profit rate of the petroleum-producing enterprise was 5.4 percent. The comparable rate for natural gas producers was 9.3 percent. Coal mines were actually operating at losses of 17 percent and required a subsidy. After the 1967 price increases, oil and natural gas profit rates rose to 27.8 percent and 64.5 percent, respectively, and coal was again in the black with a profit-to-capital ratio of 7.3 percent. With prices fixed and costs rising, however, those rates had, by 1978, fallen to 11 percent for petroleum, 17.8 percent for natural gas, and a 3.2 percent loss for coal.

Consequently, the Soviet planners in Gosplan, who allocate investment funds, have been reluctant to satisfy the demands of Soviet energy ministries. After all, the official data told them that the energy ministries were not using their existing capital resources effectively. Naturally, this stance was vigorously contested by officials in such energy ministries as the Ministry of the Petroleum Industry. Pointing to the rising world price and the critical role of petroleum in the Soviet balance of trade, they argued that their potential profitability was much higher than that dictated by official prices and indicated by the official data. They pleaded with Gosplan, Gosbank, and the Ministry of Finance for an increased allotment of ruble and hard currency investment funds for their industry.[2]

It was not that all investment funds were cut off, or that there was no expansion or purchase of new equipment; far from it. Yet it was too much to expect that Soviet planners would completely disregard their main operating indicators: foreign exchange allocations for the petroleum industry were generally limited to such relatively traditional purchases as pipe, drill bits, and submersible pumps (to remove the ever-increasing percentage of water). Officials refused to fund multimillion dollar allocations for the purchase of such new capital projects as a drill bit plant. Negotiations with American and

2. Discussion with Soviet and Western energy specialists. See also *Petroleum Economist* (1980: 9).

French manufacturers to build such a plant had begun as early as 1973, and the Minister of the Petroleum Industry was prepared to sign a contract, but Gosplan would not allocate the funds.

The need for a drill bit plant was undoubtedly real. Traditionally, the Soviets have had difficulty in generating innovative products and in keeping up with Western energy-producing technology. It is true that the Soviet Union has factories that produce more drill bits per year than any American factory, but these plants produce only two varieties. In contrast, American factories produce as many as six hundred varieties. American product differentiation reflects the varied needs of different drilling sites. The Soviets, despite their impressive production figures for drill bits, spend more time replacing worn-out bits than drilling. In addition, the predominant use of the turbo drill limits Soviet drilling efforts to depths of about 2,000 meters. Soviet well casing pipe is of such poor quality that it is extremely difficult to use other techniques to drill much beyond this depth. Consequently, petroleum or gas deposits in the 3,000- to 5,000-meter range are literally beyond the reach of most Soviet drilling teams.

Lack of innovation, quality control, and product differentiation is an old story for those familiar with the Soviet economy. Constrained by their planning and incentive system, Soviet managers and planners are interested only in fulfilling arbitrarily defined production targets. Any experimentation with new products produced in the laboratory threatens the experimenter with underfulfillment of his quota for previously standardized products. That is why the Soviets cannot move production operations from the laboratory to the factory floor, even though they have made some important theoretical advances in secondary recovery techniques. It helps explain why they find themselves restricted to the use of the turbo drill, poor well casing pipe and drill bits, and water injection technology. The incentive system places insurmountable barriers in the way, not of invention itself, but of the *adoption* of production innovations.

Alternatives for Increasing Soviet Energy Production

Given all the obstacles to increased energy output and to conservation in the Soviet Union, considerable substance underlies the CIA's warning of an impending Soviet energy shortage. But however perceptive the CIA reports, they do not consider how the Soviet Union would be able to pay for so much imported petroleum. Today, net petroleum exports account for 50 percent of total Soviet hard currency earnings. Without those exports, Soviet hard currency receipts for 1979 would have amounted to approximately $8 billion (excluding exports of gold and munitions)—leaving a deficit of $10 billion after hard currency imports of about $18 billion. If, in addition, the Soviets had to import 3.5 to 4.5 million barrels per day of petroleum, their deficit would be increased by some $37 to $45 billion per year for an intolerable total annual deficit of between $44 and $52 billion.

The Soviets could not pay for that much petroleum. This fact subsequently caused the CIA to reduce its estimate of eventual bloc imports to 1 million barrels per day by 1985. Even then, however, the Soviet Union would find itself saddled with an annual hard currency deficit of about $20 billion. Some of their petroleum needs conceivably could be satisfied through the barter of Soviet weapons and factories. After all, the Soviets have been engaged in such barter with countries like Iran, Iraq, Libya, and Algeria for some time. But however attractive this prospect, it is unlikely that OPEC countries would agree to more than modest amounts of such barter. Thus, the Soviets have a powerful incentive to find a solution to the energy-supply predicament highlighted by the CIA. Western nations also have a need to review Soviet options, for if the Soviet Union cannot satisfy its petroleum needs through normal foreign trade, there may be important political and military consequences for all of us.[3]

One of the major foundations of the CIA's conclusions is that it does not expect the Soviets to find major new petroleum reserves in the near future. Despite encouraging reports of reserve potential in deep regions of the Caspian Sea, not to mention the Pacific and Arctic Oceans, the first CIA report takes no account of possible offshore deposits. It also pays scant attention to the promising onshore regions of East Siberia that were thought to be the main source of future Soviet supplies before the West Siberian deposits were dis-

---

3. Presumably, the Soviets could cut back on their exports for a time, particularly as the world price of petroleum continues to increase. After all, they export 25 percent of their production, including about 18 percent to noncommunist countries. Thus, in the first half of 1979, Soviet petroleum exports to the OECD countries were down by 30 percent over the first half of 1978. Yet total hard currency earnings were up 20 percent due to OPEC's 50 percent price hike in early 1979. The Soviets will probably continue to favor Eastern Europe, at least until they find that exports have cut into their own consumption.

covered. Similarly, no allowance is made for the discovery of oil at depths greater than 2,000 meters. Yet there is reason to believe that once they gain increased access to Western drilling technology, the Soviets will be able to accelerate their exploration efforts and to drill beneath already producing gas fields, where many geologists expect to find petroleum.

The Soviet Union is a vast country and Soviet prospecting technology is outmoded; hence much of the country remains inadequately explored. But if new reserves were found, could they influence the Soviet energy supply by the mid-1980s? Some experts say no, not until the late 1980s, even though this answer ignores the accomplishments of the North Sea developers who brought their oil to market in just three to seven years' time. True, access to many untapped deposits hinges on the use of foreign technology. To the extent that the post-Afghanistan embargo on the sale of U.S. technology denies them the critical petroleum technology they need, the CIA's assumption may prove to be correct. But there are few who argue that the United States has a monopoly on the technology that the Soviets require. When the U.S. government took too long to issue a license for the export of an American gas lift system (a form of secondary recovery that reduces reliance on water injection), the Soviets shifted their contract to a French firm. In another case, the French were also apparently prepared to take on the construction of a drill bit plant when the United States temporarily refused to issue a license. Clearly, then, the Soviets could improve their geological exploration, the speed and depth of their drilling, and their use of apparently depleted reserves without American help.

The Soviets have gradually come to appreciate their need for foreign technology. They now permit foreign firms to participate in joint ventures on Soviet territory. Some of these ventures—in which the foreign partner bears most of the costs—are at an advanced stage. A Japanese-American-Soviet team has already found petroleum and gas off the shore of Sakhalin Island, and a Canadian firm has been drilling the Soviet north for some time. That the Soviets have agreed to such joint ventures and are considering more after having banned them from Soviet territory since the 1940s shows how far they are now prepared to go to acquire oil-drilling technology.

Conservation is another area of possible improvement in Soviet energy policy. Some commentators have argued that the Soviet automotive stock is so small that they do not suffer much from unnecessary consumption. While we in the United States have one car for every two people, they have about one car for every forty-two. But these critics overlook the enormous waste of energy within Soviet industry. It will not be easy to reduce energy usage in Soviet industry, but the potential is there; the CIA itself has shown that the Soviet Union has already been able to reduce the ratio between energy growth and GNP growth by stressing conservation (Central Intelligence Agency 1978: 6). A fall in the energy growth/GNP ratio means that the Soviet Union will have less need to increase petroleum production.

The CIA report also tends to underplay the Soviet ability to substitute other sources of energy for petroleum. Although it is true that recently faltering coal production has hampered Soviet efforts to increase coal usage, they have been quite successful in increasing their reliance on natural gas and nuclear energy.

Whatever the ultimate size of the Soviet Union's petroleum reserves, there is no dispute about its natural gas reserves—they are the largest in the world. The Soviet Union is estimated to contain about 40 percent of all the natural gas reserves in the world (*Petroleum Economist* 1979: 313). Soviet planners are increasingly substituting gas for petroleum as a source of energy at home and in Eastern Europe. It is true that until the overthrow of the Shah, the Soviet Union imported about 9.4 billion cubic meters of natural gas a year from Iran and about 2.5 billion cubic meters of gas from Afghanistan. But these supplies were mainly intended for the southern regions of the Soviet Union that border Iran and Afghanistan. These regions were adversely affected by the disruption that followed the Iranian revolution. The Soviets experienced first-hand what energy security means. It was a particularly pointed lesson because a disruption of a natural gas pipeline flow is more difficult to cope with given the critical role played by the pipeline. If the flow in a petroleum pipeline is cut off, there are alternative means of delivery. Fortunately for the Soviet Union, they could eventually reverse the pipeline flow to the Caucasus and bring in natural gas from the north. But it took time and caused some serious inconvenience along the southern border.

As the Soviet Union's allies in Eastern Europe use more gas, they are able to stretch their petroleum supplies further than would otherwise be the case. In Hungary, for example, new Soviet gas delivered through the Orenburg pipeline provides the energy equivalent of about 25 percent of Hungary's petroleum imports from the Soviet Union (*The Review of Sino-Soviet Oil* 1978: 55).

Nuclear energy, too, has become an important energy resource for the Soviet Union and Eastern Europe. There is no uncertainty about its application, as in the United States. Soviet engineers are energetically rushing toward completion of two assembly plants—one for themselves and one for the Czechs—that would mass-produce nuclear power reactors. When they are completed, these plants will each produce as many as eight 1-million-kilowatt units every year. As Professor Harvey Brooks of Harvard University points out, sixteen such reactors would displace almost 500,000 barrels of petroleum per day. Of course, not all Soviet electric power stations are fueled with petroleum. But once the Soviets are able to set up these reactors, within ten years they will more than make up for the 4.5 million barrels per day shortfall in petroleum imports predicted by the CIA. At present, the Soviets are far behind schedule, but it is clear that they are determined to substitute nuclear power for petroleum and natural gas in generating electricity.

In 1979, nuclear energy constituted 4 percent of all Soviet electricity generated, but planners expect that 10 percent of all the electricity generated in the European part of the Soviet Union will soon be produced by nuclear reactors. By the end of the tenth Five-Year Plan, which closes in 1980, the Soviets believe that nuclear reactors will provide as much as one-third of the increase in the electrical-generating capacity of this region. Similarly ambitious efforts are being pressed in Eastern Europe, and some Soviet nuclear plants are being built along the border so that their output can be sent directly to East European consumers.

This emphasis on nuclear energy reflects the Soviets' belief that reactor safety is not a serious concern. It would shock Americans to learn that, in fact, reactors are being built close to the city centers of Gorky and Voronezh in order to supply steam heat as well as electricity. What caution Soviet scientists do express focuses more on the disposal of waste than on reactor operation. Their attitude is perhaps another indication that the nuclear accident that took place in 1957–58 may have been the result of an explosion that dispersed nuclear wastes stored underground (*The New York Times* 1980b: A8). Even the President of the Soviet Academy of Sciences, Anatoly Alexandrov, professes to be mystified over the American reaction to safety matters, and especially to the mishap at Three Mile Island. As he sees it, the fuss "had nothing to do with safety. . . . The actual reason behind the whole fight over nuclear construction is entirely different. The development of large nuclear power stations could endanger the profits of the fuel-producing monopolies" (*Soviet News* May 15, 1979: 150-151). By implication, there is no such problem in the Soviet Union. Soviet scientists would not build such plants if they were not safe, so *ipso facto* there is nothing to worry about. What might not be safe is a public protest over the safety of nuclear energy.

The Future

However significant the CIA reports' neglect of Soviet potential may have been, perhaps the most bittersweet omission was the failure of the CIA to recognize the effect of its message. The reports are now likely to become a self-defeating prophesy. This is because Soviet officials and scholars tend to give more weight to Western analyses of Soviet problems than to their own analyses.

Some Soviet scholars, such as Academician A. E. Krylov, had been warning planners of virtually the same energy problems the CIA was to write about one year later.[4] We also saw how officials in the Ministry of the Petroleum Industry failed to prove their dire need to Gosplan, Gosbank, and the Ministry of Finance. But the appearance of the CIA energy report in April 1977 was apparently the answer to the Ministry of the Petroleum Industry's prayers. However ambiguous the Soviet Union's own data may have been, the CIA report was clear. It did not matter that the Soviet Union was at the time the largest producer in the world; it was, according to the CIA, approaching an energy crisis. Armed with the CIA's report, Soviet petroleum officials immediately rushed off to Gosplan.[5] Coincidentally or not, after more than four years of frustration, Gosplan and Gosbank began to see the need for petroleum technology. First, the Ministry of the Petroleum Industry found $144 million in hard currency for its drill bit plant. Soon thereafter, $226 million was authorized for

---

4. Evropa-Sibir' (1976: 153-180). He subsequently repeated the same warning in 1980 (*The New York Times* 1980a: D12).

5. Based on reports of executives from Western petroleum companies.

gas lift equipment to replace the water injection process, while new efforts and funds were authorized for offshore drilling and joint ventures.

Whether or not the CIA analysts prove to be correct, there are some important implications in all of this for American policy. There is no doubt, for example, that if the Soviet Union solves its energy problems, it will increase its economic and military strength as well. Some analysts therefore suggest doing everything we can to hamper Soviet economic development, especially holding back petroleum technology (Huntington 1980: 20). But will such an embargo work? Remember that little petroleum technology is under the exclusive control of the United States today. Thus, when the American government took its time in deciding whether or not to license the export of the $226 million gas lift equipment, the Soviets simply but decisively switched their order to a French company. Similarly in 1980, when a historic contract for a joint drilling venture in the Caspian Sea was about to be signed by the Soviets and two American companies, a French company immediately stepped in with an offer when the U.S.–Soviet arrangement was postponed because of the invasion of Afghanistan. More and more, we have less and less control over the sale of such technology.

But even if we did have such a monopoly, is it in our own interest to see the Soviet Union run out of petroleum? An equally good case can be made for doing everything we can to facilitate the development of Soviet energy resources. If the Soviets were able to continue satisfying their own energy needs, they would have less need to compete either militarily or economically with the rest of the world for Middle East petroleum. And the more petroleum produced in the world, the better for energy importers like Japan, Western Europe, and the United States. Of course, the Soviet Union could scarcely be considered a reliable supplier. But are Iraq, Libya, and Iran any more reliable?

Even if the Soviet Union is somewhat more reliable than the more unpredictable members of OPEC, that does not mean that importing energy from the Soviet Union is riskless. When it has seemed politically expedient to do so in the past, the Soviets have not hesitated to cut off the flow of energy to long-time customers. There is every reason to suspect that the Soviet Union would do the same thing again. Soviet petroleum earmarked for Yugoslavia and China was cut back sharply after the political break between those countries and the Soviet Union. Shipments to Israel were halted permanently after Israel's invasion of the Sinai in 1956. Oil was withheld from Finland in 1958 until Finland agreed to a more accomodating political stance.

Western suppliers face the same tactics today. The noncommunist countries whose energy security will be most vulnerable in the future are those who are most heavily dependent on the Soviet Union for their energy. Heading the list are Finland and Iceland, which, in 1979, imported over 60 percent of their crude oil and product from the Soviet Union. Next would be Austria, with 21 percent of its imports from the Soviet Union, and Switzerland with 17 percent. Italy and West Germany import much larger quantities of Soviet petroleum but rely on the Soviet Union for less than 10 percent of their total imports; they should be able to adjust without much difficulty to any suspension in the flow.

Although the major NATO countries would be little affected by a halt in Soviet petroleum exports, they might find themselves more rudely pinched by a shutoff of natural gas. Reliance on a natural gas pipeline reduces a consumer's flexibility, and Austria imports almost all of its natural gas from the Soviet Union. West Germany imports about 17 percent of its gas from the Soviet Union and is seeking to increase its imports substantially.

While the noncommunist world concerns itself with the threat of a Soviet cutoff, there are undoubtedly many in the Soviet Union who also worry about the security of Soviet supplies, particularly if the CIA proves to have been correct. Several analysts think that anticipated need for new sources of petroleum is the main explanation for the invasion of Afghanistan and the apparent Soviet drive to the Persian Gulf. But as we have seen, the Soviets have economic and geologic solutions open to them. Therefore, it appears unlikely that the invasion of Afghanistan was predicted in any large part on an attempt to secure future energy supplies. This conclusion is not to deny that the Soviet Union might like to generate a credible threat to the assured flow of Persian Gulf oil to Western Europe, Japan, and the United States, a threat which it could invoke to counter threats to its vital interests in other areas.[6] But given the petroleum production potential of the Soviet Union, it seems unlikely that the Soviet Union invaded Afghanistan primarily to position itself to grab Iranian oil for itself, much less for the East Europeans.

6. See Chapters 3 and 12 in this volume.

Those who predict that the Soviet Union and Eastern Europe will need massive quantities of imported oil tend to discount the economic and geological solutions that are available to the Soviets. There is no doubt that the Soviets have some serious problems, but that is not the same as saying that there are no cheaper solutions than military aggression. Moreover, the difficulties that the Soviets are supposed to have by 1985 have been projected on the assumption that the Soviets will be unable to do anything about them. In other words, both CIA reports assume no dynamic response by the Soviets.

For a time, admittedly, the Soviets did seem to be self-confident and inert. They needed a major jolt to prod them into more effective action, and the April 1977 CIA report apparently did the trick. Even if it was not the chief stimulus, it certainly helped focus the attention and resources of senior Soviet planners on the petroleum problem. However, the Soviet Union cannot always depend on the CIA. Ultimately, it will have to reform its fundamental planning and incentive system. The Soviets have long resisted this solution, but there are now signs that they may be willing to tamper with the planning process in order to bring about more effective use of their energy resources. The Soviets are redesigning the incentive system so that geologists will be rewarded for finding petroleum, not merely for digging holes. Along the same lines, responsibility for offshore drilling has been consolidated under the control of the Ministry of the Gas Industry. With one ministry in charge instead of the three, there may finally be some offshore exploration.

Concern for heightened efficiency was also very much in evidence when an overall planning reform was introduced in July 1979. Under the new mechanism, much less emphasis is to be devoted to increasing gross output, or "val." Instead, key targets will be spelled out in terms of what the Soviets call "net normative output"—our "value added." Premiums will henceforth be based on the extra value added to production. If a manager wants to be rewarded, he will now have to conserve, not squander, his material inputs. Continuing this emphasis on conservation, the Soviets are discussing the need for a wholesale price hike in raw materials such as petroleum, natural gas, and coal. With higher prices, Soviet managers will be stimulated to increase production and diminish consumption; they should also find it easier to win increased investment allocations of both domestic and foreign funds.

There is no denying that the Soviet Union has a long way to go and that it will not be able to solve all its energy security shortcomings overnight. Nonetheless, we in the United States should not be too patronizing. After all, our own energy problems are even more difficult and our plans for coping with them are hardly impressive. Our efforts at increased conservation, exploration, research, and production leave much to be desired. Nor have we had the courage to adjust energy prices to world levels. Maybe someone can convince the KBG to write a report about *our* energy problems.

REFERENCES

Central Intelligence Agency. 1977a. *Prospects for Soviet Oil Production.* Washington: Central Intelligence Agency, April, p. 1.

_____. 1977b. *China: Oil Production Prospects.* Washington: Central Intelligence Agency, June, p. 1, 23.

_____. 1977c. *Soviet Economic Problems and Prospects.* Washington: Central Intelligence Agency, July, p. 22.

_____. 1978. *The Soviet Economy in 1976–77 and the Outlook for 1978.* Washington: Central Intelligence Agency, August, p. 6.

Evropa-Sibir'. 1976. *Ekonomika i organizatsiia promyshlennogo proizvodstva.* April, pp. 153–180.

Huntington, Samuel. 1980. "The Danger from Soviet Armed Forces." *The New York Times* (February 2): 20.

The New York Times. 1980a. February 13: D12.

_____. 1980b. February 14: A8.

_____. 1980c. May 1: D3.

Park, Choon-ho, and Jerome Alan Cohen. 1975. "The Politics of the Oil Weapon." *Foreign Policy* no. 20 (Fall): 33, 40.

Petroleum Economist. 1979. August: 313.

_____. 1980. January: 9.

Petroleum Intelligence Weekly. 1980. Special Supplement (May 19): 2.

Pravda. 1978. November 10: 2.

_____. 1979. November 10: 2.

The Review of Sino-Soviet Oil. 1978. November: 55.

Sotsialisticheskaia industriia. 1979. October 5: 2.

Soviet News. 1979. May 15: 150–151.

The Washington Post. 1978. October 10: 13.

5 ENERGY SECURITY IN NORTH AMERICA

Fen Hampson
Kevin J. Middlebrook

The energy security concerns of the United States reflect its position as the principal Western economic and military power and the world's largest consumer of petroleum. The diversity of these concerns is mirrored in its energy relations with its two North American neighbors. Like Western European countries and Japan, Canada poses the problem of policy coordination with an industrialized nation that is also a political and military ally. The Canadian government is faced with a complicated array of energy-related problems that includes the rational use of domestic energy supplies and the management of import needs, the development of alternative energy resources, and the regional political and socioeconomic problems associated with rising energy costs and the shift to alternative energy sources. Canadian strategies to deal with these varied problems may offer useful lessons to the United States.

Energy relations with Mexico, on the other hand, illustrate the complex problems that oil-exporting developing countries pose for the United States. Mexico is a relatively secure potential source of important oil and natural gas for the United States, but, as with oil-exporting developing countries in the Middle East and elsewhere, its pressing socioeconomic problems and development needs significantly affect its decisions about production levels and pricing strategies. Furthermore, the frequently conflictive history of U.S.-Mexican relations ties energy security concerns inextricably to other bilateral issues such as immigration, foreign investment and technology transfer, and trade.

Although Canada and Mexico present very different issues and problems, they both form part of the broader context of North American energy relations. Are there ways that U.S. energy and security concerns might be addressed within a North American framework? As the sections that follow suggest, formal arrangements such as a "North American energy common market" or a "trilateral framework for North American interdependence" are unlikely to be adopted soon for a variety of economic, historical, and political reasons. Nonetheless, in designing measures to prepare for emergency disruptions of the world petroleum market, the United States may find opportunities for constructive leadership toward North American energy cooperation. The possibility of constructing formal arrangements at some point in the future depends in large part upon U.S. relations with each country on a broad range of issues that includes, but is not restricted to, energy.

I

CANADIAN ENERGY SECURITY POLICIES

Fen Hampson

Canada's federal energy policies are aimed at the long-term goal of achieving self-sufficiency sometime in the 1990s through a combination of conservation, substitution, and diversification. But self-reliance has proven an elusive goal, for political as well as technical and economic reasons. Canada's oil and gas policies have been sucked into the political whirlpool of federal–provincial conflict. Electoral instability has also frustrated the timely development of adequate energy security policies. As a result, Canadian reliance on foreign sources of crude is growing. Of obvious concern to Canadians, this trend is important for the United States as well because, in the event of a supply disruption, Canada could help the United States only marginally and the economy of the United States' largest trading partner would be seriously affected.

CANADIAN IMPORT LEVELS AND TRENDS

At first glance, Canada's overall energy situation appears to be relatively favorable; its energy trade balance has always been positive. (See Table 5–1.) In 1979, Canada's trade surplus in energy commodities reached $4 billion, a surplus made possible by sizeable exports of natural gas, uranium, and electricity.[1] But this broad picture is misleadingly optimistic from a security standpoint. In the mid–1970s,

I would like to thank Professor Antal Deutsch, McGill University, and Professor Jorge Dominguez, Harvard University, who commented on drafts of this chapter. As well, I would like to thank those members of the Canadian Department of Energy, Mines and Resources, the Department of National Defence, the Department of Finance, the Department of External Affairs, and the Government of Alberta who granted me interviews while I was preparing this chapter.

1. Unless otherwise indicated, all figures are in Canadian dollars. One Canadian dollar was equal to about 85 U.S. cents in 1980.

Table 5–1. Canadian energy trade balances.

Value	Petroleum	Natural Gas	Coal and Coke	Electricity	Uranium	Total
		(C $ millions)				
1970	129	201	-135	22	-34	183
1973	647	343	-9	103	69	1,153
1974	1,045	488	84	170	83	1,702
1975	171	1,084	-160	91	121	1,307
1976	-624	1,607	-13	153	241	1,364
1977	-1,064	2,028	-66	362	208	1,467
1978	-1,427	2,190	-8	477	646	1,878
1979	-1,533	2,889	-184	728	969	3,869
Volume	Million Barrels	Billion Cubic Feet	Million Tons	Billion Kwh		
1970	-2.8	756	-14.7	2.3		
1973	131.6	1,016	-4.4	13.0		
1974	83.3	952	-2.2	12.2		
1975	15.5	939	-4.5	4.3		
1976	-47.7	945	-3.3	7.5		
1977	-73.9	994	-3.9	15.5		
1978	-90.1	883	1.3	20.4		
1979	-27.2	995	-4.0	30.6		

Source: Department of Finance (1980); *Statistics Canada* (1980a, 1980b).

Canada became a net importer of oil, and 95 percent of it came from OPEC.

Despite important crude discoveries in Alberta's West Pembina fields in 1977, the production capacity of Canada's oil fields has steadily declined. Western Canada's remaining oil reserves total some 5 billion barrels (Energy, Mines and Resources 1979a) (see Figure 5–1). Some of the production losses from conventional crude reserves will be offset by new crude sources such as the tar sands and offshore oil of eastern Canada. Even so, these "unconventional" sources will not contribute to overall domestic production until the late 1980s or early 1990s because of the time required to develop them. Forecasts that domestic production is likely to decline from 1.4 million barrels per day in 1978 to 1.3 million barrels per day in 1985 are probably accurate (Energy, Mines and Resources 1979b).

Canada's daily consumption of oil was 1.8 million barrels in 1978 and 1.9 million barrels in 1979. As production from conventional

Figure 5-1.   Current energy balances (primary energy).

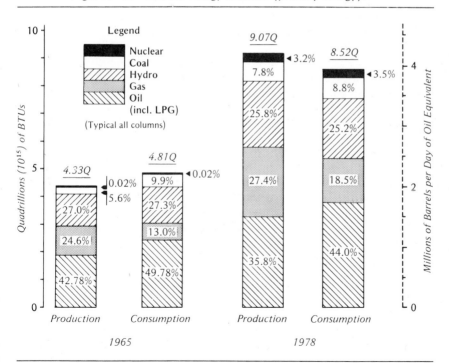

Source: Energy, Mines and Resources (1979c).

Table 5−2.   Canada's gross crude imports by source[a]
(*percent of total*).

	September 1973 (pre-crisis level)	1976	October 1979
Algeria	—	—	3.2
Egypt	—	—	—
Iraq	2.4	4.0	—
Kuwait	—	.3	4.8
Libya	6.0	2.8	—
Qatar	—	—	—
Saudi Arabia	8.7	15.0	31.0
United Arab Emirates	5.2	8.0	2.5
Total OAPEC	22.3	30.1	41.5
Total OPEC	95.3	93.2	79.3
Other	4.7	6.8	20.7
TOTAL	100.0	100.0	100.0

a. These figures reflect gross imports which take into account oil swaps between U.S. companies and their affiliates in Canada. Net imports (imports−exports) are somewhat lower.

Source: International Energy Statistical Review (1980).

reserves declines, net imports are expected to increase from current levels of 150,000 barrels per day to some 600,000 barrels per day in fiscal year 1985−86. (See Table 5−2 for current gross import levels from OPEC sources.) Net imports, now at 10 percent of total domestic oil consumption, are expected to rise to between 30 and 40 percent in 1985−86. Thus, Canadian energy security will go from bad to worse over the next five years despite a continuing energy trade surplus.

The Canadian government seems aware of the need to curb the growth of its oil imports. At the International Energy Agency (IEA) meeting in March 1979, Canada accepted the 5 percent reduction in total imports for all members.[2] At the Tokyo summit in June 1979, it agreed to keep net oil imports down to 600,000 barrels per day in 1985, a level that would allow only a 1 percent annual rate of growth in oil consumption. But Canada will probably have to default on

2. Canadian authorities have interpreted the IEA commitment to be a 5 percent reduction in imports *as a percentage of total consumption.*

these commitments if it continues its current pricing policies. At a time when most of Canada's allies are feeling the pinch of higher oil prices, Canadian consumers still enjoy very low prices. As of January 1, 1980, the domestic price for a barrel of crude was $14.75, compared to a world price of $25.65. The federal government's pricing formula raises the domestic price $1 per barrel every six months, but at this rate Canadian prices would never even approach world prices.

Canada's Department of Energy, Mines and Resources (EMR) predicts that current pricing policies could encourage oil imports to reach 641,000 barrels per day in 1985, a level that would violate the import reduction commitments made at the Tokyo summit. However, EMR predicts that imports could be reduced well below this level if Canadian prices were gradually brought to international market levels by the mid–1980s, and if gas production were accelerated to provide a substitute for oil.[3]

THE EVOLUTION OF CURRENT POLICIES

During the fifties and sixties, Canadian oil producers sought greater access to protected U.S. markets. In the early seventies, however, seeing finally that Canadian reserves were not unlimited, the government began the gradual elimination of oil exports to the United States. These exports will end in 1982.

The government acted on other fronts following the Arab oil embargo of 1973–74 (see Energy, Mines and Resources 1977). To reduce the dependence of Montreal refiners on imported sources of oil, the government proposed to extend the Interprovincial Pipeline from Sarnia, Ontario to Montreal. This was completed in 1976. It also created a formal program of energy conservation and research and development, set up an Energy Supplies Allocation Board to deal with major disruptions in imports, established a state-owned oil company, PetroCanada (PetroCanada 1976, 1977, 1978, 1979), and initiated oil export taxes.

---

3. Projections of future demand and import levels, of course, depend on assumptions about world price trends, prices of interfuel substitutes such as gas, levels of economic growth, and so forth. For a variety of projections of future import levels see Energy, Mines and Resources (1979b).

In addition, a single oil price was set for the entire nation. Previously, the Canadian market had been divided into two parts. Consumers living west of the Ottawa Valley line were supplied with high-priced Albertan oil; consumers east of the Ottawa Valley were supplied with imported oil and paid international prices. The single price eliminated these differentials. Eastern refiners of what had rapidly become expensive imported oil were compensated for the difference between international and domestic prices by the new Oil Import Compensation program.

The higher oil prices that resulted from the energy shocks of 1973−74 and 1979−80 led to serious and continuing conflict between the federal government and the producing provinces over oil and gas revenues. Under the Canadian Constitution (the British North America Act), natural resources fall under provincial jurisdiction. The provinces used their power over natural resources to alter fiscal regimes and to capture the bulk of the windfall from price increases. The federal government actively resisted these efforts and tried to obtain a greater share of petroleum revenues for itself, but with limited success. In 1978, for example, the federal share of revenues from oil and gas production was 9.5 percent; the provincial share (including bonuses and rentals) was 46.3 percent; producers received the remaining 44.2 percent.[4] In cash terms, the federal government earned slightly less than $1 billion while more than $4 billion went both to the provinces and to producers. Under current pricing policies, this arrangement would allow 1985 producer revenues to be $11.6 billion; provincial revenues, $11.7 billion, and federal revenues, only $3.2 billion.

Had Canadian prices not been kept below world levels, the magnitude of the transfers to the producers and to the oil- and gas-producing provinces would have been much greater. Higher domestic prices would also have meant increased equalization payments from the federal government to the poorer provinces.[5] These payments come from the federal government's general revenues, and the provinces contribute to the system only to the extent that their residents pay federal taxes.[6]

4. These figures are drawn from Energy, Mines and Resources (1979c).

5. The equalization payments system attempts to maintain the per-capita revenues of "revenue-poor" provincial governments at the national average so that all Canadians may receive a potentially comparable level of provincial services.

6. See Breton (1977: 105−113). Proposals upon the system are presented in Courchene and Melvin (1979), and Helliwell (1980).

The equalization payments system, the reluctance of the federal government and the oil-consuming provinces to see the oil-producing provinces become any richer, and the obvious desire of Eastern consumers for low energy prices have all mediated against higher energy prices in Canada. Increasing energy prices would also hurt economic growth (currently forecast at 0.5 percent of GNP for fiscal year 1980–81), and the resulting inflation would cut into manufacturers' profits and add to the cost of consumer goods.

There are, however, economic forces that encourage higher prices. Most significant is the differential between domestic and world prices that threatens the economy with oil-import compensation payments of more than $4 billion in 1980–81. This sum would greatly exceed revenues from the gasoline excise tax and the oil-export charge. After its electoral victory in February 1980, Prime Minister Pierre Trudeau's Liberal government proposed a "blended price" scheme as a remedy to this undesirable trend. The plan would progressively incorporate the costs of the Oil Import Compensation program while maintaining a single price for all Canadian consumers, subject only to transportation cost differentials (see House of Commons Debates 1980: 5–6). The "made in Canada" price would average the costs of easily recoverable domestic, imported, and the more difficult to recover and thus higher cost crudes, narrowing the current differential between the domestic price and world price and reducing the net import subsidy now provided under the Oil Import Compensation program.

The ill-fated Conservative government of Joe Clark, which held office for barely one year, promised to raise domestic prices by $4.00 in 1980 and by $4.50 per year for the next four years. The Conservative government's budget also provided for automatic adjustments of domestic oil prices to 75 percent of the world price in 1983 and 85 percent in 1984. Alberta stood to gain considerably from these proposals. The Liberals, however, favor significantly more moderate price increases. At the time of this writing, the federal government has been unable to reach agreement with the producing provinces for a new pricing, taxation and revenue-sharing regime. And the outcome will depend more generally on current efforts at constitutional reform.

It is unlikely that the government will attempt to promote conservation by increasing the excise tax on gasoline and transportation fuels, at least in the near future. Consumer opposition to Conservative Party plans to do exactly that contributed importantly to its defeat at the polls in February 1980. Both during and since that election campaign, the Liberals publicly opposed Clark's proposal for an $.18 per gallon excise tax on gasoline. As the public memory of election rhetoric fades, however, the government will most likely feel less committed to adhering to its campaign promises.

RESOURCES FOR SELF-RELIANCE: TAR SANDS AND NATURAL GAS

The federal government is publicly committed to accelerating development of such alternative energy resources as natural gas, hydroelectric power, nuclear energy, coal, and nonconventional crudes. These sources may well play a large role in Canada's energy future, but they are long-term rather than short-term substitutes for oil. The more immediate question is to what extent Canadian energy security can be quickly enhanced by the development of indigenous nonconventional sources of oil such as tar sands or by the use of more immediately available oil substitutes, particularly natural gas in conventional producing areas.

The tar sands of northern Alberta are, quite simply, a mixture of sand and crude (see Figure 5-2). They are estimated to contain some *900 billion* barrels of oil. With surface mining techniques, 26.5 billion barrels of this treasure should be recoverable, but the development of *in situ* recovery methods could multiply this yield by a factor of ten. To date, technological, economic, and political constraints have prevented rapid development of the tar sands. Two synthetic oil-producing plants, Syncrude and Suncor, are currently producing a total of 150,000 barrels per day, but both facilities have been plagued by technical problems. Disputes between the federal and provincial governments over prices and royalties have delayed plans for two more commercial oil sands facilities and a heavy oil project. Some experts believe that with an appropriate pricing policy and fiscal regime, oil production from tar sands could reach 700,000 barrels per day by 1990-91. But unless federal/provincial disputes over prices and royalties are resolved soon, tar sands development could be delayed still further.

Canada's natural gas resources also appear to hold considerable promise for the near future. At the end of 1979, the National Energy Board (NEB) estimated Canada's remaining gas reserves to be 86.3 trillion cubic feet, of which 71.8 trillion cubic feet are within con-

Figure 5-2. Oil and natural gas projects.

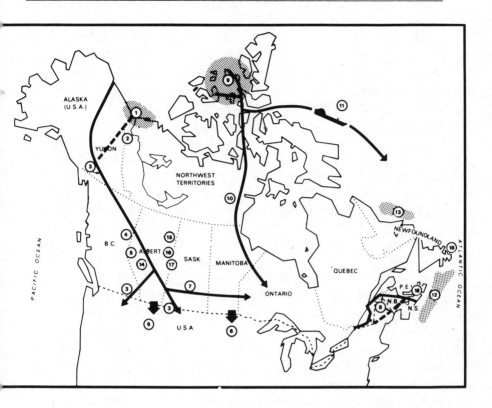

A. *Western Arctic and Alberta Gas—Routes and Markets*

1. Delta/Beaufort Gas
2. Dempster Pipeline Proposal
3. Alaska Highway Gas Pipeline Proposal
4. Westcoast Transmission—Grizzly Valley Pipeline
5. "Conventional Areas" Gas Development
6. Gas Sales
7. TransCanada PipeLines
8. Quebec and Maritimes Gas Pipeline Extension

B. *Arctic Islands and Eastern Offshore Gas —Routes and Markets*

9. Panarctic Exploration Program
10. Polar Gas Project

B. *(continued)*

11. Arctic Pilot Project
12. Petro-Canada and Mobil Oil Scotia Shelf Exploration
13. Eastcan Exploration Program

C. *Oil Development*

14. "Conventional Areas" Oil Exploration and Development (e.g., West Pembina)
15. Tar Sands development sites
16. Cold Lake heavy oil project proposal
17. Heavy Oil Development, Upgrading: Saskatchewan and Alberta Sites
18. Oil Storage and Trans-shipment Wabanex and/or Canso sites

Source: Energy, Mines and Resources Canada (1978: 69).

ventional producing areas. The more remote reserves in the Mac-Kenzie Delta–Beaufort Sea and Arctic Islands regions may be even larger than expected, but they will not be deliverable until the late 1980s, or even later.

Canadian energy security would certainly be enhanced by greater substitution of natural gas for oil, particularly in Quebec, and there is some movement toward this end. The federal government is publicly committed to extending existing natural gas pipelines into Quebec, and the National Energy Board recently approved a Quebec and Montreal (Q&M)–TransCanada proposal to extend the TransCanada pipeline as far as Quebec City.[7] Deliveries to Quebec through this pipeline could reach 300 million cubic feet per day in 1981—the BTU equivalent of 60,000 barrels per day of oil.

The Arctic Pilot Project is another proposal to provide eastern markets with natural gas. It calls for the production and liquification of 250 million cubic feet per day of natural gas from the Drake Point fields off Melville Island. The gas would be moved by liquified natural gas (LNG) icebreaking tankers to regasification terminals in eastern Canada. Most experts consider the project feasible, especially given its comparatively low initial capital costs. However, deliveries would begin in 1986 at the earliest. Once Arctic gas displaced gas delivered from western Canada in eastern markets, the western gas could then be sold through existing pipeline and distribution facilities to the United States.

Far more ambitious is the Polar Gas Project. Its sponsors have proposed the construction of a pipeline system to transport gas from the Arctic Islands to markets in eastern Canada. Costs would exceed the projected construction costs of the Alaskan pipeline, now estimated at US$20 billion, and detailed studies of the environmental and socioeconomic effect of the pipeline have yet to be conducted. For these reasons, there is little chance that the project will be approved any time soon; Arctic gas will not be needed to meet Canadian needs until the 1990s anyway.

The discovery in late 1979 of sizeable reserves of oil at the Hibernia and Ben Nevis fields off the coast of Newfoundland (estimated by some to be as high as 10 billion barrels), as well as the discovery of significant gas reserves at Sable Island off the Nova Scotia coast, have

7. The pipeline sponsor's proposal to build the line all the way to Nova Scotia was temporarily denied.

further complicated Canada's energy alternatives. Development of these new fields would result in new energy supplies by 1985, at the earliest, but would probably also delay progress on Arctic gas development projects.

Canadian gas exports to the United States now average 2.7 billion cubic feet per day, and volumes could reach 4.7 billion cubic feet per day by 1982 under the NEB's current export policies. Late in 1979, the NEB approved the export of 3.75 trillion cubic feet of gas to the United States over a seven-year period. Half of this volume, however, was approved for export through the pre-built sections of the Alaskan pipeline in southern Alberta. This decision was intended to help facilitate pre-building of the southern part of the line. The Canadian federal government, however, hesitated to authorize construction of the pre-build for fear that if the Alaskan pipeline were not built, Canadian excess capacity would be committed to the United States. This gas would be unavailable for Canadian needs at a time when gas substitution was being encouraged in Canada. Following a Congressional resolution reaffirming the U.S. commitment to construction of the line, the Canadian government gave approval for the pre-build in July 1980.

Financing difficulties for the overall construction of the line have yet to be resolved. Current negotiations between producers of Alaskan gas and the U.S. government have stalled over the issue of equity participation and whether gas conditioning costs can be included in the price paid by consumers. When (and if) completed, the pipeline would carry 2.4 billion cubic feet per day of Alaskan gas into U.S. markets. Construction of the proposed Dempster spur to the Mac-Kenzie Delta in Canada could provide an additional 1.2 billion cubic feet per day for Canadian customers.

Given the lead times involved in most of these tar sand and natural gas projects, Canada's ability to become self-sufficient in energy within the next five years or so is highly doubtful. Although Canada is rich in nonconventional oil and natural gas, its endowment may be like Tantalus's fruit: hanging just out of reach when it is needed most. It is essential, therefore, that Canada, like other oil-importing nations, develop policies to minimize the danger of oil import disruption.

EMERGENCY ENERGY POLICIES

Due to their relatively small size, the cushion provided by international market mechanisms, and Canada's hitherto modest dependence on oil imports, supply interruptions have so far gone almost unnoticed in Canada. As its overall dependence on foreign sources of oil increases, however, Canada's vulnerability to future supply interruptions grows day by day. Its emergency energy security policies are pinned on the hope that the IEA sharing system will work, an issue discussed in Chapter 13.

Domestic Canadian security policies in effect or under consideration are of three types: oil reserve policies and mechanisms; efforts to diversify sources of supply; and measures for supply allocation and rationing. It is possible, too, that Canada would play a military role in some kinds of oil emergencies, as discussed at the end of this section.

Under the IEA, Canada is committed to maintain a reserve equivalent to ninety days of oil imports. This provision may sound prudent, but the definition of reserves is rather loose. Many countries include operating stocks in calculating their total reserves on hand. Unfortunately, normal operating stocks (those used to keep refineries operational) and real safety stocks (those that could be used to deal with emergencies) are actually very different. Operating stocks would not be available for use during supply disruptions because they are needed to keep refineries, pipelines, and distributional systems functional. Not surprisingly, perceptions of minimally acceptable stock levels vary considerably. The issue is further complicated by seasonal variations in demand and many other factors. The U.S. Department of Energy estimates that for Western Europe and Japan, roughly 25 to 30 percent of normal total operating stocks would be unobtainable in the event of a supply disruption. For the United States, because of geography and greater transportation distances, minimum working stocks are about 50 percent of total operating stocks.

In order to obtain a clearer picture of its own operating stocks and to develop estimates of readily available "excess" stocks, the Canadian government surveyed refiners in 1976. It found that estimates of excess stocks varied enormously from refinery to refinery. A more recent survey, based on a modified questionnaire, is in the process of being analyzed; the results have yet to be released. Based on data provided by participating countries in the IEA and published in *IEA Quarterly Oil Statistics,* the U.S. Department of Energy calculates that Canada currently has working stocks equivalent to some eighty-two days of consumption (see Table 5–3). But out of total working stocks, Canadian pumpable stocks (stocks above minimum operating levels) would be sufficient to provide only about seventeen days of consumption.

Given its growing dependence on foreign crude, Canada must soon make crucial decisions about its reserve capacity. The government could encourage the building of emergency stocks in a variety of ways. It could, for example, impose mandatory inventory requirements on refiners. This policy would probably involve some tax breaks or other incentives, since refiners would be reluctant to assume the costs of higher inventory levels. Alternatively, the government could develop its own stockpiling program, which would probably best be administered through PetroCanada, the state-owned oil company. Yet another possibility would be a strategic reserve of crude oil and oil products administered by a new public corporation similar to that.in West Germany (see Chapter 6).

Whatever reserve policy the government chooses, it will have to solve at least one tricky distribution problem. Because the Interprovincial Pipeline only extends to Montreal, the Maritime Provinces are more vulnerable to supply disruptions than the rest of Canada (as was illustrated during the Iranian crisis when Maritime refineries

Table 5–3. Total working petroleum stocks and estimated useable stocks in canada.[a]

	Days of Consumption		
	1978	*1979*	*1980*
Working stocks	90	79	82
Estimated useable stocks	25	14	17

a. These figures are based on statistics reported in the *Quarterly OIL Statistics* (1980) and were obtained from an internal memorandum on "Petroleum Stock Levels in Major Consuming Countries" (U.S. Department of Energy 1980).

found themselves short of crude). Refineries in this area have only about seven days' worth of reserves.

Oil from Montreal could conceivably be shipped to the Maritimes by tanker, but only if the disruption had the courtesy to occur in the warmer months; the St. Lawrence River freezes over at Montreal. Rail and highway routes to the Maritimes are insufficient for a major transportation effort. Oil could be shipped from Vancouver via the Panama Canal, as in 1973, but this process is time-consuming, depends on the Canal being open, and requires spare tanker tonnage on the west coast.

One promising solution would be to develop a strategic reserve in the Maritimes. The U.S. and Canadian governments discussed developing such a facility as part of the U.S. Strategic Petroleum Reserve (SPR) program, but the discussions were halted in July 1979. Nevertheless, a Maritime SPR could be mutually advantageous to Canada and the United States. Oil from the SPR could be used to meet Maritime needs as well as those of New England in an emergency, and Albertan oil could be supplied to the U.S. Midwest as part of a "swapping" arrangement. Studies have shown that ideal storage and transshipment facilities are available in salt domes near the Canso Straits in Nova Scotia and also at the abandoned Wabana iron ore mine at Bell Island, Newfoundland.

In addition to developing adequate national reserves, Canada can also enhance its energy security by developing sources of supply that are independent of OPEC. Canada recently signed an agreement with Mexico, under which shipments of 50,000 barrels per day of Mexican oil are scheduled to begin in 1980. But, as seen in Chapter 2, government-to-government deals are usually tied to a broader package. As part of this agreement, for instance, Canada must accept heavier and less desirable forms of crude from Mexico. Government-to-government deals also introduce rigidities into the international distributional system and prevent the majors from spreading shortages fairly equally among all oil-consuming states. During the 1979 crisis, Canada benefited from such systemic flexibility. Furthermore, government-to-government deals enhance security only to the extent that the supplier country is willing to live up to its export commitments and only as long as the political climate in the supplier country is favorable. To date, the Canadian government has not actively pursued government-to-government deals, but it does expect Petro-

Canada to enter into such agreements with any country that expresses a preference for them.

A key element in any nation's emergency energy policy is the mechanism it uses to allocate supplies. In Canada, the Energy Supplies Allocation Board maintains contingency plans in readiness for an emergency (Energy Supplies Emergency Act 1979). When the Cabinet deems that an emergency exists, a mandatory allocation program is activated. The Board takes control of all supplies of crude coming into the country and allocates them to the refiners. It can set priorities for the use of controlled products, mandate the distribution of products down to the consumer level, set prices, and regulate the use of alternative fuels in cooperation with provincial authorities. The Board can also ration gasoline and transportation fuels at the retail level.

Would Canada be better off letting the market deal with domestic shortages? As pointed out in Chapters 9 and 10, there are obvious advantages to allocating shortfalls by decontrolling prices. The U.S. response to the Iranian oil shock showed that allocation schemes may well be unworkable. Economic efficiency and equity probably could be enhanced by price decontrol, if standby legislation were developed to tax oil companies to reduce windfall profits and provide rebates to consumers during a supply disruption. And the administrative costs of this strategy would be comparatively minor. Nevertheless, our review of current policy development suggests that there would be serious economic and political obstacles to any Canadian effort to decontrol oil prices.

Still, shortfalls in supply induced by a major disruption in imports would greatly widen the margin between the domestic and the world price. The government would need to be able to raise the domestic price in some way in order to encourage conservation and greater efficiency. With a blended price system that automatically averaged the domestic and the world price, there would be upward pressure on price without deliberate government action. A "disruption tariff" on imports to bring demand and supply into equilibrium and capture part of the windfall that would go to OPEC from higher prices might also be politically more acceptable than a mandated increase in domestic prices. Disruption tariffs would work rather like the proposed blended price system, which anticipates the imposition of a federal tax on all refiners. In a period of import supply interruption, a disruption tariff could be imposed in order to take the shortfall into account. If applied only to imports, however, it would have inequitable regional effects because only eastern Canada is dependent on oil imports. The tariff would probably have to be levied on all refiners (which, strictly speaking, would make it a tax rather than a tariff). A plan to provide rebates to consumers would make the system more politically acceptable.

Of course, successful implementation of a disruption tariff scheme would depend on some sort of international agreement among major oil importers not to undercut each other. They would all have to impose a disruption tariff in concert if they were to have any chance of reducing imports enough to control the rapidly escalating prices that accompany disruptions. There would clearly be a real incentive to avoid complying with the scheme in order to enjoy the "free rider" benefit of lower prices. In the Canadian case, the levy—to the extent it applied as a tax on oil company profits—would also have to be structured in such a way as to ensure that the marginal tax rate imposed on foreign-owned oil companies would not be higher than the tax rate imposed on oil companies in the home country (in this instance, the United States). If taxes were higher, they would obviously encourage companies to shift profits and direct shipments so as to minimize their global tax liabilities.

Despite the difficulties of designing a fair and workable price mechanism for Canada, the serious problems the United States experienced in administering gasoline allocation plans in 1979 strongly suggest that any allocation scheme not based on price will create more problems than it is supposed to solve. The best strategy for Canada might be to develop emergency legislation that would simply raise the excise tax on gasoline and diesel fuel to bring demand into equilibrium with the shortfall of supply.[8] Such legislation would remain in effect only during the six months or so needed to prepare a coupon-rationing plan for implementation. Thus, higher prices in the short term would be offset with the promise that within six months the price of gasoline would go down. Such a plan might prove easier to sell to the provinces as well, since they would also realize that the federal government's increased revenues were the result of a temporary tax. If desired, the government could also enact a rebate to con-

---

8. It would be desirable to include diesel fuel in such a scheme because of its importance in commercial and private automobile transportation.

sumers from the tax. Higher gasoline prices would be desirable on other grounds as well. They would stop the flood of U.S. motorists seeking to buy cheap gasoline in Canada—something that is already a problem because of current price differentials between the two countries. Considerations of equity recommend that this proposal be applied to auto fuels only. Heating fuels and other products would probably be better controlled through some sort of allocation mechanism.

We should remember that Canada might also be called on to contribute in military or diplomatic ways to curbing major energy supply disruptions. Canada could play an important, if marginal, military role in an emergency situation that called for the use of force, especially in the Persian Gulf. The United States cannot assure access to the Gulf by itself; any major military operation would require participation by other members of NATO. In such an emergency, Canada could quickly increase its forces in Europe if British and French troops were engaged in the Gulf. Under existing agreements, Canada has a commitment to dispatch 4,000 troops to Norway in the event of any hostilities involving NATO. Its mobile command of about 17,700 land and air combat troops could be used to further augment its current European forces of one mechanized brigade and three fighter squadrons.

Canadian participation could also probably be relied on in any sort of peacekeeping operation. At this point, Canada has troops in Cyprus, Egypt, Syria, and Lebanon as part of U.N. peacekeeping operations.

Canadian reaction to a crisis may, however, be conditioned by selective embargoes. Canada's reaction to events and its willingness to commit troops overseas will depend on policymakers' perceptions of the national interest and the tenor of federal and provincial relations at the time.

CONCLUSION

Although Canada has enormous reserves of nonconventional oil and sizeable reserves of natural gas in frontier areas, production from these reserves will not significantly reduce Canadian dependence on foreign sources of crude in the short term. For the time being, therefore, Canada's vulnerability to import interruptions is bound to increase as production from conventional reserves declines.

Under these conditions, a common North American market in energy is improbable. At the moment, the only formal cooperative mechanism at the bilateral level is the Energy Consultative Mechanism, established in April 1979. Discussions in this body have focused principally on the construction of the Alaska pipeline, oil swaps, and problems arising from gasoline price differentials in the two countries. Canada and the United States have also developed memoranda of understanding on oil sands and coal technology that outline possible areas for further bilateral cooperation in the development of new technologies.

In the case of oil, Canada barely has the resources necessary to meet its own needs, let alone those of its southern neighbor. Any sort of U.S. proposal for a "common market" that might, for instance, involve a joint development of the tar sands would meet considerable political opposition in Canada. Canadians are extremely nervous about the degree of foreign ownership in their economy. A Foreign Investment Review Agency was created in 1973 to screen foreign takeovers, and the creation of Petro Canada was motivated in part by the government's desire to increase the Canadian participation in energy resource development.

In any case, a common market would do little to enhance energy security in the short term. Even a massive crash program to develop the tar sands would hardly put a dent in North American oil imports, given the long lead time and the technological, economic, and political barriers that have to be surmounted to make synthetic oil-producing facilities productive. Bilateral cooperation may prove fruitful for limited, but important, projects such as the Maritime SPR, and perhaps for developing long-term oil substitutes. But for now, Canada's energy security problems are best addressed through domestic programs to develop reserves and to plan for emergency allocation.

To date, Canadian emergency energy policies have been based on the assumption that the best way of handling supply shortages is through rationing and other allocation mechanisms not based on price. The problems the United States encountered in administering allocation schemes in the aftermath of the Iranian revolution should cause Canadian decisionmakers to reflect on the utility of such approaches. Chapter 10 provides constructive suggestions for using price-responsive mechanisms to handle shortages. However, price decontrol is probably not feasible for political and economic reasons in Canada. Therefore, alternative mechanisms such as disruption tariffs and emergency taxes on gasoline and diesel fuel are probably the best solutions open to the Canadian government.

In the process of considering all of its emergency energy security alternatives, the Canadian government will undoubtedly have to answer arguments from those who think that Canada should devote all its efforts to resource development. There is some merit to these claims. Nevertheless, Canada's dependence on foreign crude will increase significantly over the next five years, despite the continued development of nonconventional crude sources and substitute sources of energy. To remain secure, Canada must soon commit itself to effective short-term responses to deal with the growing risk of supply interruptions.

II

ENERGY SECURITY IN U.S.-MEXICAN RELATIONS

Kevin J. Middlebrook

The emergence of energy resources as a critical factor in U.S. national security has coincided with the discovery of large new petroleum resources in Mexico. Since the formal announcement of these new finds in 1976, energy issues have joined migration, trade, and foreign investment as the principal issues in U.S.-Mexican relations. The total size of Mexican oil and natural gas reserves is still unknown. Although initial claims regarding their probable impact on world supplies and the U.S. market have been shown to be unrealistic, the hope remains that Mexican petroleum may in some way ease the energy security dilemma of the world's largest importer of crude oil.

A discussion of U.S. energy security with respect to Mexico appropriately involves two somewhat different meanings of "security." In the more traditional sense, energy security refers to the availability of dependable sources of petroleum imports. The first part of this section, therefore, analyzes the size of Mexico's proven and potential reserves, its current and future production levels, and the quantity and destination of its petroleum exports. In addition to the quantitative importance of Mexican oil and natural gas for the U.S. market, Mexico's rate of petroleum resource development and future export capacity are of special relevance to U.S. energy policy. The relative

This section is based in part on field research conducted in Washington, D.C. and in Mexico in June and July 1980. This research included a number of interviews with past and current officials in the U.S. Department of State and Department of Energy, officials in Petróleos Mexicanos and other Mexican government agencies, and Mexican social scientists and political commentators. I am grateful to all those individuals who shared with me primary materials and personal opinions regarding Mexican petroleum policy.

I also wish to thank David A. Deese, Jorge I. Domínguez, David Mares, Joseph S. Nye, Raymond Vernon, Van R. Whiting, and Donald Wyman for comments on an earlier version of this chapter.

security of Mexican petroleum reserves from international conflict and foreign military threat are also particularly important.

But because questions regarding petroleum resources are inextricably linked to the overall character of U.S.–Mexican relations, energy security concerns must necessarily address the role that new-found petroleum resources will play in contemporary Mexican development. The second part of this section examines the impact of these new resources on future national economic development, especially industrial expansion and agricultural modernization, and the sociopolitical consequences of petroleum-based development. Here the analysis specifically examines socioeconomic dislocation at the regional and national level as a result of the rapid expansion in petroleum production and the impact these developments may have on political change and future political stability in Mexico.

Finally, this section discusses the question of Mexico's petroleum resources in a broader foreign relations context. The nation's rapidly expanding oil export capacity has been a major factor in its recent foreign policy. Mexico's policy toward OPEC is a continuing concern for U.S. energy policymakers. Petroleum exports have paved the way for Mexican commercial initiatives toward Japan, Western Europe, and other Latin American countries. Energy is also the principal focus of recent speculations regarding the possibility of a North American common market.

PETROLEUM IN THE FUTURE OF U.S.–MEXICAN RELATIONS

Reserves

Mexico's proven petroleum reserves have increased dramatically since the mid-1970s. Petroleum production began in Mexico in the late nineteenth century, and by 1921 Mexico's production of 530,000 barrels per day was second only to that of the United States. Mexico remained a petroleum exporter for decades, but during the early 1970s—with domestic consumption growing rapidly and reserves declining—Mexico was actually a small net importer.[9] However, in

9. For a general treatment of the historical development of the Mexican petroleum industry, see Mancke (1979: 17–57). Data on long-term trends in production and exports are available in *Petroleum Economist* (March 1979: 105); *Comercio Exterior de México* (October 1979: 391–407); and Lajous Vargas and Villa (1978).

1972–73 *Petróleos Mexicanos* (PEMEX, the state-owned oil company formed in 1938 just after the nationalization of the petroleum industry) made major new discoveries in the southeastern region. By late 1980 Mexico had increased the size of its proven petroleum reserves to 60.126 billion barrels (see Table 5–4).

There is considerable optimism in official Mexican circles that even larger petroleum resources will ultimately be discovered. PEMEX estimates that only one-tenth of all potential petroleum-producing areas have been adequately evaluated, and the firm continues to conduct explorations in Mexico's continental shelf areas and in every

Table 5–4.   Proven Mexican petroleum reserves, 1970–1980[a] (*in billion barrels*).

	Total Reserves	Percent Change	Percent Oil in Total Reserves[b]
1970	5.568	—	59.1
1971	5.428	−2.5	59.6
1972	5.388	−0.7	60.1
1973	5.432	0.8	60.2
1974	5.773	6.3	61.3
1975	6.338	9.8	62.4
1976	11.161	76.1[c]	65.2
1977	16.002	43.4	65.2
1978	40.194	151.2[c]	70.7
1979	45.803	14.0	73.2
1980	60.126[d]	31.3	NA

NA = Not Available.

a. Includes crude oil, condensates, and natural gas.

b. Includes crude oil and condensates.

c. In addition to PEMEX's new discoveries as a result of expanded exploration, the very large percentage increases in proven reserves in 1975–1976 and 1977–1978 occurred as a result of a reclassification of reserves according to prevailing international standards. This reclassification expanded the area of proven reserves corresponding to each well drilled and included, as proven reserves, those confirmed reserves not yet actually in production; del Villar (1979: 135), Stewart-Gordon (1979: 263).

d. Proven reserves as of September 1, 1980.

Source: 1970–1978. Secretaría de Programación y Presupuesto (1979: Table II.30, p. 146); 1979, Petróleos Mexicanos (1979: 8); 1980: *New York Times* 16 September, 1980: D13.

state but Tlaxcala and the Federal District.[10] Mexico's potential reserves (including proven reserves and 38.042 billion barrels of probable reserves) may reach some 250 billion barrels (*Petróleos Mexicanos* 1980a: 5-14; 1980c: 7-27; 1979: 1-7; Secretaría de Programación y Presupuesto 1979: 117; *New York Times*, 16 September 1980: D13.

Production

Mexican petroleum production has increased rapidly since the announcement of these major new reserves in 1976, reaching almost 2.3 million barrels of oil per day in September 1980 and making Mexico the world's fifth largest oil producer after the Soviet Union, Saudi Arabia, the United States, and Iraq (see Table 5-5). In 1977 the López Portillo government (1976-1982) announced a 1982 oil production goal of 2.25 million barrels per day; in 1978 this target was moved forward to 1980. However, actual production levels have consistently surpassed official projections as a result of rapidly expanding proven reserves, the extraordinary productivity of the new producing areas in southeastern Mexico, growing domestic demand for petroleum (especially gasoline and other refined products), and new export sales commitments negotiated as part of Mexico's effort to diversify its economic relations. In March 1980 President José López Portillo announced that a consolidated production platform would allow a 10 percent increase over the previously announced production limit, for 1982 production of no more than 2.7 million barrels per day (*El Mercado de Valores* 1980: 257-259). The government's concern with the inflationary effects of rapidly growing petroleum export earnings may in fact hold production at this level, but there is also considerable evidence that production could approach 2.5 to 2.7 million barrels per day in 1980 alone; by 1982 it could reach approximately 4 million barrels per day.

Production levels beyond 1982 will depend on domestic refining capacity, the ultimate size of proven reserves, the construction of new transportation facilities, the profitable use of associated natural

10. The largest new discoveries were made in the southeastern states of Tabasco and Chiapas and in offshore areas in the Bay of Campeche. But major new oil and natural gas resources have also been discovered in Tamaulipas, Veracruz, Coahuila, Nuevo León, and the Baja California peninsula. PEMEX recently announced that there are also substantial amounts of hydrocarbons in the northwestern states of Jalisco, Colima, Nayarit, and Michoacán.

Table 5-5.   Mexican petroleum production, 1970–1980.[a]

	Average Daily Petroleum Production (thousands of barrels)	Average Daily[b] Oil Production (thousands of barrels)	Annual Petroleum Production (millions of barrels)
1970	851.4	486.6	310.6
1971	838.6	485.7	306.0
1972	865.8	505.6	317.1
1973	895.8	524.6	326.8
1974	1061.0	652.8	387.2
1975	1237.0	806.2	451.5
1976	1315.8	894.2	481.6
1977	1495.2	1085.6	545.6
1978	1841.9	1329.6	672.3
1979	2201.3	1618.0	803.5
1980	2976.0[c]	2276.0[c]	NA

NA = Not Available.

a. Includes crude oil, condensates, gas liquids, and natural gas (natural gas at crude oil equivalent of 5,000 cubic feet = 1 barrel).

b. Includes crude oil, condensates, and gas liquids.

c. Daily petroleum production as of July 21, 1980 includes 2,276,000 barrels per day of oil and approximately 3,500 million cubic feet of natural gas.

Source: 1970–1978: Secretaría de Programación y Presupuesto (1979: Tables II.32, p. 148; II.34, p. 151; II.36, p. 153); 1979: Petróleos Mexicanos (1979: 8 and Tables II-3, II-4, pp. 70-71); 1980: Excélsior (22 July, 1980: 4).

gas, and domestic political constraints.[11] Mexican refining capacity, expanding rapidly since the mid–1970s, is scheduled to reach 1.67 million barrels per day by 1982 (Williams 1979: 27), but the government's desire to refine petroleum domestically may tie production to the future expansion of that capacity. Concern about reserves, on the other hand, will probably not constrain production in the near future. The extraordinary success rate in exploration in southeastern Mexico indicates that proven reserves may continue to expand rapidly. Moreover, Mexico's reserves-to-production ratio remains conservative by international standards, suggesting that current proven reserves could support a higher rate of production than now planned (Congressional Research Service 1979: 13).

11. For varying estimates regarding future Mexican petroleum production, see Williams (1979: 26); Mancke (1979: 94); Congressional Research Service (1979: Table 4); and National Economic Research Associates, Inc. (1978: 12).

Exports

Since Mexico has announced its intention to fulfill its domestic needs before exporting petroleum, future export levels will depend on the growth rate in domestic consumption as well as on the expansion of transportation and port facilities. Nonetheless, a considerable share of future oil production will be exported. Mexico's large foreign debt payment obligations, continuing balance-of-payments problems, and growing food imports all increase the need for such exports. Crude exports will reach at least 1.306 million barrels per day in 1980 and may rise to 1.35 million barrels per day or more in 1981 (See Tables 5−6 and 5−7). Although Mexico may have the technical capacity to export a considerably larger volume by 1985, official concern about inflation and the pace of national economic development could constrain future export levels. In 1977 and 1978 some 86.7 percent and 88.8 percent, respectively, of Mexico's oil exports went to the United States (*Unomásuno* 27 May 1989; Secretaría de Programación y Presupuesto 1979: Tables III.38, p. 326; III.40, p. 328). However, de-

Table 5−6.   Mexican petroleum exports, 1970−1980.

	Annual Total Oil (thousands of barrels)	Daily Average Oil (barrels)	Annual Total Natural Gas (millions of cubic feet)
1970	0	0	38,845.4
1971	0	0	20,411.5
1972	0	0	9,852.6
1973	0	0	2,048.2
1974	5,804	15,901	423.8
1975	34,382	94,197	0
1976	34,470	94,438	0
1977	73,736	202,016	2,401.4
1978	133,248	365,063	0
1979	194,485	532,835	0
1980	NA	857,424[a]	109,500.0[b]

NA = Not Available.

a. Daily average for June 1980.

b. Estimate for annual total based on 300 million cubic feet per day exports as of March 18, 1980.

Source: 1970−1978: Secretaría de Programación y Presupuesto (1979: Tables III.1, p. 289. and III.37, p. 325); 1979: Petróleos Mexicanos (1979: 19); 1980: *Excélsior* (July 8, 1980: 4).

Table 5–7.   Destination of Mexican oil exports, 1980.[a]

Country	Volume (barrels per day)	Percentage of Total
United States	733,000	56.1
Spain	160,000	12.3
France	100,000	7.7
Japan	100,000	7.7
Israel	45,000	3.4
Brazil	20,000	1.5
Costa Rica	7,500	0.6
Nicaragua	7,500	0.6
Yugoslavia	3,000	0.2
Sweden	70,000[b]	5.4
Canada	50,000[b]	3.8
Jamaica	10,000[b]	0.8
Total	1,306,000	100.1

a. Data refer to contracted sales as of July 1980; actual sales to Yugoslavia were to begin in the second half of 1980.

b. Letters of intent signed with Sweden, Canada, and Jamaica were to be formalized as contracts in second half of 1980.

Source: Petróleos Mexicanos, Oficina de Comercio Exterior.

spite the greater relative profitability of exports to the United States, Mexico's active efforts to diversify its export markets are likely to reduce the U.S. share of oil export sales to approximately 50 percent or less in the future. (Table 5–7 lists Mexico's current export markets.)[12]

Mexican exports have closely followed OPEC price increases. Although Mexican official prices are higher than those of some OPEC members, due to low transportation costs U.S. imports from Mexico have generally been at somewhat lower final prices than those of all OPEC sources except Venezuela. Higher tanker rates in the 1980s will increase Mexico's oil price advantage over Saudi Arabian oil from $0.58 per barrel at the end of 1978 to approximately $1.70 (in constant dollars) by the year 2000 (Congressional Research Service 1979: 25–26).

12. For a complete list of Mexico's export markets for various petroleum products, see *Foro Internacional* 78 (October–December 1979: 321), and Secretaría de Programación y Presupeuesto (1979: Table III.40, p. 328).

The export situation with regard to natural gas is somewhat less clear. There is a high proportion of associated gas in the new Mexican petroleum finds, and expanded oil production will necessarily produce large quantities of natural gas. Some 7 percent of gas production is still flared, although stepped-up gas reinjection efforts and the completion of additional pipeline networks have apparently reduced this flare-off considerably from previous levels (*Proceso* 25 June 1979: 35; *Petroleum Economist* March 1979: 113; *Unomásuno* 12 May 1980; 23 June 1980).

After the breakdown in gas export negotiations with the United States in 1977, the Mexican government placed much greater emphasis on the domestic industrial use of natural gas. The gas pipeline from the southeastern petroleum-producing areas to the U.S. border was subsequently redirected and justified in terms of the domestic use of this gas, and the volume of domestic natural gas sales during January through April 1980 rose 29.2 percent over the same period in 1979. Mexico has no immediate plans to construct gas liquefaction facilities, so the United States will remain the only export market for natural gas in the foreseeable future. The 1979 agreement on price arrangements between the United States and Mexico may smooth the way for increased exports, but future export levels will depend on the amount of natural gas that remains after meeting domestic demand.[13]

Domestic political considerations will also significantly influence future production and export levels. The López Portillo administration has to date advocated a conservationist strategy in the development of the nation's petroleum reserves as a result of concerns that rapidly increased production could contribute to inflationary pressures and exacerbate problems in areas such as railroad transportation and shipping facilities. However, a major debate concerning the rate of petroleum resource development surfaced in early 1980. PEMEX apparently argued that a production rate of 4 million barrels per day by 1982 would be feasible with little additional investment or infrastructure development, and that this production level would be necessary to meet rapidly expanding domestic demand and

---

13. *Proceso* (8 May 1978: 26); Petróleos Mexicanos (1980b: Table 7, p. 53). Petróleos Mexicanos (1979: 20) contains a summary of the 1979 U.S.–Mexican price agreement regarding natural gas sales. First-quarter 1980 exports of natural gas to the United States reached 300 million cubic feet per day at $3.63 per million Btu; in March this price was raised to $4.47 to equal the cost of U.S. natural gas imports from Canada.

export needs. This expanded production would, in turn, increase PEMEX's own corporate resources, power, and prestige. Within the president's cabinet, the conflict pitted PEMEX director Jorge Díaz Serrano against the ministers of finance, planning, industrial development, and trade, all of whom opposed the production increase due to concerns regarding its likely negative economic consequences (*Latin American Weekly Report* 25 January 1980: 1–2; 8 February 1980: 1; *New York Times* 7 February 1980). López Portillo finally rejected the option of increasing planned production levels substantially and instead raised the production target for 1982 by only 10 percent, to a total of 2.7 million barrels per day. But PEMEX continues to expand production, and even if the López Portillo administration holds production at this new level, the debate is certain to resurface under a new president in 1982.

Unless the largest current estimates of possible Mexican petroleum reserves are finally proven correct, it is unlikely that Mexico's oil and gas resources will make a substantial difference to the world petroleum market. Even with a total production of 3.9 million barrels per day in 1985 (with exports of 2.6 million barrels per day), Mexican supplies would constitute less than 4 percent of total world production at that time (Stobaugh and Yergin 1979: 32–33). Increasing domestic consumption and efforts to diversify its export markets will almost certainly keep Mexico's share of U.S. imports well below levels predicted by initial optimistic reports. Through mid–1979 crude oil imports from Mexico accounted for only 6.6 percent of total U.S. imports (CIA 1980: 12). However, it is possible that there may be some regional variation in the importance of Mexican oil and natural gas for the United States, and Mexican supplies may be an attractive alternative to the rapidly growing southwestern "Sun Belt." PEMEX has also shown interest in developing this market by expanding its distribution and sale of a wide range of petroleum products.

But from the perspective of U.S. energy security, Mexico continues to be of special interest as a secure source of supply in an increasingly uncertain world. Petroleum moving from Mexico to the United States would travel over land or over comparatively short and easily protected sea lanes, and Mexico remains politically stable. These are important considerations, but several qualifications should be made. First, in the wake of the Iranian Revolution, other oil-importing countries also view Mexico as a dependable source of supplies and are entering into more vigorous competition with the United States for Mexican exports. Second, the security of Mexican energy supplies depends on the national socioeconomic and political consequences of the oil boom and the overall character of U.S.-Mexican relations.

In the past, Mexico has acted in accordance with U.S. security needs, including emergency oil and natural gas sales during the difficult winter of 1976–1977 and sales for the U.S. Strategic Petroleum Reserve (Williams 1979: 9, 73; *Excélsior* 10 June 1978; *Petroleum Economist* March 1979: 111). There is, however, no assurance that this cooperation will continue in all cases in the future. Mexico's willingness to make these 1976–1977 sales may have been influenced by its desire to encourage a successful gas deal at the time. Future Mexican cooperation in this regard depends heavily upon the overall state of U.S.-Mexican relations.

PETROLEUM RESOURCES IN CONTEMPORARY MEXICAN DEVELOPMENT

After a decline in historically high rates of economic growth in the mid-1970s and the shock of a major exchange rate devaluation in 1976, Mexican policymakers look to petroleum as the basis for future economic growth. Energy and food production are among the López Portillo government's highest development priorities, and petroleum resource development is the government's principal strategy for overcoming what has been characterized as a structural economic crisis. (Secretaría de Programación y Presupuesto 1980: 7–8, 44, 143–146, 149–150). In addition to large new export earnings, the future diversified development of the petroleum sector will provide the basis for a wide variety of complementary and derivative industrial activities. Rapid, diversified economic growth is crucial if Mexico is to solve a wide range of problems: unemployment and underemployment of at least 25 to 30 percent of the economically active population, a large foreign debt (approximately US$31.1 billion in 1980), and continuing balance-of-payments deficits (Beltrán del Río 1980: Table 9, pp. 34, 37). The government's 1980 "Global Development Plan" and prospects for creating millions of new jobs are clearly centered on the availability of large earnings from petroleum exports, and Mexico's renewed economic growth (an 8.0 percent increase in real gross national product in 1979, compared to 2.1 percent in 1976 and 3.3 percent in 1977) is the direct result of the oil boom (Secretaría de Programación y Presupuesto 1980: 48).[14]

The level of petroleum exports will also significantly affect federal government resources for capital expenditures. Since the public sector is currently responsible for roughly half of the country's gross annual fixed investment, this clearly has a major impact on the overall rate of economic growth. These new resources are to contribute to sectorally and geographically diversified industrial growth, port development, agricultural modernization, and an expansion in the tourist industry.

PEMEX itself will play a major role in Mexico's future economic development. Its share of net internal product rose from 5 percent in 1976 to 16 percent in 1979, while its contribution to public sector savings increased from 28 percent to 69 percent, and crude oil and basic petrochemical sales rose from 16 percent to 49 percent of total exports over the same period (*Proceso* 26 March 1979: 36–37). PEMEX's share of total public expenditures (including those of the federal government and decentralized state agencies) doubled from 10 percent in 1970 to 19.2 percent by 1979 (*Proceso* 23 July 1979: 18; *El Día* 25 February 1979).

PEMEX's domestic pricing policy for petroleum products also plays an important role in national economic development. The difference between domestic and international prices varies considerably by product, but domestic prices for petroleum products are less than one-half of world market levels (*Comercio Exterior de Mexico* September 1979: 317).[15] Current government policy calls for a gradual increase in domestic prices to reduce this difference and so restrain domestic demand and the inflationary consequences of the oil boom. But domestic petroleum product prices will remain below international levels to stimulate national industrialization and economic growth. PEMEX has also agreed to make a direct contribution to a "National Employment Fund" (*El Día* 19 June 1979).

14. Net revenues from the export of crude oil, oil products, and petrochemicals rose 117 percent from US$1.837 billion in 1978 to US$3.987 billion in 1979 (Petróleos Mexicanos 1979: Table IV–6–A, p. 113).

15. For further details on PEMEX's pricing policies, see del Villar (1979: 130–132).

However, a number of negative economic consequences may be associated with petroleum-led national development.[16] Although in the short run earnings from petroleum exports have eased Mexico's balance-of-payments deficit, these consequences may be particularly severe for Mexico's already difficult long-term balance-of-payments situation. The rapid growth of the petroleum industry has in itself increased import needs, and the earnings from petroleum exports could undermine efforts to modernize the traditional agricultural sector by making increased food imports an easier short-term solution to stagnating agricultural production. Petroleum revenues may also support an overvalued exchange rate vis-à-vis the U.S. dollar, further encouraging imports and penalizing nonpetroleum exports to the U.S. market where the existing balance-of-payments deficit is largest.

Mexico's relatively large industrial economy, its growing population and expanding domestic market, and its diversified export structure should absorb some of the disruptive effects of large petroleum revenues. But in 1980 public expenditures exceeded those in the comparable 1979 period by 70.1 percent, and the estimated 1980 inflation rate of at least 25 percent both exceeded official predictions and undercut the gains made in 1977−1978 (*Unomásuno* 13 May 1980; *Wall Street Journal* 21 July 1980; Beltrán del Río 1980: Table 6, p. 19). Rising domestic prices resulting from excessive demand and liquidity and various structural bottlenecks (such as railroad transportation) may reduce the competitiveness of other export products, especially labor-intensive manufactured goods, ultimately reducing the diversity of the Mexican economy.

Some of these problems are already apparent. In the first third of 1980, petroleum export earnings accounted for 63 percent of the value of all Mexican exports. And while petroleum exports increased dramatically, the rate of increase in manufactured exports in early 1980 declined significantly in comparison with previous years (*Unomásuno* 13 May 1980; 28 June 1980; *El Día* 24 June 1980; 1 July 1980). Perhaps the greatest danger in this regard may be the temptation to increase petroleum exports to ease the economic problems created by petroleum-led growth. Rapid growth in the petroleum

16. For a discussion of the economic consequences of petroleum-led economic development in Mexico, see del Villar (1979: 155–158); Solís (1979: 238–242); Beltrán del Río (1980, especially Tables 5–7); Randall (1979). For a comparative treatment of this issue, see Bosch et al. (1979: 105–126).

sector may also lead to distortions in the domestic labor market, disequilibria among internal factors of production, and increased income concentration. Increasingly unequal income distribution has been a persistent problem in the history of Mexican economic development. It is likely to be an especially difficult problem in the future.

Rapidly growing petroleum revenues also increase the potential political problems associated with rising popular expectations. In their dealings with the international community and in bilateral discussions with a number of countries, Mexican officials have emphasized the limitations and dangers of petroleum-led growth and the importance of developing petroleum reserves in an orderly fashion. However, in pronouncements to labor and peasant groups within Mexico, government officials have held out petroleum as the final answer to problems that have defied solution since the Mexican revolution (1910–1917) (*Excélsior* 2 October 1978; 31 March 1978; 28 September 1978). In the short run, the availability of large new financial resources may help the government satisfy immediate socioeconomic demands. But high rates of inflation, inequalities in income distribution and geographic development, widespread unemployment, and the continuing need for large imports of basic foodstuffs are problems that will not be easily resolved in the near future despite the availability of petroleum revenues. These are also issues that raise difficult political questions regarding the future direction of Mexican development.

Timing the growth of the petroleum sector therefore emerges as an especially difficult issue for Mexican decisionmakers. They perceived rapid expansion of petroleum production as essential to reestablishing national economic equilibrium following the 1976 devaluation. Petroleum export earnings provided the basis for renewed economic growth, and the prospect of continued economic expansion has been a major element in recent increases in foreign and domestic private investment. But rapid increases in petroleum production and export sales aggravate the domestic inflation rate and a continuing balance-of-payments problem. To the extent that the capital goods needs of the rapidly expanding petroleum industry must be met through foreign imports, national industry loses an opportunity for further expansion and employment generation. The tension between the immediate needs of the petroleum sector and long-term, balanced development of the national economy remains a critical issue for Mexican policymakers.

The socioeconomic problems associated with rapid petroleum development are a major source of concern for Mexican political leaders. Problems of rising popular expectations, spiralling inflation rates, and rapid socioeconomic change have appeared in petroleum-producing countries elsewhere, both in industrialized countries such as Norway and in developing economies such as Venezuela. Mexico itself has experienced the disruptive consequences of oil booms twice before: in the Tampico region in the 1920s and 1930s, and in Guanajuato after the construction of a refinery at Salamanca in the mid–1950s.[17]

The most obvious socioeconomic consequences of the current oil boom have so far been in the areas that hold the bulk of the newly discovered reserves—the states of Tabasco, Chiapas, and Campeche. However, similar problems have recently appeared in the Minatitlán-Coatzacoalcos area of southern Veracruz as the petroleum industry expands there (*Unomásuno* 21 May 1980; 8 July 1980). The prospect of petroleum discoveries throughout much of Mexico suggests that, in the future, socioeconomic dislocations resulting from petroleum production may spread widely.

In southeastern Mexico, the promise of new employment opportunities in petroleum exploration and exploitation has produced a dramatic influx of workers and their dependents, straining social and community resources to the breaking point. Sewage and drainage facilities, the potable water supply, housing, and other social services are inadequate for the needs of the suddenly increased population. Alcoholism and prostitution have placed additional strains on the traditional social fabric.

As a result of this massive population increase and the huge financial resources PEMEX devotes to the development of the region's petroleum reserves, southeastern Mexico has also suffered from very high rates of inflation. Workers employed in the petroleum industry and related activities earn several times more than those employed in more traditional economic activities. The combination of higher wages in the petroleum sector, the massive inflow of external resources, and the fact that petroleum-related activities have not

---

17. For a general discussion of the socioeconomic and political problems accompanying petroleum-led development, see Whitehead (1978: 655–677). Details on the Tampico and Salamanca experiences, respectively, appear in *Proceso* (6 March 1978: 12–15; 13 August 1979: 10).

yet generated sufficient employment opportunities to meet increased demand produced an inflation rate of 30 percent per year in southeastern Mexico in 1978, well above the national average.

In addition, recent petroleum exploration and production have occurred in agricultural and coastal areas, resulting in pollution and damage to natural waterways, lagoons, and cultivated areas. Fishing areas, oyster beds, and shrimp grounds have been especially affected. As a result of higher wages in petroleum-related activities, inflationary pressures, rapid urbanization in the area, and pollution, the southeastern region's traditional agricultural economy—based on the production of coffee, bananas, cocoa, fruit, coconuts and copra, sugarcane, and livestock—has been significantly disrupted.[18]

The conclusion that Mexican petroleum resources are a secure source of supply rests on the assumption of continuing Mexican political stability. The institutional strength of Mexico's political system will certainly be an important factor in absorbing the socioeconomic tensions produced by the oil boom. Yet, like other petroleum-producing countries, Mexico is likely to experience important political changes as a result of rapid petroleum-led growth. The socioeconomic disruptions in the southeastern producing areas have, for example, produced a number of regional protest movements. Complaints regarding PEMEX's operations have been so numerous in Tabasco that a special claims commission has been formed to deal with them. Many of these demands, frequently channelled through organizations such as the "officialist" National Peasants' Confederation and the Independent Peasants' Confederation, often stem from delayed or insufficient payment of damage compensation. On some occasions, protesting peasants have blocked access roads and occupied PEMEX installations to press their claims for damages and land expropriation payments (*Proceso* 28 November 1977: 27–28; 9 January 1978: 19–20; 26 February 1979: 26; 9 July 1979: 13, 15–16; *Excélsior* 19 March 1978).

The petroleum boom has also resulted in a major increase in PEMEX's power and operating autonomy within the state sector. The company has historically enjoyed a somewhat privileged position among state-owned enterprises and decentralized agencies, but the recent massive expansion in the size of the hydrocarbon sector has

18. On these various problems in southeastern Mexico, see Michel and Allub (1978: 691–709; *Proceso* (14 November 1977: 18; 19 June 1978: 16, 19; 26 February 1979: 26; 2 July 1979: 12–15; 9 July 1979: 11–16; 16 July 1979: 33; 23 July 1979: 16).

produced major increases in its budgetary resources and personnel. Although López Portillo has taken greater personal responsibility in decisions regarding petroleum resource development, increases in PEMEX's corporate resources and the growing national and international importance of petroleum-related affairs have expanded PEMEX's power within the state bureaucracy, especially vis-à-vis the Ministry of National Property and Industrial Development. For example, PEMEX was granted extensive authority to expropriate property without prior judicial review in the process of exploring for and developing petroleum resources, including the construction of the gas pipeline from southeastern Mexico to the U.S. border. PEMEX's prominent role in petroleum-producing areas also raises the possibility of mobilizing important local and regional allies behind its policies.

Significant changes have also occurred within the national petroleum workers' union (STPRM). As with PEMEX, the union's resources have increased enormously. Between 1973 and 1979 PEMEX employment and union membership rose from 78,609 to 93,762 workers; by 1980 the union represented approximately 100,000 regular workers (Secretaría de Programación y Presupuesto 1980: Table IV.1, p. 377; *Unomásuno* 28 June 1980).[19] STPRM agreements with PEMEX allow the union to control over 40 percent of those drilling contracts granted to subcontractors through 1983 and provide the union with 2.5 percent of the value of all subcontractors' work as remuneration for union-supplied social welfare services (*Excélsior* 24 May 1977; *El Día* 12 November 1977; *Proceso* 24 October 1977: 12–13). These arrangements have greatly expanded the financial resources controlled by the national union leadership, allowing it to increase its control over union affairs and providing corrupt union leaders with new opportunities for self-enrichment. The national union leadership has virtually eliminated internal opposition groups that had often been affiliated with minority political parties and that had provided channels for the articulation of rank-and-file discontent during the early and mid–1970s (*Unomásuno* 28 June 1980). Furthermore, the STPRM leadership has also substantially increased its local and regional influence in the principal petroleum-producing areas.

19. STPRM is the acronym for Sindicato de Trabajadores Petroleros de la República Mexicana ("Mexican Petroleum Workers Union").

This expansion in union resources and power has to date reinforced STPRM's long-term role as a major source of pro-government
labor support. The union leadership continues to enjoy widespread
control over labor matters, including hiring for PEMEX, in exchange
for labor peace. On several occasions union leaders have publicly announced their support for the López Portillo administration and its
petroleum development policy, including the vigorously debated gas
pipeline to the U.S. border. From 1976 to 1979 STPRM also pursued
a policy of wage restraint, despite high inflation rates, in support of
the government's anti-inflation program (*Excélsior* 27 October 1977;
19 March 1978; 27 January 1978; *El Día* 21 July 1977; 13 July 1980).
In return, López Portillo hailed the union leadership's "exemplary
performance," and in 1980 STPRM received a 25 percent increase in
wages and benefits—the largest single contract increase granted to
any major union since 1976 (*Unomásuno* 19 March 1980; 21 July
1980). Although there have been cases of general but unorganized
dissatisfaction with this partnership among petroleum workers, the
increased resources available to the union leadership, its key role in
a critical economic activity, and the active political support of the
federal government make a successful challenge to the "officialist"
union leadership from the rank-and-file unlikely in the foreseeable
future. Rivalries, tensions, and factionalism within the union leadership as a result of increased competition for control over STPRM's
new resources may be a more likely source of instability within the
union in the future.

While none of these recent changes poses an immediate threat to
Mexico's longstanding national political stability, the long-term consequences and sociopolitical changes resulting from an era of rapid
economic expansion and social change are difficult to evaluate. However, the rise of petroleum as a central focus of national development
strategy has, in the short run, produced a public debate regarding
energy policy which has few parallels in recent Mexican history. One
consequence of this has been a significant increase in the relative
importance of the Cámara de Diputados (Chamber of Deputies) as
a forum for debate. PEMEX director Jorge Díaz Serrano has twice
appeared before the Cámara, once to explain and defend official
petroleum policy following allegations of conflict of interest (regarding his alleged continued participation in the drilling firm responsible
for the Ixtoc 1 blow-out and oil spill), and a second time to justify
the construction of the gas pipeline to the United States.(*Proceso* 31

October 1977: 10—11; 17 September 1979: 25). Opposition groups and parties have entered this national debate with alternative proposals for national energy policy, and this expanded public debate has affected PEMEX operating procedures.

Spurred by public controversy about pollution and socioeconomic dislocations in the Southeast, PEMEX has sought to reduce the environmental damage resulting from its exploration and exploitation activities. In 1977–1979 it spent some US$350 million on various environmental protection and pollution control measures (*Petróleos Mexicanos* 1980a: 31). PEMEX has also proposed a regional development plan for its future operations in the Chicontepec region in Veracruz, although little detailed work has been done on this plan to date and PEMEX alone lacks the authority to coordinate various state agencies' activities in a coherent regional development project. The longer term consequences of these sociopolitical changes are difficult to predict, but continued large-scale unemployment and inflation, corruption, the lack of union channels for expressing internal opposition, and the organizational activities among labor and peasant groups by minority parties officially recognized by the 1977 political reform could eventually create serious problems for the established regime.

ENERGY AND MEXICAN FOREIGN RELATIONS

Mexico's recent emergence as a petroleum-exporting country has had important consequences for the nation's foreign relations. Petroleum resources have expanded Mexico's negotiating power and flexibility in international affairs. Until the late 1950s and early 1960s, Mexican foreign policy was essentially defensive and defined largely with respect to the United States. Membership in the Latin American Free Trade Association and sponsorship of the 1968 Olympic Games helped redefine this orientation. Under the Echeverría administration (1970–1976), Mexico took an aggressive international position regarding developing countries' socioeconomic and political rights. The Echeverría regime sponsored the "Charter of the Economic Rights and Duties of Nations" and played an active role in the formation of the Latin American Economic System (SELA) (Ojeda 1977: 40). Although López Portillo has displayed a less flamboyant style in foreign affairs, he has clearly indicated Mexico's continuing concern with the influence of international relations on national socioeconomic development. His September 1979 proposal to the United Nations General Assembly for a "World Energy Plan" to join petroleum-producing and consuming nations in cooperative research, production, distribution, and consumption of different forms of energy has been his principal multilateral initiative in this area. But the López Portillo government has also placed increasing emphasis on economic relations with Western Europe, Canada, Japan, and other Central and South American countries in an effort to reduce Mexico's dependence on the United States.

The Organization of Petroleum-Exporting Countries (OPEC)

Since the discovery of its large new petroleum reserves in the early 1970s, Mexico's relations with OPEC have been a continuing source of speculation. There was some discussion of Mexico's seeking observer status or even full membership in OPEC during the last years of the Echeverría administration, and Venezuela argued publicly in favor of such a move (Congressional Research Service 1979: 26; *Proceso* 1 January 1979: 14). However, although it has followed OPEC oil price policies closely, Mexico has carefully avoided either close public association with or membership in OPEC. This policy allows Mexico to benefit fully from the organization's pricing policies without incurring a number of direct and indirect costs: loss of trade subsidies under the terms of the 1974 U.S. Trade Act (for which Venezuela and Ecuador, as OPEC members, are not eligible), political ill-will from the United States and other consumer nations, and the constraints on national export and development policies that could result from production cutback decisions made by OPEC. Nevertheless, this position may come under increasing strain in the future. Over the longer term, as Mexican petroleum production rises and production by countries such as Saudi Arabia declines, the rising marginal importance of Mexican production in the world oil market may result in pressure for Mexico to define more clearly its position regarding OPEC pricing decisions.

Western Europe, Canada, and Japan

Mexico is actively seeking to diversify its commercial relations and expand economic ties with various West European countries (especially France, Spain, and Sweden), with Canada, and with Japan. In recently completed bilateral economic agreements with these countries, Mexico has offered oil exports in exchange for access to technology, development assistance, training for Mexican workers and technicians, and broad-based financing for various development projects. The López Portillo government has shown particular interest in coinvestment projects that combine technology transfer, financing, and opportunities for export promotion.

Mexico recently increased petroleum sales to Spain to 160,000 barrels per day, and in 1980 PEMEX began to export 100,000 barrels per day of oil to France and 70,000 barrels per day to Sweden. In exchange, France agreed to provide Mexico with nuclear technology and equipment and assistance in the development of its uranium resources. Sweden signed an economic cooperation agreement with Mexico covering technology transfer and industrial cooperation, technical training for Mexican workers in a number of industries, and Swedish investment in Mexican tourism projects. Negotiations with West Germany, Great Britain, and Canada have also focused on exchanging crude oil for assistance with uranium enrichment and nuclear reactor technology, shipbuilding, pipeline construction, hydrocarbon exploration and development, and other industrial and agricultural development projects. Japan continues to seek a substantial increase in the quantity of crude oil it imports from Mexico, and Mexico has received long-term loans and credits from Japan. These two nations have also held extensive discussions regarding Japanese assistance in building Mexican industrial ports and electrifying the Mexican railroads (projects that would eliminate two of Mexico's largest development bottlenecks), the joint operation of a supertanker fleet, and Japanese investments in agriculture, petrochemicals, and the petroleum machinery industry.[20]

Mexican petroleum sales to these countries have so far been limited to crude oil. But during his May 1980 trip to Europe, López Por-

20. *Petroleum Economist* (January 1979: 39; February 1979: 71–72); *Latin America Weekly Report* (25 January 1980: 7; 8 February 1980: 7; 29 February 1980: 7); *Uno-másuno* (25 May 1980; 16 July 1980); *Excélsior* (8 April 1980); *El Día* (10 July 1980).

tillo discussed the possibility of also marketing refined petroleum products in France, West Germany, and Sweden. The recent PEMEX agreement to purchase 34.3 percent of the stock of Spain's Petróleos del Norte opened the way for such sales in Spain and perhaps in other European countries as well. PEMEX has also undertaken preliminary discussions regarding Mexican access to refining capacity in France and Germany (*Unomásuno* 24 May 1980; 27 May 1980; 13 July 1980). In these discussions PEMEX pays close attention to various factors affecting the profitability of such operations, and it appears to show some preference for arrangements with firms whose diversified, vertically integrated production and marketing structures parallel its own. While PEMEX has also considered the possibility of refined product sales in the southwestern United States, Mexican interest in these other markets—which have traditionally played a minor role in Mexico's commercial relations—clearly constitutes an effort to lessen Mexico's economic dependence on the United States.

Central America and the Caribbean

Mexico's petroleum resources have increased its importance as a regional power in Central America and the Caribbean. In January 1980 Mexico agreed to provide Nicaragua with about half of its current oil requirements, or 7,500 barrels per day, as part of a broader assistance package that included technical aid for exploring Nicaraguan energy resources, university-level training programs, and other support. Costa Rica has proposed the construction of a natural gas pipeline between it and Mexico, while Mexico and Jamaica have agreed on an oil-for-bauxite contract which also involves the training of Jamaican technicians in petroleum technologies.[21]

These deals are small, both in absolute terms and as a percentage of Mexican production and exports. But they do constitute important shares of national consumption for the other parties to the agreements. They also suggest the new role that petroleum resources may permit Mexico to play in Central America and the Caribbean. Like Mexico's negotiations with industrialized countries, these deals have been made with the criteria of economic interest and financial

21. *Latin America Weekly Report* (15 February 1980: 3; 22 February 1980: 9, 12); *El Día* (26 June 1980; 5 July 1980); *Unomásuno* (27 June 1980); *Excélsior* (11 January 1980; 14 April 1980; 1 July 1980).

viability clearly in mind. But the attached political considerations at the regional level have also been clearly important.

Following lengthy discussions, Mexico and Venezuela have recently agreed to share equally in meeting the petroleum import requirements of Central American and Caribbean nations. The total volume involved is estimated at between 160,000 and 200,000 barrels per day. Although the oil exported under this arrangement will be supplied at international prices, Mexico and Venezuela will provide long-term financing for 30 percent of all sales and may extend further credit assistance on a bilateral basis. This agreement is consistent with Venezuela's longstanding efforts to help oil-importing developing countries bear the cost of spiralling international oil prices. It also constitutes a regional test of López Portillo's 1979 United Nations proposal for international energy cooperation among petroleum-exporting and importing nations.

ENERGY IN U.S.-MEXICAN RELATIONS

Unlike other petroleum-exporting developing countries, Mexico shares a 2,000 mile border with the United States. Relations between the two nations concern numerous and complex issues: migration, trade, foreign investment, the transfer of technology, and specific border-related issues such as pollution and smuggling. Discussions on issues such as these are complicated by a long history of often difficult bilateral relations. Memories of the loss of over half of Mexico's territory to the United States following the Mexican–American War (1845–1847), the U.S. Navy's occupation of Veracruz in 1914, and Pershing's 1916–1917 military expedition into Mexico remain deeply imprinted in the Mexican public consciousness. Mexico's economic dependence on the United States has been constant throughout its history, and the large U.S. business presence in Mexico today is an important domestic political issue.[22]

U.S. energy security concerns regarding Mexico are inextricably imbedded in this larger context of bilateral relations. Discussions concerning Mexican petroleum resources in the contemporary international context might be difficult at best, but from Mexico's per-

---

22. See Wyman (1978) and Fagen (1977). For a more detailed discussion of this theme, see Meyer Cosío (1978), especially pages 579–580.

spective this issue is colored and further complicated by intensely felt nationalistic sentiments and memories of the hostile U.S. response to the nationalization of U.S.- and British-owned oil company holdings in 1938.[23] Many of the public statements made to date by U.S. officials regarding bilateral energy relations appear to recognize Mexico's right to determine how it will use its natural resources. Yet actual U.S. conduct is often at odds with these public statements.

Mexican sensitivities were aggravated during the 1976–1977 negotiations for the sale of Mexican natural gas to the United States. The Mexican representatives in these negotiations may well have underestimated the complexities of the American political process on this question, and the construction of a gas pipeline from the southeastern oil and natural gas fields to the U.S. border area may have been precipitous. But U.S. policymakers' handling of the affair only deepened many Mexicans' reservations regarding the proposed transaction (Fagen and Nau: 382–427). Although an agreement was finally reached in September 1979, the episode will continue to influence Mexican perceptions and negotiating positions. When Mexico's January 1980 crude oil price increases were openly criticized by Department of State spokesman Hodding Carter, López Portillo responded that "Mexico has, does and will control its oil resources independently" (Latin America Weekly Report 11 January 1980: 2).

Understanding the complexities of U.S.–Mexican relations and the likely socioeconomic and political consequences of rapid Mexican petroleum-led development is a necessary first step in the formulation of mutually satisfactory arrangements on energy matters. The United States should not allow energy issues to dominate bilateral relations, and it cannot assume it has a "special relationship" with Mexico that gives it access to Mexican petroleum resources. Nor should U.S. officials think that recent proposals for a "North American energy common market" or a "trilateral framework for North American interdependence" are necessarily adequate or mutually attractive solutions to the energy problem. It is unlikely that either Canada or Mexico would consider such an arrangement for energy resources alone, and a broader agreement encouraging the free flow of factors of production across national borders would involve very difficult political issues for all parties involved, including the United

23. For a more general historical treatment of petroleum in U.S.–Mexican relations, see Meyer Cosío (1972).

States. Both Canada and Mexico have therefore rejected the common market concept as premature and unsatisfactory (*Unomásuno* 27−28 May 1980). Cooperation on specific energy projects might be a more acceptable arrangement in the immediate future. Such agreements might include U.S. technological assistance on border-area electricity generation and the development of Mexican solar and geothermal sources.

Mexico's past behavior suggests that it might well be willing to enter into special arrangements with the United States in the event of a prolonged, severe disruption of petroleum supplies from other sources. But the lessons of past U.S.-Mexican negotiations on such issues and the somewhat more open context in which Mexican national energy policy is now formulated indicate that such arrangements may be difficult to negotiate in advance of an actual emergency. The high political sensitivity of this issue would make it difficult for Mexico to sustain any long-term commitment. Furthermore, any new Mexican president would probably not feel bound by an agreement negotiated by his predecessor.

A recent study of U.S.-Mexican energy relations by the Rand Corporation advocates the creation of Mexican surplus production capacity and surge capability under International Energy Agency supervision to alleviate the effects of a major disruption in the world petroleum market (Ronfeldt et al. 1980). In his March 18, 1980, speech commemorating the nationalization of the Mexican petroleum industry, PEMEX director Jorge Díaz Serrano commented that given continuing uncertainty in the world energy situation, it might be useful for Mexico to have a surplus production capacity. However, Mexico's concern for sovereign national control over the use of its petroleum resources would make the supervision of its production decisions by an international agency politically impossible. It is also questionable whether Mexico could maintain surplus capacity for emergency use; the domestic socioeconomic and political pressures to develop this capacity in order to generate additional revenues for national development might be difficult to contain. For both political reasons and economic self-interest, then, it is unlikely that Mexico would greatly increase its exports to the world market during an emergency disruption in an effort to hold down rising prices. On the other hand, Mexico could be expected to make some provisions for extraordinary sales as part of its overall responsibility to the international community.

A perceived linkage among different problems in the overall context of bilateral relations will continue to affect both U.S. and Mexican officials' handling of energy issues. The existence of large Mexican petroleum reserves has heightened U.S. policymakers' concern with the broad array of problems that affect bilateral relations and has increased Mexico's confidence in its dealings with the United States.[24] This situation will challenge the political leadership of both nations even under normal conditions. In an oil supply disruption, the United States government might be tempted to exert strong pressures on Mexico to guarantee its own supply. But the United States should not hope to use trade, migration, or border issues as points of leverage in negotiations regarding Mexican petroleum production and export policy. It is unlikely that domestic political factors would allow the Mexican government to respond to U.S. energy requirements in the face of such pressures, and negotiating tactics of this kind might well do permanent damage to bilateral relations between the United States and Mexico.

REFERENCES

Beltrán del Río, Abel. 1979. "Mexican Oil Policy: Its Prospective Macroeconomic Impact, 1979-1980." Philadelphia: Wharton Econometric Forecasting Associates, Inc.

_____ . 1980. "The Mexican Oil Syndrome: Early Symptoms, Preventive Efforts and Prognosis." Wharton Econometric Forecasting Associates, Inc. Paper presented at conference on "Trade Prospects among the Americas: Latin American Export Diversification and the New Protectionism," São Paulo, Brazil, March.

Bosch, Pedro, Manual Lapiedra, and Miguel A. Ortega. 1979. "La experiencia de seis economías exportadoras de petróleo." In El Petróleo en México y en el Mundo, Consejo Nacional de Ciencia y Tecnología, México.

Breton, Albert. 1977. "The Federal-Provincial Dimension of the 1973-1974 Energy Crisis in Canada." In The Political Economy of Fiscal Federalism, edited by Wallace E. Oates, pp. 105-113. Toronto: D.C. Heath.

Central Intelligence Agency. 1980. International Energy Statistical Review. National Foreign Assessment Center, March 12.

Comercio Exterior de México. 1979. Vol. 25, no. 9 (September).

_____ . 1979. Vol. 25, no. 10 (October).

---

24. For an analysis that stresses the strategic importance of Mexican petroleum resources for the United States, see Saxe-Fernández (1980: 132-133, 135).

Congressional Research Service. 1979. *Mexico's Oil and Gas Policy: An Analysis*. Report prepared for the U.S. Senate Committee on Foreign Relations and Joint Economic Committee, December 1978. Washington, D.C.: Government Printing Office.

Courchene, Thomas, and James R. Melvin. 1979. "The Heritage Fund: Consequences for the Rest of Canada." Paper prepared for the Conference on the Alberta Heritage Savings Trust Fund, University of Alberta, October 18–19.

del Villar, Samuel I. 1979. "Estado y Petróleo en México: Experiencias y Perspectivas." *Foro Internacional* 77, Vol. 20, no. 1 (July–September).

Department of Finance. 1980. *Economic Review: A Perspective on the Decade*. April, Ottawa.

El Día. 1977. July 21.

_____. 1977. November 12.

_____. 1978. January 13.

_____. 1979. February 25.

_____. 1979. June 19.

_____. 1980. June 24.

_____. 1980. June 26.

_____. 1980. July 1.

_____. 1980. July 5.

_____. 1980. July 10.

El Mercado de Valores. 1980. Vol. 40, no. 12 (March 24): 257–259.

Energy, Mines and Resources. 1977. *An Energy Strategy for Canada: Policies for Self-Reliance*. Ottawa.

_____. 1978. *Energy in Canada: An Overview*. Ottawa.

_____. 1979a. *Background to a New Energy Strategy*. November, Ottawa.

_____. 1979b. *Canadian Oil and Gas Supply/Demand Overview*. November, Ottawa.

_____. 1979c. *Taxation and Revenue Sharing*. November, Ottawa.

Energy Supplies Emergency Act. 1979. *Canada Gazette* 4, no. 7 (Part III).

Excélsior. 1977. May 24.

_____. 1977. October 27.

_____. 1978. January 27.

_____. 1978. March 19.

_____. 1978. March 31.

_____. 1978. June 10.

_____. 1978. September 28.

_____. 1978. October 2.

_____. 1980. January 11.

_____. 1980. April 8.

_____. 1980. April 14.

_____. 1980. July 1.

_____. 1980. July 8.

_____. 1980. July 22.

Fagen, Richard R. 1977. "The Realities of U.S.-Mexican Relations." *Foreign Affairs* 55, no. 4 (July).

Fagen, Richard R., and Henry R. Nau. 1979. "Mexican Gas: The Northern Connection." In *Capitalism and the State in U.S.-Latin American Relations*, edited by Richard R. Fagen. Stanford, California: Stanford University Press.

Foro Internacional 78. 1979. "México: Las Promesas y los Problemas del Petróleo," in "Documentos." Vol. 20, no. 2 (October-December): 321.

Helliwell, John F. 1980. "The Distribution of Energy Resources Within Canada." Paper prepared for presentation at the Seminar on Canadian-U.S. Relations, Harvard University, February 19.

House of Commons Debates. 1980. "Speech from the Throne" (Hansard). April 14: 5-6.

International Energy Statistical Review. 1980. National Foreign Assessment Center, U.S. Central Intelligence Agency. Washington, April 9.

Lajous Vargas, Adrián, and Victor Villa. 1978. "El Sector Petrolero Mexicano, 1970-1977: Estadísticas Básicas." *Foro Internacional* 72, Vol. 18, no. 4 (April-June).

Latin America Weekly Report. 1980. January 11: 2.

_____. 1980. January 25: 1-2, 7.

_____. 1980. February 8: 7.

_____. 1980. February 15: 3.

_____. 1980. February 22: 9, 12.

_____. 1980. February 29: 7.

Mancke, Richard B. 1979. *Mexican Oil and Natural Gas: Political, Strategic, and Economic Implications.* New York: Praeger.

Meyer Cosío, Lorenzo. 1972. *México y los Estados Unidos en el Conflicto Petrolero, 1917-1942*, 2nd ed. México: El Colegio de México.

_____. 1978. "El Auge Petrolero y las Experiencias Mexicanas Disponibles: Los Problemas del Pasado y la Visión del Futuro." *Foro Internacional* 72, Vol. 18, no. 4 (April-June).

Michel, Antonio, and Leopoldo Allub. 1978. "Petróleo y Cambio Social en el Sureste de México." *Foro Internacional* 72, Vol. 18, no. 4 (April-June): 691-709.

National Economic Research Associates, Inc. 1978. "Mexico: Potential Petroleum Giant." September 15.

New York Times. 1980. February 7.

_____. 1980. September 16: D13.

Ojeda, Mario. 1977. "México ante los Estados Unidos en la Coyuntura Actual." In *Continuidad y Cambio en la Política Exterior de México: 1977*, Centro de Estudios Internacionales. México: El Colegio de México.

PetroCanada. 1976. *Annual Report.*

_____. 1977. *Annual Report.*

_____. 1978. *Annual Report.*

_____. 1979. *Annual Report.*

Petróleos Mexicanos: 1979. *Memoria de Labores, 1979.*
_____ . 1980a. "Report of the Director General." March 18.
_____ . 1980b. "Informe al Consejo de Administración." March–April.
_____ . 1980c. *Plan de operación para 1980.*
Petroleum Economist. 1979. Vol. 46, no. 1 (January): 39.
_____ . 1979. Vol. 46, no. 2 (February): 71–72.
_____ . 1979. Vol. 46, no. 3 (March): 105.
Proceso. 1977. No. 51 (October 24): 12–13.
_____ . 1977. No. 52 (October 31): 10–11.
_____ . 1977. No. 54 (November 14): 18.
_____ . 1977. No. 56 (November 28): 27–28.
_____ . 1978. No. 62 (January 9): 19–20.
_____ . 1978. No. 70 (March 6): 12–15.
_____ . 1978. No. 79 (May 8): 26.
_____ . 1978. No. 85 (June 19): 16, 19.
_____ . 1979. No. 113 (January 1): 14.
_____ . 1979. No. 121 (February 26): 26.
_____ . 1979. No. 125 (March 26): 36–37.
_____ . 1979. No. 138 (June 25): 35.
_____ . 1979. No. 139 (July 2): 12–15.
_____ . 1979. No. 140 (July 9): 11–16.
_____ . 1979. No. 141 (July 16): 33.
_____ . 1979. No. 142 (July 23): 16.
_____ . 1979. No. 145 (August 13): 10.
_____ . 1979. No. 150 (September 17): 25.
Quarterly OIL Statistics. 1980. Organization for Economic Cooperation and Developments, International Energy Agency. First Quarter.
Randall, Laura. 1979. "The Political Economy of Mexican Oil, 1976–1979." Hunter College, unpublished manuscript.
Ronfeldt, David, Richard Nehring, and Arturo Gándara. 1980. *Mexico's Petroleum and U.S. Policy: Implications for the 1980s.* Santa Monica, Calif.: The Rand Corporation.
Saxe–Fernández, John. 1980. *Petróleo y Estrategia: México y Estados Unidos en el Contexto de la Política Global.* México: Siglo XXI.
Secretaría de Programación y Presupuesto. 1979. *La Industria Petrolera en México.* México.
_____ . 1980. *Plan Global de Desarrollo, 1980–1982.* México.
Solís, Leopoldo. 1979. "Comentario." In *Las Perspectivas del Petróleo Mexicano,* El Colegio de México. México: El Colegio de México, Centro de Estudios Internacionales.
Statistics Canada. 1980a. *Exports–Merchandise Trade.* Annual catalog. No. 65–202.
_____ . 1980b. *Imports–Merchandise Trade.* Annual catalog. No. 65–203.

Stewart-Gordon, J. 1979. "El Petróleo Mexicano: Mitos, Realidad y Futuro." In *El Petróleo en México y en el Mundo*, Consejo Nacional de Ciencia y Tecnología, México.

Stobaugh, Robert, and Daniel Yergin. 1979. *Energy Future: Report of the Energy Project at the Harvard Business School.* New York: Random House.

Unomásuno. 1980. March 19.

_____. 1980. May 12.

_____. 1980. May 13.

_____. 1980. May 21.

_____. 1980. May 24.

_____. 1980. May 25.

_____. 1980. May 27.

_____. 1980. May 28.

_____. 1980. June 2.

_____. 1980. June 23.

_____. 1980. June 27.

_____. 1980. June 28.

_____. 1980. July 1.

_____. 1980. July 8.

_____. 1980. July 13.

_____. 1980. July 16.

_____. 1980. July 21.

U.S. Department of Energy. 1980. "Petroleum Stock Levels in Major Consuming Countries." Internal memorandum, April 21.

Wall Street Journal. 1980. July 21.

Whitehead, Laurence. 1978. "Petróleo y Bienestar." *Foro Internacional* 72, Vol. 18, no. 4 (April-June): 655-677.

Williams, Edward J. 1979. *The Rebirth of the Mexican Petroleum Industry.* Lexington, Mass.: Lexington Books.

Wyman, Donald L. 1978. "Dependence and Conflict in U.S.-Mexican Relations, 1920-1975." In *Diplomatic Dispute: U.S. Conflict with Iran, Japan, and Mexico*, edited by Robert L. Paarlberg, Harvard Studies in International Affairs, No. 39. Cambridge, Mass.: Center for International Affairs.

6 WESTERN EUROPE

David A. Deese
Linda B. Miller

The 1973 oil crisis caught all Western governments unprepared. Yet that embargo was the logical climax of developments that had been taking place for decades: the gradual substitution of Middle East petroleum for domestic coal, the rise of the independent oil companies, and the decline of the majors vis-à-vis the oil-producing nations. The Europeans paid heavily for their lack of preparedness. They found it nearly impossible to develop oil substitutes rapidly and to devise contingency plans smoothly. Frantic scrambles for bilateral deals with OPEC revealed their political as well as industrial vulnerability.

Since that first oil shock, Europe's understanding of the energy security threat has grown, but its stock of solutions—especially those that would strengthen European ties with the United States and Japan—is no more impressive than it was almost ten years ago. Understandably, most major West European countries are now groping for answers under time pressures that narrow the margin for mistakes. Yet the persistent tendency to strive for government-to-government deals may seriously damage the Western alliance.

DEFINING THE CHALLENGE

Energy vulnerability poses as great a threat to the security of Western Europe as the missiles and armies of the Warsaw Pact. Western Europe now depends on the energy security policies of the Organization of Economic Cooperation and Development (OECD) nations, especially the United States, as much as it does on NATO's military posture in Europe. The extent of dependence on foreign oil means that supply interruptions will hit Western Europe especially hard; only Japan is more vulnerable than Western Europe to potential damage. Geographical proximity to the Middle East and the Soviet Union makes the prospect of a world war over Persian Gulf supplies alarming to West Europeans, but they are relatively helpless to prevent violence and conflict in the Gulf. Differences among the energy-related situations of the nations within Europe make policy coordination difficult and, in certain areas, unlikely.

The sources of Europe's present dilemma lie in the past several decades of European and global history. While Western colonial empires finally disappeared during the 1960s, the oil-exporting countries were beginning to assert their independence. By the early seventies, when Britain was forced to relinquish its political and military control of the Persian Gulf, the United States was already deeply involved in Vietnam. With seemingly few other options at the time, the United States decided, in 1971, not to replace the British in the Gulf but to rely on regional powers, particularly Iran, to act as the Gulf's policemen.

This shift in the regional military balance coincided with America's loss of dominance in strategic weapons and with the transition from domestic coal to Middle East petroleum in the major consuming nations. Western demand for imported oil increased from 25 percent of total energy use in 1950 to 67 percent in 1973, a year that marked the end of an unprecedented three-year period of strong worldwide economic growth.

The October War of 1973 and the associated embargo and production cutback dramatized Western Europe's plight, for America could no longer assume the role of oil supplier of last resort as it had in the Suez Crisis of 1956–1957. The OECD nations were lulled into inaction by the decrease in real oil prices between 1975 and 1978. Europeans reduced oil consumption over these years, but their savings were due at least as much to poor economic performance as to effective conservation policies.

The Iranian Revolution of 1979 and related disturbances in the world oil market revived anxieties about oil supply and political unrest in the oil-exporting countries. The Soviet invasion of Afghanistan raised concerns about Moscow's intentions in the Persian Gulf region and injected East–West strategic competition into the local military balance.

Under these conditions, it is urgent for European nations to reconsider their definitions of energy security and preparations for responding to energy emergencies. A definition of European energy security as access to adequate amounts of hydrocarbons at a price that ensures a standard of living and rate of industrial growth comparable to that enjoyed since the 1960s is inadequate in several respects. First, this definition concentrates on absolute size of supply rather than continuity and preparations for disruptions. Second, it assumes that prices can and must be held down. Third, it ignores the foreign policy and military dimension of energy security. Unless Europeans define their energy security more realistically, they may singly and collectively prepare themselves, like army generals, to refight the last war.

In view of their severe dependence on foreign imports, West Europeans will continue to face the likelihood that rising costs; deliberate supply interruptions; or accidents, wars, revolutions, and natural disasters will deny them foreign oil. The interruption lasting a year and amounting to only 5 million barrels per day, which was assessed in Chapter 1, would have enormous economic and political effects. A shortage of 15 million barrels per day, or the equivalent of the combined daily production in 1979 of Saudi Arabia, Kuwait, the United Arab Emirates, Qatar, and the Neutral Zone could be an economic and political disaster for Western Europe. Strong emergency steps might help, but unless effective preparations are already in place when the disruption occurs, governments will be forced to act in ways that are likely to aggravate the shortfall.

With or without future supply disruptions, European security is also threatened by rapid increases in the price of oil. Although the exact causes of the world recession of 1975 and the economic slowdown of 1979 and 1980 remain unclear, it is generally agreed that the 400 percent increase in nominal oil prices in 1974 and the 130 percent increase in 1979 and early 1980 played a vital role. Table 6—1 shows the dramatic slowdown in GNP growth rates and increases in unemployment after the oil embargo in late 1973. Most estimates attribute at least half of Western Europe's reduction in economic growth rates and half of its increases in inflation.

With the exception of West Germany, Western Europe's increases in inflation are ominous. Economic reports indicate an average inflation rate of 9.2 percent in the last quarter of 1979, compared to 6.2 percent for the same period of 1978. Table 6—1 shows the growth rates in inflation for 1978—1980. The combined trade deficit for Western Europe grew from $4.3 billion for 1978 to $21.7 billion for the first nine months of 1979.

Even before the unexpected deepening of the recession in the United States, gloomy economic projections emerged for Western Europe in 1980. The oil price rises, combined with the lack of energy conservation from 1974 to 1978, led to an expected overall average growth rate of only 1.9 percent in 1980 and to an inflation rate of over 10 percent. Given Western Europe's continuing need for oil, these adverse economic effects will persist. Of all oil imported into Western Europe in 1977, 61 percent came from the Persian Gulf (see Table 6—2); the figure for 1979 was 63 percent. Expectations that this dependence will be no less than 62 percent in 1985 starkly confirm Europe's long-run economic vulnerability.

This condition has serious internal political implications. In the future, it will be increasingly difficult to maintain consensus among interest groups and sustain governing coalitions among political parties. Energy price increases almost certainly contributed to the troubled political circumstances that faced the governments of Britain, France, Italy, Sweden, and West Germany in 1980. European energy security policies must therefore soon address ways to limit the social, economic, and political damage caused by past and future oil price increases.

Western Europe's energy problems threaten to undermine not only its internal politics but also its foreign policies. Competition with the United States, Japan, and perhaps the Soviet Union for scarce resources like oil could rob European nations of their remaining independence in foreign policy, especially in the Middle East. The capacity of the oil-exporting countries to influence the foreign policies of Western Europe has expanded because the international oil

Table 6–1.   Economic performance in Western Europe.

	Growth Rates in GNP, 1960–1979	
Country	1960–1973 Annual Average	1974–1979 Annual Average
France	5.7	2.9
West Germany	4.8	2.3
Italy	5.2	2.5
United Kingdom	3.2	1.1
Japan	10.5	4.1
United States	3.9	2.3

	Unemployment Rate	
Country	1960–1973 Annual Average	1974–1979 Annual Average
France	2.1	4.8
West Germany	.8	3.2
Italy	3.4	3.4
United Kingdom	2.9	5.1

	Inflation (percent change in consumer price indices) 1960–1979	
Country	Increase 1960–1973 (14 years)	Increase 1974–1979 (6 years)
France	80	59
West Germany	53	23
Italy	88	102
United Kingdom	90	88

	Inflation Rate 1978–1980 Percentage Change from Previous Year		
Country	1978	1979	1980
France	9.3	10.8	11.5
West Germany	2.6	4.5	5.0
Italy	12.1	14.8	16.5
United Kingdom	8.3	12.3	15.5

Source: Adapted from OECD, (1979 and 1980).

companies can no longer allocate oil during supply interruptions or selective embargoes, as they did in the early 1970s. Other changes in the oil market during the last six years have also strengthened the leverage of the OPEC nations. The shift toward producer government control over production and oil sales has enabled the oil exporters to put continuous pressure on the industrial democracies of Europe.

VARYING PATTERNS OF CHALLENGE AND RESPONSE

Although they share some common problems as oil importers, the countries of Western Europe differ in many important respects, among them ethnic diversity, economic growth rates, industrial structures, and military strength. In general economic terms, the much stronger growth of GNP in West Germany and France, as compared with Britain and Italy, is reflected in stronger industrial production and lower rates of inflation and unemployment. Varying national perceptions of the energy challenge and differing preparations for energy emergencies undermine the prospects for successful regional cooperation.

The major nations of Western Europe differ significantly with respect to five indicators of energy security. No single indicator by itself portrays a realistic picture, whereas together they allow accurate comparisons among countries. The simplest measure is the *degree of dependence on foreign sources of energy*, and for imports of crude oil in particular (see Table 6−2).[1] Britain and Norway are more nearly self-sufficient in all respects than the others. The Netherlands and West Germany import about 50 percent of their energy; France, Italy, and Belgium, over 75 percent. The European Community (EC) as a whole was 57 percent dependent on foreign energy sources in 1976.

A second measure of energy security is the *diversification of oil import sources* (see Table 6−3). The importance attributed to this measure depends on the effectiveness of the International Energy Agency (IEA) and EC sharing plans in allocating oil, and of market forces in raising prices and equalizing supplies during an interruption.

1. Dependence on imports of petroleum products is also important, but not as directly related to energy security since most products are imported from within Europe and since the spot market for products is most important during slack periods in the world oil markets.

Table 6-2.   Oil dependence in Western Europe, 1978.

	Oil as Percentage of Total Energy Use	Percentage of Oil Imported	Percentage of Oil Imported from OPEC	Percentage of Oil Imported from Persian Gulf
West Germany	54	95	58	31
France	63	99	84	70
United Kingdom	45	55	67	60
Italy	68	99	80	61
Belgium and Luxembourg	56	100[a]	—	—
The Netherlands	50	98[b]	72	57

a. Belgium only.

b. 1977.

Source: CIA (1980); The Committee for Energy Policy Promotion (1980); and British Petroleum Statistics (1978).

Table 6–3.   Crude oil imports, by source (1979 and 1980 in percentages).

	West Germany (June 1980)	France (May 1980)	United Kingdom (January 1980)	Italy (4th Quarter) 1979	Netherlands[a] (1979)	Spain[a] (1979)
Abu Dhabi	–	5.8	2.4	–	–	–
Algeria	6.2	3.8	–	2.1	0.1	2.9
Egypt	0.6	–	4.0	–	–	–
Iraq	5.4	25.2	8.3	17.5	2.3	11.2
Kuwait	1.1	4.4	15.1	7.7	10.4	3.0
Libya	14.3	0.4	–	12.1	1.4	10.6
Qatar	–	0.6	–	0.9	1.4	2.7
Saudi Arabia	24.4	38.2	53.3	33.9	21.6	33.0
U.A.E.	8.9	–	–	4.8	4.9	9.5
Other	0.7	0.8	–	–	–	–
Total OAPEC	60.6	79.1	83.2	79.1	43.0	72.8

Table 6–3.   continued

Gabon	1.5	—	.1	0.6	0.8
Iran	3.6	—	2.4	6.4	8.5
Nigeria	12.9	2.2	2.4	15.0	.4
Venezuela	1.0	5.9	1.2	0.9	4.2
Total OPEC	78.2	87.3	85.1	66.0	86.8
United Kingdom	11.5	—	—	—	—
Norway	3.0	—	—	—	—
Canada	—	—	—	0.3	.1
Other	6.0	8.7	14.9	33.7	13.1
Total	100.0	100.0	100.0	100.0	100.0

a. Includes estimated imports of crude oil and refined products.

Source: Adapted from CIA (1980: 4–8).

These considerations aside, heavy reliance on single sources of oil imports increases vulnerability to cutoffs below 7 percent of consumption, to foreign policy pressures, and to price increases.[2] These vulnerabilities are most important early in a crisis, when national leaders must try to maintain public confidence and when panic buying by one or two countries could rapidly raise spot market prices.

Even West Germany—with well-diversified sources including Libya, Nigeria, Britain, and Algeria—is vulnerable. Its oil and gas imports from Algeria are under daily threat of disruption due to political turbulence, and recent political changes in Libya ring ominously for future stability and oil export capabilities. Such unpredictability is precisely what makes diversification valuable, but diversification alone is insufficient. France and Italy face the greatest concentration of oil import sources. About 80 percent of all French oil imports come from the Persian Gulf, with 50 percent from Saudi Arabia and Iraq.[3] Nearly 80 percent of Italian imports also come from the Persian Gulf, with Saudi Arabia, Libya, Iraq, and Iran the prominent suppliers. The Netherlands and Spain are typical of most other West European nations; their dependence on oil imports from the Persian Gulf ranges from 75 to 85 percent of their total oil imports.

In theory, dependence can be mutual; oil suppliers could come to rely on their largest markets. Most exporters, however, have wisely sought diversification among their customers. The notable exceptions are Libya, exporting heavily to West Germany, Italy, and Spain; Algeria, with exports mainly to West Germany; and, to a lesser extent, Iraq, which sells large quantities to France and Italy.

A third measure of energy security is the *distribution of primary energy sources* on which a nation relies. This indicator varies widely among the countries of Western Europe (see Table 6–4). Italy, France, and most of the smaller countries rely heavily on oil; the Netherlands emphasizes gas; and West Germany, Britain, and Belgium burn relatively large amounts of coal. Britain has substantially increased its reliance on North Sea oil. Britain and France are the main users of nuclear power, although France is the only European country whose nuclear power program appears to offer a serious prospect of displacing oil imports in the 1980s.

---

2. The trigger level for the IEA sharing agreement is 7 percent of consumption. See Appendix A.

3. As of this writing, the war between Iran and Iraq has eliminated the 25 percent of French oil imports which came from Iraq.

Table 6-4.   Consumption of primary energy resources in Western
Europe, 1978 (*million tons of oil equivalent*).

	Oil	*Gas*	*Coal*	*Hydro*	*Nuclear*
West Germany	142.7	42.1	48.0	3.6	8.2
France	119.0	20.9	28.2	15.0	6.4
United Kingdom	94.0	37.9	70.4	1.2	7.9
Italy	99.5	24.4	10.2	12.2	1.1
The Netherlands	37.2	34.0	3.0	–	0.9
Belgium and					
Luxembourg	28.4	10.5	9.4	0.1	2.7

Source: British Petroleum Statistics (1978); The Committee for Energy Policy Promotion (1980).

A fourth measure for assessing energy security is the *distribution of final uses of energy.* West European countries use 9 to 12 percent of primary energy to produce electricity; U.S. usage is about 30 percent. Energy use in transportation varies little within Europe but is generally 10 percent less than in the United States. This distinction is critical for the analysis of measures that could be taken to reduce oil consumption during supply interruptions. Industrial uses of energy are relatively low in Britain and France, higher in West Germany, and very high in Italy. In case of a major supply disruption, the United States may have a definite advantage due to its relatively low industrial use; Italy and Japan, on the other hand, may not be able to curtail consumption without cutting into the productive sectors of their economies. Japan, Italy, and the United States use relatively less energy for household and commercial purposes than Britain, West Germany, and France.

Although energy import and use patterns vary considerably among the nations of Western Europe, *differences in government energy policies*—the fifth indicator—may be much more important. The degree of government intervention in energy markets is very great in some countries, almost nonexistent in others. West Germany, Britain, and Switzerland pursue free market energy policies; France, Italy, Spain, and the Netherlands exert strong control; Belgium and Austria have mixed market policies. National oil companies either already exist or are being established in almost all West European countries. They tend to be run almost exclusively as independent commercial ventures in the free market countries, and with varying degrees of government control elsewhere. These basic differences in government policies complicate the working of such cooperative measures as the IEA emergency allocation system because free market countries tend to draw oil away from other countries during emergencies.

Government and industrial research and development policies in energy technology and long-range energy planning also differ. In real terms, the largest increases in government research and development budgets from 1974 to 1977 took place in Sweden, Ireland, the Netherlands, Italy, Norway, Denmark, and West Germany. Research and development budgets actually decreased over the same period in Britain, Belgium, and Spain. And while the principal countries of Western Europe still concentrate extremely high percentages of government research funds on nuclear technology, they are pursuing very different technological options. Public concern and foreign policy positions on nuclear matters also vary tremendously.

Given the differing situations of the West European countries in all these respects, it is hardly surprising that they differ in their definitions of energy security and in the extent of their readiness to deter or respond to oil supply disruptions, including the use of military force. France, Britain, and perhaps the Netherlands could deploy military power in the Indian Ocean; West Germany and other countries might act indirectly by relieving U.S. military responsibilities in Europe, as described in Chapter 12.

Defining the energy security challenge must be a dynamic experience for the West Europeans. If they could ignore the behavior of the superpowers in the Middle East, for instance, their task of selecting options to maximize access to oil at tolerable prices would be far simpler. But increasingly, Europeans face the delicate job of supporting a strong Western deterrent in the Gulf while simultaneously restraining American and Soviet impulses that could kindle local revolutions and regional conflicts. Furthermore, the last decade has shown that the Europeans may have very little control over other problems that could threaten their energy interests: the depletion of Soviet energy resources, for example, or changes in U.S. policy on nuclear reactor safety standards, technology transfers, and sales of enriched uranium. Thus, Europe's freedom of action is circumscribed. Policymakers and observers who look for European principles rather than ad hoc reactions to external pressures are frustrated.

In seeking to gear emergency preparations to the shifting challenges that face them, the West Europeans have displayed a penchant for potentially competitive, rather than cooperative, responses. Moreover, their separate national emergency plans, as yet untested, are weakened by a general reluctance to exchange information in advance of a crisis.

PREPARING FOR EMERGENCIES IN WEST GERMANY, FRANCE, AND GREAT BRITAIN

European preparations for supply disruptions will be important in protecting the security of individual countries and the OECD countries as a whole. Since West Germany, France, and Britain are the largest energy consumers and the most influential international actors of Western Europe, their preparedness is of overriding importance. These nations may also provide models—for emulation or avoidance—for other countries, notably the United States. The plans of West Germany, France, and Britain are especially interesting because they grow out of different economic, industrial, and political systems.

West Germany. The West German stockpiling system, which carried the equivalent of over 100 days of oil consumption during the first nine months of 1980, operates largely under coordinated industrial management. EC directives, as incorporated into West German law, require reserves of ninety days of oil consumption. The IEA requires member countries to hold ninety days of net imports which, for most European countries, is essentially equivalent to ninety days of consumption. By contrast, the IEA requirement for the United States is equivalent to only forty-five days of oil consumption. Both the EC and the IEA allow countries to count commercial inventories (or working stocks) as part of overall reserves, despite the fact that most of these stocks are required to keep the oil distribution system working.[4]

West German law avoids the ambiguity—and sidestepping—of treating commercial inventories as reserves by establishing a special category of oil reserves, usually called emergency, strategic, or com-

---

4. The commercial inventories required for normal refinery operation range from about sixty days in the United States to forty-five days for Western Europe overall, and twenty-five days in West Germany.

Table 6−5.   West German oil stocks.

Oil refiners	25 days
Government and consortium	65 days
Total compulsory stocks	90 days
Commercial inventories	14 days
Total all stocks (May 1, 1980)	104 days

pulsory stockpiles. Compulsory stocks include crude oil and products held by three separate groups: importers and refiners, the government, and the industry consortium (see Table 6−5).

In 1968, importers and refiners were required to hold the equivalent of sixty-five days of oil use in their operating inventories. This provision was modified in 1972 to ninety days of inventories.[5] A new public law in 1979 requires refiners to hold the equivalent of twenty-five days of their production of finished products from imported crude in the prior year, and the government and a special oil industry consortium to hold a combined total of sixty-five days of oil use. The government program is designed to create a stockpile of 8, or perhaps eventually 10, million tons (60 to 70 million barrels, or twenty-five to thirty days of net imports). In 1980 it held over 6 million tons (about 40 million barrels or twenty days of net imports) in salt domes in northern Germany.

The overall total of ninety days of compulsory stocks is stricter and more meaningful than in other countries since it specifically *excludes* all commercial inventories. Another indication of the German government's serious attitude toward stockpiling is that it encourages holding reserves in excess of legal requirements. The government has urged consumers to hold their own stocks, and government ministries, industries, commercial ventures, and other productive sectors of the economy are asked to keep at least fourteen-day stockpiles.

The industrial consortium, or Erdoelbevorrantungsverband (EBV), was established by law in 1978. Membership is mandatory for all companies that import or refine oil in West Germany. The consortium arranges for all storage space and manages the stocks. Central to its operation is the financial arrangement that frees the oil industry

5. West German government regulation ABI No. 20 of February 6, 1980, p. 330 in Nr. L. 308/14, December 23, 1968.

Table 6—6. National emergency storage programs for crude oil and petroleum products.

Country	Obligatory Stocks (days of use as of May 1980)	Relationship to Commercial Inventories	Ownership
West Germany	90	Combined	Government/Industry Consortium
France	90	Amalgamated	Industry
Italy	90	Amalgamated	Industry
Netherlands	90	Combined	Industry Consortium
Japan	90	Segregated	Government Industry
United States	6[a]	Segregated	Government

a. This is equivalent to about twelve days of U.S. net oil imports.
Source: Adapted from Krapels (1980).

and the government from the burden of carrying the oil stocks on their books (Krapels 1980). EBV is completely debt-financed, with only the normal government guarantees and services given to any German corporation. Interest on the loans is paid through uniform storage fees collected from the companies. Not only does this arrangement keep the oil industry from having to carry the reserves on its books, it also sets the oil apart administratively, in a form that government planners can constantly monitor (see Table 6—6).

West German emergency allocation and conservation systems are based on two principles. First, shortages will be absorbed to the greatest possible extent by nonproductive sectors of the economy. Second, government intervention will be dictated by the severity of a supply disruption. Crises are divided into three types—light, medium, and heavy—on the basis of total oil consumption (see Table 6—7). The relation of West German shortfall to world shortfall is based on the assumption that the IEA allocation system works as planned. The categories are not defined precisely since uncertainty about the depth and duration of an interruption is always high. The crisis of 1973—1974, which affected Germany heavily through the embargo and production cutback targeted on the Netherlands, would be defined as a Type I, or light, interruption.[6]

6. Interviews with officials in the Ministry of Economics, West German Government, May 1980.

Table 6-7.   Oil supply disruptions in West Germany.

Type of Crisis	West German Shortfall	World Shortfall
I. Light (10-15% of free world oil consumption)	280,000-420,000 bd	Up to 5-7 mbd
II. Medium (up to 25-35%)	Up to 700,000-980,000 bd	Up to 17 mbd
III. Heavy (over 25-35%)	Over 700,000-980,000 bd	Over 17 mbd

Consistent with West Germany's free market approach to energy, Type I crises are expected to require only limited government intervention. Government agencies would meet with consumers and provide policing functions as necessary, but they would avoid formal bureaucratic action. The government would intervene much more actively in a Type II crisis, however, in order to maintain the productive sectors and continue the delivery of such essential services as fire, police, and hospital operations. A Type III crisis would essentially give the government war powers over the economy. Two laws provide the government with authority to act in such emergencies. Both grant the government the authority to control everything from the production to the pricing of all fuels.

Detailed preparations for a Type I crisis include fuel switching, voluntary conservation of jet fuels and industrial feedstocks, and gasoline conservation measures such as Sunday driving bans, speed limits, and appeals for carpooling or greater use of trains. Preparations for a Type II interruption will eventually encompass stronger restrictions on the use of gasoline and heating fuels, but little or no direct government intervention in most industrial and commercial sectors. Plans for rationing gasoline and diesel fuels were still incomplete as of mid-1980, in part because the subject is very sensitive—after all, 20 percent of all GNP comes from the automotive industries. An unpublished government directive in preparation would give a base level gasoline or diesel fuel allocation to each registered car, saving approximately one-half of all available gasoline for special allotments to commercial and other priority users. The rationing plan is based on transferable coupons, but the Economics Ministry has not yet decided how they will be distributed or who will adminster the coupon system.

Government policy on light fuel oil—the fuel used for residential and commercial space heating—has, however, been determined. It is based on a government note, published in 1976, directing all consumers to retain heating bills for two years. If a Type II crisis makes rationing necessary, local dealers will make a quarterly allocation to each consumer based on a fixed percentage of past consumption. The government will not be involved, except to settle disputes and to set overall priorities. At present, those priorities require that the total available quantity of middle distillates first be used to produce diesel oil for industrial use; light fuel oil for heating is then to be removed for essential services such as hospitals; commercial uses come next; military and civilian uses must come from the remaining light fuel oil. No acceptable plans for allocating residual fuel, naptha, or jet fuel have been devised since these fuels are all used directly and indirectly for industrial and commercial purposes. Coal and gas could replace some naptha.

The presumption that wartime conditions would exist under a Type III crisis seems to have provided an excuse for avoiding detailed preparations for a truly heavy disruption. Plans for the civilian sector have not been thought through, although Type II preparations provide a start and the government does have clear authority to act in emergencies. Only military preparations for a Type III emergency are reported to be in place. These presumably include close coordination with the United States for any action beyond West German borders, as well as mobilization at home. The government would have the authority to reduce civilian demand as necessary to support military operations.

France.   The French oil stockpiling system is rather different. Government control over the import of crude oil and products derives from a law passed back in 1928 (Comité Professionel du Pétrole 1976). Stockpiling directives of 1951 and of 1958, as modified in 1975, comprise a system that requires all importers to hold stocks equivalent to 25 percent of their inland sales during the prior twelve months. This system is the model for the obligatory EC stockpiling requirements passed in 1968. Crude oil and oil products are imported under licenses granted by the French government. Market shares for imports are set within restricted ranges for each company to maintain a balance between the international oil companies and France's two national oil companies. The longstanding stockpile requirements are met largely by the major oil companies, with approximately equal shares held by the national companies and the majors.

The government allows at least some of the companies' storage expenses to be offset by adjustments of the price ceilings set on petroleum products. Ceiling prices are set by the French energy agency (the Direction des Carburants) on the assumption that companies hold sixty-five days of emergency stocks and twenty-five days of commercial inventories dispersed through their inventories, or the equivalent of ninety days of consumption. This parallels the ninety days of compulsory stocks held in West Germany (see Table 6–6). The French system is thus tightly regulated by the government, yet managed by and completely integrated with companies. There are no separate facilities for emergency reserves.

Stockpiling is not the only policy instrument the French employ. In times of supply disruption, they look to external sharing arrangements, adroit management by the international companies, and internal allocation and conservation mechanisms to help meet the crisis. Because France's energy security situation is more precarious than that of Britain or of the United States, the government assumes that it must be prepared to act quickly under a wide variety of circumstances, including those requiring military responses.

Government policy relies on diversifying external sources of oil imports, although heavy dependence on Saudi Arabia will continue. Officials also hoped for an agreement, especially with Iraq, on the use of shut-in oil production capacity in emergencies. However, Iraq would only make such arrangements in exchange for concessions on a Middle East settlement. It remains unclear how the Iran–Iraq war will affect French policy, but it is likely to lead to a shift away from relying heavily on such bilateral relationships.

The French contemplate their options in terms of supply crises of three types: (1) up to 15 percent of noncommunist world oil production, or about 7.5 million barrels per day; (2) up to 30 to 40 percent, or about 15 million barrels per day; and (3) anything above 15 million barrels per day. These categories are for discussion purposes only, similar to those apparently used by the U.S. government, and are not a formal mechanism like West Germany's for structuring and triggering responses. The French believe that the political systems of the Persian Gulf are closely related. If conflict or revolution occurs in an exporting country, French leaders assume that most other producers will be affected.

Since July 1, 1979, a heating fuel regulation system has restricted homes and offices to no more than 90 percent of 1978 use. Although details of emergency response programs are secret, there is apparently a plan to impose increasingly stringent ceilings on heating fuel for homes and offices through the current regulation system. A second emergency program is a coupon rationing system for gasoline, administered through car registration records. This arrangement was attempted during the 1956 crisis, but the period of its operation was too short and the number of cars involved too small to help in current planning. Government officials openly acknowledge that gasoline rationing would not be operational until six months to one year after initiation.

These two programs, together with plans to decontrol home heating oil gradually and thus allow the market prices to operate for all products, seem to represent the extent of France's plans for serious interruptions. Nevertheless, like the well-prepared West Germans, the French state that their military preparations are complete. It is not clear whether these plans include projecting force into the Persian Gulf or other producing regions, but such action seems to be implied as the last resort in the case of very large interruptions. This resolve is not reassuring because the French appear not to have more moderate alternatives available to them.

Great Britain.   Like their German and French counterparts, British officials have given time and thought to the need for emergency preparations. They are somewhat reluctant to divulge specific plans because they fear that their present comparative strength in oil supplies would commit them in advance to put substantial North Sea oil supplies at the disposal of the other EC countries.[7] This posture is consistent with the British refusal to sell North Sea oil to EC partners at concessionary rates in normal times. British officials argue that doing so would only foster the mistaken idea that energy can still be had cheaply.

---

7. Interviews with Department of Energy officials and Foreign Office officials, London, June 1980.

Britain's active role in the IEA managerial group has partially mitigated the image of selfishness engendered by these stances. Britain is helping to draft plans to draw down existing stocks, share imports, and possibly temporarily reallocate North Sea oil during any crisis that would deprive EC members of large amounts of their normal supplies. In keeping with the traditional muddle-through approach to foreign policy questions, the British are reluctant to agree in advance to increase North Sea production during crises. If disturbances do occur, they might temporarily allow gas to be flared in the North Sea in order to furnish EC members with 50,000 to 100,000 barrels of oil per day.[8]

Rather than worrying about emergencies, the British are still sorting out the dimensions of a national oil depletion policy. Deciding whether to expand North Sea exploration, delay development, or control production levels seems a more urgent task than contingency planning. In addition, British political leaders, whether Labor or Conservative, rely on a distinction between two threats—the complete interruption of supplies and a "pre-crisis" strained market with continued price rises. Again, British energy planners resist the setting of IEA target figures as bases for sharing before a crisis develops, and they believe it is premature to create spare production or "surge" capacity in the North Sea. Furthermore, they emphasize that uncoordinated national stockpiling keeps pressure on prices, especially in periods of short supplies, but perhaps even in periods of glut.[9]

The British are more concerned about labor problems, technical factors, and a hostile physical environment that constantly endangers North Sea production. These attitudes clearly distinguish Britain from its less well-endowed allies and could cause more serious friction if others want to press ahead now with costly collective programs to deal with emergency requirements. The British are unlikely to make further headway in forging or revealing emergency preparations until a simmering controversy over the future of the British National Oil Company (BNOC) is resolved. If the national oil company should be denationalized, as the Tory Government wishes, and its trading and development functions spun off, much greater gov-

8. Interviews with Department of Energy officials and Foreign Office officials, London, June 1980.

9. Interviews with Department of Energy officials and Foreign Office officials, London, June 1980.

ernment-to-industry coordination would be required to plan for emergencies.

Britain's oil wealth will reach its maximum limits in the 1990s, and even now oil imports continue because British refineries cannot process additional amounts of "sweet" North Sea crude oil without expensive conversion that officials have decided to avoid.[10] Although producer Britain retains a consumer mentality, making further estrangement from France and Germany on emergency planning unlikely, additional joint planning does not seem plausible either. The British will continue to cooperate on nuclear reprocessing with France and Germany and pursue bilateral uranium deals with Australia, but these arrangements will not substantially improve Europe's energy security in this century.

PROSPECTS FOR COOPERATION

To non-Europeans, it may seem self-evident that the member countries should coordinate their energy security policies as closely as possible in the European Community, and that they should not allow their varying resource endowments, needs, and attitudes to hinder the urgent business of reducing their vulnerability to severe disruption. Nevertheless, Europeans have not made the Community an effective vehicle for the development of a common European energy policy. Pursuit of national interests and unwillingness to share supplies characterized European responses to the 1973 embargo. Since then there has been little in the way of cooperative improvement of their energy security position.

The differing resource endowments of the members produce different priorities. Some members believe that enhancing the Community's authority would interfere with national energy prerogatives. Britain does not want the Community to make any demands on British oil, and others are equally adamant in their refusal to allow the Community to decide where to send nuclear waste or whether they may sell reactors in exchange for oil. Several nations are hostile to Community nuclear regulations that could serve as a stimulus to further integration in other fields.

10. Interviews with Department of Energy officials and Foreign Office officials, London, June 1980.

These differing national approaches help explain why the Community's Commission has produced a spotty record in promoting a common energy policy. The Commission, as part of a clumsy and complex internal decisionmaking structure involving the Council of Ministers, the Energy Committee, and technical experts, has nevertheless called for national stockpiles of ninety days' supply, restriction of oil and gas use in national power stations, and stricter conservation measures. In a more daring move, the Commission has suggested promoting research on conservation and energy sources by means of loans or a tax on the consumption, production, and importation of oil products.

However important these recommendations may be, they could suffer the fate of the Commission's 1974 document, "Energy Policy Objectives for 1985." That document urged members to reduce their dependence on external energy suppliers to 40 percent and to develop nuclear power as an alternative to imported oil, while increasing natural gas and domestic oil production. In so doing, the Commission discounted both the labor and investment problems plaguing the European coal, gas, and oil industries and the rising domestic opposition to nuclear power. As a result, members tended to disregard those proposals.

Expressions of Community political will are apt to be intermittent. The smaller countries like the Netherlands, Belgium, Italy, Denmark, and Ireland have been most interested in a Community approach, although not all for the same reasons. The larger countries are much less interested because they differ on how to proceed. France favors a "dialogue" with the Arabs. Britain, with its own oil, wants a less conciliatory attitude toward OPEC. The Germans have been caught in the middle. Some Community members believe that it is necessary to endorse the specific political objectives of the Arab oil producers, and others do not. There have also been differences over the Camp David accords. More broadly, policymakers cannot agree on whether a European energy policy should start with a common internal policy, especially common regulation of the oil market, or with a common front to the outside that masks internal differences. Under these circumstances, it is no wonder that the Community does not command the members' allegiance and attention in energy matters and that the United States is dissatisfied with the Community as a negotiating partner in energy security matters.

Short-term reactions to the oil crisis of 1973 reinforced the tendencies of the West Europeans to resist yielding control to nonstate actors like the European Community. Even so, the revival of the Atlantic tie, demonstrated in the establishment of the International Energy Agency in 1974, revealed a growing acceptance of the stark facts of middle-rank status, of Europe's military weakness, and of its susceptibility to economic disruptions, which even staunch Gaullists have recently acknowledged. Facing unpalatable choices in the early 1970s, the Europeans, with the exception of France, found that tolerating the American desire for an IEA was less risky than placing cherished dreams of growth and prosperity in the hands of OPEC.

The brief history of the IEA, like that of the EC, underscores the elusive quality of both European and Atlantic unity. During the Iranian crisis, when the French urged cooperation among consumers as a prelude to consumer–producer solidarity, this new realism was severely shaken by the American move to subsidize U.S. imports of middle distillates by about $5 a barrel. The fine print revealed nothing sinister about American intentions, but European reaction was hostile. Outraged at Washington's apparent bad faith, the French charged the Americans with setting the stage for an oil war among the Western governments. The incident illustrates how easily differing consumer interests can frustrate attempts at coordination and how intensely sensitive energy matters are in international relations. It may also have been symptomatic of a tendency for Europeans to view their interests as increasingly distinct from those of the United States.

Summit meetings have emerged as an important symbolic step toward coordinated policies among the major energy consumers. The Europeans, the United States, and Japan reached agreement on national and collective oil import limitations at Tokyo in July 1979. The 1980 Venice Summit recommended a doubling of coal use by 1990 and eschewed quick fixes in favor of the development of alternative energy sources. Unfortunately, that path ignores the likelihood of oil supply interruptions, and the goal of doubling coal production by 1990 was adopted in the face of persistent environmental risks and passionate opposition. The skepticism of the European Community's spokesman about attaining the Venice goal, given the costs of converting power plants, casts doubt on the realism of the joint objectives and forces European nations to fall back on the inadequate solution of devising their own national emergency preparations in isolation.

Neither the European Community, the IEA, nor consumer coalitions seem able to mobilize domestic European constituencies and encourage them to face the hard decisions that energy security demands. At present, there is little congruence among national energy policies in Western Europe and little incentive to go beyond bilateral deals for oil and uranium. For its part, the IEA will probably remain an important focus for stockpiling and sharing oil, but each European nation will go its own way with respect to nuclear power, coal, and natural gas. Only a real crisis—something more than short supply interruptions, for which Western Europe is somewhat better prepared than it was in 1973—1974—could substantially change this picture.

BILATERALISM AND FOREIGN POLICY

Reluctant to help create or rely on a common European energy policy, a number of West European countries are relying heavily for their energy security on bilateral arrangements with producers. They hope to make oil producers more dependent on them by investing in their economies and assisting in their industrial development. The growth of such bilateral arrangements may seriously complicate the international energy system and relations among Western nations. As discussed in Chapter 2, these agreements tend to reduce the ability of the international oil market to deal with crises. Another crucial issue, difficult to assess, is the extent to which these deals may force countries like France and West Germany to adopt Arab political objectives in return for the writing and fulfillment of energy contracts. As bilateral arrangements become more common, it will be increasingly important, though often difficult, for the United States to understand which ones pose real threats to Western alliances and which, if any, might benefit our allies without seriously threatening national and international security.

In 1973, the main reason for the Europeans to seek bilateral deals with the oil-producing governments was to assure a steady supply of crude oil. After the crisis eased, the scope and number of such transactions continued to grow because of concern about price. Today, bilateralism in the form of government-to-government deals has become a permanent fixture of the oil marketing and consumption pattern for many European states. It is not yet clear how the dramatic

shift to bilateral oil deals will affect the probability of directed embargoes by producer governments, but political changes in the turbu-
lent Middle East and North Africa seem likely enough to make us
doubt that bilateral links will truly enhance energy security for West
European countries.

Whatever the value of such arrangements in assuring supplies, they
failed to address the rapidly escalating price levels of 1979 and 1980.
Other benefits to consumers are possible, of course. Bilateral deals
may offset the balance-of-payments deficits incurred through oil imports, or even promote the dependency of the oil-exporting nations
themselves. Italy, for example, participated in Iranian construction
projects valued at almost $3 billion in 1980.

Even in the absence of explicit political concessions, these new
relations may have adverse effects on international security. Western
Europe exports large quantities of sophisticated conventional weapons to Iraq, Libya, and Saudi Arabia. Aid to the nuclear power programs of oil exporters is in some cases also a dangerous form of
Western Europe's industrial development assistance. Iraq is now the
beneficiary of a large French nuclear research reactor with highly
enriched fuel, and the Italians are promoting a power reactor deal
with the Iraqi government. The export of more advanced nuclear
technology may lead to the military use of that technology.

Gauging the political consequences of Western Europe's accelerated export policy is a complicated exercise. The European Community's ultimate refusal to impose real trade sanctions on Iran in 1980
was a stunning instance of trade commitments influencing a foreign
policy decision of major importance to the United States. Reliance
on bilateralism also aggravates tensions among European nations
which may deepen divisions within NATO in times of crisis.

France exhibits the most consistent devotion to bilateral deals,
with controversial results. Some sources claim that France has pursued and concluded secret deals with Iran and Iraq. Other observers
claim that France's gains are moot.[11] Oil has flowed, but the French
have received no obvious special advantages. In 1973–1974, while
the Dutch were embargoed, all Europeans—including the French—
experienced somewhat even reductions. In any case, other Europeans are not convinced that French policy is better than combining
domestic, bilateral, and multilateral techniques.

11. See, for example, Lieber (1980: 139–163).

The fact that a pro-Arab stance has not restored French autonomy in the energy sphere has not been lost on other European governments. Iran, Iraq, Saudi Arabia, Libya, and later Pakistan have often demanded trade terms, advanced weapons, and nuclear technology, which the French have frequently found unacceptable. Key Arab producers have not wanted to limit their purchases of technology and industrial goods to France, nor have they offered the French substantially lower oil prices. The French preference for a Euro-Arab dialogue has not worked out, nor have they been able to lead other countries away from an Atlantic perspective.

Outside OPEC, the major participant in European bilateral energy arrangements is the Soviet Union. It has become an important trading partner, and both sides expect cooperation in energy to increase. There are mutual advantages to enhanced European-Soviet trade relations. The Soviet Union will gain much-needed hard currency and possibly also the sophisticated technologies needed to tap its oil and gas supplies. Western Europe will gain an additional energy supplier and an expanded market for its exports. Europe's need for primary commodities and energy resources, together with the Soviet Union's need for manufactures and advanced technology, creates natural trade opportunities that are far greater than those between the American and Soviet economies.

As the most highly industrialized European nation, West Germany has the greatest stake in the trade issue. As of this writing, West German companies were pursuing a contract for a $13.3 billion gas pipeline in the Soviet Union, despite Soviet refusal to withdraw troops from Afghanistan and American pressure to limit technology trade. This 3,000 mile natural gas pipeline from Siberia to the Soviet Union's western border would supply 40 billion cubic meters of gas, or about 10 percent of West European gas consumption in 1978, to Western Europe beginning in the mid-1980s.

This economic cooperation does not surprise most observers. Germany has been transferring technology and selling equipment to Russia for well over a century. It is by far the leading Western supplier of machinery and equipment to the Soviet Union, providing nearly one-third of such Soviet imports. Likewise, the Soviet Union is West Germany's single most important communist trading partner after East Germany. Among the larger German-Soviet deals are West German exports of energy technology and collaboration on nuclear energy research. Even stronger than West Germany's economic motivation in trading with the East is its desire to maintain and improve relations with East Germany.

Some U.S. officials are concerned that expanded oil and gas output might increase the military potential of the Soviet Union. In Western Europe, there is little, if any, debate about such issues. This difference in perspectives reflects the greater dependence of West European economies on trade and our allies' tendency to separate trade from political considerations. The United States, for its part, views commitments to trade relations as secondary in importance to political or military responsibilities.

The Soviets will continue to conclude as many deals with the West as they possibly can to secure high technology equipment for oil and gas prospecting, recovery, and especially offshore operations. In 1978, a French company, Technip, won one of the largest single Soviet orders placed with a Western company: a $213 million contract for gas-lift installations to improve oil recovery levels in Western Siberia. Great Britain's technology exports to the East, which include gas pipeline and secondary recovery equipment for oil, are expected to increase along with North Sea oil production. Recently, the Soviet Union has shown interest in acquiring such advanced Western prospecting hardware as seismic mapping equipment and field units to assist in the recovery and analysis of seismic data. A number of computers have been sold to the Soviet Union to provide this analytical capability. Soviet experience and technology lag far behind that of the West in all phases of offshore work; hence Soviet imports of offshore equipment are particularly significant.

Since the Soviet Union benefits so much from European technology and equipment, the probability is slight that it would, under normal circumstances, use its energy exports to do more than exert subtle, and possibly divisive, political influence. War in Europe or the Persian Gulf, on the other hand, would almost certainly end all Soviet energy exports to Western Europe. The loss of oil would be manageable, but gas supplies could be threatened more seriously. Therefore, new gas exports to Western Europe should be monitored closely and military planners should carefully assess the implications for emergency mobilization of the West European economies.

The political sensitivity of Soviet–West European relations was demonstrated by Europe's hesitation to punish the Soviets for invading Afghanistan. This caution, together with European reluctance to resist OPEC, has opened a rift among the OECD nations. The economic and political pressures of oil have undercut several IEA, EC, and Western summit initiatives. Bilateral energy arrangements could seriously affect the course of American–European relations, perhaps unintentionally undermining Western security. Continued vigilance is obviously necessary.

CONCLUSION

Interruptions of oil supply, energy price increases, and diminished foreign policy flexibility pose a new and serious security threat to Western Europe. Despite their marginally greater creativity and progress in domestic and some multilateral preparations for future disturbances, the Europeans will remain more vulnerable to this threat than the United States. Germany is reasonably well prepared to meet the threat, but many other European nations are not. As a result, Europe is exposed to strong pressures to accommodate Arab political goals and to avoid confrontation with the Soviet Union. If its vulnerability is to be reduced, Europe's oil stockpiles and emergency conservation schemes must be supplemented by carefully planned and well-coordinated responses involving all members of the European Community and the NATO Alliance.

Yet even revitalized U.S.–European coordination of foreign policies can only go so far. Fundamental differences in resources and perspectives will persist. The United States must continue to maintain certain international political and military commitments that are of less interest to Europe, and Europe must similarly protect some unique trade and cultural ties with Eastern Europe and the oil-exporting countries. Western Europe's expanding foreign policy independence from Washington should not be fought. To do so would be futile. Rather, the allies should explore new or broader European roles in deterring Soviet aggression and political upheaval in the Persian Gulf, in meeting energy-related economic and political problems of the less-developed countries, and, to some extent, in negotiating arms control and security issues with the Soviets. The United States still has much to learn from its European allies about how to prepare for emergencies. More bilateral and multilateral discussion would greatly strengthen Western initiatives in stockpiling, demand restraint, emergency supplies, and allocation programs. Some diplomatic initiatives directed at the producer nations—creating surge production capacity and providing quiet military advisory services—may best be coordinated by our allies.

For their part, the West European countries may be expected to continue their pragmatic rather than ideological approach to energy security, an approach built on a mixture of unilateral, bilateral, and multilateral tactics. For the short term, it follows that realistic definitions of the challenge and suitable domestic and international preparations for emergencies should be a minimum goal. Over the longer term, incentives to cooperate more fully with the United States and Japan must be created, and the opportunities provided by the European Community, the International Energy Agency, and annual economic summits must be captured.

REFERENCES

British Petroleum Statistics. 1978. London: British Petroleum.

Central Intelligence Agency. 1980. *International Energy Statistical Review.* August 26. Washington, D.C.

Comité Professionel du Pétrole. 1976. *Réglementation Pétrolière: Régime de l'importation des produits pétrolières.* Part A, Article 1. Paris: Comité Professional du Pétrole.

The Committee for Energy Policy Promotion. 1980. *Japan and the Oil Problem.* Tokyo, Japan.

Krapels, Edward W. 1980. *Oil Supply Security.* Washington, D.C.: Johns Hopkins University Press.

Lieber, Robert J. 1980. "Economics, Energy and Security in Alliance Perspective." *International Security* (Spring): 139–163.

OECD. 1979. *OECD Observer.* July.

_____ . 1980. *OECD Observer.* January.

7 JAPAN

Joseph S. Nye

No industrialized country has an energy security problem as large as Japan's. Poor in natural resources, the second largest economy in the free world depends heavily on trade. Fully 99 percent of Japan's oil is imported, and three-quarters of those imports come from the fragile Persian Gulf area. If supply interruptions threaten the United States with economic dislocation, they pose absolute catastrophe for Japan, which is four times more dependent on energy imports (88 percent compared to 22 percent) and more heavily dependent on oil (75 percent of total energy compared to 50 percent) (Committee for Energy Policy Promotion 1980).

Any disruption of the steady stream of oil imports floating daily into Japan's harbors would impose three general kinds of costs to this society: direct damage to life, health, and public order; economic strains caused by wealth transfers and the disruptive effects of rapidly rising prices; and the unwilling alteration of foreign policy in order to secure a resumption of energy supplies. Since its vulnerability to interruptions is greater than that of the United States, direct damage to the health and safety of the public is a greater concern in

I am grateful to the following persons for comments or assistance, though the responsibility remains mine: Faneuil Adams, Mark Brown, Kent Calder, Toyoaki Ikuta, Munemichi Inoue, Kunisada Kume, Amiyoshi Okumura, Keichi Oshima, Hisashi Owada, Tadashi Yamamoto, and others.

Japan. Conversely, foreign policy damage is a more significant hazard for the United States. Therefore, any Japanese efforts to diminish vulnerability to direct damage by altering foreign policy positions pose a potentially dangerous source of friction for the economic and political relations between these major free world allies.

Japan's sense of vulnerability is reinforced by a number of circumstances. Its economy depends on events in the distant Middle East and along the precarious sea routes through the Straits of Hormuz and Malacca, yet its constitution restricts its military establishment to "self-defense forces" near the Japanese islands. Even arms exports are impossible, given the postwar antimilitary consensus of the Japanese public. So Japan lacks some of the political and military instruments the United States can bring to bear in the complex tacit bargaining of oil diplomacy.

To compound the problem Japan is dependent on foreign oil companies. Up to the autumn of 1978, international oil companies provided 70 percent of Japan's supplies. When those companies lost access to crude oil supplies in Iran and Nigeria, they were forced to cut back on sales to third parties in order to supply their own affiliates. Many of these third parties were independent Japanese refiners who felt a sense of panic. Today international companies supply about 40 percent of Japan's imports.

Still, Japan has some important assets to deal with its energy problems. Not only does its economy abundantly produce goods and technology desired by oil producers, but its giant trading companies have a long tradition of flexibility in putting together bilateral package deals. Domestically, Japan has responded to crises creatively with social solidarity. This success reflects both Japanese cultural patterns and the inescapable nature of the problem the country faces. Unlike the United States, Japan has been willing to let prices rise to constrain demand and has pursued macroeconomic and labor policies that maintain economic growth while controlling inflation.

Yet another asset—although one considered debatable by some Japanese—is the Ministry of International Trade and Industry (MITI), which acts as Japan's energy department. Indeed in 1977, MITI preserved its bureaucratic position by successfully resisting Prime Minister Fukuda's efforts to create a separate energy deparment. While MITI's power does not fit the role implied by the crude caricature of "Japan, Inc.," its bureaucrats are engaged in a continual dialogue with industry. They reflect a consensus viewpoint, and their power rests more on persuasion than on law or formal orders. The resulting "administrative guidance" on prices, gas station closings, and industry restructuring creates more flexible government–business relations in the energy area than is true in the more legalistic and arms-length political culture in the United States. MITI's "guidance" on prices, for example, is loosely applied by a small bureaucracy and designed to ensure that any windfalls in the acquisition of cheaper crude oil are passed on to consumers and used to moderate price increases. Otherwise, importers expect MITI to allow them to pass along increases in international prices to the domestic market. Consumers accept this arrangement as the basis of the prices they pay.[1]

Japan's sense of vulnerability and concern about energy security have increased greatly over the last decade. Three series of events accelerated the process. First came the Arab oil embargo of 1973. Then, in the mid–70s, were disputes with Canada and the United States over nuclear nonproliferation policies which threatened uranium supplies. Finally, at the end of the seventies, came the complex series of events triggered by the Iranian Revolution. By 1980, energy security had become a major issue in Japanese politics.

THE EVOLUTION OF JAPANESE ENERGY POLICY

Before 1973 Japanese energy policy concentrated primarily on price, not security of supply. Low energy prices were essential to government's strategy of encouraging investment in heavy, energy-intensive industries (Tsurumi 1978). Cheap imported oil was favored over indigenous coal or hydroelectric resources. As a result, Japan's dependence on energy imports rose from 26 percent of total consumption in 1955 to 46 percent in 1960 and 90 percent in 1973 when the oil crisis struck.

Oil policy was based on the local refining of imported crude. Under the Petroleum Industry Law of 1962, the Ministry of International Trade and Industry was given authority to license entry into refining, approve production plans, and set standard prices. MITI used this authority to encourage Japanese firms to engage in refining and to discourage any domination of the industry by oil majors or

---

1. Based on conversations with MITI and oil industry officials, Tokyo, July 1980.

the general trading companies. The resulting fragmentation of the refining industry was supposed to keep domestic petroleum product prices low. The price of kerosene (which is used as a home heating fuel) was kept low for political reasons (Porges 1980).

Internationally, Japan relied primarily on the large multinational companies (the "majors") for supply while the international oil market was in a condition of glut. Although MITI sought to promote exploration by Japanese companies, it preferred to diversify its efforts rather than give special support to the Arabian Oil Company that had been privately established by Japanese in 1958. As international markets began to tighten and government diminished its emphasis on heavy industry in the early 1970s, a new MITI minister promoted efforts to reduce dependence on the majors and to foster exploration by Japanese banks and trading firms through subsidies from the Japan National Oil Corporation (JNOC) that had been created in 1967. However, in 1973, the majors still supplied 80 percent of Japan's oil (Tsurumi 1975).

The Arab oil embargo of that year was a severe shock to Japan. Previous politically instigated shortfalls in 1956 and 1967 had been buffered by surplus American capacity, but that surplus no longer existed in 1973. Moreover, Japan was surprised that its low diplomatic profile in the Middle East had not spared it the wrath of the Arab nations. The initial Japanese response was a voluntary 10 percent conservation program by industry and the closing of gas stations on holidays. Subsequently, Japan tried to relieve itself of the embargo's pressures by altering its foreign policy. On November 22, Japan issued a cautiously worded statement endorsing Palestinian rights and indicating that it might have to "reconsider its policy toward Israel" (Juster 1977; Nau 1979). Coming right after a visit by Secretary of State Kissinger, this action was widely regarded as the most serious breach in bilateral relations since the Second World War.

Although its diplomatic efforts, including visits to the Middle East and promises of aid, earned Japan a transfer to the Arabs' "friendly nation list" by December 25, they did not really solve Japan's problem. The real relief came through the efforts of the international oil companies to distribute available oil supplies as equitably as possible. Contrary to popular political belief in Japan, the companies' actions allowed Japan to suffer less than other countries: it experienced only a 3 percent shortfall below forecast supplies, compared to an 11 percent shortfall for the United States and a 19 percent shortfall for Europe (Stobaugh 1975: 193). By the time of the Washington Energy Conference in February 1974, Japanese officials had realized the advantages of cooperating with the United States. They were active in launching the IEA and designing its Emergency Plan which was agreed upon in September 1974.

Following the 1973 oil crisis, Japanese energy policy began to cope with the security problem, though at a rather restrained pace. Some of the conservation effects of the initial price increase were limited by exchange rate changes which subsequently reduced the costs of crude oil imports. Price controls instituted in the inflationary period following the crisis were officially removed in 1975, but MITI continued to shelter kerosene and jet fuel from the full effect of rising prices. By 1977, the prices of gasoline and kerosene had doubled their 1970 levels, roughly in proportion to consumer prices in general. But since there was a 50 percent rise in real incomes over the same period, the effects on personal incomes were not severe. In the case of industry, however, heavy oil prices rose to three times their 1970 level (in comparison with a 69 percent increase in the wholesale price index over the same period (Kaya 1979: 10). In addition, MITI acted to discourage the further domestic expansion of such weak energy-intensive industries as copper smelting and aluminum refining. In the three years after 1973, Japan's overall energy consumption per real unit of GNP declined by 10 percent. Between 1973 and 1978, when the gross domestic product grew 3.6 percent per year, total primary energy consumption grew by 1.2 percent and oil consumption, 0.4 percent. Oil imports declined 0.9 percent (International Energy Agency 1980).

To increase the domestic supply of energy, the Japanese government launched ambitious programs in nuclear and renewable energy sources. Project Sunshine, initiated in 1974, focused on developing solar, geothermal, coal conversion, and hydrogen technology (Momota 1979: 20). Its original target was to provide 1.6 percent of Japan's total energy supply by 1990. The 1970 nuclear program called for 60 gigawatts (GW) of power by 1985, but siting problems and lengthening construction times forced this goal downward to 30 GW. Coal imports remained stagnant, while imports of liquified natural gas (LNG) rose from 3 to 14 million tons of oil equivalent between 1973 and 1978. Thus, Japan's energy supply problems clearly continued to center on oil.

The government took a number of steps in relation to the security of oil supply. In 1973, Japan had only forty-five days of imports in stock. New legislation required companies to hold ninety days in stocks (the IEA target) by 1980 and the government planned to build its stockpiles to 20 million kiloliters by 1985. MITI, if not public opinion, took a less restrictive attitude toward the majors and increased government subsidies for Japanese firms to explore abroad. By 1980, however, such firms produced only 10 percent of Japan's oil imports. Diplomatically, the government fostered ambitious aid and investment programs in oil-producing countries and negotiated a number of direct government-to-government agreements for the purchase of oil. At the same time, Japan cooperated with the United States through bilateral research and development arrangements in the multinational IEA.

The Iranian crisis of 1979 dealt Japan a second oil shock. Cut off from their traditional sources of crude oil by Iran and other OPEC countries, the majors curtailed sales to third parties in order to supply their own affiliated refineries. Since Japan had discouraged large refining efforts by the majors, many of those third parties were independent Japanese refineries. The majors supplied 44 percent of Japan's oil supplies at the beginning of 1980—down from 70 percent in 1978 (MITI 1980; see also Institute of Energy Economics 1979: 12–15). The result was panic on the part of Japanese firms. They paid extreme spot market prices for what oil they could get and submitted to extraordinary contract terms. Their continuing buildup of oil stocks helped exacerbate the market tightness caused by the Iranian revolution.

CURRENT JAPANESE STRATEGY

The recent turmoil in Iran produced a renewed commitment among the Japanese to reduce their oil dependence and devise a strategy to cope with the unavoidable security problems raised by their energy needs. The goals of Japanese energy policy are, by 1990, to reduce oil dependence from the current level of 75 percent to 50 percent and to increase the uses of Asian oil from 20 percent to 30 percent of total oil imports. In concert with other developed countries attending the Tokyo Summit in July and the IEA Ministerial Meeting in December 1979, Japan established oil import ceilings. Its target was set at 6.3 to 6.9 million barrels per day in 1985, allowing a 17 to 28 percent increase over the current level of 5.4 million barrels per day. Subsequently, the Japanese government announced its intention to meet the lower target level. Its strategy to achieve this goal includes measures to diversify energy sources, restrain demand, and enhance the security of its oil supply (MITI 1979; 1980). Table 7-1 shows the planned changes in energy supply.

Oil will remain the dominant energy source for Japan but the importance of coal, nuclear power, and natural gas is scheduled to nearly double over the course of the eighties. Although successful completion of this plan would still leave Japan dependent on oil and on imported energy, the diversification of fuels and import sources should reduce its vulnerability to disruptive events in fragile areas such as the Persian Gulf.

The official targets for alternative energy sources are very ambitious. Domestic coal production is to be maintained at 20 million tons, but imports of steam coal will have to increase from 1 to 53 million tons per year by the end of the decade. Coal-fired thermal plants will be encouraged; new oil-fired plants will be discouraged. Large investments will be required to develop overseas coal production, build an infrastructure for the drastic increase in coal imports, and convert present oil-burning industrial facilities to coal. Japan's hopes for other power sources are also ambitious. Plans call for expanding current nuclear generating capacity from 15 GW to 30 GW in 1985 and 53 GW in 1990. Liquified natural gas imports are scheduled to increase from 14 to 45 million tons of oil equivalent by the end of the decade. The 1974 "Sunshine Project" devoted to such novel energy sources as solar power and coal liquefaction is expected to account for 5 percent of total energy supply by 1990.

Table 7-1. Changes planned in the sources of Japan's energy supply.

| | Percentage of Total Energy Supply | | | |
	1977	1985	1990	1995
Oil	75	63	50	45
Coal	14.8	16.1	17.8	18.3
Nuclear power	2	6.7	10.9	14.3
Liquified natural gas	2.9	7.2	9	8.7
Hydroelectric power	4.8	4.7	4.6	4.6
Solar, geothermal/and other sources	.1	1.3	6.5	9.4

Source: Ministry of International Trade and Industry (1979).

Table 7−2.   Two projections of alternative energy supply in 1990.

		Government's Program	Ikuta's Estimate
Hydroelectric power	GW	26	20
Domestic coal	MT	20	18
Geothermal energy	GW	3.5	0.6
Domestic oil and natural gas	MT	9.5	9.5
Imported steam coal	MT	53.5	28−33
Liquified natural gas	MT	45	32
Liquified petroleum gas	MT	26	15
Nuclear power	GW	53	30−35

Source: Ikuta (1980).

In 1980, the Japanese government increased its energy budget by 30 percent to 740 billion yen. Special funds and a "New Energy Development Authority" are now being established to promote alternative energy sources. Unfortunately, the targets for alternative energy supplies will probably not be achieved unless current government policies are changed. Table 7−2, prepared by Toyoaki Ikuta, President of Japan's Institute of Energy Economics, is an estimate of the energy that may actually be supplied by alternative energy sources in 1990. The realism of Ikuta's estimates is confirmed by other private Japanese sources, such as the Industrial Bank of Japan.[2]

Ikuta predicts the largest absolute shortfalls from nuclear energy and steam coal imports. Japan has 15 GW of nuclear capability operating and 5 GW more under construction. Plants with another 10 to 15 GW have been or are about to be approved, but construction on them has not yet started. Since building a nuclear reactor now takes close to ten years, it is difficult to see how Japan's nuclear capacity could exceed this total by 1990.

The outlook for energy from imported steam coal is not so pessimistic—if government policy changes. Japan currently uses oil to generate some 53 percent of its electricity. Although it is MITI policy not to approve new utility applications for oil-burning plants, twenty are now under construction and another thirteen have been approved in the blueprint stage.[3] Unless official policy is more strictly

2. Ikuta (1980); and interviews in Tokyo, July 1980.

3. Interviews, Industrial Bank of Japan, Tokyo, July 1980.

interpreted and enforced, Japan will continue to build new oil-burning plants through 1986. Local political and environmental concerns seem to be the main obstacles to more rapid conversion to coal. MITI is currently engaged in consultations that may produce a consensus on more rapid conversion from oil to coal. But since Japan uses ten times more energy per unit of habitable land area than the United States, the environmental issue is serious (Kanoh 1979).

However difficult the energy supply situation, demand trends may turn out better than expected. Pessimists argue that Japan's per-capita energy consumption of 3.2 tons of oil equivalent is well below both the IEA average of 4.9 tons and the United States consumption of 8.2 tons. With rapidly rising personal income, they suggest, consumers will want to purchase more air conditioners, appliances, and larger homes. Furthermore, there is comparatively little room for conservation because Japan's industries represent a high 58 percent of total energy consumption and are already more energy efficient than their counterparts in other countries. More optimistic forecasters point to the greater price responsiveness of Japanese industry, its flexibility in purchasing energy-intensive components from abroad, the encouragement that MITI and rising prices give to a shift toward a less energy-intensive industrial structure, and heavy investment in new energy-saving processes.

The early returns favor the optimists. Total energy consumption declined in the first half of 1980, despite positive economic growth. Japan may well exceed its conservation goals of saving 15 percent of what would otherwise have been the energy consumption level in 1990 (Committee for Energy Policy Promotion 1980). A new Energy Conservation Act passed in October 1979 requires large factories to appoint energy managers who report regularly to MITI, provides tax incentives and assistance for energy savers, and sets building and vehicle efficiency standards. Also during 1979, the gasoline tax was increased by 25 percent, the aviation fuel tax was doubled, and kerosene prices were deregulated (International Energy Agency 1980). In addition, in February 1980, the government announced short-term measures such as reduced room heating and automobile use in an effort to curtail oil consumption by 7 percent. Electrical prices were raised 50 percent so that individual customers would pay $.13 per kilowatt hour (*The Economist* 1980: 77).

The government has also taken a number of measures to deal with possible oil supply interruptions. Private oil stocks rose to slightly

Table 7–3.   Japan's stockpile promotion system.

Finance Capital for Stockpile Oil Purchases	Interest; 2.1% (5% interest subsidy) Finance ratio: 90%
Financing the cooperative stockpile company installations	Public investment Two-thirds of suitable land price (limited to 20% of total construction costs)
Financing individual company installations	Interest: 7.15% Finance ratio: 80% Limit: 2000 million yen per 100,000 kl tank
	Interest: 7.15% Finance ratio: 70% Limit: 1300 million yen per 100,000 kl tank (1500 million yen for especially costly newly reclaimed land, etc.)

over 100 days' supply by mid–1980, well over the required level of 90 days. Other aspects of the stockpiling program are listed in Table 7–3. MITI annually determines stockpile goals for the next four years and requires importers and refiners to submit implementation plans which it has the power to revise. The government encourages the growth of private stocks through long-term, low-interest loans for 90 percent of the costs of the oil and 70 percent of the cost of the facilities. In addition, one-third of the normal property tax is waived on storage facilities. When several industries recently established a joint stockpile corporation, for example, the Japan National Oil Corporation provided two-thirds of the cost of purchasing the site.

The performance with respect to official reserves has been less impressive. The program has lagged behind schedule because of difficulties in finding storage sites and obtaining oil under tight market conditions. In 1980, the Japan National Oil Company had about 33 million barrels (approximately seven days' imports) stored in twenty surplus tankers.[4] The government target, however, is 120 million barrels (roughly twenty days' imports) in storage by 1982 and a forty-day public stockpile by a later but still unspecified date.

In an emergency, Japan's first priority is to avoid social panic. The government's tools to that end are three: publicity encouraging conservation; price increases and gentle administrative guidance to business in order to minimize disruptive social effects; and full-scale rationing. The value of each strategy varies with the severity of the disruption. Ideally, the government's philosophy is to use market forces as much as possible, so it considers the extent of its involvement in the second strategy as flexible. The 1979 disruptions were small enough to be handled by voluntary conservation and price-induced demand restraint; the government's role was only minor. But macroeconomic policy and monetary policy were quickly adjusted to take increased energy costs into account.

Rationing coupons have been printed for use during a large emergency, but the idea of rationing is so unpopular that little detailed planning for implementation has been accomplished. Nor has much attention been given to taxes or tariffs to restrain demand and prevent any large transfer of wealth to overseas producers. MITI officials explain that public opinion is not focused on wealth transfer and that a tax might be resented by consumers, especially if it fell heavily on industry and caused unemployment. Pointing out that emergency planning is MITI's responsibility, its critics charge that it resists more open and detailed planning in order to avoid giving other groups or bureaucracies an excuse for further involvement in what it considers its own business. Also, MITI bureaucrats officially committed to the IEA are fully prepared to encourage increased oil purchases in the world market if the sharing plan fails. In addition, they plan to make bunkers available to vital Japanese shipping in times of crisis.[5]

Stockpiles and demand restraint are but the short-term components of Japan's energy security strategy; conservation and the development of alternative energy supplies are its long-term hopes. In the ambiguous intermediate term, the main components of Japan's strategy are diplomatic and business measures to diversify and assure supply. Undertaken so far are government-to-government oil deals (for instance with Mexico); energy and related industrial investment proj-

---

4. Department of Energy estimates, March 1980.
5. Based on interviews, Tokyo, July 1980. See also, Nomura Research Institute (1980).

ects in OPEC countries (such as large petrochemical plants in Saudi Arabia and Iran); and exploration projects in Communist countries (China and the Soviet Union) and in OECD countries (like Canada).

Development assistance to Indonesia, for example, is also designed to help assure access to oil supplies. Japan hopes to use its industrial and economic power to replace its dependent relations with producers with more interdependence. There are limits to this process, of course, as the difficulties over the Mitsui petrochemical plant in Iran have proven. Nonetheless, it is one of the few mid–term instruments available to Japan. Even if the Japanese gain little leverage from these efforts, their investments in energy production facilities will help alleviate generally tight market conditions and diversify the sources of oil supply. More might be done in this area, but Japanese officials are uncertain what role to assign to the oil companies and what diplomatic posture they should adopt in dealing with the United States and the oil producers.

A number of these officials realize that, contrary to popular belief, the majors tended to play a stabilizing role at the time of the 1973 crisis. Their ability to control the flow of oil through their complex global distribution network diminished the effectiveness of the political embargo and equalized the burden of shortage in a way that governments would have difficulty duplicating. By acting as a buffer between politics and oil allocations, the majors can help reduce friction between governments. But as the role of the majors declines—probably irreversibly—the prospect for heightened tensions increases. The emergency sharing plan of the IEA rests upon the capabilities of the thirty-four reporting companies for its implementation. If these companies become too small a part of the Japanese market, doubts arise about the plan's chances for success.

Yet the pressure for direct deals continues to mount, fed by the interest of both producers and consumers. Some Japanese see direct deals and government-to-government arrangements as allowing some degree of consumer leverage. In this view, at least the Japanese can bargain with producers at a time of crisis rather than merely accept the allocation decisions of the majors. A new factor in the Japanese situation, one that combines some of the advantages of government-to-government deals and the market-sensitive operations of the majors, is the increasing role of small Japanese oil companies and the giant general trading companies which, by early 1980, accounted for 44 percent of oil imports. The trading companies are enormously flexible distribution systems able to provide equipment, technology, and services in return for access to oil. In many cases, they work closely with the majors; in other instances, they are involved in third-party sales of their own. As they are drawn into the IEA network, they can help provide some of the declining flexibility in that system while still providing Japan with direct leverage.

At the same time, the trading companies are difficult to control, and MITI is reluctant to see its control of the oil industry diluted by too large a share for the trading companies. The alternatives to greater trading company involvement are direct deals by the relatively small Japanese-capitalized oil companies and government-to-government deals. Although the latter are often urged by the producer governments and are attractive to some Japanese government officials, others are aware of the dangers of political extortion that can arise when a country as dependent as Japan loses market buffers.

Problems of political leverage also limit Japan's projects with its communist neighbors, particularly the Soviet Union. Despite Soviet resources, Japan is wary about increasing its vulnerability to Soviet pressure. Cooperation in the development of natural gas in Yakutsk and oil offshore Sakhalin Island was agreed on among the Soviet Union, Japan, and the United States in the mid–1970s, but Japan has not agreed to Soviet proposals for bilateral development of Tyumen oil in West Siberia. With regard to China, low production levels and poor crude quality have been major disappointments. At present, China supplies only 3 percent of Japan's oil, though Japan remains eager to increase both oil and coal imports from China (Miwa 1980).

Another major issue for Japan's intermediate-term energy security strategy is the proper diplomatic distance to maintain from the United States. Japan counts on friendly relations with producers and a low diplomatic profile overall. At the same time, Japan needs close cooperation with the United States both inside and outside the IEA to achieve a degree of energy security and military protection. These conflicting needs frequently present policy dilemmas. Japan would profit from consultation on energy security as part of a broader relationship with the United States, but it does not wish to be seen in a military or confrontational role by Middle Eastern states.

In the past, for understandable historical and political reasons, Japan has been reluctant to become involved in the foreign policy dilemmas relating to the security of the Persian Gulf. Nevertheless, former Foreign Minister Miyazawa has observed that "the Japanese have only recently become aware of the fact that a major economic power cannot shun a certain degree of political responsibility."[6] Since actions of any sort in the Persian Gulf are bound to have a strong effect on Japan, it would be in Japan's best interest to develop bilateral and multilateral consultation procedures encompassing a broad range of energy security measures.

A great deal of consultation in energy matters already occurs before and during the annual economic summits. At the ministerial level, bilateral and multilateral meetings occur under IEA auspices. At the technical level, the United States and Japan cooperate on fusion technology, coal conversion, high energy physics, solar and geothermal power, and other energy problems—again, bilaterally and through the programs and projects of the IEA. Nonetheless, some current aspects of the energy relationship, particularly its broader security aspects, are not given enough attention. Yet Japan is not sure whether it wants to remedy this situation. Although there has been increased interest in improving local defense capabilities (incidentally freeing some U.S. naval forces for use in the Indian Ocean) (The Comprehensive National Security Study Group 1980), MITI and others resist the open discussion of defense issues in the context of energy because they believe that this step would politicize the oil issue even more.

CONCLUSION

Japan faces the worst energy security situation but it compensates somewhat for its objective difficulties with impressive social solidarity, flexible government–business relations, and a sensitive responsiveness to price that may lead to greater conservation than the government expects. Still, local political forces have inhibited Japan's effective response to the pressing dangers that could ruin its economy. The tradition of consensual decisionmaking has delayed Japan's nuclear program and the conversion of oil-fired facilities to coal. These domestic political problems may cause acrimonious international problems in the future if Japan fails to develop enough alternative energy sources to meet its Tokyo Summit commitment to limit oil imports. Increasing exports to pay for additional oil could

6. "To Meet the Challenge," speech to the Trilateral Commission, London, March 23, 1980.

also encourage Japan's trading partners to introduce severe protectionist pressures against Japanese goods. Movement of Arab capital directly to Tokyo security markets could alleviate this problem but not solve it.

In the intermediate term, Japan's ability to avoid these lurking foreign policy problems will depend on improved conservation and further imports of coal. Moreover, both have important security benefits. Liquified natural gas is subject to some of the same dangers of interruption as oil. Nuclear supplies are unlikely to be constrained by disputes over nonproliferation policy now that Japan and her suppliers have formed a basis for compromise that reflects the outcome of the International Nuclear Fuel Cycle Evaluation.[7] Nonetheless, nuclear energy remains vulnerable to the political reverberations of an accident anywhere in the world. Conservation, on the other hand, is pure "home-produced" energy equivalence. And while coal is imported and there are only seven significant exporters, imports can be diversified among politically stable states such as Australia and the United States (Wilson 1980).

Next to sensible domestic policies, including large stockpiles, the most important factor increasing Japanese energy security would be close cooperation with the United States. The U.S. alliance is fundamental to overall Japanese security and provides an additional incentive for U.S. cooperation in the case of an energy emergency. Despite temptations to hold the United States at diplomatic arm's length and avoid a higher political profile in energy issues, Japan will retain a strong interest in energy cooperation with the United States (Nye 1980). Together, the United States and Japan represent half the free world's oil imports. They cannot escape this market interdependence. Thus Japan should actively pursue the bilateral and IEA plans for dealing with oil market disruptions. Japan is the most dependent industrial state, but like the prospect of hanging, extreme dependence can help clarify the mind.

---

7. For a detailed discussion, see Imai and Rowen (1980); and Rockefeller Foundation and National Institute of Research Advancement (1979).

REFERENCES

Committee for Energy Policy Promotion. 1980. *Japan and the Oil Problem.* Tokyo, February.

The Comprehensive National Security Study Group. 1980. "Report on Comprehensive National Security." Tokyo, July.

The Economist. 1980. "Japan: Rising Sun." (June 21): 77.

Ikuta, Toyoaki. 1980. "Energy Problem of Japan." May. Mimeo.

Imai, Ryukichi, and Henry Rowen. 1980. *Nuclear Energy and Nuclear Proliferation (Japanese and American Views).* Boulder, Co.: Westview Press.

Institute of Energy Economics. 1979. *Energy in Japan.* no. 47, December.

International Energy Agency. 1980. *Country Report on Japan.* IEA/SLT (79) 78.21, Paris, February 13.

Juster, Kenneth. 1977. "Foreign Policy-Making During the Oil Crisis." *The Japan Interpreter* XI (Winter).

Kanoh, Tokio. 1979. "A Japanese Perspective." Paper presented at "Energy: Fact, Fantasy and the Future," Toronto, October 1.

Kaya, Yoichi. 1979. "Japan's Energy Consumption Structure and the Direction of Energy Conservation." *The Wheel Extended* (Autumn).

Ministry of International Trade and Industry. 1979. *Japan's Energy Strategy Toward the 21st Century.* Tokyo, March.

_____ . 1979. "Provisional Long-Term Supply and Demand Outlook." Interim report, Tokyo, August 31.

_____ . 1980. "Oil Imports Inventory." Tokyo, January.

_____ . 1980. *Energy in Japan: Facts and Figures.* Tokyo, February.

Miwa, Yoshihiko. 1980. "Oil Trade Between Japan and China." Paper presented at Workshop on Cultural Development in ASEAN, University of the Phillipines Law Center, June.

Momota, Tsuneo. 1979. "Japan's Development of Alternate Sources of Energy." *The Wheel Extended* (Autumn).

Nau, Henry R. 1979. "U.S.-Japan Relations in the 1973-74 Energy Crisis: Bilateral Confrontation and Multilateral Cooperation." George Washington University. Unpublished manuscript.

Nomura Research Institute. 1980. *Cutoff of Oil Supply: A Systematic Analysis of Energy Crisis Management.* Tokyo.

Nye, Joseph S. 1980. "Energy and Japan-U.S. Relations." Paper prepared for the Japan-United States Economic Relations Group, July.

Porges, Amelia. 1980. "Case Study No. 2: The Petroleum Industry Law and the Naptha War of 1977-79." Harvard Law School.

Rockefeller Foundation and National Institute of Research Advancement. 1979. *Future U.S.-Japanese Nuclear Energy Relations.* Tokyo.

Stobaugh, Robert. 1975. "The Oil Companies in the Crisis." *Daedalus* (Fall).

Tsurumi, Yoshi. 1975. "Japan." In "The Oil Crisis in Perspective," edited by Raymond Vernon. *Daedalus* (Fall).

_____ . 1978. "The Case of Japan: Price Bargaining and Controls on Oil Products. *Journal of Comparative Economics* 2.

Wilson, Carroll, ed. 1980. *Coal: Bridge to the Future.* Cambridge, Mass: Ballinger Publishing Company.

8 THE OIL-IMPORTING DEVELOPING COUNTRIES

David A. Deese

When we speak of a developing country, we mean one that faces serious social, economic, political, and technological constraints internally and a high level of dependence on trade, foreign aid, and foreign investment externally.[1] Most Westerners view the importance of these countries in terms of the balance of power between the superpowers and assume that developing economies have very little need—if any—for the oil that drives our giant industrial economies.

These assumptions are wrong. The oil import burden on most developing countries now poses a first-order problem of energy and security for the world. The insecurity of the eighty-five oil-importing developing countries (OIDCs) that are net importers of oil or commercial energy—a significant problem in its own right—indirectly threatens the stability of OPEC, our allies, and ourselves.[2] Furthermore, the problem cannot be solved any time soon; we will be lucky to keep it from growing worse over the next decade. Of all the countries laboring under the strain of dependence on imported oil, the

1. The World Bank classifies developing countries with per-capita GNPs below about $360 as low-income and from $360 to about $3,500 as middle-income.

2. The group of OIDCs does not include the thirteen members of OPEC—Algeria, Ecuador, Iran, Iraq, Gabon, Indonesia, Kuwait, Libya, Nigeria, Qatar, Saudi Arabia, United Arab Emirates, and Venezuela—and the other energy self-sufficient or oil-importing less-developed countries—Angola, Bahrain, Brunei, Congo, Egypt, Malaysia, Mexico, Oman, Syria, Trinidad and Tobago, Tunisia, and Zaire.

229

OIDCs will remain the most threatened and the least able to define and control the sources of their misfortune.

World war, a battle for Europe, and upheaval in the Persian Gulf are not the only threats to our national security. We must also try to avert regional disruptions and conflicts that could be triggered by energy-related social and political stresses. National social and political cohesion can be shattered by sudden economic contractions (the threat to the OIDCs) as well as by rapid economic growth (the threat to the oil-exporting nations). Vital U.S., as well as local and regional, interests are at stake. Disruption in Turkey undermines the NATO alliance and weakens our ability to reinforce the Persian Gulf; turmoil in the Philippines could end our use of the critical naval base in Subic Bay; and war in South Korea, Central America, or the Caribbean is likely to involve the United States directly. Furthermore, political upheaval or military conflict in bordering countries could directly or indirectly stop oil exports from producers such as Indonesia, Gabon, Libya, Algeria, or Nigeria. The disruption of exports from Libya, for example, would slash almost 10 percent of U.S. and 15 to 20 percent of West German oil imports and trigger the International Energy Agency (IEA) emergency allocation system. Thus the problem of the economic and political cohesion of the OIDCs cannot be detached from that of political change in the oil-exporting countries.

ENERGY AND SECURITY IN THE DEVELOPING COUNTRIES

The OIDCs face the same general national security threats from energy as other oil-importing countries: direct disruption of normal social and economic conditions due to oil shortages; economic and political turmoil caused by unexpected and rapid increases in oil prices; and foreign policy costs, including war. Unlike most developed countries, though, many OIDCs would be severely threatened by even continued moderate increases in the real price of oil. Of course, despite these very general similarities, no two countries among the eighty-five OIDCs would define the energy security issue in the same way. These countries are distinguished by enormous cultural, economic, political, and military differences.

Direct Damage

The disruption of normal social, economic, and political conditions caused by the loss of oil imports can come about in OIDCs in at least three different ways. First, many of these nations are unable to pay for oil, even under normal market conditions, and so are forced to do without needed supplies. Second, small interruptions of oil supplies in the international market tighten national distribution systems and result in shortages. Third, the severe shortages accompany larger disruptions.

Financial and distribution difficulties plagued Turkey, Pakistan, and Kenya throughout much of 1980. Turkey operated its economy with working oil inventories at emergency levels of about fifteen days' supply. Many other developing countries simply bought less oil and learned to live with shortages. The late seventies witnessed increasing distribution problems and other shortages of electricity, fossil fuels, and even fuelwood, kerosene, and other fuels used for cooking and space heating. These shortages cut directly into the commercial and industrial sectors of many developing economies. Brownouts are now common, for example, in urban India and Kenya. These effects, and the accompanying sharp price increases, disrupt life in the countryside and the city and strain the capacity of local, state, and national political systems.

Economic and Political Effects

The threat of economic and political upheaval in OIDCs arises from the various effects, both direct and indirect, of oil price increases. Although most OIDCs import relatively small amounts of oil, these imports can be just as essential to the economy of a one- or two-crop agricultural-exporting nation like Ghana as they are to a newly industrialized nation like South Korea. Within the group of eighty-five OIDCs, almost fifty depend on imported oil for 90 percent or more of their commercial energy use. With some exceptions, such as India, Pakistan, South Korea, and Zambia, the other OIDCs depend on oil imports for between 50 and 90 percent of consumption.

In 1979, the OIDCs used almost 8 million barrels of oil per day, or not much more than the imports of the United States alone. They produced about 4.7 million barrels and imported about 4 million barrels per day, or about 15 percent of all oil traded internationally. About sixty of the OIDCs imported fewer than 10,000 barrels per day; the remaining twenty-five were fairly evenly divided between those that import up to 20,000 barrels and those that import between 20,000 and 60,000 barrels per day. In 1975, only seven nations—South Korea, Singapore, Taiwan, Hong Kong, Brazil, Argentina, and Jamaica—accounted for over one-half of all commercial energy consumption in the OIDCs.

The economic situation of many OIDCs now seems precarious. While attempting to continue adjusting their economies after the worldwide recession and inflation experienced in 1974 and 1975, they now confront a new round of recessionary and inflationary forces brought on in part by the real oil price increases and the economic slowdown of 1979 and 1980. Oil price increases, especially rapid escalations over short periods, seriously affect all or most OIDCs because their economies are heavily dependent on trade, aid, and foreign investment.

We can identify five critical effects of the oil price increases. First in importance is the slowdown in the economic growth rates of the industrial nations, which adversely affects the growth of two-thirds of the OIDCs' export markets. These export markets are the most important element in the developing nations' overall economic growth and their only real hope of absorbing the new oil import burden. Related to this problem is the second most significant effect of increasing oil prices: weakening terms of trade (stagnant or declining rates of growth in prices received for exports as compared to more rapidly growing prices paid for imports). The third adverse effect is that oil payments come to represent an increasing share of the importers' foreign exchange earnings. Fourth, the shortage and increased cost of energy have slowed national economic growth rates and forced government officials to raise the price of gasoline, diesel fuel, kerosene, and other products. Finally, lower growth rates in developed countries and a decline in the real price of oil from 1975 to 1979 undercut OPEC's foreign aid programs while making commercial banks in the developed countries more cautious about loans to the OIDCs.

Unfortunately, the economic shocks of 1979 and 1980 must be expected to inflict major new damage on OIDC economies and political systems. The oil price increases from about $13 to $35 per barrel in 1979 and 1980 were rapid and enormous in absolute terms. Worldwide recessionary and inflationary pressures are now likely to continue at least into the early 1980s. Many experts forecast continuously tight oil markets and real price increases of perhaps 5 percent per year over the next five to ten years, and their estimates rely on the shaky assumption (assessed in Chapters 1 and 3) that oil markets will not be disrupted again in the 1980s. Since growth rates in the OECD countries are now predicted to be no higher than 2 to 3 percent per year in the 1980s, or at least until 1985, the growth in demand for primary products will be weak, and access to the markets of developed countries for manufactured goods may be restricted by protectionist measures.

Meanwhile, rapid real price increases continue for imported goods, especially food, petrochemicals, machinery, and manufactured products. The OIDCs will have to devote a larger and larger fraction of their foreign exchange earnings to imports during a period when their export growth rates will be decreasing. The percentage of all import costs consumed by fuels in the OIDCs increased from an average of 7 to 12 percent in 1972 to 15 to 30 percent in 1976 (World Bank 1979: 4). Table 8-1 demonstrates the severity of this trend for a selected group of less developed countries. Table 8-2 compares the proportion of merchandise export earnings consumed by energy imports in 1960 and 1977 for twenty countries. To make matters worse, the price booms experienced by some OIDCs in their commodity exports of 1973-1975 are not available in 1979 and 1980 to help compensate for the higher prices of oil and other imports.

The direct burden of increasing real prices for oil imports threatens to create enormous—perhaps even insoluble—balance-of-payments and debt service problems. Current account deficits in the OIDCs jumped by at least $33 billion, from $27.1 billion in 1978 to over $60 billion in 1980—an enormous shock to absorb over only two years. The overall annual debt service of the OIDCs grew from about $10 billion in 1973 and 1974 to over $30 billion in 1978. Furthermore, the level of reliance on external financing, especially from private sources, has skyrocketed at the same time when opportunities for commercial borrowing appear to be declining.[3]

Table 8-2 shows troubling data for twenty-one OIDCs: increases in their interest payments from 1970 to 1977; debt service a rising percentage of GNP and of exports; and growing energy imports as a

3. Debt service on commercial loans to the OIDCs grew from less than $6 billion in 1973 to over $23 billion in 1978.

Table 8–1. Structure of merchandise imports (*percentage share of merchandise imports*).

	Food		Fuels		Other Primary Commodities		Machinery and Transport Equipment		Other Manufactures	
	1960	1977	1960	1977	1960	1977	1960	1977	1960	1977
(OIDCs attempting to overhaul agricultural sector)										
Bangladesh	—	18	—	24	—	6	—	13	—	39
India	21	16	6	26	28	15	30	19	15	24
Pakistan	22	17	10	16	2	7	27	28	39	32
Philippines	15	10	10	24	5	7	36	26	34	33
Thailand	10	5	11	22	11	10	25	30	43	33
(OIDCs with heavy requirements for capital equipment imports)										
Jamaica	22	20	8	29	9	6	24	12	37	33

Source: Adapted from World Bank (1980: 128, 129).

| | Interest Payments on External Public Debt (millions of dollars) | | Debt Service as Percentage of: | | | | Energy Imports as a Percentage of Merchandise Exports | |
| | | | GNP | | Exports of Goods and Services | | | |
	1970	1978	1970	1978	1970	1978	1960	1977
Argentina	121	513	1.9	3.5	21.5	26.8	14	12
Bangladesh	—	42	—	1.3	—	11.7	—	48
Bolivia	6	83	2.2	8.5	10.9	48.7	4	1
Brazil	136	1,725	0.9	2.2	13.5	28.4	21	37
Burma	3	17	1.0	1.2	16.1	18.0	4	12
Chile	78	290	3.1	7.3	18.9	38.2	10	25
Costa Rica	7	63	2.9	7.2	9.7	23.0	7	13
El Salvador	4	13	0.9	0.8	3.6	2.6	6	10
Ethiopia	6	13	1.2	0.8	11.4	7.5	11	27
Guatemala	6	15	1.4	0.4	7.4	1.7	12	15
India	189	342	0.9	0.8	20.9	9.4	11	26
Jamaica	8	70	1.1	7.0	2.5	17.9	11	32
Kenya	11	45	2.6	2.4	7.9	8.3	18	24
Pakistan	76	179	1.9	2.1	21.6	12.2	17	33
Panama	7	130	3.0	25.2	7.7	39.2	—	—
Peru	43	317	2.4	7.4	11.6	31.1	4	23
Philippines	25	167	1.4	2.8	7.5	13.4	9	33
Sudan	13	36	1.2	1.4	10.7	9.4	8	26
Thailand	16	96	0.6	0.9	3.3	3.7	12	29
Turkey	42	182	1.3	0.9	16.3	11.0	16	79
Zaire	9	160	2.0	6.5	4.4	31.3	3	16

Source: World Bank (1980: 122, 123, 134, 135).

percentage of often weakening merchandise export earnings. Annual debt service is rapidly becoming a great drain on the economies of many OIDCs. And as oil price increases consume more and more of their export earnings, countries are borrowing on increasingly harder terms to fund unmanageable annual debt service and oil import requirements. The inability to cover oil imports with export earnings is already a serious problem for several countries. If it continues and spreads to others, it could become a severe structural dilemma for the international financial system.

Even before the Iranian Revolution, real balance-of-payments deficits in the OIDCs were three times higher in 1976–1977 than in 1972–1973. An overall oil import bill for the OIDCs of $30 billion in 1978 will help push the total current account deficit in 1980 over $68 billion, with oil imports easily topping $100 billion by 1985. These strains are reflected in an increase of debt service problems in the 1970s. The number of countries that have fallen behind in their multilateral debts jumped from three in 1974 to eighteen in 1978, and this increase occurred before the oil price shock of 1979 and 1980.

Creditworthiness will become a concern for both the relatively few middle-income countries enmeshed in commercial debt markets and many other OIDCs in the International Monetary Fund (IMF), World Bank, and other multilateral credit markets. Official aid can help, but it will not balance the deficits in the many countries without access to commercial debt because OPEC and OECD aid flows have not been increasing consistently. U.S. foreign aid problems threaten even traditional levels and channels, leaving no serious prospect for near-term improvement.

Yet another reason for a pessimistic prognosis for the OIDCs in the 1980s is the combination of high and persistent world and OIDC inflation and high interest rates. Aggregate average inflation levels over the period 1974 to 1977 increased from 7 to 11 percent per year for the industrial countries; from 7.5 to 14.8 percent for the oil exporters; and from 7.7 to 25 percent for the OIDCs. Brazil faced a 41 percent inflation rate in 1978 and over 80 percent in 1979. Higher interest rates now limit the previously positive effects of inflation in increasing real government revenues and reducing foreign debt.

By 1980, many OIDCs therefore faced declining or stagnant growth rates and dramatic inflation rates. (See Table 8–3.) But they are also beset by other economic and social ills that the energy situa-

	GDP—Average Annual Growth Rate (percent)		Average Annual Rate of Inflation (percent)		Income Distribution[a] (percent shares of household income)	
	1960–1970	1970–1978	1960–1970	1970–1978	Highest 20%	Highest 10%
Argentina	4.2	2.3	21.8	120.4	50.3	35.2
Bangladesh	3.6	2.9	3.7	17.9	–	–
Bolivia	5.2	5.6	3.5	22.7	–	–
Brazil	5.3	9.2	46.1	30.3	66.6	50.6
Burma	2.6	4.0	2.7	13.7	–	–
Chile	4.5	0.8	32.9	242.6	51.4	34.8
Costa Rica	6.5	6.0	1.9	15.7	54.8	39.5
El Salvador	5.9	5.2	0.5	10.3	–	–
Ethiopia	4.4	1.8	2.1	4.0	–	–
Guatemala	5.6	6.0	0.1	10.8	–	–
India	3.6	3.7	7.1	8.2	48.9	35.2
Jamaica	4.6	-0.8	3.8	16.9	–	–
Kenya	6.0	6.7	1.5	12.0	–	–
Pakistan	6.7	4.4	3.3	14.6	–	–
Panama	7.8	3.4	1.6	7.5	–	–
Peru	5.4	3.1	9.9	22.2	61.0	42.9
Philippines	5.1	6.3	5.8	13.4	53.9	–
Sudan	1.3	2.7	3.7	7.4	–	–
Thailand	8.2	7.6	1.9	9.1	–	–
Turkey	6.0	7.1	5.6	21.5	56.5	40.7
Zaire	3.6	1.3	29.9	26.2	–	–

a. These data are unreliable; quality and comparability are limited.

Source: World Bank (1980: 110–113, 156, 157).

tion will probably only aggravate in coming years. The lack of progress in income distribution and rapid rates of urbanization shown in Table 8−4 are especially threatening. A large number of middle-income OIDCs have one or two huge and very densely populated cities with a socially and politically explosive combination of paralyzed human services, underemployment, and unemployment. Some of these petroleum-reliant nations−especially those in Latin America−are experiencing rapid urbanization, rising social expectations, and the world's largest relative decreases in annual economic growth rates. By the late 1980s, almost 40 percent of the LDC populations will live in urban slum areas. Table 8−5 reveals striking decreases in annual GDP growth after 1974 for Latin America, even without removing oil-exporting countries such as Ecuador, Trinidad and Tobago, and Venezuela.

It is tempting to underestimate the serious plight of the very low-income OIDCs because of their small size and relative unimportance in international financial and commercial markets. Although they raise less attention and concern, their balance-of-payments and economic growth rate problems are the most virulent of all the oil-importing countries. Their primary commodity export markets are the weakest and most vulnerable to disruption by oil price increases and other fluctuations in the international economy. Official aid from developed countries, which these countries desperately need, consistently declines when their need is greatest. Countries such as Kenya and the Philippines are now being forced to drop or drastically revise economic development plans built on years of economic expectations and political commitment. When cuts must be made, human service programs are among the first to be abandoned.

As economic conditions change, especially abruptly, they affect and then are affected by a range of political variables. Economic factors lead directly or indirectly to such political events as protests, demonstrations, strikes, coups and revolutions, and crises, conflicts, and wars between nations. One working hypothesis to explain this phenomenon is that economic deterioration aggravates regional, ethnic, and religious tensions within a society. Abrupt fluctuations in real wages and inflation−whether up or down−seem to be particularly conducive to political change.[4]

4. See, for example, Davies (1962 and 1979); Duff & McCamant (1968); Gurr (1968, 1970); Miller (1977 & 1979); Tilly (1978); Olson (1963); and Goldstone (1980).

Urbanization

| | Urban Population | | | | Percentage of Urban Population in Cities of over 500,000 | | Adult Literacy Rate 1975 (percent) |
| | As Percentage of Total Population—1975 | | Average Annual Growth Rate (percent) | | | | |
	1960	1980	1960–1970	1970–1980	1960	1980	
Argentina	74	82	2.0	1.8	54	60	94
Bangladesh	5	11	6.5	6.6	20	51	26
Bolivia	24	33	4.1	4.3	0	44	63
Brazil	46	65	4.8	4.3	35	52	76
Burma	19	27	3.9	4.0	23	29	67
Chile	68	81	3.1	2.4	38	44	88
Costa Rica	37	43	4.2	3.4	0	64	90
El Salvador	38	41	3.2	3.4	0	0	62
Ethiopia	6	15	6.1	6.9	0	37	10
Guatemala	33	39	3.6	3.7	41	36	47
India	18	22	3.3	3.3	26	47	36
Jamaica	34	50	3.5	3.6	0	65	86
Kenya	7	14	6.6	6.8	0	57	40
Pakistan	22	28	4.0	4.3	33	52	21
Panama	41	54	4.4	3.9	0	33	78
Peru	46	67	5.0	4.4	38	44	72
Philippines	30	36	3.9	3.6	27	36	87
Sudan	10	25	6.9	6.8	0	31	20
Thailand	13	14	3.7	3.5	65	68	84
Turkey	30	47	5.1	4.6	32	42	60
Zaire	16	34	5.2	7.2	14	38	15

Source: World Bank (1980: 110, 111, 148, and 149).

Table 8–5. Latin America: Annual variations in gross domestic product[a], by countries, 1961–1978 (*percentages*).

Country	1961–1965	1966–1970	1971–1974	1975	1976	1977	1978[b]
Argentina	4.5	4.3	5.1	-1.3	-2.9	4.2	-4.1
Bahamas	NA	NA	NA	-6.8	2.1	3.5	5.9
Barbados	2.4	7.5	2.6	1.3	3.8	4.7	4.3
Bolivia	3.9	6.4	6.0	5.5	6.4	3.6	3.1
Brazil	4.5	7.7	12.2	5.7	9.0	4.7	6.0
Chile	5.0	3.9	2.4	-11.3	4.1	8.6	6.0
Colombia	4.7	5.8	6.7	3.8	4.6	4.8	7.9
Costa Rica	4.6	7.4	7.1	2.1	5.5	7.8	5.9
Dominican Republic	3.1	7.7	10.0	5.2	6.4	4.4	3.6
Ecuador	5.3	5.7	12.1	3.4	9.7	6.4	6.8
El Salvador	6.9	4.5	5.4	5.6	3.9	5.2	4.4
Guatemala	5.3	5.8	6.5	1.9	7.4	8.4	5.2
Guyana	3.3	3.9	1.9	11.1	5.0	-6.0	-1.0
Haiti	0.7	1.0	3.7	0.4	7.3	3.1	4.9
Honduras	5.5	4.3	3.4	-1.6	7.4	7.0	7.9
Jamaica	4.7	6.3	3.0	-1.0	-6.7	-4.0	-3.0
Mexico	7.2	6.9	6.1	4.1	1.7	3.2	6.6
Nicaragua	10.1	3.8	6.5	2.2	5.6	6.1	-5.9
Panama	8.2	7.7	6.0	0.6	-0.3	0.9	2.7
Paraguay	4.8	4.2	6.4	5.0	7.5	11.8	9.8
Peru	6.7	4.4	5.4	4.3	3.4	0.3	-1.8

Trinidad and Tobago	4.9	3.2	1.9	6.8	10.8	7.0	6.1
Uruguay	−.9	2.3	−0.1	4.4	2.6	3.4	2.3
Venezuela	7.3	4.6	4.7	5.2	7.8	6.8	6.5
Latin America	5.3	5.9	7.5	3.1	4.7	4.5	4.3

a. At constant market prices with reference to the base year used by each country. For Latin America, the figures were calculated by converting national values into dollars of 1976 purchasing power.

b. Preliminary estimates.

NA = Not Available.

Source: Inter-American Development Bank, based on official statistics of the member countries.

Reprinted from *Economic and Social Progress in Latin America*, 1978 report (Inter-American Development Bank, Washington, D.C.).

Even lacking much of the evidence required to show causal relations, it is possible to isolate economic conditions or indicators that warn of impending political change. Rapid increases in the price of oil imports, for example, may or may not be passed on to consumers by a national government. If passed on, price increases in essential commodities such as kerosene for heating and cooking or diesel fuel for transport and electrical generation can trigger the entire range of political protest and violence. When passed on only in part or not at all, oil import costs are subsidized by governments. In many OIDCs, such subsidies are causing increasingly severe burdens on government revenues, public and private investment (especially in energy resource development), the foreign exchange available for imports, the balance-of-payments, and debt service burdens. Governments are thus forced to reduce economic growth rates, borrow heavily in international capital markets, or both. Most OIDCs have only one option—borrow as much as possible from the IMF and then cut economic growth as necessary.

In short, when higher energy prices are not passed on to the consumer, the resulting economic problems undercut the political system's ability to maintain normal social and economic activity and public order. When these costs are passed on, protests and demonstrations against the government frequently result. Specific examples of this pattern are numerous: the demonstrations in the Philippines in the early and late 1970s and in Jamaica in 1979; strikes in Jamaica and Peru in 1979; and violent protests in the Philippines in the 1970s and in Brazil and Jamaica in 1979.

Foreign Policy Costs

Internal political change interacts directly and indirectly with foreign policies and international political events (Snyder and Diesing 1977: 510–530; Goldstone 1980). A weakened coalition government, for example, may be more likely either to invite coercion by another country or to take similar action against a neighbor to gain control of domestic political events. Such actions may, in turn, induce direct or indirect intervention by a regional power or a superpower. Regional balances of power and disputes, especially over boundaries, are also aggravated by the location of energy resources. Crises and even conflict in the Third World may now become increasingly visible and threatening to international security (Hopple and Rossa 1979). OIDCs thus face some of the same types of internal, regional, and international energy and security threats as the Persian Gulf nations reviewed in Chapter 3.

For the OIDCs, the foreign policy costs of their energy dependence include heavy pressure for acceptance of Arab political positions as a price for special concessions and aid. Meanwhile the United States and the Soviet Union offer vitally needed aid—for a price, too. Perhaps most important for the longer term bargaining power of the OIDCs is their gradual split with OPEC over oil price increases. Their unique foreign policy challenge is to maintain their alignment with the oil exporters on general resource management issues while preventing and coping with the effects of oil price increases.

Political instability and foreign policy costs in the OIDCs can also affect U.S. foreign policy and security. At stake are vital U.S. trade and financial interests, rights to military bases and facilities, foreign policy objectives, and the overriding commitment to avoid war. If growth continues to be constrained in the OIDCs, trade will suffer worldwide. The fastest growing trade sector for many industrialized countries is with the less-developed countries. U.S. exports to the Third World reached $42 billion in 1977, including 50, 60, and 70 percent respectively of wheat, cotton, and rice exports. Over the 1970s these U.S. exports grew at an average annual rate of 22 percent, as compared to 15 percent for exports to industrialized nations.

No matter what conditions prevail in the oil market, balance-of-payments financing and international monetary stability link the vital foreign policy interests of the OIDCs with those of the OECD countries. The United States has special powers, responsibilities, and risks through the commercial banking institutions, the public international banks, and even the Eurocurrency market. As discussed in Chapter 11, creditworthiness and liquidity already demand attention as threats to the economic stability of at least several OIDCs. In the event of a major disruption of oil supplies, this problem could be severely aggravated, forcing many OIDCs to curtail economic growth drastically.

Revolutions, coups, or even cabinet changes in countries such as Turkey, the Philippines, and Panama could end or severely limit American use of critical military bases. Communications stations and air force bases in Turkey, air stations and a large naval base in the Philippines, and many other facilities worldwide could be shut down as abruptly as the U.S. bases in Iran. In many OIDCs, especially those with severe economic problems, foreign military bases are themselves a political liability for the governing regime since they provide a continual target for use in mobilizing political opposition groups.

Third World crises, instability, or shifts in alignment caused by economic or energy problems and by pressure from OPEC nations can be controlling factors over U.S. foreign policy objectives. Our ability to muster votes in the U.N., mediate the Middle East peace negotiations, verify strategic arms control treaties, and maintain military alliances all depend on the economic and political capacity of OIDCs such as India, Turkey, and Brazil. Our supreme foreign policy objective of avoiding war also demands attention to numerous territorial disputes such as those in the South China Sea or the Aegean Sea, which are aggravated by energy resources, and to regional crises and conflicts involving countries such as Pakistan, Thailand, and the Sudan. When added to massive refugee problems and other results of regional conflict, economic strains from oil imports can easily trigger regime changes. Existing and emerging commitments in South Asia, Central America and the Caribbean, and East Africa may draw the Soviet Union and the United States into regional conflicts.

ECONOMIC AND POLITICAL EFFECTS
IN KEY COUNTRIES

The patterns of energy production and consumption in the OIDCs obviously vary widely. It would be impractical to discuss every one of these eighty-five nations' energy security problems. Nor would it be particularly helpful to divide up the OIDCs into groups and discuss representative countries, since various analysts have proposed any number of classification schemes and none of them has won general acceptance. Therefore, we will demonstrate the economic and political effects of oil price increases by sketching the situations of four OIDCs of particular importance to the United States and to regional security: Brazil, Turkey, the Philippines, and Pakistan. Each of these important countries suffers from severe oil import burdens. In 1977, over 30 percent of their aggregate merchandise export earnings were consumed by energy imports; in Turkey, that figure reached 80 percent. They also span a wide range of national income levels, from 1978 per capita GNP of $230 in Pakistan to $1270 in Brazil.

Brazil

In 1980, Brazil confronted an extraordinary and alarming situation: its oil imports of $7 billion and debt service obligations of some $13 billion exceeded all export earnings. And yet, as Table 8—5 shows, until 1977 Brazil's GDP had grown faster than that of any other country in Latin America. Balance-of-payments deficits, interest payments, and foreign borrowing had been increased rapidly since 1973 in order to support the maximum feasible rate of economic growth.

Brazil imported about 800,000 barrels of oil per day in 1973. That oil cost $600 million. By 1979, oil imports had increased to only 960,000 barrels, but those barrels cost about $7 billion (*The Economist* 1980: 21—32). Even the 15 percent annual average growth in exports from 1974 to 1979 could not long sustain the levels of economic growth recorded in Table 8—5. Inflation was rampant in 1979 and 1980, and net debt service alone consumed about two-thirds of all export earnings. Foreign debt grew at an average of over 25 percent per year from 1974 to 1979; while total debt service increased over 500 percent, total private debt grew over 600 percent between 1972 and 1978.

Despite strong and relatively successful efforts to slow the growth of oil imports and continued heavy international borrowing, the Brazilian economy is now contracting. Growth rates were progressively reduced to 5 percent or even less by 1980 despite the fact that 7 percent is required to provide jobs each year for only the new entrants into the labor market. Even if continued borrowing to cover annual debt service and strong export growth are possible, export earnings will be more than consumed by the costs of petroleum imports and debt service for the foreseeable future.

The combined pressures of escalating unemployment, unprecedented inflation, rapid urbanization, and high population growth rates are aggravating crime, violence, and opposition to the government. Labor groups and opposition parties are increasingly active and successfully eroding the political support for the government's national party. It remains unclear what will happen to Brazil's military authoritarian government before and during the election due in 1982. Its fate is important to the international financial system, U.S. foreign policy, and regional security.

Turkey

With sixty years of experience with democratic government and a 1978 per capita income of $1200, Turkey falls right on the dividing line between developing and developed nations.[5] In 1980, it too confronted an extraordinary set of economic conditions. Even holding annual debt service payments aside, the cost of imports was *several times* that of all export earnings. Like Brazil, Turkey enjoyed rapid economic growth through the mid-1970s—averaging 6.5 percent per year from 1947 to 1977 and 7.7 percent from 1970 to 1976. From 1974 to 1977, growth in the commercial energy sector was based on oil imports for 70 percent of all consumption.

Turkey has long relied on the economic strategy called import substitution: manufacturing local goods to replace imports while placing little emphasis on export markets, including tourism. This approach created a severe vulnerability to external shocks. Faced with the crisis of 1973 and 1974 and the world recession of 1975, the Turkish government chose to maintain rapid economic growth through deficit financing and public sector spending. The domestic economy was insulated from oil price increases through a special fund to subsidize the price of gasoline. This fund helped support real wages and profits for a while, but it intensified the effect of the oil crisis on the balance of payments since it weakened any possible incentives to substitute other fuel for oil. Monetary supply was increased in part to help keep several major public enterprises solvent. The only means to allow the chosen high levels of domestic consumption was to use foreign reserves and then borrow, even in the Eurodollar market.

Although politically popular in the first few years, this economic strategy could not be maintained. Inflation was estimated at 40 percent in 1977, 50 percent in 1978, almost 60 percent by 1979, and 100 percent in 1980. As the inevitable cuts in imported petroleum

---

5. Turkey's per capita income in 1978 was less than two-thirds that of Portugal, and the lowest among the OECD countries.

and other raw materials were made, industrial capacity became 50 percent idle by 1979 and unemployment grew from about 14 percent in 1978 to over 20 percent in 1979 (Szaz 1979; World Bank 1978).

In 1970, export earnings covered about two-thirds of the bill for imports; remittances from workers in other countries, especially in Western Europe, covered the rest. As the recession hit all OECD countries in 1975, Turkey's export markets in these countries lagged and many of the workers abroad lost their jobs and returned home. By 1976, exports covered only 40 percent, and remittances 20 percent, of import costs. Workers' remittances, which decreased from $1.4 billion in 1974 to $1 billion, declined to about 15 percent of imports by 1977. Current account deficits were growing rapidly even before a large jump in 1978. Export earnings in 1977 amounted to only $1.7 billion as compared to import costs of $5.8 billion. The cost of energy imports alone in 1977 consumed 79 percent of all export earnings (World Bank 1980).

Outstanding debt reached $10 billion by 1977 and $12 billion in 1979. By 1977 and 1978 Turkey began to fall behind in debt service payments. The first major rescheduling of debt, at the $1.2 billion level, consisted of two steps: a stabilization program enacted with the IMF in April 1978 to allow Turkey to draw on the Compensatory Financing Facility, and an overall agreement with the consortium of OECD nations leading to the bilateral rescheduling of debts and loans. Several months later it became obvious that old and new debts, combined with critical current imports, exceeded all resources. More help was essential. West Germany emerged from the Summit Meeting of January 1979 in Guadaloupe as the leader of another economic rescue mission.

Since this package of about $1.5 billion in rescheduled dents, new loans, and economic assistance was delayed and new problems arose with the IMF, the Ecevit government decided to impose a new austerity program in early 1979. The plan helped meet IMF and bilateral economic conditions, as well as cope with obvious problems. Prices of petroleum, especially gasoline, and other products were raised sharply as a means of allocating severe shortages. New emphasis was directed to controlling the rate of increase in domestic consumption, reducing inflation, accelerating exports and investments by foreign companies, cutting unemployment, and using productive capacity more efficiently.

Coincident with the U.S. arms embargo of Turkey and the 1975 worldwide economic recession was a dramatic increase in antigovernment demonstrations and riots. Four major demonstrations and five riots occurred during 1975. Economic improvements during 1976 were accompanied by a sharp decrease in such demonstrations and riots. Tightening economic conditions since 1977 may have been reflected in the sharply increasing number of demonstrations, riots, and assassinations. These events may indicate social and political strains induced in part by oil price increases.

The agricultural sector has for some time been hampered by low incomes and structural problems such as weak public and private investment. Economic difficulties since the mid-1970s accelerated the flight of rural poor into the cities, contributing to an explosive combination of rapid urbanization, high population growth rates, inflation, and unemployment. Compared with trends over the past twenty years, the recent levels of general crime and violence, urban terrorism and gang warfare, and protest against the government are unprecedented. Over 2,000 people died in political violence in Turkey during the first eight months of 1980.[6]

There can be little doubt that Turkey's oil import burden and rapidly deteriorating economy in the late 1970s were important background factors to the military coup of September 1980. On two prior occasions, in 1960 and 1971, the military temporarily seized control to stabilize economic and political conditions. In both cases the government was returned to civilian control.

Yet since the second return to civilian control in 1973, neither the Social Democratic Government of ex-Prime Minister Demirel nor the more conservative Government of Ecevit has been able to capture a majority in Parliament. The result has been weak governing coalitions and an average of over one change in government per year in the 1970s. This increased the need of each government to rely on smaller, more extreme parties, and decreased their capability to manage the economy.

For the two months prior to the bloodless military coup in September 1980, Parliament was unable to select a new president. The economy seemed out of control, with inflation running at about 130 percent, and political violence was rampant. The political system was

6. In September 1980 the military government announced that the actual number of deaths from political violence during this period was 5,000.

so paralyzed that many people seemed relieved when the military finally followed through on their many threats to again seize power for an interim period.

The Philippines

Despite optimistic estimates that Philippine oil production will increase from 15,000 barrels per day in 1979 to 100,000 in 1985, current dependence on oil imports is over 80 percent of all energy use. In 1976, the Philippines imported about 200,000 barrels per day at a cost of over $850 million. By 1978 oil import costs topped $1 billion. At then-current prices, the bill for their 210,000 barrels per day of imports in 1979 would be about $2.5 to $3 billion. Energy imports consumed over one-third of all export earnings and over one-fourth of all import costs in 1977. The government recently revised the goal of its energy development program to reduce oil imports to 50 percent of all energy use by 1985 rather than by 1990.

Given their strategic location and the strength of their human and natural resources, the Philippines' economic growth rates have never been impressive. The per capita GNP in 1978 was $510, about the same as that of Bolivia and Thailand. Average annual growth rates of GDP were 5.1 percent from 1960 to 1970 and 6.4 percent for 1970 to 1977. If the Marcos regime is reporting accurate statistics, growth rates held at about 5.6 percent for 1978, and 6.5 percent for 1979.

The government's strategy for coping with increasing import costs emphasizes productive capacity and export-led growth. Recent approaches imitate the Japanese and South Korean trading companies with major public loans and tax credits. Manufactured goods and related products have grown well since 1975, providing 40 percent of export earnings in 1979 and perhaps 50 percent in 1980. Other exports, however, have done much worse. Coconuts, sugar, minerals, and forest products face protected markets and fluctuating prices. Low sugar prices in 1979 and weak coconut oil prices in early 1980 cut export earnings severely.

Rather than reduce economic growth further, the government has expanded the money supply, imposed new taxes, and borrowed heavily in international capital markets. Inflation averaged over 13 percent from 1970 to 1978 and reached about double that level in 1979. Price controls have been eased, but the price of petroleum products—the principal accelerator of inflation—cannot rise without government approval. Despite some recent price increases, basic food products and most petroleum products are still heavily subsidized.

Current account deficits increased to $876 million in 1978, about $1.5 billion in 1979, and may exceed $2 billion for 1980. Total debt service and total private debt service have also increased dramatically, including heavy borrowing in the Eurodollar market, and may rise again from $1.56 billion in 1979 to about $2 billion in 1980 (*Far Eastern Economic Review* 1979).

President Marcos clearly prefers IMF-imposed economic conditions to rapid price increases, especially for petroleum products. The Philippines was the first country to complete a three-year IMF stabilization program. In 1979 it became the first nation to obtain a second agreement, which provided medium-term funds through the Extended Fund Facility in return for the imposition of even stricter economic conditions.

Each government attempt to raise prices for petroleum products invokes immediate and strong public reaction. Prior to Marcos's imposition of martial law in late 1972, a number of such announced price increases provoked antigovernment demonstrations and violent riots. In February 1980, a major presidential speech proposing a 50 percent increase in gasoline prices to over $2.00 per gallon and smaller price increases for other products touched off panic buying, shortages, and protests. Similar events were sparked in July of 1980 by proposed increases in taxes and levies on petroleum products. Just before and after Marcos's state of the nation address, students led demonstrations and ultimately clashed with police and crowd dispersal units. These actions also reflect more fundamental pressures arising from massive urbanization problems in Manila, rapid population growth rates, accelerating inflation and unemployment, and losses in real wages due to inflation. They may be important indicators of latent problems and opposition because all such political activity is banned and treated seriously under the longstanding conditions of martial law.

Pakistan

Pakistan's 1978 per capita GNP of $230 ranks it in the middle of what the World Bank terms the low-income countries. Its oil imports averaged about 77,000 barrels per day in 1976, representing an annual growth rate of less than 1 percent since 1970. Oil use per capita in 1976 was one-fourth of that in the Philippines, one-sixth of that in Turkey, and one-eighth of that in Brazil.

But by 1976 fuel imports reached 18 percent of all imports, and in 1977 they exceeded one-third of all merchandise export earnings. These trends are reflected in weakening terms of trade and a doubling of interest payments on public debt between 1970 and 1977, even though the deficit on current account was essentially unchanged between 1970 and 1977. Overall debt service and total private debt service increased relatively little, except in 1978. The explanation for this relatively strong performance centers on workers' remittances. During 1972 and 1973, about 138,000 Pakistanis worked abroad. By 1978 and 1979 this number had risen to between 1.7 and 2.7 million, about 80 percent of whom reside in OPEC countries. Although much of the remitted funds end up in real estate and other local investments, the net effect is a major export industry for Pakistan.

Even so, Pakistan faces very rapid population growth, slow economic growth, and increasing inflation. Demonstrations, strikes, and violent protests have been staged against the government for most of the last five or six years.

POLICY RESPONSES

Given the economic structure and needs of most OIDCs over the next decade, energy self-sufficiency is an unrealistic, if not counterproductive, goal. Most OIDCs will continue to rely on current or even greater levels of petroleum imports, especially of the light products that cannot be produced locally. More energy can and must be produced locally, and much remains to be done in the management of demand, especially product pricing.

But these necessary steps do not exhaust the practical responses that can be made to limit, and ultimately to reduce, the OIDCs' increasing vulnerability to external shocks. A combination of domestic, bilateral, and multilateral policy measures must be tailored to the specific circumstances of each OIDC. These developing nations and others interested in their welfare and stability must do what they can, knowing that everything they do attempt may be overwhelmed by any severe oil supply disruptions in the 1980s.

Domestic Responses

Every OIDC should develop a domestic energy security program with at least four components. Most important are preparations for short-term disruptions of oil supplies. Finding substitutes for oil is a critical element of these preparations. There should be continuing efforts to displace gasoline and diesel in the transportation sector and new emphasis on substitutes in industrial and agricultural uses and in electricity generation. Small- and large-scale hydroelectric power and even coal can displace oil in current and future power stations. Nuclear power stations may also eventually replace oil for electrical generation in a few OIDCs, but not on a time scale relevant to the energy security problem.

It may be prohibitively expensive to hold large stockpiles of crude or oil products, but the option should be considered seriously. Direct embargoes by oil producers against OIDCs may be unlikely, but producers do use oil exports as tools of their foreign policies and accidental interruptions affect OIDCs at least as quickly as they do other oil-importing countries. Brazil, for example, lost a staggering 400,000 barrels per day of oil from Iraq—almost one half its imports—as a result of the war with Iran in 1980. In all OIDCs, but particularly where large stockpiles are financially difficult, preparations should also be made for emergency taxes to reduce demand and for short-term emergency distribution plans to allocate oil for essential uses such as fire, police, and medical services.

The second set of advisable energy security measures addresses demand management. There may well be serious political opposition to energy price increases in many OIDCs, but realistic pricing policies are absolutely essential to macroeconomic management. Low prices distort both demand and supply and help create shortages, which are also politically explosive. If prices do not approach world levels, it is extremely difficult for many countries to maintain current oil production levels and to attract foreign investment for new exploration and production. There may be clear cases for exceptions, such as kerosene or naptha used by the poor for heating, but even here some price signals may become necessary to encourage improved efficiencies in consumption and the introduction of substitute fuels.

Access to crude oil refining capacity, required refined products, and transportation for crude and products forms a third set of issues.

The OIDCs must improve both their own capabilities and their access to foreign capabilities in all three areas. In the cases where OIDCs have some local refining capability, simpler technology produces a greater proportion of heavier products. This makes them highly vulnerable to disruptions in types of imports, especially the lighter products, as well as in quantities. During supply disruptions, they may be quickly forced into spot markets for access to the most expensive products. This calls for upgrading of local refineries or arrangements for access to products or refinery capacity elsewhere.

The trend of increasing government-to-government contracts discussed in Chapter 2 is particularly strong in the OIDCs. During past supply interruptions, OIDCs have generally had access to oil in producing countries if they could find adequate tankers and refining capacity. They must, therefore, also pursue arrangements now that would provide emergency transportation.

The final domestic response to the energy security emergency should be to control permanently or reduce oil imports. In many cases, OIDCs will be hard-pressed over the next decade to do so. For the middle-income countries in particular, economic growth rates are high and energy use per unit of production is much greater than in the industrial nations. As income levels rise and urbanization and industrialization accelerate, many OIDCs will demand more energy.

We are already beginning to see an accelerating shift away from traditional fuels and toward oil in many developing countries. Better forestry and land management programs to halt environmental degradation could do much to preserve traditional energy sources.

Bilateral Responses

Beyond the prudent management of energy security policies at home, the most important remedial actions that OIDCs can take are bilateral. Three in particular demand urgent attention: concessional oil prices; access to trade markets; and guarantees of oil supplies during emergencies. Iraq provided over $170 million in long-term interest-free loans to poor OIDCs in 1979 to offset surcharges on oil contracts. Other OPEC producers kept sales to OIDCs at official contract prices in 1979 to help on access and price. Venezuela and Mexico have provided some oil to regional OIDCs at reduced rates, but most assistance takes the form of grants and loans to offset price increases. Many of these transactions are done quietly, with the express intent of avoiding wider pressure for price concessions. The real extent of such arrangements is unknown.

Trade questions are also best handled bilaterally. In negotiations with the oil exporters, OIDCs must work to uncover new export markets and create every possible opportunity for barter deals and local investment. With OECD and COMECON countries, the developing nations should find new exports, gain access to markets for manufactured products, and maintain reasonably steady demand for traditional exports. None of these areas offers bright prospects due to slowed economic growth in industrial countries and conservative financial and monetary policies in most oil-producing nations. Even so, more may be gained between countries than on the broader multilateral level. Continuing increases are also essential in the growing trade and investment between OIDCs.

Bilateral assistance should also be accelerated in developing renewable and commercial energy resources and in managing traditional fuels. Producing countries can be drawn on for increasing technical assistance, especially in oil production and contract negotiations with the multinational companies. This assistance should also be extended to refining industries and transportation arrangements. OECD countries can do much more serious training of OIDC officials in energy security planning and management.

Multilateral Responses

Broad international efforts toward operational activities are frequently inefficient or impossible, but less ambitious multilateral agreements can become invaluable catalysts of much-needed reform. OPEC in particular is a crucial forum for negotiations to avoid sharp price increases for OIDC oil imports, to support bilateral or even broader concessions on oil prices, and to motivate increasing purchases by oil producers of real and financial assets in the OIDCs.

The OECD, including the IEA, can at least clarify and emphasize OIDC needs for help from the industrial countries. OECD efforts in comparative data collection and distribution can help on aid flows, macroeconomic policies, trade policies, and foreign investment affecting the OIDCs. The OECD should be used even more by Western industrial governments as a forum for exchanging commitments to avoid behavior harmful to the OIDCs, especially strongly deflationary policies; protection by OECD governments of weak traditional sectors in their industry and agriculture; and decreasing aid flows. It can also be used to offset the unconstructive policies of other organizations, such as the severe European Community barriers to agricultural imports from Turkey and other oil-importing countries.

An increasingly urgent result of oil price effects on OIDCs is a requirement for careful monitoring of balance-of-payments financing and international debt management. International financial policy responses to these problems are assessed in Chapter 11. Although the magnitude of the financing requirements in the 1980s can only be met by the commercial banks, the IMF and the World Bank must clearly also become more involved. Reductions in the conditions and increases in the volumes of IMF balance-of-payments financing can help. Yet allowing countries continually to roll over debt service commitments and in effect to finance increasing debt service with loans on harder terms will not solve the problem. Unless there is real progress in increasing OIDC exports, gaining concessional oil-import pricing, and improving bilateral foreign aid flows, the international financial institutions are unlikely to be able to handle the recycling burden alone. Recycling was handled surprisingly well in the mid–1970s, but strains on the system are accumulating in unprecedented fashion. New oil supply interruptions in the 1980s, which are quite likely, will further strain the system. Advance preparations for larger, but temporary, international financial assistance are absolutely essential if these interruptions are not to have disastrous consequences.

Foreign aid and cooperative resource development projects form a further set of multilateral responses. The new World Bank program in commercial fuels development can be important if it facilitates local OIDC initiatives, multinational corporate investments, regional development bank projects, and bilateral assistance. Arguments that OIDC absorptive capacity is saturated in energy programs and investments do not stand up to empirical evidence. Much more can be done, especially with programmatic rather than specific project assistance. The OECD, the European Community, OPEC, Arab development funds, UN organizations such as the UNDP, and various cooperative arrangements among the OIDCs must also stimulate private sector investment and contribute badly needed funds to energy development in the OIDCs.

These institutions are also essential catalysts for multilateral and bilateral programs in technology transfer, such as in solar energy and in energy planning and management. Even when the institution itself cannot provide assistance directly, it can stimulate government tax incentives, local business ventures, and loans from regional development banks.

CONCLUSION

Only in the late 1970s did some of the industrial countries and nongovernmental organizations begin to focus on energy problems in the OIDCs. For various reasons, most of the OECD, centrally planned, and OPEC countries have been obsessed with nursing their own economies since the oil embargo of 1973. In order to assert solidarity with OPEC on broad international economic and political principles, the OIDCs avoided any public discussion of energy issues until after the second round of price increases in 1979. Even now, many OECD countries are only concerned about possible competition from the OIDCs for scarce oil in the next decades.

The World Bank, a leader among multilateral organizations, started its fossil fuels development program in 1979—almost six years after the 1973—1974 watershed. The social, economic, political, and security implications for the OIDCs and the OECD countries of the world oil market after recent events in Iran demand quicker and deeper action by governments and other organizations worldwide.

Energy resources are, more than ever before, international commodities. Their rates of production, consumption, and conversion in many countries affect the economic growth and social well-being of people around the world. Pricing of and access to petroleum now dominate the activities of nations in the international economy and have enormous welfare and security implications for countries worldwide. Under both normal and disrupted oil market conditions, issues of creditworthiness and liquidity in the OIDCs link their vital foreign policy interests with those of the OECD nations, especially the United States. The OIDCs are finally calling for assistance from other countries, the private sector, and international organizations in managing energy problems. The importance of cooperation in such areas as developing and marketing new energy technologies is now apparent. What may not yet be clear is that the OIDCs, as well as the OECD nations, must be prepared for new and worse oil supply and price disruptions in the 1980s.

For at least the next decade, OIDCs will remain extremely vulnerable to external energy price and supply shocks. Countries such as Turkey and the Philippines will face severe pressure to adopt foreign policies sympathetic to the goals of the oil exporters, especially to cut all ties with Israel and to support an independent Palestinian state. Weaker economic growth in the OECD and COMECON nations will only make OIDC problems worse: the growth of OIDC export earnings is unlikely to keep pace with increasing import costs, especially for petroleum, and harder economic times will weaken foreign aid flows from the industrial nations. Aggravated by increased energy costs, economic pressures on OIDCs will intensify. Even with prudent macroeconomic management, governments may face untenable political opposition to the direct and indirect effects of increasing energy prices. As crime rates, student and union protests, and violent rioting confront governments, it may become increasingly difficult to hold governing coalitions together and to enact sound fiscal and monetary policies.

The OIDCs' stake in energy and security issues will increase faster than their power to influence international events. Therefore, they need help in defining their individual energy security problems and domestic policy responses. Urgent attention must be paid to stockpiles and allocation plans for oil supply and price emergencies. Special bilateral arrangements must be negotiated between oil producers and the world's poorest oil consumers. And international agencies must start making up for the time they have lost. Only by becoming directly involved in these preparations can U.S. foreign policy help contain imminent threats to international security.

REFERENCES

The Economist. 1980. May 17: 21-32.

Davies, James C. 1962. "Toward a Theory of Revolution." American Sociological Review XXVII (February): 5-19.

_____. 1979. "Communication." American Political Science Review 75: 825-830.

Duff, Ernest A., and John F. McCamant. 1968. "Measuring Social and Political Requirements for System Stability in Latin America." American Political Science Review 62 (December): 1125-1143.

Far Eastern Economic Review. 1979. September 14: 58.

Goldstone, Jack A. 1980. "Theories of Revolution: The Third Generation." World Politics 32: 425-453.

Gurr, Ted Robert. 1968. "A Causal Model of Civil Strife: A Comparative Analysis Using New Indices." American Political Science Review 62 (December): 1104-1124.

_____. 1970. Why Men Rebel. Princeton, N.J.: Princeton University Press.

Hopple, Gerald W., and Paul J. Rossa. 1979. "International Crisis Analysis: Recent Developments and Future Directions." International Studies Association, Annual Convention paper.

Inter-American Development Bank. 1978. Economic and Social Progress in Latin America. Washington, D.C.: Inter-American Development Bank.

Miller, Abraham H., Louis H. Bolce, and Mark Halligan. 1977. "The J-Curve Theory and the Black Urban Riots: An Empirical Test of Progressive Relative Deprivation Theory." American Political Science Review 71: 964-82.

Miller, Abraham H. and Louis H. Bolce. 1979. "Communication." American Political Science Review 73: 818-21.

Olson, Jr., Mancur. 1963. "Rapid Growth as a Destabilizing Force." Journal of Economic History 23: 529-552.

Snyder, Glen H., and Paul Diesing. 1977. Conflict Among Nations. Princeton, N.J.: Princeton University Press.

Szaz, Z. Michael. 1979. NATO Security and the Turkish Economy. Washington, D.C.: American Foreign Policy Institute.

Tilly, Charles. 1978. From Mobilization to Revolution. Reading, Mass.: Addison-Wesley.

World Bank. 1978. The Foreign Exchange Gap, Growth and Industrial Strategy in Turkey: 1973-1983. Staff Working Paper No. 306, November.

_____. 1979. Energy Options and Policy Issues in Developing Countries. Paper No. 350, August.

_____. 1980. World Development Report 1980.

U. S. ENERGY
SECURITY POLICY

9 IMPORT MANAGEMENT AND OIL EMERGENCIES

William W. Hogan

Oil emergencies capture public attention. A sudden loss of production, chaos on the world market, dizzying jumps in prices, gasoline queues, freezing in the dark, economic collapse, war. The spiral downward is easy to imagine but difficult to face. During the seventies we were surprised by the severity of our oil problem. Today we are confused by the complex variety of programs to meet the security threat to our oil supply.

A main assumption of U.S. energy policy in the seventies was that reducing oil imports would directly improve oil security. From Project Independence in 1973 to the Energy Security Act of 1980, long-run, expensive programs to increase domestic supply and reduce domestic demand appealed for support in the name of national security. But the connection between oil insecurity and dependence on imports may be weaker than we thought. At least two characteristics of the oil market suggest that we may have overemphasized import reduction policies and neglected the actions that are needed to truly improve oil security.

First, dependence is not necessarily vulnerability. If world oil production were distributed among many small producers, each unlikely

I thank Alvin Alm, Michael Barron, Francis Bator, Hung Po Chao, David Deese, Glen Hubbard, Henry Jacoby, Joseph Kalt, David Kline, Henry Lee, Thomas Neville, Joseph Nye, Lucien Pugliaresi, Henry Rowen, Thomas Schelling, James Sweeney, Thomas Teisberg, John Weyant, and Daniel Yergin for their comments and contributions.

261

suddenly to cease producing, even a high level of oil imports would reflect little vulnerability to supply interruptions. Although we are not likely to reach this condition soon, it does illustrate the distinction between *import dependence*, which is not dangerous in itself, and *import vulnerability*, which is. Even in the present oil market, with a few large but insecure sources of supply, protection from cut-offs could be found by creating excess capacity in the oil system. With a large strategic oil stockpile, for instance, the United States could weather a supply interruption at low cost; under such conditions, our vulnerability would be low even though we continued to be highly dependent on imports. It follows therefore that import reduction policies that neither create excess capacity nor lower the likelihood of interruption may provide few security benefits.

Second, energy autarky is an illusion. The world oil market is an integrated system, and our security depends very much on the security of our allies. A large reduction in oil imports would not protect the United States, or any other country, from a proportionate share of the total loss in supply during an interruption. Even if we had the market power, we could not stand idly by and watch our allies bear the full brunt of a supply interruption; we would share our oil with them. Hence, only by reducing the dependence of *all* importing countries can we begin to achieve energy security. But even the most optimistic observers do not foresee the world's early weaning away from the 20 million barrels per day produced in the Persian Gulf. Complete oil independence is not within our reach.

The challenge, then, is to develop policies that achieve reduced dependence *and* reduced vulnerability. This chapter summarizes how import-management programs and preparations for meeting an oil emergency can contribute to the success of such an energy policy.

OIL IMPORT REDUCTIONS

The United States should reduce its oil imports. The present import subsidy through the entitlements program drains our national wealth and increases our dependence on unstable sources of oil supply.[1]

---

1. In an effort to equalize costs for all sources of oil, the entitlements programs gives a refiner an "entitlement" to more cheap domestic oil with every barrel of expensive oil imported.

Domestic oil prices in January 1980 were $11 below the price of imported oil, and the entitlements program provided an effective subsidy for imports of $5.28 per barrel. The first step in rationalizing the oil market must be to decontrol U.S. crude oil prices, forcing domestic oil demand to adjust to the unpleasant reality of high world oil prices. The nation is now embarked on this course; we should not turn back.

But how far should the United States go to restrict its imports? Several circumstances in the world oil market make the true cost of imported oil greater than its market price. A high level of oil imports may exacerbate inflation and balance-of-payments problems; the world price does not reflect these costs. In addition, greater import dependence increases our vulnerability to an interruption of oil supplies, which imposes large economic costs. The events of 1979–1980 have increased our appreciation of these costs and reinforced recommendations for aggressive import-reduction programs.

Oil import reductions in advance of a sudden supply curtailment may help reduce the costs of a disruption, but the connection is not necessarily obvious. In the best of circumstances, an import reduction may prevent a supply interruption. This is the argument of many who support improved energy conservation and greater domestic supplies as means of reducing our oil import vulnerability. But in the worst case, an import-reduction program may eliminate secure sources of supply, serving only to deprive us of our demand cushion and increasing the cost of supply curtailments when they come. This latter case is not far-fetched: unfettered world market operations and the sharing plans of the International Energy Agency (IEA) suggest that effects such as these are to be expected.

Steps to reduce imports gradually may have quite different impacts than a quick demand reduction in response to a supply curtailment. A strategic stockpile, for example, which could reduce import demand for a short period, should have different costs and benefits than our long-run program to subsidize synthetic fuels and to improve the efficiency of automobiles. Yet it is easy to confuse one program with another, calculating the benefits of an oil stockpile as justification for the costs of a synthetic fuels program.

Uncertainties about many parameters, especially our estimates of the timing and scale of supply interruptions, further complicate our analysis of the benefits of import reductions. Legitimate differences in judgment may lead to vastly different conclusions; yet these dif-

ferences in judgment are seldom stated explicitly enough for evaluation and resolution. In this chapter, we will focus the debate on the
value of import reductions in advance of an interruption by applying
a simple model and accounting structure for calculating costs and
benefits.[2] We include the link between reduced dependency and reduced vulnerability, that is, the mitigating effect of import reductions on the costs of supply interruptions. Since the United States
has no existing strategic oil reserve and no plans for quick, inexpensive reductions of demand in case of an oil emergency, we assume
that there are no contingency plans and that the market will balance
supply and demand with higher prices during an oil emergency.

There are many ways to reduce imports prior to an emergency.
For a market or for efficient government programs, the least important uses of oil will be eliminated first. Although government policies
have not always been so benign, it simplifies the analysis to assume
that the reduction in imports would be achieved by imposing a tariff
on oil imports and rebating the proceeds to all consumers.

Our focus is on calculating the optimal level of imports, or the
optimal premium, considering both the pre-interruption costs and
benefits and the expected costs of various supply interruptions. We
summarize the main arguments in the next section, saving the detailed calculations for the Technical Appendix.

COMPONENTS OF AN IMPORT PREMIUM

The dynamics of the world oil market complicate the analysis. Over
a period of years, as national economies grow and domestic oil supplies dwindle, either oil imports will grow or oil prices will increase
to maintain a long-run equilibrium in the market. Working against
this trend, consuming countries can increase or decrease their demand for oil, putting themselves on a new long-run equilibrium
path. Simultaneously, oil-consuming countries face the possibility
of an accidental or intentional interruption of oil supplies that would
drive up prices in the short run and create costly macroeconomic
reverberations.

2. There is an extensive literature, still developing, on one or more components of an
import premium. The major attempts at a comprehensive taxonomy are in Stobaugh and
Yergin (1979), Nordhaus (1980), Neville et al. (1980), Rowen and Weyant (1980), and Teisberg (1979).

Each long-run equilibrium trend has its own associated opportunity costs and benefits, externalities that can create a wedge between the true cost of imports and the price on the world oil market. In a similar manner, the cost of a supply interruption can depend in part on the level of oil imports. This additional externality, adjusted to reflect the likelihood of occurrence, also adds to the wedge which is the optimal import premium or optimal import tariff. In our accounting framework, we separate the components of this optimal import premium to distinguish the arguments and assumptions that support each estimate. By thus dividing the premium, we hope to win, or at least clarify, the debate surrounding the importance of import-management programs. First we examine the long-run costs of imports in terms of inflation, balance of payments, and the price of oil. Then we examine the costs associated with vulnerability to supply interruptions.

Inflation

Because oil is an important and expensive commodity, a long-run trend of rising oil prices will contribute significantly to the general inflation of all currencies—both directly, in price increases for baskets of goods including oil products, and indirectly, as other prices and wages rise in attempts to recoup lost purchasing power. The large costs of this inflation come from the unsought redistribution of income and from government attempts to prevent it by slowing economic growth and dampening the price inflation. (We need not agree on the optimal macroeconomic policy response to agree that the costs could be high).

In estimating the oil price inflation premium, our attention focuses on the difference in effects between long-run oil price regimes rather than on the one-time costs of a transition from one regime to another. These transition costs may be large; the cost of the supply shock in 1979 is a case in point. And the costs of transition may balance some of the benefits of the new price regime. For example, if we use an oil tax to lower the level of imports, the tax itself adds to the short-run inflation problem. But most policies for managing imports focus on the long run and will have little effect on the path between one long-run trend and another. We wish to isolate the inflation costs of being on one trend and not another.

It is common to point to the high burden of inflation as an important reason for reducing oil imports. The United States might have to forego over $100 billion of GNP to remove one percentage point from its general inflation rate.[3] However, the attribution of these costs to oil imports is problematic. It is price change that determines inflation, not price or quantity level. And although the production quantity level usually determines the import price level for a depletable resource like oil, the long-run rate of price change is primarily a function of the nominal interest rate.[4] Even if we reject the theory of depletable resources and adopt the production target theory of oil producer behavior—that is, that production is fixed and prices increase only with increasing demand—a permanent shift in the demand curve produces a one-time change in the price, but no change in the *trend* of prices, after the transition.[5] In either case, therefore, no long-run inflation benefit accrues because there is no change in the rate of oil price increase and because, unless we can find a costless, nonprice mechanism for making the transition, we absorb additional inflation costs in the short run as we move from a high import regime to a lower.

The effect of oil import levels on the rate of oil price inflation is only half the story. Although there are many opportunities for conserving oil, they are probably not sufficient to avoid a second effect of oil price inflation: by changing the demand for oil we change its value in the economy. For instance, if we impose a tariff on oil, demand will decrease but the total expenditures on oil and related products, including the tariff, will probably increase. It is this total value of expenditures that governs the transmission of oil price inflation to general inflation. If oil and related products amount to

3. The estimate of $100 billion per point of inflation can be found in Nordhaus (1980). It follows from a Philips curve assumption of two points of unemployment needed to remove one point of inflation, a conservative shading of Okun's law to 2.5 points of lost output per point of unemployment, and a $2500 billion potential GNP. ($2500 × 2.5 × 2 × 0.01 = $125.)

4. For a depletable resource with no production costs, the only cost is the scarcity value or the backstop price of an alternative. According to Hotelling's result, the initial price is determined by the backstop price but the price grows at the nominal rate of interest. This result holds for the competitive case. If the demand elasticity is constant over time, it also holds for the case of a monopolist producer.

5. For the production target model, the price growth rate is determined by the growth rate of demand. A one-time shift in demand will produce a one-time shift in the price level but, if the shift is proportional in each period, no change in the growth rate of demand or prices.

10 percent of the economy, then a 10 percent annual growth in oil prices will add 1 percent to the overall rate of inflation and stimulate further wage and price increases. At the same time, any increase in the relative value of oil must produce an equal decrease in the relative value of other inputs to the economy and, therefore, a reduction in their contribution to inflation. The ultimate result will depend on many adjustments in the economy. But without substantial reductions in the price, higher levels of oil imports should increase the rate of general price inflation.

The higher rate of inflation does not translate immediately into a cost attributable to oil imports. The inflation premium depends upon the reaction of our planners. In the most optimistic assessments, we hope for full accommodation of the inflation and dextrous use of transfer payments to correct any distortions caused by rising prices. Such efficient management of the economy would avoid any inflation premium. However, if our planners cannot manage this herculean task and choose to accommodate only half of the price increases, the oil inflation premium could mushroom to over $20 per barrel. This may be an extreme case, but a premium range of $0 to $15 per barrel is arguable, albeit subject to a high degree of uncertainty.[6]

Balance of Payments

The ambiguities of the inflation calculation have analogies in the estimation of the balance-of-payments and exchange rate effects of oil imports. Higher imports contribute to the problem of maintaining a balance of payments. Higher oil imports at higher prices increase the need to export goods and services or to receive investment payments in anticipation of future exports. But we can expect oil producers' total demand for goods and services to be less than their total revenues for a long time: oil producers in the aggregate will run a surplus, and oil-consuming countries will run a deficit.

---

6. These inflation estimates are sensitive to macroeconomic policy assumptions for which we have no definitive theory. And small changes in the partial equilibrium model used in the Technical Appendix can have significant effects on the premium estimate, largely because of the high cost of inflation (see footnote 2). This suggests that the partial equilibrium model may be too simple for the task here; the current estimates are subject to a high degree of uncertainty.

There is an arithmetic definition stating that the total deficit of the oil-consuming countries must be balanced by the total surplus of the oil-producing countries. Total net payments will be zero. But this equivalence will not hold true for every country. Strong currencies will attract more than their share of investments; weak currencies, less. So some countries will have a surplus and some a deficit in transactions with the oil producers. Public and private financial institutions bear the burden of using the surpluses to finance the deficits.

For the incremental barrel of long-run oil imports, the rule in the aggregate does not apply. Each country has an incentive to reduce oil imports: only a fraction of the nation's payment for the incremental barrel will be returned to it. For countries with strong currencies, like West Germany and Japan, the fraction returned will be large; for countries with weak currencies, Brazil and the Philippines for instance, the fraction will be small. But in each case the portion returned will be less than the payment, with the balance going to other countries that will see the increased flow of funds as a free good, a positive externality created by the imports of their neighbors. Acting alone, therefore, each oil-importing country sees that the last barrel of oil (or the incremental expenditure on any imports) works to the consumer's disfavor in the adjustment of exchange rates.

Some adjustment will be necessary for such an oil-induced and permanent shift in the balance of payments. Nordhaus (1980) argues that the result will be a deterioration in the exchange rate to maintain the present value of the balance of trade. Imports will become more expensive and exports cheaper; it will take fewer yen to purchase a dollar. This result will impose a real cost on the U.S. economy; only part of this cost will be the real resources payment for increased imports.

Whether or not a significant import premium arises turns on a number of factors. If the oil producers are willing to hold dollars, say, by making investments in the United States, there need be no change in exchange rates and no premium. Or if the export and import levels of other goods and services are sensitive to small changes in exchange rates, then the current account comes into balance with only a small premium. Finally, the existence of a premium depends on the extent to which oil producers adjust the dollar price of oil in response to shifts in exchange rates. If they do not adjust, then they bear the extra cost whenever they spend their dollars outside the

United States. It is possible, therefore, to describe plausible conditions that produce no import premiums for the United States — or, as in Nordhaus (1980), that result in a premium that approaches half the price of oil.

Of course, a one-time increase in the dollar exchange rate caused by a reduction in oil imports provides a one-time decrease in the overall price level. As with a one-time increase in the long-run trend in oil prices, this transition effect may be significant. But the temporary benefit should be of the same magnitude as the temporary costs of inflation incurred in reducing oil imports through a tariff. Therefore, we ignore the transition costs and assume that the entire balance-of-payments premium is captured in the long-run costs. For the sake of present discussion, we adopt a $0 to $8 per barrel as the range of legitimate uncertainty for the balance-of-payments premium.[7]

Price Protection

The oil-producing countries have, and use, market power to drive oil prices above marginal costs in order to extract monopoly rents from the oil-importing nations. The obverse of their market power is the power of consumers. Countries with a large share of world imports, or all importing countries acting together, could affect the world oil price by changing the volume of their oil purchases. And since the resulting price difference would be paid on all oil, the true cost of the incremental barrel is higher than the market price.

For example, if a 1 million barrel per day increase in U.S. oil demand raises the world price by $.50 per barrel, then the United States must pay the higher price on all 8 million barrels per day of its imports. In short, the cost of the incremental barrel would be $4.50 more than the world price. If we count the increased payments consuming countries make on all 30 million barrels of OPEC's daily production, the incremental barrel would cost $15 more than the world price, a substantial import premium.

The argument for the existence of this import premium appears sound on the surface, but the estimate of its size flounders in evalu-

---

7. Nordhaus (1980) estimated the balance-of-payments premium as $8 when oil price was $16. He did not give his elasticity estimates. We continue his assumption that an aggregate oil price increase affects all countries equally and produces no balance-of-payments deficit. See the Technical Appendix for detailed calculations.

ating the response of producers faced with different import demand levels. If producers behave according to the theory of markets for depletable resources, by adjusting prices to equate present and future revenues, then a shift in oil demand produces only a small change in the price; reduced production accommodates the reduced demand, and the import premium may be as low as $1 per barrel. However, if producers adhere to a production target, a shift in demand may force them to lower prices substantially in order to maintain sales. In this case, the premium could be as high as $5 per barrel.[8] Of course these premiums are for a country (the United States) acting alone; the collective importing country premium could be three times as high.

Even this range of uncertainty understates the difficulty of predicting producer response. If, for example, we take seriously the notion that producers adhere to revenue targets and are not fully exploiting their market power, then a reduction in oil demand could produce an increase in oil prices. Or, as another example, a consumer tariff might be interpreted as a declaration that oil is underpriced and as a political challenge to the producers to raise their prices further. In either case, the implied import premium would be negative.

Even if we give little weight to these latter theories, they caution us against overestimating the import premiums that could arise from use of the consumers' market power. For the United States acting alone, anywhere from $1 to $5 per barrel is a plausible estimate of the premium, with a higher probability on the lower end of the range.

Vulnerability: Cost Reduction

The social costs of oil imports in normal times complement the costs of oil imports during a sudden interruption of supplies. Although the precise timing and scale of such interruptions are unpredictable, observers of the world oil market consider large, precipitous drops in oil supply very likely. Even if these supply interruptions were only temporary, they would impose stupendous costs on the oil-consuming countries, creating an economic catastrophe on the scale of the Great Depression.

---

8. The low price protection premium follows from intertemporal optimization models of oil producer behavior; for example, Salant (1980). The higher figure follows from assumptions of models with production targets and low elasticities of demand; for example, Stobaugh and Yergin (1979).

The primary policy implication of this risk is that the consuming countries should make the prevention of interruptions a cardinal military and foreign policy objective. And they should be willing to pay heavily to achieve it.

At the same time, there is a need to manage imports so that the costs of a supply curtailment could be mitigated. The scope of the potential economic costs of any interruption will be affected by the level of imports at the start of the emergency. More imports mean more barrels for which we would have to pay a suddenly higher price. The loss of a few million barrels per day could raise the oil price by $10 per barrel; the loss of the whole Persian Gulf could push the price of oil over $100 per barrel. Paying such a price on incremental imports would create an even greater drag on the economy, exacerbating the short-run macroeconomic effects. Therefore, even if import management does not reduce the size of the interruption, it can reduce its cost.

The size of the implicit import premium for vulnerability cost reduction depends upon a number of factors. How likely is the interruption? How large will it be? How long will it last? How much will the indirect macroeconomic effects add to the direct resource costs? How quickly and how well will the consuming countries adjust to the supply interruption? Plausible answers to these questions suggest a range of estimates for the import premium. If the chance of a one-year interruption is less than 10 percent in any given year, and if only the direct economic costs matter, then best estimates of the adjustments possible in the United States yield an import premium of as low as $1 per barrel. But if the probability of interruption is closer to 33 percent and indirect losses are as great as the direct resource costs, the premium could be as much as $10 per barrel.[9]

Vulnerability: Interruption Reduction

The best way to avoid the costs of a supply interruption is to avoid the interruption altogether. This certainly does not suggest a policy of energy self-sufficiency for any individual country, however. In the world oil market, no country is an island, including the United

9. See the Technical Appendix for details. A part of this premium is a cost that will be borne by the oil importer if an interruption occurs. In a rational expectations model, the cost would be considered in the consumption decision and not be part of the premium. This would reduce the vulnerability cost reduction estimates by 30 to 50 percent.

States; the goals of Project Independence were an illusion. The oil-importing countries are bound together by the forces of the market and by international agreement. A supply interruption anywhere will affect everyone everywhere.

Although no one can escape the effects of a supply interruption, a reduction in oil imports could lessen the size, and the cost, of the interruption when it comes. An import reduction in advance of the emergency could create excess capacity in the world system—capacity that could and would be brought into production in the event of a supply interruption. To the extent that a long-term reduction in oil imports lessens the effective size of an oil emergency, an import premium and further benefits to a program of import management materialize.

Just how these benefits will be realized is uncertain. If cutting imports results in reduced output in an especially unstable country, such as Iran in 1979, then exposure to accidental interruptions may be reduced. If, as is more likely, the reduction in production comes from Saudi Arabia, we must depend on the Saudis' goodwill to maintain large amounts of excess capacity and to use it to stabilize the market during a supply interruption. Given the Saudis' domestic situation and the pressures their fellow producers would probably exert, it is easy to envision a reluctance in Riyadh to use excess capacity to dampen oil price increases. At best, events will depend on the political circumstances of the moment.

In the worst of situations—political use of the oil weapon—a program of import management may have no effect on the size of the supply interruption. We may succeed only in eliminating the easiest domestic adjustments to a supply curtailment, guaranteeing that the costs of the interruption will be higher than without import management.

The uncertainty about the size of any reduction in vulnerability combines with other counterproductive incentives for individual countries considering management of oil imports. According to IEA agreements, all participating countries must share oil shortages in proportion to their oil consumption or imports depending on the size of the interruption. This diplomatic rule reinforces both the general pressures of the oil market and the apparent tendencies of the international oil companies. And it reduces the incentive for any country to reduce oil demand. Any reduction imposes costs which that country must bear alone, but the resulting decrease in the size of any potential interruption will be shared with all. The United States, for example, would see less than half the benefit of any reduction in its imports, even if the reduction were fully effective in decreasing the size of the total supply loss.

These special problems, combined with the uncertainties clouding the calculation of the premium for vulnerability cost reduction, increase the difficulty of calculating the premium for vulnerability interruption reduction. At the low end, where there is no reduction in the interruption, the premium is zero. At the high end—in a dangerous world, with poor macroeconomic policy, and with the benevolence of our friends in Saudi Arabia—the oil import premium for vulnerability interruption reduction may be as high as $10 per barrel.[10]

Stockpiles

The best place to create excess capacity is in the hands of the oil-importing countries. This capacity can take many forms, but the most attractive surely is a ready stockpile of oil that can be drawn upon to replace interrupted supplies.

A stockpile has several advantages over import reductions that create excess capacity in the world. First, we can control its use. Second, unlike increased, or "surge," production from Saudi Arabia, a stockpile would allow us to avoid the wealth transfer and attendant macroeconomic problems. Third, we need pay for the stockpile only once, until it is used and replaced, but we must pay for import reductions every year. Finally, a large stockpile may deter political supply interruptions. Its greatest value may be in preventing the need for its use.

Of course, this partial solution has its own problems. A stockpile would be of little value without a plan and a will to use it. And unless it were very large, it would only be a nuisance to a determined foe. Despite these potential drawbacks, however, the premium we should be willing to pay today, when our stockpile is miniscule, to add to our petroleum reserve is far above the premium for long-run, permanent import reductions. For instance, under conditions where

---

10. See the Technical Appendix for details. This premium tends to complement the premium for vulnerability cost reduction. It is unlikely that both effects will be large.

vulnerability premiums are near zero, the premium for stockpiled oil is over $10 per barrel. Assuming a more pessimistic view of the world, this figure can jump to as much as $25 — and that is for the United States acting alone, with the benefits shared by all oil consumers! If all oil importers were to work together, the range of the stockpile premiums would jump to $20 to $70 per barrel.[11]

PREMIUMS AND OIL POLICY

One premium affects the value of others. If, for example, we impose a vulnerability tariff and reduce oil imports, we reduce the price protection premium because the price rises apply to a smaller quantity of imports. Therefore, the optimal tariff is less than the sum of the components. (The main results of the detailed estimates in the Technical Appendix are summarized in Table 9–1.) The possible range for a long-run import reduction premium is from $2 to $40 per barrel for the United States acting alone.

This is a large range of uncertainty. Unfortunately, it reflects arguable differences in judgments about parameters and assumptions that lie behind the debate over the importance of reducing oil imports. The range of input assumptions behind Table 9–1 is roughly compatible with the range of assumptions made by different analysts; however, the range of premium estimates is narrower. The first reason for this narrowing is that we must distinguish between average and marginal costs of oil imports. That is, inflation costs may be high, but we may not be able to affect them much by changing the long-run demand for oil imports. The second explanation is to be found in our concentration on permanent changes in oil demand. The costs of transition, such as those of short-run supply shocks, may be much higher, but there is little we can do now to affect these costs. Most proposals for import management will take many years to have a significant effect. So in evaluating policy options, we need to focus on the benefits of long-run import reductions.

One might ask if Table 9–1 is comprehensive. Does it cover all the social costs of oil imports above the direct price on the world oil market? After all, we have no entries for "political," "foreign pol-

---

11. See the Technical Appendix for details. We have assumed that the costs of holding the stockpile are balanced by its appreciation in value.

Table 9—1. Import premiums for the United States acting alone (*in dollars per barrel*).

Components of an Import Premium	Low	High
Inflation	$0	$15
Balance of Payments	0	8
Price Protection	1	5
Vulnerability		
Cost Reduction	1	10
Interruption Reduction	0	10
Total Range	2	40
Stockpile Premium	13	70

Note: For details of the calculation, see the Technical Appendix. The total range is less than the sum of the components because a large premium in one dimension reduces the premium in others.

icy," or "national security" premiums. These omissions reflect the view that these items are not additional costs of the incremental barrel of oil but alternative mechanisms for avoiding the social costs of oil imports. Presumably the high economic cost of oil motivates the use of political, foreign policy, and defense options. If we do nothing with oil imports, we incur the costs identified in Table 9—1. These other options may reduce the import premium.

Our narrow view of oil supply interruptions suggests that the figures in the table might be too high. More complicated strategies than we have examined—wherein oil producers cut back production to inflict a certain level of damage on oil importers—could negate the value of import reductions or stockpile buildups. Or there might be some benefits from higher oil imports that we have ignored. Is, for example, the net environmental effect positive? Although there may be a few minor adjustments to the taxonomy, and many disagreements on the estimates, Table 9—1 should be an acceptably comprehensive catalog of the total cost premium of imported oil. If we leave aside the more complex interruption strategies for separate treatment elsewhere, we can consider the policy implications of the oil import premiums.

Given the remaining uncertainty in the premium estimate, an uncertainty not likely to be resolved by gathering more facts or conducting more analysis, policy should flow first from the qualitative implications of the premium analysis. The most striking feature of the table is the large difference between the import reduction premium and the stockpile premium. If one discounts the inflation and balance-of-payments premiums as avoidable costs and accepts the low end of the import premium range as more likely, or if one believes in the high end of the range but is pessimistic about the ability of the U.S. government to impose a large tariff or manage an effective subsidy program, one must be discouraged and dismayed by the almost total concentration on reducing oil imports at the expense of preparing for oil emergencies.

In mid–1980, the United States has no significant strategic stockpile and no public plan for completing its stockpile on anything approaching an emergency basis. Nor has it any credible plans for responding to an oil supply emergency, either in terms of providing for its energy needs or of minimizing the macroeconomic costs of a supply interruption. And even the hard-won programs for import reduction will have almost no effect in the short run; import reductions may come later, but the danger of a large supply interruption is here now. The United States, together with its allies, should reverse this misordering of priorities. After a long search for cheap, equitable ways to reduce oil imports, the country should now devote its intellectual, political, and physical resources to improving its ability to deal with oil supply interruptions.

As part of this policy initiative, we should redouble our efforts to fashion effective international agreements to capture the benefits of import reductions and develop measures for meeting oil emergencies. Most potential effects of reduced imports or effective emergency actions have the features of a public good—the costs are borne by one country, but the benefits are shared by all. The inflation and vulnerability cost reduction premiums might not be affected by cooperative action, but the value of price protection could triple and the value of vulnerability interruption reduction could double if all oil-importing countries worked together. The total import reduction premium might be twice as high as for the United States acting alone, and the higher range for the stockpile premium would be the more likely case. In elemental terms, the oil-importing countries have an overriding collective interest in avoiding internal competition in order to reduce the vast wealth transfers to oil producers.

In developing these domestic plans and international agreements, the critical need is to focus on what could be done soon to meet the threat that is here now. The supply shock of 1979—1980 was expensive. Any repetition would be bad enough, but an even worse emergency could erupt at any moment. The threats are many and the options few. But there *are* steps that the importing countries can and should take now to mitigate, if not eliminate, the costs of oil emergencies.

MEETING AN OIL EMERGENCY

While we wait for the oil stockpile to grow, while we promote the creation of excess capacity everywhere possible, and while we fashion defense and foreign policies to minimize the chance of a supply interruption, we can also consider what we would do if an oil emergency confronted us tomorrow. The United States has given this subject too little attention. Our lack of preparedness demonstrates a lack of conviction that the threat of interruption is real, serious, and here. Most of the proposals we have considered for meeting such an emergency, like rationing, will flounder in the conditions likely to prevail during a serious interruption of oil supplies. We need to establish now the priorities and principles for meeting an oil emergency.

Buy Time

The immediate energy past may be a guide to the energy future. In that past, a pervasive uncertainty marked our oil supply interruptions. During crises, we did not know the size, intent, or duration of the supply interruptions; in fact, we still do not know many of those important details. This uncertainty was particularly evident during the critical early days, weeks, and months—when we made many of the most important decisions extending price controls, implementing domestic allocations, jawboning refiners, creating a special distillate entitlement, and so on. There is every reason to believe that this uncertainty will be repeated in the next supply interruption. Can we really expect a future emergency to unfold without ambiguity or confusion?

No doubt the next oil supply interruption will come as part of a wider, more complex crisis: a new war in the Middle East, or another revolution in Iran. The oil supply cutoff will be entangled with delicate foreign policy and military issues. Even for very large supply interruptions the loss of oil may be the least serious concern, for every decision we make will risk the danger of a precipitous decline into war. The first goal of any emergency plan, therefore, would be to buy time, to provide breathing space for collecting information and evaluating options. If war may be imminent, we do not want the president preoccupied with gasoline lines. Nor do we want the decisionmaking agenda cluttered with many complicated and difficult choices concerning the management of our oil market.

Besides diverting us from the most pressing problem, the need to make hard choices early in an oil emergency increases the chances that wrong decisions will be made. If confusion reigns, it will be difficult to call for extraordinary sacrifices. Imagine an American president with the courage and support to impose, quickly, a $1 per gallon tax on all oil products because of an outbreak of hostilities in the Persion Gulf and a sudden skyrocketing of spot market prices. It would be far more likely for him to do as other presidents have done: attack the messenger or promise easy solutions, for example, to establish allocations based on historical use, making the short-run problems worse and creating inefficiencies that we would pay for over many years. We hope instead to defer the hard political calls in order to improve the chances of making good choices. The emergency plan should be as automatic as possible.

Decentralize Decisionmaking

One of the best ways to buy breathing space for the central decisionmakers and to ensure an automatic oil emergency system is to decentralize decisionmaking. Given the nature of the U.S. oil market, most of the data needed to make day-to-day or week-to-week allocation decisions are located far from the central computers of the Department of Energy. Emergency management plans that depend on the rapid collection and central processing of these data are doubly flawed.

First, the very act of bringing the data to the federal government focuses the decisions, creating the expectation and the need for top decisionmakers to deal with the details of supply allocation. When something goes wrong, the press will turn to Washington, demand an explanation, and clamor for corrective action. Centralized allocation will increase the pressure on the president at the worst time.

Second, something will surely go wrong. A sophisticated data collection and evaluation system adequate to allocate U.S. oil supplies is beyond the state of the art, and the problems will not be solved with more and bigger computers. We hardly know the data needed to capture, in real-time, the abrupt emergency-induced changes in the patterns of oil use. Confronted with this dilemma, central decision-makers resort to a simple formula that requires very little information: allocation fractions applied to historic use. This ready answer virtually guarantees misallocation. Far better decentralized decisions could be made in the existing system.

Be Efficient

The misallocation of supplies during an oil emergency could be very expensive. Given a large shortfall, even seemingly essential uses will be affected. The stakes will be high. It will take more than a little rearrangement of driving patterns to accommodate the loss of all Persian Gulf oil—a loss that could mean a shortage of 6 million barrels per day, one-third of our current consumption. In a large interruption, it will be especially important to allow the available oil to flow to the most valued uses. To the extent that the emergency system fails the efficiency test, large costs will accrue and, again, unwanted pressure will build for the government to take precipitous actions—economic, diplomatic, and military—to solve the problem.

Be Fair

No emergency system that does not provide for an equitable sharing of the burden will survive long. We must share the costs fairly across sectors and income groups. This political fact dominates the design of many emergency plans even though this goal is in sharp contrast to the goal of efficiency. The presumption of fairness, for example, is one of the strongest arguments for gasoline-rationing plans. Apparently, our political collective is willing to sacrifice a great deal of efficiency to create even the appearance of equity. Hence, the burden of proof rests with anyone proposing an emergency plan that efficiently allocates supplies to high priority uses. We must demonstrate that the plan also has a chance of clearing the equity hurdle standing in the way of implementation.

Capture the Rents

A sudden loss of oil supplies will push up the price of all the remaining barrels we import, creating a monumental transfer of wealth that will complicate every other problem. Economists in importing countries imagine many ways to capture these bonuses in order to prevent this transfer of wealth to the oil producers. The IEA agreements, for example, contemplate emergency demand-reduction measures that will accommodate any oil shortage and prevent the ruinous competitive bidding that produces the same oil allocation but makes OPEC the tax collector.

A tariff might drive a suitable premium between domestic and world prices, preventing the wealth transfer. But the tariff must be imposed quickly, and we have seen that quick action is unlikely. Other demand-management programs offer some hope, but the import reductions they achieve would have to be large and price bidding might still take place at the margin. Again the stakes are high. Despite the difficulties, any emergency plan should be able to help stanch the flow of economic blood from the importing countries.

Protect the Economy

The loss of oil, the income drain of the higher oil payments, and the burst of inflation will create severe macroeconomic management problems. If, for example, we restrict the money supply to dampen inflation and fail to replace the demand lost in payment for oil, we could create severe unemployment in a sharp recession, a loss that could be avoided and that depends only indirectly on an oil shortage. This indirect loss could be greater than the direct economic costs of the oil shortage. Such was the lesson of 1974. The fiscal and monetary authorities, not the Department of Energy, control the most important tools for meeting an oil emergency. Any emergency plan must recognize this dimension of the problem. It may be possible to marry macroeconomic policy and energy policy, as, for example, in using tax rebates to create a measure of equity while providing a fiscal stimulus to maintain full employment. This same package might also allow the monetary authorities to accommodate a one-time burst of inflation and minimize the macroeconomic effects of the oil shock.

Cooperate with Allies

The oil-importing countries have a strong common interest in meeting an emergency. We have seen how joint action could mitigate the costs of supply interruptions; a failure to cooperate will guarantee higher costs to all. We recognized this principle in the organization of the IEA, but there should be further opportunities to fashion international agreements. Our leaders must recognize the existence and importance of these cooperative efforts.

To date, the record of the United States has not been good. Our unwillingness to share our Alaskan oil with Japan during relatively good times does little to build confidence that we will share our oil during bad times. Our creation, in 1979, of the special "distillate entitlement" to subsidize imports to the United States violated the spirit of the IEA agreements.[12] Furthermore, there is no evidence that the government has prepared the public to support the IEA sharing agreements if they are ever invoked. This lack of preparation is dangerous. Our emergency plans should include credible, enforceable provisions for cooperation with our allies.

Withdraw Gracefully

Eventually the emergency will pass, either because production will be restored or because we will make the short-run transition to a new long-run market regime. Seven years of oil price controls in the United States demonstrated that decisions made in an emergency can have long-run consequences. If we make our policy on the run, that policy will surely not be addressed to long-run concerns. But by

12. The details of the distillates entitlement decision can be found in the case study prepared by Paul Starobin (1980).

developing emergency plans now we can give attention to this issue. Other things being equal, a better program for meeting emergencies will be one that exploits, or at least accommodates, the eventual transition out of the emergency condition. The program's adjustment of oil uses should be consistent with the long-run efficient solution, and it should avoid spawning groups interested in preserving the emergency measures. Consider the difficulty of eliminating special subsidies for the small refiners that sprang up under the U.S. price controls and entitlements program. Or imagine the problem of eliminating tax rebates or ration coupons if we discover that oil prices will be permanently higher. It behooves us to consider now the problems of terminating an emergency plan after the crisis has passed. We should act early to avoid prolonging the costs of adjusting to the post-emergency period.

CONCLUSION

Imported oil has costs that exceed its market price. Therefore, in addition to decontrolling domestic oil prices, we should further reduce our imports. Although we have not examined the details of import-reduction programs, we have summarized the main contributors to an oil import premium. Unfortunately, our analysis does not narrow the range of import premium estimates enough to provide a sharp rule for setting the optimal tariff or subsidy; judgments on key uncertainties are required to produce a single estimate.

The macroeconomic costs of oil imports, through inflation and the balance of payments, could be the largest components of a long-run import premium. But there is a high degree of uncertainty in our estimates of the inflation premium. The implication of the highest estimate is that we should search first for better macroeconomic policies to deal with energy-induced inflation, and only then look to oil import reductions.

The security component of the import premium depends critically on the degree to which long-run import reductions reduce the size of supply interruptions. Since dependence is not the same as vulnerability, reduced dependence contributes to oil security only by reducing the costs of interruptions or by creating excess capacity that could reduce the effective size of a given interruption.

The uncertainty in our estimate of the import premium does not translate into a similar uncertainty regarding the nature of the premiums or the major policy implications. For almost all the components of the import premium, the actions taken by one oil-importing country produce costs and benefits for all oil-importing countries. This relationship suggests that the oil import premium for a country acting alone will be much less than for a group of countries acting together. Workable international arrangements for reducing oil imports and meeting the costs of an oil emergency should receive high priority from energy policymakers.

Furthermore, under every assumption we have examined, the stockpile premium is larger than the import reduction premium. The stockpile serves as a proxy for any program that reduces the size of an oil interruption or contributes substantially to reducing its costs. This weighting of the benefits in favor of emergency preparation is quite at odds with the weighting of U.S. energy policy in the seventies. We need to redirect our attention away from nearly exclusive concentration on import management and begin urgently building our capabilities to meet oil emergencies.

The most pressing need in energy policy is for a program to weather the dangerous early days of a large supply interruption. Without a program to mitigate the pressure from the energy sector, precipitous decisions could complicate a very bad situation in the short run and lock us into costly policies over the long run. Most proposals for meeting oil emergencies, such as programs for gasoline rationing, betray misunderstandings about the nature of supply interruptions and of the critical demands that will be placed on us during a major oil emergency. Our criteria for emergency programs are intended to serve as a guide to designing policies now that will help us meet any imminent interruption.

Finally, we see the need for defense and foreign policy initiatives to improve our energy security. The cost of an oil supply interruption will be high, and energy policy alone can do little more than reduce this cost at the margin. There is faint hope for using energy policy to eliminate completely our vulnerability to oil supply interruptions. If there is any hope for eliminating this vulnerability, it must come from other policies that improve the stability of the Persian Gulf oil supply. Our energy policy can complement defense and foreign policies. It cannot replace them.

REFERENCES

Landsberg, H. et al., *Energy: The Next Twenty Years*. Ballinger Publishing Co., Cambridge, Mass., 1979.

Neville, T., J. Blankenship, M. Barron, W. Lane. 1980. "The Energy Problem: Costs and Policy Options." Working Paper, Office of Policy and Evaluation, Department of Energy, March 1980.

Nordhaus, W.D. 1980. "The Energy Crisis and Macroeconomic Policy." *Energy Journal* 1, no. 1, January 1980.

Pindyck, R. 1980. "Energy Price Increases and Macroeconomic Policy." M.I.T. Energy Laboratory Working Paper, MIT-EL 79-061WP (revised), May 1980.

Rowen, H., and J. Weyant. 1980. "Reducing Our Dependence on Persian Gulf Oil: Need and Opportunities," Working Paper, Stanford University, March 1980.

Salant, S. 1980. "Imperfect Competition in the International Energy Market: A Computerized Nash–Cournot Model." *Operations Research*, forthcoming, 1980.

Starobin, P. 1980. "Managing the Oil Crisis: Distillate Entitlements." Case Program, Kennedy School of Government, Harvard University, 1980.

Stobaugh, R., and D. Yergin (eds.). 1979. *Energy Future*, Random House, New York, 1979.

Teisberg, T. 1979. "A Dynamic Programming Model of the U.S. Strategic Petroleum Reserve." Working Paper, M.I.T., October 1979.

TECHNICAL APPENDIX

There are many ways to reduce imports prior to an oil emergency. For a market or for efficient government programs, the least important uses of oil will be eliminated first. Although government policies have not always been so benign, it simplifies the analysis to assume that the reduction in imports is accomplished by imposing a tariff on oil imports, with the tariff proceeds rebated to all consumers. Our focus is on calculating the optimal level of imports, or the optimal tariff, considering both the pre-interruption costs and benefits and the expected costs of the range of possible supply interruptions.

THE LONG-RUN MARKET

The dynamics of the world oil market complicate the analysis. Simplifying as much as possible, we consider only two time frames: the long-run market and the short-run of an interrupted market. For a typical year in the long-run market, we use a conventional description of oil import supply and demand (see Figure A9−1).

Consumer Benefits

There is an inverse import demand function which relates prices to quantities,

$$p(q),$$

where q is in millions of barrels per day and p is in dollars per barrel.

The benefit from import level q is the gross consumer value, the area under the demand curve,

$$\int_{o}^{q} p(\hat{q}) d\hat{q} \ .$$

Figure A9-1.   A "normal" market.

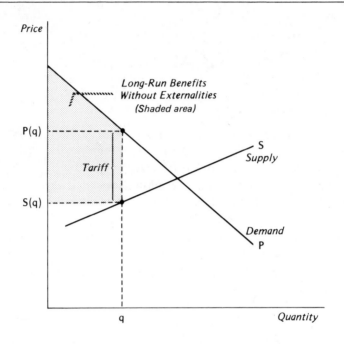

Import Resource Costs

The inverse import supply curve relates the quantity of oil supplied by the world market to the price of imports,

$$s(q) \ .$$

The steady-state cost of a given level of imports is

$$s(q)q \ .$$

Inflation

Long-run inflation in the price of oil will create a sympathetic inflation in the prices of related products; for example, natural gas. With full accommodation, the resulting impact on the general level of inflation will be in proportion to the value share of oil and related products. Let:

s = supply price;

γ = inflation rate of oil import prices;

$\bar{p}$ = price of oil and related products including the tariff;

$\bar{q}$ = quantity of oil and related products (millions barrels per day);

ω = value share of oil and related products;

n = elasticity of demand for oil and related products;

λ = first-round contributions to inflation from all sources.

Then the contribution to inflation from oil import prices is

$$\gamma \, \frac{s}{\bar{p}} \, \omega \ .$$

If I is the first-round price increase of all other input factors, then

$$\lambda = \gamma \, \frac{s}{\bar{p}} \, \omega + I \, (1 - \omega) \ .$$

Now,

$$\omega = \frac{\bar{p}\bar{q}\,(.365)}{GNP} \ .$$

Therefore,

$$\lambda = \gamma \, \frac{s\bar{q}\,(.365)}{GNP} + I\left(1 - \frac{\bar{p}\bar{q}\,(.365)}{GNP}\right) \ .$$

If first-round nominal price increases of other input factors are not affected by oil prices, then

$$\frac{\partial \lambda}{\partial q} = \frac{.365}{GNP}\left[\frac{\partial \gamma}{\partial q}\, s\bar{q} + \gamma \frac{\partial s}{\partial q}\, \bar{q} + \gamma s \frac{\partial \bar{q}}{\partial q} - I\left(\frac{\partial \bar{p}}{\partial q}\, \bar{q} + \bar{p}\, \frac{\partial \bar{q}}{\partial q}\right)\right] \ .$$

According to the usual theory of depletable resources, $\gamma \approx r$, where r is the nominal interest rate; hence γ is independent of q. However, we may adopt a different theory of producer behavior. As an opposite extreme we might hypothesize that oil producers meet a production target. But even in this case, a permanent shift in oil demand would provide a one-time change in the level of prices but would not change the trend in prices. Therefore, under either theory,

$$\frac{\partial \gamma}{\partial q} = 0 \ .$$

For our purposes, we assume

$$\frac{\partial \gamma}{\partial q} = \delta \ ,$$

where δ is a small number.

By definition of the producer response in supplying oil imports,

$$\frac{\partial s}{\partial q} = s'(q) \ .$$

If 80 percent of the import reduction is in the form of demand reduction,

$$\frac{\partial \bar{q}}{\partial q} = .8 \ .$$

Therefore,

$$\frac{\partial \bar{p}}{\partial q} = \frac{\partial \bar{p}}{\partial \bar{q}} \ .8 = .8(n^{-1})\frac{\bar{p}}{\bar{q}} \ .$$

With these assumptions, we have the change in annual inflation per million barrels per day:

$$\frac{\partial \gamma}{\partial q} = \frac{.365}{GNP} \left[\delta s\bar{q} + \gamma \bar{q} s'(q) + .8(\gamma s - I\bar{p}(1 + n^{-1})) \right] \ .$$

Our Philip's curve assumption is that it requires two points of unemployment for one year to eliminate one point of inflation from an exogenous price change. Using an "Okun's law" of 2.5 points in output lost for each point of unemployment, we obtain a five to one ratio of lost output per point of inflation reduced.

As Nordhaus (1980) observed, full accommodation of this inflation is not likely, nor is no accommodation at all. The former would impose politically unacceptable burdens, for example, in the inflationary redistribution of wealth. The latter would cause a great loss in real output. If we let $(1 - \theta)$ represent the optimal degree of accommodation of inflation, then the loss in real output and the dollar per barrel inflation premium is:

$$5(\theta) \ \frac{GNP}{.365} \ \frac{\partial \lambda}{\partial q} \ = \ 5\theta \left[\delta s \bar{q} + \gamma \bar{q} s'(q) + .8(\gamma s - I\bar{p}(1 + n^{-1})) \right] \ .$$

Balance of Payments

Following Nordhaus (1980), we assume that an increase in oil imports will lead to a partial increase in exports, as the oil producers recycle their revenues, and a partial depreciation of the dollar to restore a balance of payments. Let:

p_d = domestic dollar price level;

p_f = foreign currency price level;

e = exchange rate (p_f/p_d);

s = dollar price of imported oil;

q_E = quantity of exports;

q_I = quantity of nonoil imports;

q = quantity of oil imports (in MMBD);

n_E = price elasticity of exports demand;

n_I = price elasticity of imports demand .

A balance of payments (with units on a daily basis) requires,

$$p_d \ q_E \ (p_d \ e) - \frac{p_f}{e} \ q_I \left(\frac{p_f}{e} \right) - sq \ = \ 0 \ .$$

Suppose that β percent of any increase in oil import payments is returned by oil producers through higher exports. Then, with perfectly elastic supply functions, at the margin the change in exchange rates must satisfy

$$p_d \ \frac{\partial q_E}{\partial (p_d e)} \ \cdot \ p_d \ \frac{\partial e}{\partial q} + \frac{p_f}{e} \ \frac{\partial q_I}{\partial \frac{p_f}{e}} \ \frac{p_f}{e^2} \ \frac{\partial e}{\partial q} + \frac{p_f}{e^2} \ q_I \frac{\partial e}{\partial q}$$

$$- \frac{\partial s}{\partial e} \ \frac{\partial e}{\partial q} \ q - (1 - \beta)(s + \frac{\partial s}{\partial q} q) = 0,$$

or

$$(n_E \, p_d \, q_E \; + \; (n_I + 1) p_d q_I) \frac{\partial lne}{\partial q} \; - \; \frac{\partial lns}{\partial lne} \cdot \frac{\partial lne}{\partial lnq} s \; - \; (1-\beta)\,(s + \frac{\partial s}{\partial q} q) = 0 \; .$$

Now the first term is the change in imports and exports valued at the domestic dollar price. The last term is the real resource cost of the incremental oil imports (excluding the β percent recycled immediately and not adding to the balance-of-payments deficit). The middle term, therefore, is the balance-of-payments premium, which consists of the elasticity of dollar oil prices as a function of the exchange rate and the elasticity of the exchange rate as a function of import levels.[13]

From this last equation we obtain

$$\frac{\partial lne}{\partial lnq} = \frac{(1-\beta)\,(s + \dfrac{\partial s}{\partial q} q)\, q}{n_E \, p_d \, q_E \; + \; (n_I + 1) p_d q_I \; - \; \dfrac{\partial lns}{\partial lne} q \; s} \; .$$

Hence, if the elasticity of demand for exports or imports is high, or β is close to 1, then the elasticity of exchange rate with respect to import quantity is low. But if β, n_E, and n_I are small, then the reverse holds true.

The elasticity of oil price to exchange rate is uncertain. If the oil producers are willing to fix the price in dollars or to make purchases only in the United States, possibly later, then this term should be near 0. If oil producers' dollars are converted to other currencies, and the producers wish to maintain the purchasing power of their oil, then this elasticity is 1.

The balance-of-payments import premium per barrel is

$$s \; \frac{\partial lns}{\partial lne} \frac{\partial lne}{\partial lnq} \; .$$

Combined Long-Run Costs and Benefits

The two components, inflation and balance of payments, will be combined in the import premium component $\bar{t}$. The net long-run

---

13. We have ignored the second-order effect of the partial recycling of balance-of-payments premium.

costs and benefits of imports are

$$\int_{0}^{q} p(\hat{q}) d\hat{q} - \bar{t}q - s(q)q \quad . \tag{1}$$

AN INTERRUPTED MARKET

The long-run level of imports defines a reference point for short-run supply and demand curves in an interrupted market (see Figure A9–2). The short-run import demand curve for quantity q_s at price w, relative to pre-interruption price $p(q)$ and quantity q, is assumed to be linear with slope c; that is,

$$q_s = q - c(w - p(q)) \quad .$$

Figure A9-2.   An interrupted market.

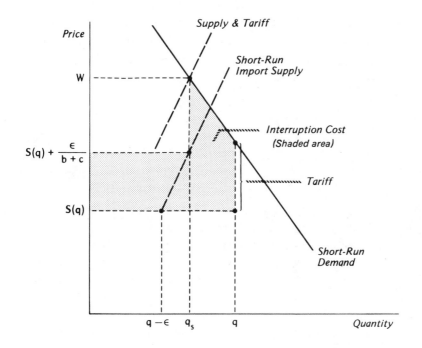

This yields the inverse demand function

$$w = p(q) - \frac{1}{c}(q_s - q) \ . \tag{2}$$

We assume the interruption lasts for one year. The short-run supply function during an interruption is determined by the size of the interruption, ϵ, and a short-run response relative to the import price, $s(q)$. The short-run supply of imports is very inelastic; a large change in price produces a small increment in curtailed supply. We further assume that the pre-interruption price difference $p(q) - s(q)$, is maintained during the interruption; hence, the short-run supply curve with slope b is

$$q_s = q - \epsilon + b(w - s(q) - p(q) + s(q)) \ .$$

This yields the inverse supply curve,

$$w = p(q) + \frac{1}{b}(q_s - q + \epsilon) \ . \tag{3}$$

With these definitions, the market-clearing quantity during an interruption is q_s and the shaded area in Figure A9−2 represents the direct social cost of interruption. This area is equal to

$$\frac{1}{2}(q - q_s)\left(\frac{\epsilon}{b+c}\right) + (q - q_s)(p(q) - s(q)) + q_s(w - p(q)) \ ;$$

or, simplifying,

$$\frac{c\epsilon}{c+b}(p(q) - s(q)) + q\frac{\epsilon}{b+c} - \frac{1}{2}\frac{\epsilon^2 c}{(c+b)^2} \ . \tag{4}$$

These interruption costs are the direct costs, that is, the wealth transfer to oil producers and the deadweight loss of consumer surplus. However, when imposed suddenly, these large costs may create a drain on aggregate demand (to the extent that payments for imports are not recycled immediately for real goods and services) and accelerate inflation, compromising our ability to maintain a full employment economy. These indirect costs, which result from our inability to manage the economy in the short run and which may be different than the long-run costs discussed above, are real and could be of the same order of magnitude as the direct costs. As a first approximation of these effects, we include a multiplier, m, to scale up the direct costs to give the total costs of interruption,

$$m \geq 1 .$$

OPTIMAL IMPORT LEVELS

The size of interruption is a random variable, with the most likely case in any year being no interruption at all. To describe this uncertainty, we assume that these are n different interruption levels, ϵ_i, $i = 1, 2, \ldots n$, each to occur with probability ρ_i, $\sum_{i=1}^{n} \rho_i \leq 1$.

With this characterization of the uncertainty, we postulate that the objective of the United States is to choose the import level that maximizes the net expected benefits minus costs,

$$\text{Max}_{q} \int_{0}^{q} p(\hat{q})d\hat{q} - \bar{t}q - s(q)q - m \sum_{i=1}^{n} \rho_i \left[\frac{c\epsilon_i}{c+b} (p(q)-s(q)) + q\frac{\epsilon_i}{c+b} - \frac{1}{2} \frac{\epsilon_i^{2} c}{(c+b)^2} \right] . \qquad (5)$$

We are interested in calculating the optimal import level, q, and the optimal import tariff, which captures the effects of all our costs,

$$p(q) - s(q).$$

If we differentiate the objective function with respect to q, set the derivative equal to 0, and solve for the optimal tariff, we obtain

$$p(q) - s(q) = \left[1 - m \sum_{i=1}^{n} \rho_i \frac{c}{c+b} \frac{\partial \epsilon_i}{\partial q} \right]^{-1} . \qquad (6)$$

$$\left[\bar{t} + s'(q)q + m \sum_{i=1}^{n} \rho_i \frac{\epsilon_i}{c+b} \left(c(p'(q) - s'(q)) + 1 \right) \right.$$

$$\left. + m \sum_{i=1}^{n} \rho_i \left(\frac{q}{b+c} - \frac{\epsilon_i c}{(c+b)^2} \right) \frac{\partial \epsilon_i}{\partial q} \right] ,$$

or

$$p(q) - s(q) = t_1 + t_2 + t_3 + t_4 ; \qquad (7)$$

where

$$\phi = \left[1 - m \sum_{i=1}^{n} \rho_i \frac{c}{c+b} \frac{\partial \epsilon_i}{\partial q} \right] ,$$

which adjusts the loss of tariff payments for changes in the size of the interruption;

$$t_1 = \frac{1}{\phi} \bar{t} , \tag{8}$$

the tariff component from inflation and balance of payments costs;

$$t_2 = \frac{1}{\phi} s'(q)q , \tag{9}$$

the tariff component for the monopsony power of the United States to affect prices;

$$t_3 = \frac{1}{\phi} m \sum_{i=1}^{n} \rho_i \frac{\epsilon_i}{c+b} (c(p'(q) - s'(q)) + 1) , \tag{10}$$

the tariff component caused by the economic loss due to dependence or the scale of imports; and

$$t_4 = \frac{1}{\phi} m \sum_{i=1}^{n} \rho_i \left(\frac{q}{c+b} - \frac{\epsilon_i c}{(c+b)^2} \right) \frac{\partial \epsilon_i}{\partial q} , \tag{11}$$

the tariff component caused by the effect of imports on vulnerability or the size of the interruption.

This accounting scheme helps us isolate the key judgments that could contribute to different estimates of the optimal tariff.

PARAMETERS

We can apply this summary model if we have rough estimates of the various parameters. In this section we present such estimates, with key uncertainties indicated.

Inflation and Balance-of-Payments Components

We assume:

$$q \;=\; 8 \text{ million barrels per day}$$
$$\gamma \;=\; .10$$
$$I \;=\; .06$$
$$\bar{q} \;=\; 20 \text{ million barrels per day}$$
$$s \;=\; \$25/\text{barrel}$$
$$\bar{p} \;=\; \$25/\text{barrel}$$
$$.1 \leq \theta \leq .5$$
$$n \;=\; -.5$$
$$0 \leq \delta \leq .005$$
$$s'(q) \;=\; \text{see below.}$$

Therefore, the inflation component of the premium is

$$5(.1 \text{ to } .5) \Big| (0 \text{ to } .005)(25)(20) + (.1)(20)(.2 \text{ to } .6)$$
$$+ .8((.1)(25) - (.06)(25)(1-2))\Big|$$
$$= \$1.80 \text{ to } \$17.25 .$$

For the balance-of-payments component, we assume that $-3 \leq n_E \leq -2$, $-2 \leq n_I \leq -1$. Nordhaus (1980) states that $\beta = .25$. Finally, we assume $-1 \leq \frac{\partial lns}{\partial lne} \leq -.5$. Hence, for 1978 balance-of-payments data (on an annual basis),

$$\frac{\partial lne}{\partial lnq} = \frac{(.75)(25 + .6(8))(8 \times .365)}{(-557 \text{ to } -284) - (-1 \text{ to } -.5)(25)(8 \times .365)}$$

or

$$-.31 \leq \frac{\partial lne}{\partial lnq} \leq -.13 .$$

Therefore,

$$\$1.63 \leq s \frac{\partial lns}{\partial lne} \frac{\partial lne}{\partial lnq} \leq \$7.75 .$$

For our purpose, which is to examine the likely range of import premiums, we might consider the fine tuning of long-run inflation and balance-of-payments benefits as beyond the ability of government. In addition, we can envision a less perfect response by oil producers and other foreign holders of dollars with a resulting transfer of the inflation and balance-of-payments losses to the foreign holders of dollars. Finally, at the larger end of the premium range, the partial equilibrium assumptions will not hold; for example, a deterioration of exchange rates may increase oil imports in other countries and reduce our balance-of-payments deficit. Recognizing these caveats, which are only partially addressed in our analysis, we adopt a range for the combined premium of

$$0 \leq \bar{t} \leq \$20.00 \ .$$

Demand Elasticities

Import demand is the residual of domestic demand minus domestic supply,

$$q(p) = q_1(p) - q_2(p) \ .$$

We assume that the long-run demand elasticity, at 18 MMBD, is $-.5$ and the supply elasticity, at 10 MMBD, is .1, each at \$25/BBL. Hence,

$$q_1'(p) \frac{25}{18} = -.5, \text{ or } q_1'(p) = -.36 \ ;$$

$$q_2'(p) \frac{25}{10} = .1, \text{ or } q_2'(p) = .04 \ .$$

Therefore, $q'(p) = -.40$, or $p'(q) = -2.50$.

Or, a 1 million barrel per day reduction in demand would accompany each \$2.50 increase in price in the long run.

We assume a short-run domestic elasticity of $-.05$, and a short-run domestic supply of .05; hence,

$$q_1' \frac{25}{18} = .05, \text{ or } q_1' = -.036 \ ;$$

$$q_1' \frac{25}{10} = .05, \text{ or } q_2' = .02 \ .$$

Therefore,

$$c = -q'_1 + q'_2 = .056 \ .$$

Import Supply Elasticities

The prediction of the foreign oil producers' response to changes in import levels is problematic. For a revenue-maximizing monopolist, the effective comparative static supply curve is highly elastic. But many other hypotheses have been offered as to the long-run price effects of shifting import demand. We use two alternative assumptions. First, consistent with the monopolist model, we assume a very elastic supply curve with

$$s'(q) = .2 \ ,$$

that is, each 1 million barrel per day change in imports causes a \$.20 change in price. As an alternative,[14] we assume a less elastic supply curve with

$$s'(q) = .6 \ .$$

We assume a short-run import supply elasticity of .1,

$$q' \ \frac{25}{8} = .1, \text{ or } b = q' = .032 \ .$$

Vulnerability

A recent DOE study (Neville et al. 1980) suggests as analytic simplifications three views of the world regarding our vulnerability to supply interruptions. In terms of the size of one-year interruptions for the United States, these three views are depicted in Table A9−1.

Taking these probabilities as the chance in ten years of one or more events leading to U.S. supply interruptions of the given size, and assuming independence of events, the corresponding one-year probabilities are depicted in Table A9−2.

---

14. This price response compares with that of Stobaugh and Yergin (1979), who assume a 10 MMBD shift in q produces a \$6 shift in s for an average value of $s'(q) = .6$. The figure of $s'(q) = .2$ is comparable with the work of Salant (1980).

Table A9-1. Disruption world views (*decade probabilities*).

World View	ϵ_1 = 1 MMBD	ϵ_2 = 3 MMBD	ϵ_3 = 6 MMBD
1	.50	.10	.05
2	.75	.30	.05
3	.95	.50	.20

Table A9-2. Disruption world views (*one-year probabilities*).

World View	ϵ_1 = 1	ϵ_2 = 3	ϵ_3 = 6
1	.07	.01	.005
2	.13	.04	.005
3	.26	.07	.02

The second feature of vulnerability is our ability to change the exposure by reducing oil imports. Surprisingly, we may be very limited in our ability to affect exposure; in other words $\frac{\partial \epsilon}{\partial q}$ might be quite small.

In a freely operating market, assuming rough equality of demand elasticities across countries, allocation of a supply reduction will be in proportion to consumption. This natural tendency will be reinforced by the IEA sharing agreements which also allocate shortages in proportion to consumption. This rule largely determines the dependency of interruption size on the level of imports under the control of a single country acting alone.

Consider the present situation. The United States accounts for 36 percent of the free world's oil consumption (18 out of 50 million barrels of oil per day (MMBD). If the world lost 10 MMBD in an interruption, the United States would have to absorb a 3.6 MMBD cutback. Now suppose that in the absence of the interruption the United States reduced its consumption and imports by 2 MMBD. This would reduce our share of total consumption to 33 percent (16 out of 48 MMBD). How much would this reduce the U.S. shortage? We look at two cases: (1) where there is no reduction in the size of the interruption, and (2) where there is a full elimination of 2 MMBD of supply curtailment:

Table A9−3.   Shortages and import levels.

Case	Interruption Size	a U.S. Interruption (33-1/3%)	b Change (3.6-a)	$\frac{\partial \epsilon}{\partial q}$ (b/2)
1	10	3.33	.267	.134
2	8	2.64	.960	.480

Under market operations and under the IEA sharing rules, the change in vulnerability per unit change in imports is anywhere from 13 to 48 percent.

VALUE OF STOCKPILE

With these parameters, we can calculate the optimal pre-interruption tariff. In doing so, we can also evaluate the expected benefits of adding a barrel of oil to the stockpile. Under the IEA agreements, the stockpile is not shared; each barrel of oil drawn from the stockpile during an emergency reduces the size of the interruption to the country by 1 barrel. Hence the change in interruption costs is just the derivative of the objective function with respect to ϵ.

If the IEA agreement breaks down, and the stockpile must be shared, the reduction in emergency costs is in proportion to the share of consumption, denoted as α. With no sharing, $\alpha = 1$; with full sharing, $\alpha = .36$ for the United States. In addition, use of the stockpiled oil yields the full consumer surplus benefit less the direct cost of the oil.

These benefits accrue until the stock of oil is used in an emergency. Following Neville (1980) and Teisberg (1979) we provide a conservative estimate of the premium by assuming that only half the stockpiled oil will be used in an emergency. Hence, the undiscounted marginal expected premium for a barrel of oil in the stockpile is

$$\frac{1}{2} \sum_{j=1}^{10} (1 - \sum_{i=1}^{n} \rho_i)^{j-1} \ m \sum_{i=1}^{n} \rho_i \left[\alpha \left\{ \frac{c}{c+b} \ (p(q) - s(q)) + \frac{q}{c+b} - \frac{\epsilon_i c}{(c+b)^2} \right\} + \frac{\epsilon_i}{c+b} \right] ,$$

Table A9–4.   Assumptions.

Parameter	Low	Medium	High
World View	1	2	3
α	.36	.7	1.00
Demand Elasticity (LR)	−.5	−.35	−.20
$\dfrac{\partial \epsilon}{\partial q}$	0	.13	.48
$s'(q)$	.1	.2	.6
$\bar{t}$	0	10.0	20.0
m	1	1.5	2.0
q	7.3	4.7	3.2

or

$$\left[\frac{1-(1-\sum_{i=1}^{n} \rho_i)^{10}}{\sum_{i=1}^{n} \rho_i} \right] \frac{m}{2} \sum_{i=1}^{n} \rho_i \left[\alpha \left\{ \frac{c}{c+b} (p(q)-s(q)) + \frac{q}{c+b} - \frac{\epsilon_i c}{(c+b)^2} \right\} + \frac{\epsilon_i}{c+b} \right] . \quad (12)$$

CALCULATING PREMIUMS

With these accounts and parameters we are prepared to estimate the optimal tariffs. We illustrate the range of debate by examining three different combinations of assumptions, leading to three levels of the optimal tariff. We use equation (6) above and solve simultaneously for the optimal tariff and the optimal level of imports. Equation (5), scaled to an annual basis, allows us to compare the objective function with and without the interruption costs to compute the expected annual costs of interruption. The three sets of assumptions are summarized in Table A9–4.

The resulting premium or tariff estimates appear in Table A9–5. Hence, if we believe the assumptions associated with the low estimate, which is consistent with world view one, then we should be

Table A9–5.   Import and stockpile premiums ($ *barrel*).

	Low	Medium	High
t_1	0	10.21	25.40
t_2	.73	.94	1.95
t_3	1.23	3.08	5.33
t_4	0	1.42	10.45
Total	1.97	15.66	43.13
Annual Expected Cost of Interruption	3.6×10^9	8.58×10^9	30.18×10^9
Stockpile Premium	12.74	34.27	70.38

willing to impose only $2 per barrel as a tariff above world oil prices in order to reduce oil import demand. But if we believe the assumptions associated with the high estimate, we should be willing to impose a tariff of $43 per barrel. On close examination, it appears that the most important security assumptions are those regarding the probability of an interruption and the degree to which import reductions mitigate the severity of supply interruptions. If import interruptions are unlikely, or if oil import reductions do not help lower the size of interruptions, then we should not, for reasons of security, be willing to pay much to reduce oil imports. But if there is a high probability of a large interruption, and reducing imports now will reduce the size of the interruption when it comes, we should be willing to pay a great deal to reduce imports—to reduce dependency in order to reduce vulnerability.

For the medium and high cases, the dominance of the inflation and balance-of-payments premium reflects the importance of the assumptions regarding the macroeconomic response. Given the assumed high cost of dampening inflation, the premium estimate turns critically on the assumed degree of inflation accomodation. The case of the largest premium may suggest a need to reexamine the macroeconomic policy more than to impose such a high import tariff.

The other message of this exercise and Table A9–5 is the high value of building the strategic petroleum reserve. In fact, the same premiums would apply to any program that could provide quick substitutes for imports in the event of an interruption.

10 COPING WITH INTERRUPTIONS

Alvin L. Alm
William Colglazier
Barbara Kates–Garnick

LESSONS FROM THE PAST

Twice in seven years the United States suffered from petroleum supply interruptions. Both times the price of imported oil shot up precipitously, and rapid inflation and a serious recession soon followed. Both times the country endured gasoline lines, trucker revolts, and the fear of heating oil shortages. Both times domestic allocation programs designed to minimize dislocations made the problems worse. Both times stocks on hand at the end of the disruption were greater than at the beginning. Both times the improvised machinery to deal with the interruption proved to be woefully inadequate.

The time for inaction and complacency has long since passed. Americans need to learn from their experience and devise effective measures to deal with the next supply interruption. This chapter reviews the events following the Iranian upheaval in an effort to develop principles for assessing response measures and then proposes a number of policy directions to make the United States more secure in the future.

We would like to thank William Taylor and his colleagues at the Department of Energy for several helpful discussions.

Damages from Supply Interruptions

When people think of an emergency shortfall, they envision gasoline lines, cold homes, and closed factories. The direct disruption of supplies not only creates personal inconvenience and hardship but also damages certain industries such as tourism, automobile manufacturing, and trucking.

A second form of damage—economic losses from higher prices—results when demand exceeds supply and OPEC is able to raise the price of oil. Sharp price increases can occur from an interruption because of the relatively slow response of demand to price. They generate substantial wealth transfers from the United States to producer countries; induce productivity losses as energy costs become a higher fraction of the cost of goods; and, by simultaneously increasing inflation and lowering growth, prevent effective use of fiscal and monetary tools by the government to promote economic recovery.

Yet another form of damage is the perilous weakening of America's foreign policy position. A supply interruption disrupts the cohesion of the Western alliance, aggravates instabilities in the Third World, and increases the likelihood of confrontation with the Soviet Union.

The shortfall in Iranian supplies inflicted all three forms of damage on the United States. The size of the loss to the world oil market is shown in Figure 10-1 (DOE 1980d: 26). Iranian production dropped 3.8 million barrels per day between the three month period ending in November 1978 and the three month period ending in March 1979. Production outside of Iran rose by 1.8 million barrels per day over the same interval, reducing the total loss to the world oil market during the first quarter of 1979 to approximately 2 million barrels per day, roughly 4 percent of free world production. In total, the world oil market lost only 150 million barrels of supply, which is equivalent to five days of OPEC production or three days of free world consumption. So the Iranian losses were small, especially when compared to possible future losses. But they set in motion a series of events that more than doubled the world oil price and transformed the world petroleum market.

Direct Disruption of Supplies. The Iranian cutbacks resulted in substantial disruptions of gasoline and diesel fuel supplies in the United

Figure 10-1. Components of total free world crude oil production (Iran versus rest of world)[a].

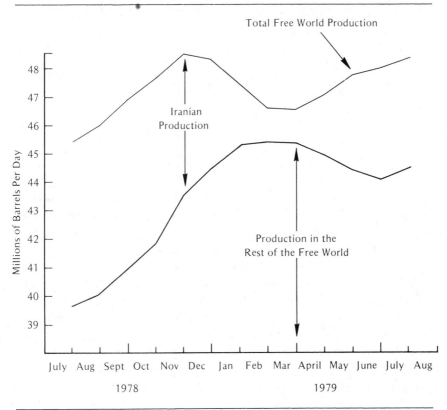

a. Each point in the figure represents the average production level over the preceding three months.

Source: DOE (1980d).

States. Stocks of distillate products, including both diesel fuel and heating oil, were at dangerously low levels at the beginning of 1979 — 17 percent below those of the previous year (DOE 1980e: 7). In the spring of 1979, farmers claimed that the supply of diesel fuel for agricultural equipment would be insufficient for crop planting, raising the spectre of increased food prices. To counter this threat, the Department of Energy (DOE) allocated diesel fuel to farmers, and the farmers took advantage of their priority allocation by increasing their own stocks. By diverting supplies to agriculture, diesel fuel shortages were shifted to truckers by late spring. Saddled with rising diesel prices and frustrated by purported Interstate Commerce Commission (ICC) delays in allowing recovery of those higher costs, the truckers rebelled. Sporadic violence forced plans for truck convoys and other measures to assure that needed products would be brought to market. Changes in ICC procedures and easing of the shortage reduced the intensity of the truckers' discontent.

The fear of future heating oil shortages caused the government in April to set a target of 240 million barrels of distillate stocks by October. This target was a clear signal to refiners that if shortages were to occur, homes and factories would be protected at the expense of motorists.

The gasoline shortage for the general public was more pervasive, long-lived, and politically volatile. The extent of the disruption was shaped by three forces: demand for gasoline prior to the shortage, government priorities for allocating cutbacks, and private stockpile policies. From late 1978 to early 1979, gasoline demand was at an all time high despite extensive publicity given to the production cutback in Iran. Consumption was 6 percent higher in February and approximately equal in March and April to 1978 demand levels. Virtually no provisions, other than requests by the government for voluntary conservation, were made to reduce gasoline consumption before the inevitable shortages occurred.

By May, the gasoline shortages began to appear in California. The Department of Energy indicated at that time that these shortages would soon disappear and could be avoided elsewhere provided that crude oil imports reached projected levels and oil companies used part of their stocks. During the early summer of 1979, the Department began urging refiners to increase their yields and to draw upon both crude and gasoline stocks. What actually happened, however, was quite different. By June, reserves were being built up; crude and gasoline stocks had climbed to their levels of one year before. But gasoline supplied was down by almost 9 percent. In August, gasoline stocks were 11 percent higher than the previous August while gasoline supplied was down by about 8 percent.

Various interpretations can be made of these data (DOE 1980d; Department of Justice 1980). Although one could argue that the oil companies were holding back supplies to profit from future higher prices, the most logical explanation is that they were merely being conservative. The industry would have been foolish to antagonize Congress and the public intentionally while the terms of the Windfall

Profits Tax were being debated, which would affect their profits for years to come. The companies had experienced heavy consumer demand for gasoline in the early part of 1979, and, being fearful of instability and uncertainties in the oil market following the Iranian cutback, they hedged by building up high stock levels. In retrospect, a prudent drawing down of stocks could have avoided much of the agony during May and June of 1979. The lesson for the United States, as well as other consuming countries, is that uncertainty will induce stock buildups rather than withdrawals, exacerbating the shortages.

In April of 1979, the Department of Energy issued a response plan describing the steps being taken to mitigate the shortages (DOE 1979). Besides voluntary conservation and efforts already underway, such as increased production at the Elk Hills Naval Petroleum Reserve, the plan called for greater fuel switching to natural gas made more available by the Natural Gas Policy Act of 1978; increased wheeling[1] of electricity from utilities with coal and nuclear power to those heavily dependent upon oil-fired generation; mandatory controls on building temperatures; and reductions in the federal use of oil. Independent of the response plan, the President initiated the gradual decontrol of domestic crude oil prices, which would be completed by October 1981.

Although the emergency response measures reduced oil use somewhat, the savings did not approach the 1.2 million barrels of oil per day projected in the response plan for the summer of 1979. Furthermore, the savings that were achieved were mainly of residual fuel oil, which was in surplus throughout the emergency. The measures in the response plan were certainly not sufficient to alleviate the loss of petroleum supplies.

The government used the 1974 regulatory authorities to allocate the reduced supplies of crude oil to refineries and gasoline to dealers. Using the market to allocate petroleum was not possible because of price controls on domestic crude oil and gasoline and uneven refinery access to crude oil supplies. As might have been expected, regulatory inflexibility often compounded the problems. For example, the Department of Energy had to allocate some crude oil supplies away

---

1. Wheeling is the transfer of electricity over high voltage transmission lines between utilities. Wheeling is normally used to balance loads on a daily or seasonal basis, and can be used during interruptions to transfer electricity from utilities unaffected by the emergency to those experiencing shortages.

from sophisticated refineries that could produce gasoline and middle distillate to smaller and less complex refineries that mainly produced residual fuel oil. Although the amounts were not substantial, residual oil was made more abundant at the expense of badly needed gasoline and distillate fuel.

Nor did the allocation regulations always allow gasoline to be distributed where it was most needed. The regulations initially used 1972 as the base year for calculating allocations. As the shortages began to pinch, the Department of Energy quickly updated the base period to 1977–1978 and created special provisions for supplies to rapidly growing areas. Nevertheless, consumption patterns during an emergency are not the same as historical usage because driving patterns change. The uncertainty about gasoline supplies discouraged vacations and even weekend outings, but outlying tourist areas continued to receive allocations based on the previous year's consumption. Hence, portions of rural America were awash with gasoline while long lines formed in the cities.

The regulatory allocation system also doled out disparities among refining regions. Gasoline is not allocated by state or region but by supplies available to each oil company. Under this arrangement, if a company in one state has enough crude oil to meet its gasoline demand while a second company can only meet part of its demand, then the state in which the first company operates will have ample supplies while the other state suffers shortages. Explaining why Maryland experienced greater shortages than many other states, a DOE official answered: "It's the luck of the draw."

Perhaps the Department of Energy could have done more in implementing the allocation program, but each refinement of the regulations extracts a high price in added confusion and uncertainty. On balance, it is unlikely that a substantially different outcome would have occurred if the regulatory program were even more finely tuned. The only certain cure for gasoline lines was deregulation of gasoline prices. Lifting of price controls would have efficiently allocated supplies and restrained demand, but at the cost of high profits by oil companies and independent service stations. In retrospect, American consumers benefited little, if at all, from the regulatory program. They bore the inconvenience of gasoline lines only for a small respite in facing higher prices.

Economic Damage. During and following the Iranian cutback in petroleum production, consuming nations and the international oil companies attempted simultaneously to meet current demands and to build up stockpiles, even beyond normal levels. The goal was to achieve some protection in an unstable and uncertain market. For example, the Japanese, many of whose contracts for oil with major oil companies were cancelled, set about building stockpiles to ninety days of supply, almost without regard to cost. Spot prices began to soar, leading to cancellation of contracts by some producer nations, higher official prices, and a two-tier pricing system. With revenues ballooning, a number of OPEC nations cut back production, further aggravating price pressures and encouraging consumers to build even larger stockpiles. Besides increasing prices, the sellers' market emboldened many OPEC countries to tie contracts to economic concessions and limitations on destination. Within one year, the world petroleum market had been fundamentally and permanently changed.

These forces raised world oil prices by a staggering 120 percent in 1979, from an average of $13 per barrel at the beginning of January to $28 by the end of December. The increase in the price of oil following the OPEC oil embargo in 1973 was larger in percentage terms, 230 percent, but smaller in current dollars, from an average of approximately $3 in 1973 to $11 in 1974.

The economic consequences of these price increases for the United States were severe. The precise magnitude of the damage is controversial among economists, but one careful analysis has found that most of the extraordinary inflation in 1974 and almost all of the recession in 1974 and 1975 were due to the first energy price shock (Mork and Hall 1980: 42). That study attributes to the energy price increases a 4 percent contribution to the 1974 inflation rate and a loss in real output of $30 billion in 1974 and $66 billion in 1975 (in 1972 dollars). Analysis is still being done on the economic effects of the 1979 price rise, but these will certainly include a loss in real output of many billions of dollars in 1979 and 1980 and a substantial contribution to the high inflation rate. The bill for imported oil alone will be $35 billion higher in 1980 than in 1978. Equally important, the inflation from oil price increases has greatly increased the difficulty of managing the economy, intensifying the 1980 recession.

In both 1974 and 1979, no effort was made to develop an international consumers' coalition to reduce price pressures. At the March meeting of the International Energy Agency, the United States succeeded in gaining agreement on a 5 percent reduction in consumption by each member nation. There was, however, no attempt to trigger the allocation system, smooth out stockpile purchases, or make a concerted effort to cap spot market prices. Evidently, few Western observers expected prices would rise so dramatically, and each nation was more concerned at that time with direct disruption of supplies than with long-term price increases. These miscalculations by the Western countries have proven to be very costly to their economies.

Weakening of American Foreign Policy. In addition to the substantial change in the power balance within the Persian Gulf, the Iranian upheaval affected American relations with Europe and Japan. Instead of leading to cooperative actions among the industrialized Western nations, the immediate result of the supply shortfall was increased competition and tension. Politicians were presented with the difficult task of satisfying domestic constituencies while protecting international interests.

The first strain in relations came from the aggressive Japanese response to contract terminations from major oil companies. Their behavior, although understandable, did lead to the bidding up of world oil prices on the spot market. Since marginal demand dictates price trends, OPEC was able to continue the upward price spiral for all customers. The President of the United States responded by publicly chastizing the Japanese for bidding up prices.

The United States may also have been guilty of an action that, at least temporarily, forced prices up. Faced with apprehension about distillate stock levels for the coming winter, and concern that heavy bidding was encouraging diversion of traditional American distillate supplies to Europe, the President authorized a $5 per barrel subsidy for U.S. imports of distillate fuel oil. The subsidy was provided through the domestic entitlements program associated with price controls, a program that the allies felt was already encouraging excess consumption in the United States. The subsidy was put into effect without even advance consultation with other Western consuming nations. Their reaction was instantaneous and vociferous. They saw the subsidy as a "beggar thy neighbor" policy. Considering the greater domestic energy base of the United States, its smaller dependence on imported oil, and its price control incentives for overconsumption, the hostile reaction from the allies was predictable. At the June Economic Summit in Tokyo, the Western nations agreed not to employ any similar import subsidies in the future.

Conclusions from Iranian Experience

Three conclusions concerning interruptions are inescapable from this retrospective look at the Iranian episode. First, a sudden supply shortfall will produce inexorable pressures for bidding up oil prices. Second, relying again only on the emergency measures used in 1979 will lead to an inadequate domestic response to the crisis. Third, divisive tensions will inevitably arise among the allies.

The experience of two interruptions has not led to the development of policy responses that will prevent a recurrence of this dismal history. The United States has not yet put into operational readiness all the emergency measures authorized in the 1975 Energy Production and Conservation Act (EPCA). After five years, there are only thirteen days' supply of imports in the strategic petroleum reserve; there is no operational gasoline rationing plan; and the one emergency conservation measure approved by Congress (Emergency Building Temperature Restriction Program) appears to be in permanent rather than standby use.

In trying to comprehend why the United States has failed to develop some protection against future supply interruptions, it is useful to elaborate on the distinction between dependence and vulnerability. The two terms are often used interchangeably in energy rhetoric, but there is a difference between them that is critical to any understanding of the energy security threat. Dependence is defined as the amount of oil imported, particularly from unstable areas. Vulnerability is defined as the expected damage from a supply interruption. There are two considerations in assessing vulnerability: the magnitude of the shortfall that the United States would sustain during an interruption, and our capacity to minimize the damage.

The physical difference between dependence and vulnerability can be illustrated with a simple calculation. In recent years, the United States has imported roughly 8 million barrels per day out of a total domestic consumption of 18 million barrels per day. A 2 million barrel per day reduction of oil imports would reduce U.S. dependence by 25 percent (2 mbd/8 mbd). But cutbacks from an interruption are likely to be allocated on the basis of total oil consumption rather than on the level of imports. Hence, a reduction in dependence by 25 percent (2 mbd/8 mbd) lowers physical vulnerability by only

11 percent (2 mbd/18 mbd). Even with feasible rates of import reduction in the 1980s, this calculation illustrates that the U.S. percentage share of a shortfall would not be much reduced.

There is little prospect that the United States, much less the Western alliance, could eliminate dependence and achieve "energy independence" in the foreseeable future. The DOE's optimistic goal for
the United States is to cut oil imports by 50 percent, to 4 million
barrels per day, by 1980 (DOE 1980a: 1–8). Some major oil companies have made a more pessimistic assessment of future import
levels because they expect a decline in domestic oil production of 2
to 3 million barrels per day over the same period (Exxon 1979: 16).
But even if the United States were able to completely eliminate oil
imports, a large supply interruption would threaten American security by weakening allies who will remain heavily dependent on imported oil for a long time to come. We have moral, legal, and political
obligations to share supplies with our allies, whose security is intertwined with ours. Therefore, reducing dependence is not sufficient
to cope with the U.S. national security problem. Entirely different
tools and approaches are needed to guard against this threat.

Why has the United States failed to develop adequate protective
measures against future petroleum emergencies? There has been no
dearth of major energy initiatives, such as Project Independence and
the National Energy Plan. But the emphasis of policy has been to
reduce dependence rather than vulnerability. Billions of dollars have
or will be spent on fusion, advanced nuclear options, synthetic fuels,
and renewable technologies which will not have an appreciable effect
until somewhere between 1990 and the middle of the twenty-first
century. Not that we should lessen our efforts to deal with the long
term decline in petroleum energy; but we should give equal emphasis
to the more immediate and potentially devastating problem of supply interruptions.

Conditions during Supply Interruptions

Managing responses to energy interruptions is an almost impossible
job. Decisionmakers never know how serious the interruption will be,
how long it will last, and what damage it will cause. Government personnel tend to be inexperienced in dealing with emergencies, and
their decisions, subject to unbearable political pressure and not tied
to precedent, tend to be ad hoc. Without the proper tools, applied

predictably, response measures are very likely to make the situation worse.

The first step in planning response measures is to appreciate the variety of potential emergencies that could arise. These contingencies range from an interruption like the one of 1979, which, although small in volume, set in motion large price rises and caused panic, to very large interruptions that would threaten economic collapse.

One analysis by the Department of Energy has estimated the likelihood of various interruptions according to three reasonable views of the world (Neville et al. 1980: 3). The estimates are summarized in Table 10−1. The three disruption cases correspond to the production loss of a small OPEC state, the loss of Saudi Arabia, and the loss of the whole Persian Gulf. For these shortfalls, the annual U.S. economic costs alone were estimated to be $85 billion, $325 billion, and $685 billion, respectively.

A majority of the energy experts who have studied the DOE report believe that World View 2 is the most realistic of the three alternatives. Although the probabilities for the large interruptions in the table are truly speculative, the experience of the past decade suggests that a small disruption is highly probable in the 1980s and that a very large interruption is far from inconceivable.

Although planning for interruptions of various magnitudes is difficult, being prepared for an unknown duration is even harder. It is possible to plan abstractly for a one-year, 3 million barrel per day shortfall. But during an interruption, decisionmakers do not know whether it will last three months or three years. If they incorrectly assume a long interruption, then they will fail to use stockpiles that

Table 10−1.   Hypothetical probabilities of oil supply disruptions.

World Views	Size of One-Year Disruption (percentage probability for occurrence at least once in decade)		
	3 mbd	10 mbd	20 mbd
1	50%	10%	5%
2	75	30	5
3	95	50	20

Source: Neville, Blankenship, Barron, and Lane (1980).

could have reduced price pressures and shortages. If they err in the other direction, the hardships may dangerously worsen as stockpiles are depleted too quickly. These judgments are critical and extraordinarily difficult to make.

A third complicating factor is the decisionmaking and management system. During the last two supply interruptions, decisionmaking and management were undertaken by people with little experience in dealing with interruptions and with no established response programs or administrative organization to back them up. It is easy to criticize the failures of the Department of Energy and its predecessors. But successful programs take many years to become established and well managed; it is folly to expect an improvised management structure, led by people under severe pressure, to perform with precision. Response planning must take this reality into account.

The political pressures during a supply interruption cannot be underestimated. Nearly everyone will be calling for the government to do something. The temptation to accede to outside demands can cause some of the most serious policy mistakes. Mechanisms must be developed in advance to prevent these pressures from derailing a reasoned response. The tendency to deal only with short term problems during an emergency can lead to further errors. Top officials are besieged with congressional hearings, White House meetings, sessions with special interest groups, and briefings in their own agencies. This focus on immediate problems can lead to a series of tactical, rather than strategic, decisions without thinking through their broader ramifications.

Principles for U.S. Responses to Oil Emergencies

Considering the experience of the past decade and the pressures on officials during an interruption, it is possible to identify principles that are critically important in planning to deter and alleviate the damages of supply interruptions. These principals will be applied to the specific policy proposals that are described in the next section.

First, emergency response measures must deal simultaneously with upward price pressures as well as with direct disruption from the shortages. Each time a decisionmaker considers a policy to increase or to allocate supplies, he or she must ask what that policy will do to the price of imported oil. Indeed, the first consideration in dealing with an interruption must be how to blunt the pressures that send prices spiralling upward. The United States has paid dearly for its failure to do so during the last two supply interruptions.

Second, planning must be sufficiently flexible to take into account the unknown duration of an interruption. Certain measures must be ready to be put into effect immediately and automatically when an interruption occurs. Other measures must be ready to be instituted when more information is available on the likely depth and duration of the interruption.

Third, emergency measures should use the marketplace to the greatest extent possible. Letting the market allocate supplies is more efficient and less cumbersome than using regulatory requirements, which are subject to political pressures and human limitations. Whenever regulatory requirements are proposed, their proponents should be required to prove that the market could not serve more effectively and efficiently, and no less equitably, within the time available.

Fourth, responses must be predictable enough to insulate the President and Congress from detailed energy management decisions and to prevent public panic. The President must have the time and opportunity to deal with the political situation that caused the interruption; that situation could easily be a threat to world peace. For private individuals and companies, uncertainty about the nature and adequacy of the government response can exacerbate the problems by causing stock hoarding and upward price bidding.

Fifth, the management structure for dealing with the supply short-falls should be established in advance. Creation of new bureaucracies during a crisis should be avoided at all cost. It may be necessary to centralize all emergency planning and operational responsibilities at the level of a presidential appointee in the Department of Energy.

Finally, U.S. response plans must contain both domestic and international initiatives. Coordinated international action will be critical in capping price increases and avoiding chaotic energy markets. At a minimum, the United States should support the International Energy Agency sharing system while exploring more comprehensive areas for international cooperation.

RESPONSES FOR THE FUTURE

So far we have touched on the large damages that an interruption can inflict, the chaotic conditions under which emergency management takes place, and the guiding principles that should underlie response measures. These principles are difficult to apply because some conflict with traditional thinking and others raise controversial political issues like raising prices or devolving authority to an international organization. But these conflicts and issues must be addressed because the probability of a future interruption is high and the United States is no better prepared now than in 1973.

Although possible responses to an interruption are almost as diverse as the uses of energy, this section will focus on coordinated international actions, domestic allocations, and stockpiles. We will also evaluate a number of potential supply initiatives and emergency conservation measures to determine how they can supplement other efforts. First, we will discuss whether import reductions prior to an emergency can help cope with the threat of a supply interruption.

Import Reductions

Reducing U.S. dependence on imported oil is important for a number of reasons. Import reductions help create slack in the world oil market and, thereby, put a downward pressure on price. The excess capacity which is created in producer states could become a valuable asset to consumers if used to offset shortages during a disruption. Having lowered production from an unstable area might also decrease the size of a subsequent interruption. Import reductions lessen the wealth transfers to producers during both normal and disrupted periods, which, for the United States, is essential for reducing the balance of payments deficits and the macroeconomic impacts from the government trying to cope with the induced inflation and recession. Thus, successful efforts by the United States to curb growth in oil consumption could result in lower long-term energy prices, greater opportunity for economic growth, smaller economic losses during supply interruptions, and decreased tension with allies over energy policy.

As discussed in the previous section and chapter, import reduction policies are not sufficient for protecting the United States against disruption of supplies in the 1980s. Thus, a large subsidy or crash program to reduce imports far beyond what is in U.S. economic interest cannot be justified on the basis of national security.

In order to determine which policies for reducing imports are appropriate, the "oil premium" discussed in Chapter 9 should be calculated in a rational and careful manner. The premium takes into account the hidden costs associated with national security, environmental quality, and the effect of import levels on world oil prices, inflation, and the balance of payments deficit. As outlined in Chapter 9, the size of the premium is sensitive to various assumptions. If the premium were accepted, whatever its value, and added to the cost of foreign oil, as with a steady-state tariff, then government intervention could only be justified on the basis of achieving least-cost energy for end-use demands. National security would be dealt with more directly with other measures such as stockpiles, disruption tariffs, emergency allocation systems, and so forth. Understanding the goals of energy policy can assure that proper resources are directed to both managing the energy transition and reducing vulnerability, a condition that unfortunately has not always been true in the past.

International Measures

The most important objectives for consumer nations during an interruption are to prevent producers from sharply raising oil prices and to share the burden of the shortfall equitably. Through the International Energy Agency (IEA), the consumer countries have addressed the distribution issue but have not focused directly on price. The tendency for prices to rise during oil crises can be mitigated by larger and coordinated use of stockpiles, implementation of a coordinated emergency oil tariff, or operation of an allocation system. The goal is to compensate quickly for the shortfall with reserves and with a reduction in demand before producers can raise prices. The international cooperation required among the energy consumers to operate such a regime has historically been difficult to achieve.

Sharing and Price Cap. The 1974 International Energy Agency sharing agreement, which focuses on the distribution issue, grew out of political exigencies following the first oil disruption. The agreement, triggered when any signatory suffers losses of more than 7 percent of its total consumption, was crafted to deter targeted embargoes, particularly by Arab OPEC members. The sharing agreement also specifies in detail how oil is to be allocated among the participating countries when there is a group shortfall equal to or greater than 7 percent of total IEA consumption. Historically, the major oil companies have distributed oil during shortages in such a way that all consuming countries received about the same reduction as a percentage of consumption. The IEA sharing formula is similar but considerably more favorable to countries with domestic oil production for large interruptions. Table 10–2 lists the approximate cutback in oil consumption by IEA countries for various world shortfalls according to both the IEA sharing formula and an allocation system based on equal percentage reductions in consumption.

In addition, each country is required to keep reserves of at least ninety days' imports, which can then be used to make up for part of its portion of the shortfall. The remainder of the shortfall must be met by demand reductions, either 7 or 10 percent of consumption depending on the size of the interruption.[2] According to the agreement, stocks in excess of the mandated level can be used by a country instead of taking demand restraint measures. For the United States, roughly 600 to 700 million barrels of stocks (ninety days of imports) would be eligible for sharing under the IEA agreement; the rest could be used exclusively to meet domestic shortfalls. The IEA definition of stocks that can be counted to meet the ninety-day requirement supposedly excludes any oil not technically available for use during a severe emergency. How closely the IEA adheres to that definition will be addressed later.

The IEA countries have reached other agreements, such as the import ceilings set at Tokyo in June 1979 (and modified in December) and the phased reduction of oil usage set at the Venice Summit in June 1980. However, none of these measures is directly designed to stem the price pressures or the disruption of supplies that arise from an oil interruption.

The IEA sharing agreement, if applied rigorously, could curb the oil price increases that spring from supply interruptions. The consuming nations would rigidly enforce the IEA sharing agreement together with an advance agreement on the maximum price for their oil purchases. Since large price increases can result from small interruptions, the agreement should take effect even for shortfalls smaller than the current trigger. While the sharing agreement would allocate existing supplies, the maximum price agreement would prevent the bidding up of oil prices on the spot market. These two agreements would try to match OPEC's power with a consumers' coalition.

---

2. For shortfalls between 7 and 12 percent of consumption, IEA member countries are required to reduce demand by 7 percent. For shortfalls greater than 12 percent, IEA countries are required to reduce demand by 10 percent.

Unfortunately, the rigorous sharing agreement with the price cap requires an unprecedented level of discipline to work. Each participating country would have to reduce oil use in the face of rising protests from its citizens. Since the hardships caused by the shortages will vary among consuming countries, pressures to cheat or to abrogate the agreement are always present and will intensify as the crisis lengthens. Producer nations have the ability to retaliate by disrupting marketing or reducing production further, probably to levels that Western economies could not tolerate. The actual motivation of states like Saudi Arabia will depend heavily on the nature of the interruption, whether it is a political or chaotic situation. Although this alternative is theoretically interesting, there is little evidence that the consuming nations have the cohesiveness to make it work.

Stockpiles. It is in the interest of the United States to encourage other consuming countries to expand both government and private reserves. Although buying the oil for these foreign stockpiles will create short-term price pressures in the world market, all consuming countries stand to benefit substantially if that reserve oil is used to moderate prices during a disruption. The United States has no guarantee that foreign stocks will actually be drawn down during an interruption, but their existence will lessen the possibility of frantic competition for supplies and bidding up of prices on the spot market.

That stockpiles are currently at historically high levels in Japan and Europe provides an opportunity to preserve and expand this option. Total European and Japanese primary oil stocks on hand at the end of each of the past three years are given in Table 10—3 in millions of barrels and in approximate days of consumption. Stockpile building has continued through the first quarter of 1980.

These figures in Table 10—3. do not indicate how much of the oil stockpiles are actually available for use in an emergency; a large portion of this oil is needed to maintain normal operations. Because they are smaller geographically than the United States, however, Europe and Japan do have a smaller percentage of their stocks tied up in the distribution systems.

Increased stockpile levels in the major consuming countries has many advantages. Used in an emergency, large Western stockpiles could reduce price pressures and increase supplies during an interruption. Upward pressure on the spot price would be reduced by dump-

Table 10-2. Cutback in oil consumption by IEA countries for various world shortfalls *(according to sharing agreement of the International Energy Agency).*

Country	1979 Total Inland Oil Consumption[a] (mbd)	1979 Net Imports[b] (mbd)	Approximate Country Shortfall for Various World Shortfalls[c] (mbd) (Upper figure is shortfall according to IEA agreement; lower figure is shortfall if allocation based on same percentage reduction in total consumption.)				
			1 mbd	3 mbd	5 mbd	10 mbd	20 mbd
Canada	1.77	.22	.034 / .034	.101 / .101	.132 / .168	.206 / .335	.267 / .670
Italy	1.61	1.99	.030 / .030	.091 / .091	.185 / .152	.422 / .305	.977 / .610
Japan	5.17	5.63	.098 / .098	.294 / .294	.566 / .489	1.257 / .979	2.825 / 1.957
United Kingdom	1.69	.44	.032 / .032	.096 / .096	.134 / .160	.227 / .320	.349 / .640
United States	18.43	7.94	.349 / .349	1.047 / 1.047	1.578 / 1.744	2.886 / 3.489	5.098 / 6.977
West Germany	2.66	2.84	.050 / .050	.151 / .151	.289 / .252	.639 / .504	1.430 / 1.007
Other IEA Members	4.47	5.27[d]	.085 / .085	.254 / .254	.504 / .423	1.139 / .846	2.607 / 1.692
Total	35.80	24.33[e]	.678	2.033	3.388	6.776	13.553

Notes to Table 10-2

a. U.S. Department of Energy, Monthly Energy Review, DOE/EIA 0035/80 (06), June, 1980, p. 86. Total inland oil consumption is approximately 93% to 95% of total IEA consumption.

b. Central Intelligence Agency, International Energy Statistical Review, ER IESR 80–010, June 24, 1980, pp. 9–11.

c. World production of crude oil and natural gas liquids outside of the centrally planned economies was 51.50 mbd in 1979. Assuming oil exports from the Soviet Union to free world countries in 1979 at roughly the same level as in 1978, 1.33 mbd, yields an approximate value for free world consumption (including addition to stockpiles) in 1979 at 52.83 mbd. It is assumed that the percentage of the world shortfall absorbed by the IEA countries as a group is equal to their percentage of free world consumption before the interruption (which may not be the case).

d. This figure includes U.S. territories and is calculated from data in the OECD Observer, January, 1980, p. 35.

e. Total net imports less bunkers was approximately 22.9 mbd.

Table 10–3.   Primary oil stocks in Europe and Japan.

	Western Europe[a]		Japan[a]	
Year	Millions of Barrels at End of Year	"Days of Consumption"[b]	Millions of Barrels[c] at End of Year	"Days of Consumption"[b]
1977	1028	102	407	79
1978	982	97	411	79
1979	1076	107	461	89

a. These figures come from the International Energy Statistical Review, National Foreign Assessment Center, Central Intelligence Agency, ER IESR 80–010, June 24, 1980. The Western Europe figures include: Belgium, Denmark, France, Italy, Luxembourg, Netherlands, Spain, Great Britain, and West Germany. Because of seasonal variations, stocks on hand at the end of a year are usually larger than the average for the year.

b. This column has been calculated by dividing the first column by the inland oil consumption for 1979. Stockpile levels for 1980 are higher.

c. Japanese stocks include government-owned strategic stockpiles estimated at about 33 million barrels and scheduled to reach 120 million barrels in two years.

ing reserve oil on the world market. Releasing that reserve oil would also help make up for the shortages and, thereby, lessen the damages and hardships resulting from the disruption of supplies. With all or most consuming nations building a coordinated stockpile, a much larger reserve would be possible. Such a reserve could result from an agreement to increase the stocks to be maintained by each country, such as increasing the IEA minimum reserve from 90 to 120 days. Equally important, the Western nations should agree on how stockpiles would be drawn-down in an emergency. If stockpile withdrawals are not coordinated, some nations unwilling to use their stocks would reap price benefits from others' stock draw-downs while maintaining their own reserves for insurance.

The creation of a large consumer reserve would face political obstacles. It would put upward pressure on the world price of oil and would require substantial budgetary outlays in a period of worldwide inflation and fiscal retrenchment, and it could be opposed by producers. But the largest obstacle would be reaching agreement on how the costs of filling and maintaining the reserve would be shared and how it would be used during an emergency. Most countries would be very reluctant to give up sovereignty over a large portion of their domestic stocks.

Coordinated Disruption Tariffs. "Disruption tariffs" are, in principle, a good way to reduce wealth transfers to OPEC during a supply interruption. A disruption tariff could take the form of an actual per barrel tariff on imports or an internal tax on oil products. Both are designed to raise prices to reduce excess demand during a supply disruption. If, at the beginning of an interruption, the major consuming nations could agree simultaneously to establish emergency tariffs high enough to bring demand and supply in balance, then producers would find it difficult or impossible to raise prices to clear the market as they did following the Iranian disruption. The tariff would raise oil prices in every consuming country, but governments could rebate the revenues to prevent the loss of disposable income and to blunt the domestic wealth transfers and other economic losses arising from the interruption.

The disruption tariff would quickly fail if some countries refused to comply, choosing instead to reap the benefits of lower oil prices and cheaper prices for their export commodities. The argument for a disruption tariff—preemptively raising prices to prevent OPEC from reaping wealth transfers—may be too sophisticated for the political discourse of the industrial democracies. It is also unlikely that OPEC would stand passively by while the consuming countries institute a disruption tariff. Furthermore, it requires a level of comity and cooperation among oil consumers that has not been achievable in the past. Despite these problems, the disruption tariff is worth considering because the potential economic losses that it could avert are in the hundreds of billions of dollars.

Spare Capacity and Supply Diversification. The spare capacity of producing nations could, if used, minimize the damages from disruptions and the severity of subsequent response measures. This capacity represents a cheaper source of reserve supply than building stockpiles and would not result in the same strains on the world oil market. If this spare capacity were diversified, that is, geographically spread across the world—Mexico, North Sea as well as Middle East—it could potentially cushion the effects of a wide variety of foreseeable disruptions. Production from reserve capacity, mainly from Saudi Arabia, prevented an even worse situation when Iranian exports were terminated.

Despite these obvious benefits to consumers, spare capacity is far from a secure supply source, particularly if the shortfall is a politically targeted embargo aimed at the United States or its allies. Even without an embargo, there is no guarantee that remaining producers will use their spare capacity to make up for a shortfall; there is a fundamental incompatibility between the economic interests of consumers and producers. Even though large windfalls are to be gained from using spare capacity during a disruption, most producers are not willing to incur the financial cost of building excess capacity and holding it in reserve.

Few producers perceive political advantages to increasing reserve capacity. If spare capacity were created, the consuming nations might pressure them to speed up production each time oil prices were increased, or threatened to increase. However, Saudi Arabia more than the other producers may see spare capacity as an opportunity to enhance its political leverage within OPEC on pricing and other issues. Furthermore, all the producing states have a stake in the world economy. A political or economic weakening of the West is ultimately a threat to their security. And most of the producing states have some combination of economic and political concessions they would like to obtain from the West such as access to its markets, immigration rights, security agreements, or technical assistance.

The United States might successfully persuade a few of the major producing states to create spare capacity if it offered them some combination of these inducements. Political and economic concessions, consistent with overall U.S. foreign policy, might be exchanged as a "quid pro quo" for establishing and maintaining excess capacity. Or the United States could, alone or in conjunction with other consuming nations, agree to reimburse some of the costs of developing and operating the spare capacity.

Diversification of oil production throughout the world should be encouraged by consumers because it would reduce vulnerability to a supply cutoff from the Persian Gulf. Furthermore, increased supply and competition puts downward pressure on world oil prices. In some developing countries, however, political opposition to potential exploitation by the oil companies and the companies' concern over expropriation or other investment risks are obstacles to rapid exploration and development. In other cases, lack of ready access to technology may be a barrier. U.S. encouragement and financing of multilateral programs to develop indigenous energy supplies helps to overcome these obstacles. This approach softens resistance to direct investment by the developed world while satisfying the pressing need of Third World countries with potential petroleum reserves to develop alternatives to imported oil.

Domestic Measures

Although international initiatives to improve energy security are important, the United States must give the highest priority to putting its own house in order. International initiatives by the United States are not credible without strong domestic preparedness. Domestic response actions can be divided into two categories: those that stockpile oil for an emergency and those that ease or distribute the pain of a shortfall. The former measures are designed to deter interruptions and to prevent their adverse impacts; the latter to minimize adverse impacts and to share burdens equitably.

Existing Stockpiles. Traditionally, the petroleum industry has maintained stockpiles of crude oil and petroleum products to sustain operations and to meet minor emergencies. In the summer of 1980, domestic primary stockpiles of 1.36 billion barrels were at the highest level ever (DOE 1980e: 6).[3] Stocks in excess of normal operating levels were 130 million barrels. Another 130 million barrels could be drawn down before jeopardizing the petroleum production and distribution system. When combined with the existing government strategic reserve, these usable stockpiles theoretically equal twenty-one days of U.S. consumption, or roughly fifty days of imports.[4] In other words, only 350 million barrels of primary and strategic stocks are currently available for use during a shortfall. The method of counting stocks for meeting IEA mandated levels of ninety days of imports clearly bears little relationship to the amount of oil actually available for use during an interruption and is a strong argument for increasing the level of stockpiles.[5]

3. Primary stocks are defined as crude oil products held at refineries, in pipelines, and at major bulk terminals. Secondary stocks are held for resale by wholesalers and retailers; tertiary stocks are held by homeowners or industry for their own use.

4. This calculation of "days of imports" is based on an import level of 7 million barrels per day, roughly the level of gross imports for 1980.

5. For the U.S., ninety days of imports equals approximately 630 million barrels. In order to have primary reserves which can be withdrawn by this amount, the United States would need an additional 280 million barrels of stockpile oil.

The Strategic Petroleum Reserve. After the 1973–74 embargo, the administration and Congress realized that private stocks were not adequate protection against a worldwide supply disruption. In 1975, Congress authorized a strategic petroleum reserve of 500 million barrels. In President Carter's National Energy Plan of April 20, 1977, the goal for the reserve was increased to 1 billion barrels by 1985. Due to technical, political and management problems, however, only 92 million barrels, equivalent to thirteen days of imports, are actually in storage in mid-1980.

A large strategic petroleum reserve is the most potent domestic measure for dealing with supply interruptions. A functioning stockpile could shelter the United States from a large and severe supply interruption as well as help meet IEA sharing requirements. If used to cover domestic petroleum shortfalls from an interruption too small to trigger the IEA sharing agreement, the 1 billion barrel reserve could replace a 1 million barrel per day loss for two and three-quarter years.

A stockpile could also reduce the skyrocketing price increases that accompany supply interruptions. Even if the United States were to act independently, the release of stockpile oil to the world market would add supply and thereby reduce the consumer panic that drives up prices. Losses to GNP in the hundreds of billions of dollars could be prevented. If a substantial strategic reserve had been available and used after the Iranian cutback, virtually all of the price increases could have been avoided.

A large oil reserve could help deter shortfalls that were created for political purposes. These interruptions are particularly dangerous because, in addition to their economic cost, they raise international tensions and the risk of war. The likelihood that a producer state will use the oil in an attempt to influence U.S. policy is directly related to its chances of success. The greatest benefit of a stockpile, like that of our nuclear arsenal, may be its mere existence.

Finally, a strategic reserve could provide flexibility during an energy supply interruption. For example, war or sabotage in the Persian Gulf might create inexorable pressures for precipitous action to restore oil supplies. If, however, the United States could shield itself from the immediate pain of an interruption with an oil reserve, it would have the time for a reasoned response. Hence, a large reserve has many benefits. Even during the period when it is being filled, merely diverting the stockpile purchases into current consumption could create surge capacity without touching a drop of oil in storage.

A large strategic stockpile cannot be created overnight. Its growth is constrained by both the feasible rates of fill and the pace of storage capacity creation. The fastest level of fill achieved so far is 300 thousand barrels per day, though that rate could be increased temporarily. Higher fill rates could not be sustained for long because of the limits on storage capacity. The strategic reserve capacity is now 250 million barrels and is projected to increase to 400 million in 1985 and 540 million in 1986. If funding is granted soon to proceed with design and purchase of land, the reserve capacity could be increased to 750 million barrels in 1989 and perhaps 1 billion barrels in 1991. The maximum withdrawal rate at present is slightly over 1 million barrels per day, but that could be raised to 1.7 million barrels per day by putting oil in the two existing storage sites that are currently empty. The maximum withdrawal rate will be approximately 3.5 million barrels per day with capacity at the 540 million barrel level (4.4 million barrels per day at the 750 million barrel level).

These limitations on capacity and fill rate are discouraging enough with a goal of 750 million to one billion barrels. But recent analysis, by calculating much higher damages from interruptions, suggests that a strategic reserve of 3 to 4 billion barrels could be justified (Office of Oil Policy, 1980). It would take thirty years to achieve a reserve of this magnitude with a fill rate of 300,000 barrels per day.

Purchases of oil for the U.S. strategic reserve were halted not long after the Iranian revolution. Due to Congressional prodding, the United States now plans to begin filling the strategic petroleum reserve again, but Congress requires a fill rate of only 100,000 barrels per day, one-third of the rate prior to the Iranian revolution. At this rate, it would take over twenty years to reach the 750 million barrel level and almost twenty-eight years to reach a 1 billion barrel level. If the recent action represents the first step in accelerating reserve purchases, then it is worthwhile. If, however, this level of fill becomes permanent, it is little more than a symbolic gesture.

The reasons for not moving ahead with the original reserve plan are apparently twofold. Economically, additional demand in the current world oil market creates price pressures that must be borne by all allies as well as by the United States. Politically, reserve purchases may create diplomatic problems with Saudi Arabia and other producers. U.S. officials have been particularly concerned that Saudi Arabia might cut back its production if the United States resumes fill of the strategic reserve.

These problems are real but they are not compelling. The initial price increases resulting from filling the strategic reserve should be small compared with the benefits that would accrue to all consuming nations during an emergency. The value of a reserve is indicated by the large premium for stockpiled oil calculated in the previous chapter. The reserve would also be an appreciating asset, since the price of oil will probably increase faster than the inflation rate and offset the costs of storage. If the United States had reached its target of 500 million barrels of oil in reserve by 1980, the U.S. government would have made an inventory profit of well over $5 billion. Furthermore, the leaders of Saudi Arabia, whose defense depends on the United States, should realize that the lack of a U.S. strategic reserve places a "hair trigger" on a future oil crisis. And the leaders of Europe and Japan should realize that the United States needs a large strategic reserve to meet the IEA sharing agreement.

Recent federal initiatives—such as phased decontrol of crude oil, reduced oil use in utility boilers, greater production of heavy oil, and conservation incentives—help to cut U.S. petroleum import demand. These initiatives, coupled with higher prices and depressed economic activity, have reduced the average level of oil imports for the United States in 1980 by roughly 1.5 million barrels per day compared to 1979. Thus, U.S. stockpile purchases would no longer place rising demands on the world oil market. While filling the reserve during the slack market that existed in early 1980 would have been optimum, there are still good reasons to move ahead now, even if some price pressures result. Certainly there is no guarantee that the market will be better for any sustained period of time in the future.

If the United States does not seize the initiative quickly by developing new storage capacity and filling the strategic reserve at a meaningful rate of at least 300,000 barrels per day, then we are likely to wonder after the next interruption why the United States was so shortsighted or blind to its own national security interests. Any potential discomfort that might be experienced now would seem small compared to the ordeal of a future large supply interruption with no protection.

Private Stockpiles. The maintenance and expansion of private stocks can also provide needed protection against interruptions, particularly while the United States has no functioning strategic reserve. The Energy Policy and Conservation Act (EPCA) already gives to the President the authority to require refiners and importers to hold in storage 3 percent of the amount refined or imported for use in an emergency, which would amount to roughly 200 million barrels. Such stocks have advantages over a government strategic reserve. There is more flexibility in having numerous sources of reserve supply rather than one, and purchases for private stocks do not create the same type of political problems with producing countries.

Maintaining and increasing private stocks, however, creates problems, both for oil companies and for government management of supplies during interruptions. Stocks are costly to build and hold because of the costs of oil at over $30 per barrel and the annual costs of storage at approximately $.80 to $1.00 per barrel. With high interest rates, oil companies may face financial incentives to draw down stocks whenever the oil market begins to appear more stable and when price decontrol becomes fully effective. Moreover, an aggressive private storage program would require considerable new steel tank capacity.

Even if oil companies maintain high levels of stocks, their availability during an emergency will be unclear as they will be outside direct government control. Historically, private stockpiles have not been used extensively during emergencies. Oil companies might choose to release stockpiles after the price has gone up rather than using them to dampen price increases. Providing incentives for industry to sell the stocks at the right moment requires a high degree of government and private sector interaction. Nevertheless, considering the urgency of gaining some security against interruptions, building up private stocks is essential, at least until the strategic reserve reaches a functioning level. And while policies to stimulate increases in private stocks are evolving, every effort should be made to maintain current high stockpile levels. Government and industry should undertake discussions on voluntary maintenance of the existing stocks.

Three other policy approaches to building an industrial petroleum reserve merit consideration. First, the government could provide incentives for private stockpiles. Assurance that subsequent regulations would not allocate stocks to other refineries would facilitate normal market incentives for stockpiles. If additional incentives were needed, consideration could be given to tax breaks or to direct subsidies, encouraging industry to hold and build high levels of stocks. These market approaches have the advantage of minimum government involvement, but they create no certainty as to levels of stockpiles that would result or how they would be managed during an emergency.

A direct approach allowing the government greater leverage would be the regulation of minimum stockpile levels, requiring, for example, 5 percent over "normal" levels for the first year, 10 percent for the second, and so forth. Or the government could regulate stock levels as a percentage of annual refinery production. To lower storage costs, the government could lease space in the strategic reserve to oil companies, lowering annual costs from $.80 to $1.00 per barrel to somewhat over $.30 to $.40 per barrel.[6] To encourage draw-downs during an interruption, federal standby regulatory authority over the use of the stocks may be necessary.

Finally, a public–private corporation similar to the one established by the Federal Republic of Germany as discussed in Chapter 6 could be created to fill a public–private reserve. The corporation could undertake filling operations, relieving refineries from raising capital and physically storing oil. Stockpile purchases could be funded by per barrel assessments on refineries.

All of these options have drawbacks. Just relying on market incentives has the positive feature of less government involvement. But government coordination of stock withdrawals is inconsistent with a policy of nonintervention. And if the government cannot intervene, the oil companies have strong incentives to hold back stockpile use until the price rises, precisely what the government is trying to prevent. Government regulation of stockpiles circumvents this problem, but it politicizes stockpile use during an emergency. Moreover, the option confronts oil companies with a new regulatory requirement and consumers with slightly higher prices from the cost of maintaining stocks in private storage. A public–private corporation might have been a good idea at the inception of the strategic reserve program. But injecting a new institution and method of financing at this late date may only delay the program for a few more critical years unless steps are taken simultaneously to assure that its momentum is sustained.

6. Figures on storage costs were rough estimates as of July 1980 provided by U.S. Department of Energy, Policy and Evaluation.

The Management of Stockpiles. The U.S. strategic petroleum reserve program was initiated without a clear mandate on how it would be managed. The general operating premise at that time was to use the reserve as a source of last resort, only making up large domestic shortfalls when other measures were no longer sufficient. Little thought was given to the fact that the United States would actually be sharing its supplies with the allies.

Reducing price pressures must be a primary goal of a strategic petroleum reserve. Consequently, a reserve's use should be predictable during the early stages of an interruption, before panic sets in. This conclusion contradicts the original concept of stockpiles when the goal was to keep them intact, even to hoard them. To provide market certainty, the United States should amend the strategic petroleum reserve plan to set forth an automatic schedule of stockpile releases based on different levels of supply interruption. This policy would encourage oil companies and the public to refrain from hoarding and building stocks during an emergency and to assure our allies that new supplies would be available to supplement world shortfalls. Because of the possibility of a prolonged shortage, the automatic releases could cease when stockpiles reached certain minimum reserve levels.

Consideration should be given to the idea of private stocks serving as a tactical reserve, aimed at reducing price pressures during relatively small interruptions. The public strategic reserve would then be employed during large emergencies, both further dampening price pressures and serving as a source of supply to a starved energy market. This approach is particularly effective during the period when the strategic petroleum reserve is still small. But it requires either that the government regulate private stock use or provide incentives for withdrawals.

The government needs to decide in advance on a pricing structure for releasing stockpile oil. If the price of strategic stockpile oil is less than the ongoing spot price of oil, American refineries will buy stockpiled oil rather than importing supplies. In addition, they will have no incentive for reducing their own stocks since bargain government prices will undercut their market. To reduce spot prices, stockpile oil should compete in that market as a new and large marginal source of supply. Undercutting the market to keep consumer prices low will result in less imports to the United States, the hoarding of private stocks, unnecessarily fast depletion of the reserve, continued difficulties in managing the shortage, and higher prices later.

Finally, stockpile policy must relate to the capacity of the refinery industry to use oils of various weights and sulfur content. Due to the high use of gasoline in the United States and tighter environmental standards, American refineries tend to use lighter and lower sulfur oil than the average in the world oil market. During a supply interruption, it is quite possible that heavier and higher sulfur crude oil will be in more abundant supply. This fact not only makes it more difficult to attain the supplies appropriate to our refineries, but can also result in refinery production of more of the heavy oil products, which are less in demand in the United States. The industry is currently making investments to convert 550,000 to 800,000 barrels per day of capacity to refine more light products from heavier crude, but these changes will take many years.[7] As these investments are made, stockpile decisions should reflect not only the current mix of refinery capacity but also the likely future capacity and variety of crudes available under various interruption scenarios.

If the United States does not develop a workable management plan for the strategic reserve, as well as for private stockpiles, the consequences are likely to be serious. The management of the strategic reserve could be so conservative that stocks are never used to depress price pressures, and hence accomplish little for the large expenditure of public funds. Or the reserve could be disgorged at cheap prices, prematurely depleting our protection against a long and deep interruption. Plans to manage stockpiles are needed before an interruption occurs.

Emergency Conservation. A number of emergency conservation measures have been assessed and proposed by the Department of Energy, partly in response to congressional legislation. These measures would achieve demand reductions primarily through regulatory controls, forcing temporary changes in American lifestyles and habits. The truly sustainable form of conservation—improving the efficiency of energy usage—cannot be implemented quickly enough for use in an emergency.

In devising demand restraint measures, the executive branch has also been constrained by Congress. Both the Energy Policy and Conservation Act of 1975 (EPCA) and the Emergency Energy Conserva-

---

7. For an article on oil refinery upgrading, refer to Anthony J. Parisi, "Oil Refining Upgrading Urged," *New York Times* (1980: D1).

tion Act of 1979 (EECA) grant the federal government the authority to undertake planning and emergency measures but then prohibit the use of tariffs, taxes, or user fees. In effect, the government has been deprived of the most effective tools to promote quick consumer action.

Impelled by the Iranian production losses, the government finally submitted to the Congress in the spring of 1979 the measures developed in response to the EPCA mandate. Of the three proposals—a ban on outdoor electrical advertising, a ban on the weekend sale of gasoline, and controls on building thermostat settings—only the latter was not rejected. The Emergency Building Temperature Reduction Program, which is still in effect, restricts temperature settings for space heating, cooling, and hot water heating in nonresidential buildings. The Department of Energy had estimated preliminary energy savings at 200,000 barrels per day of oil equivalent, but these figures are speculative and may be optimistic. The actual petroleum savings are less than the total energy saved and include savings in residual fuel which, in previous emergencies, was not in short supply.

Even though emergency conservation measures were not particularly significant in alleviating the Iranian disruption, Congress continued to push them in the Emergency Energy Conservation Act. The legislation requires state emergency conservation plans as well as a standby federal conservation plan (DOE 1980b). The federal government is also required to establish fuel conservation targets and a rationing plan. In order to reduce gasoline lines and private automobile usage during an interruption, the Standby Federal Conservation Plan mandates minimum fuel purchase restrictions and odd-even purchase limitations (both widely used by states in previous interruptions) as well as an employer based commuter plan. For a larger shortage, the plan also proposes a vehicle sticker plan and a compressed work week.

The mandated minimum and odd-even purchase requirements did shorten lines at service stations during the previous interruptions, but probably only because they either reduced panic buying somewhat or were fortuitously initiated just as shortages had begun to ease. It is questionable whether federal intervention in this area is even necessary, since state and local governments have authority to implement these measures and have done so. The energy savings of these two measures are negligible.

The employer based commuter plan would require employers of 100 or more persons to develop emergency employee transportation programs, such as carpooling and vanpooling. Laudable in its intent of enabling workers to get to their jobs during an interruption, the plan's energy savings are nevertheless small, perhaps 50,000 barrels per day (DOE 1980b: 8475). In addition, the plan does not provide the private sector with incentives to work out details before an emergency hits, nor does it assure affected employers of additional allocations of fuel to put the ride sharing into operation.

The sticker plan would preclude the use of private vehicles for one, two, or three days per week; stickers would identify which days a car could not be on the road. To be workable, all vehicles in a household would have to be banned during the same day or days. The Department of Energy estimates energy savings up to 345,000 barrels per day for the one day plan, 730,000 barrels per day for the two day plan, and 1,350,000 barrels per day for the three day plan (DOE 1980b: 8482).

These estimates necessarily make heroic assumptions about compliance. The sticker plan is not only difficult to administer, it is extremely inequitable. Motorists with access to public transportation, carpools, or other ways to get to their jobs would be unaffected or only slightly inconvenienced by the provision. Others, particularly those in suburban or rural areas, would be unable to get to work or would be stranded on the weekend. Enforcing this unpopular program would burden local police. This proposal is less flexible and more inequitable than gasoline rationing, although it could be implemented more quickly and with less government cost.

The quality of state conservation contingency planning varies widely. A review of state contingency plans required by EPCA revealed a huge discrepancy in the expertise of state energy offices. Few states have information systems good enough to indicate the amount and location of various petroleum products. Given these differences among the states, which in part are due to inadequate funding, state energy planning for an emergency does not promise to be very effective in the near future.

These series of measures will not significantly improve the capability of the United States to deal with supply interruptions. The sticker plan creates unequal burdens and lacks flexibility. The building temperature plan is worth using in an emergency, but the savings are indeterminate and lie mainly in residual fuel oil. Employer-based parking and ride-sharing programs are sensible, but their savings are small. Odd–even and minimum purchase requirements shorten gasoline lines, but federal authority is hardly necessary to accomplish that. At best, these measures can make a small contribution to reducing demand during an emergency.

Emergency Supply Enhancement. Emergency options exist to increase energy production and to accelerate fuel switching from oil to coal, nuclear, natural gas, and wood. Some measures, such as transporting electricity between utilities and using surplus natural gas supplies, can help immediately. Others, such as speeding up nuclear plants and domestic oil production, can potentially help in some types of interruptions. Synthetic fuel production from coal and shale, on the other hand, probably cannot help cope with supply interruptions in this decade because of the long lead times involved. In the past, emergency production and fuel switching have been of only marginal value, but with prices spiralling upward and longer interruptions possible, they may have greater importance.

During the Iranian crisis, the DOE response plan of April 1979 listed several supply options for increasing domestic oil production and switching from oil to alternative fuels. The five measures (with the plan's original projection for their maximum contribution by the end of 1979) are: increased production from the Naval Petroleum Reserve (20,000 barrels per day), increased capacity through the Alaska pipeline (150,000 barrels per day), phased decontrol of domestic oil (80,000 barrels per day), electricity transfers (200,000 barrels per day) and natural gas substitution (400,000 barrels per day). The projected savings were mainly in residual fuel. Implementation of the measures for increasing domestic oil production listed in the DOE Iranian Response Plan are already underway on a permanent basis. The other measures could be used in future emergencies.

For future interruptions, a combination of decontrolled prices and spiralling world oil prices could spur additional domestic supplies. Although production incentives would be powerful, the physical limitations on oil production would be restrictive. Production beyond a maximum efficient rate can damage well structures and limit future oil production. Tertiary recovery can augment supplies if there were expectations that prices would remain high over a sustained period of time. But this possibility has not been adequately analyzed.

The potential for switching quickly from the use of oil to natural gas varies seasonally and is feasible only for those industrial and utility boilers which can use natural gas as well as other fuels. The American Gas Association estimates that natural gas could substitute for 1.1 million barrels per day of oil within a year (American Gas Association 1980: 2). Being able to switch during an emergency also depends on having excess gas available and the capability to distribute it. Currently, the U.S. pipeline system runs throughout the year at roughly 10 to 15 percent below capacity, so there is some room to move extra gas. The amount of unused capacity varies among different pipelines; in some cases, it is small.

There are essentially four measures for obtaining the additional gas for an emergency: using gas in domestic storage, pumping faster from existing wells, capping domestic wells for surge capacity, or contracting with Canada or Mexico for either surge capacity or for gas to be stored in the U.S. Although there may be some potential for tapping existing storage, most of the working gas currently in storage is probably not available during an oil emergency. That gas is supposedly insurance for heating homes and office buildings during a severe winter. And borrowing between separate pipelines poses regulatory and other difficulties. During an emergency, some additional gas could be produced by faster pumping, but the amount is unknown. Already, the average pumping rate is relatively fast. If the U.S. government purchases existing wells or develops new wells for domestic surge capacity, then the capping of those wells may adversely affect existing production and consumption.

The most attractive option to augment natural gas supplies during an emergency would be to contract for excess Canadian capacity. The Alberta gas fields have spare capacity of 1 trillion cubic feet per year (500 thousand barrels per day of oil equivalent). The United States could negotiate a contract for surge capacity to be used during an oil emergency. But Canadian officials might feel that their country needs the gas during an interruption. Another more expensive option for the United States would be to purchase the excess gas now and store it in depleted domestic gas fields.

As discussed earlier, oil savings from fuel switching have resulted mainly in expanding supplies of residual fuel oil, which has been in surplus. Hence a gas reserve is not nearly as flexible as an oil reserve in providing the light products that are likely to be most in demand.

Yet creating a gas reserve neither places upward pressures on the world oil market nor raises the same types of political issues. While it represents a potentially useful emergency response, this measure requires further analysis before it can be considered a realistic alternative.[8]

On an average daily basis in mid-1980, transfers of electrical power between regions of the United States saved 300,000 to 400,000 barrels of oil.[9] This amount is close to the current physical limit, although perhaps savings of another 50,000 to 100,000 barrels per day savings is possible. The main constraints to more power wheeling are the weak interties (connecting links among major electrical power grids) in several key areas, such as across Pennsylvania, up New York State, and Florida to Georgia. Strengthening the interties would require building new transmission lines, which is not the highest financial priority of utilities or state utility commissions. Thus, while power wheeling of electricity from coal and nuclear plants to displace oil is already occurring, the potential for significantly increasing this amount in an emergency is not large.

Near term options exist for increasing electricity production from existing nuclear plants. Plants which are temporarily off-line for various checks or those which have been required to run at reduced power can be called back into service; or plants can be operated at a higher capacity than their licensed rating. Rough estimates indicate that three gigawatts of increased electrical power (primary energy equivalent of approximately 90,000 barrels per day of oil) could conceivably be produced in this way in an emergency in the early 1980s.[10]

Another longer term option, probably requiring at least six months to see any effect, would be to speed up construction and licensing of nuclear plants which are nearing completion. There are fifteen plants, each about one gigawatt in capacity, scheduled to come on line between 1980 and 1982. Because of their geographic location, many of these plants will not be displacing oil when in operation. For those

8. Private communication, U.S. Department of Energy, Policy and Evaluation, July 1980.

9. Private communication, U.S. Department of Energy, Economic Regulatory Administration, July 1980.

10. Private communication, U.S. Department of Energy, Policy and Evaluation, July 1980.

plants, wheeling of electricity would be required to effect residual fuel oil savings.

The utilization of domestic coal resources is limited by demand at present. The administration is attempting through proposed legislation, to mandate permanent conversion from oil to coal for as many fuel-burning installations as possible. By 1985, savings of 200,000 to 300,000 barrels per day of utility oil use are expected out of 400,000 to 500,000 barrels per day potentially achievable.[11] Getting oil-fired plants to burn coal on a temporary basis can be just as expensive and difficult as forcing them to do so on a permanent basis. For those utility plants unable to convert permanently to coal, for either institutional or environmental reasons, it might be possible to install coal handling facilities for emergency use. However, it would probably be easier to rely instead on oil storage as the contingency measure at those plants. Other than direct switching, emergency oil savings from coal use would have to come from electrical power wheeling.

Relaxing environmental laws in an emergency is sometimes suggested as an option for increasing fuel supplies. Gasoline production could be increased up to 125,000 barrels per day by temporarily rescinding the limits on lead as an additive (for use only in cars lacking catalytic converters). But production of other petroleum products would be reduced. Crude oil savings of only 25,000 barrels per day would result from requiring less energy in the reforming process where the octane of gasoline is enhanced.

Some have suggested relaxing requirements on the sulfur content of oil burning as a way of increasing distillate supplies during an emergency. They argue that distillate or vacuum gas oil, now blended with residual fuel oil to lower its sulfur content, could be saved if utilities could burn higher sulfur oil. There is great dispute over both the facts and the desirability of such a step. There is disagreement over how much distillate or vacuum gas oil would be saved, whether refiners would be able to use the vacuum gas oil to produce heating oil, and how much released distillate would flow into the United States from the Caribbean. Even if these issues could be resolved, the regulatory system is extremely complex and dispersed. Nevertheless,

---

11. Private communication, U.S. Department of Energy, Policy and Evaluation, July 1980.

these analytical questions should be answered since this measure is likely to reappear as an option should another distillate shortage occur.

The response measures used during the Iranian crisis can help during future interruptions, but their potential is limited. Greater production of oil and natural gas is likely if prices are very high, but again physical limitations restrict their potential. The most interesting possibility would be use of excess Canadian gas, either as spare capacity or stored in the United States. But even this option is speculative. A large and long-term supply interruption would be a different story. Under these conditions, the United States may need to launch crash programs to increase production. But dealing with the more likely and predictable interruptions requires measures that can be brought on quickly. Until more analysis is conducted on these possibilities, we should not count on much from emergency supply enhancement and fuel switching.

Allocation of Shortfalls. Until a large and functioning strategic petroleum reserve is developed, the United States will have no alternative but to allocate shortfalls among oil consumers during an interruption. In theory, of course, a government with infinite wisdom and power could allocate oil supplies in such a way as to minimize damage to the economy and inconvenience to the public. In fact, knowledge is limited, government power is restricted, and, during an interruption, political pressure to serve special interests is great. Consequently, government action could easily exacerbate rather than ease the problems.

Standby price and allocation regulations give the federal government authority to distribute crude oil to refineries, to mandate the production mix of petroleum products, to allocate products to end users, and to control prices at each stage. Despite this pervasive and awesome regulatory control, it is unlikely in the current political environment that any product other than gasoline will be extensively allocated, except in the most severe emergency. During the last two supply interruptions, petroleum products were generally available for uses other than transportation.

The premises behind government forcing gasoline users to absorb the total shortfall come from concern over jeopardizing public health if heating oil is curtailed, concern over losing jobs if industrial fuel supplies are curtailed, and a tacit assumption that there are substantial discretionary uses of energy in the transportation sector. Another political premise affecting contingency planning is that prices of gasoline will, or must, be controlled during an emergency to prevent large wealth transfers from consumers to the oil industry. These widely held premises constrain the options available to the government in dealing with supply interruptions.

The major tools for distributing gasoline are federal allocations to dealers and rationing. For shortfalls less than 10 percent of normal gasoline consumption, federal allocations can probably limit gasoline lines to a tolerable level. For larger shortfalls, when gasoline lines are unbearably long, it is generally assumed that gasoline rationing would be the only recourse.

Despite ostensible reliance on gasoline rationing for any significant shortfall, the plan submitted to Congress in June 1980 will not be in place as a standby measure until late 1981. Once ready, the rationing plan still requires ninety days to be put into operation. Moreover, rationing is authorized only for shortfalls greater than 20 percent of normal gasoline consumption, almost three times greater than the gasoline shortfall during the Iranian emergency. Additional congressional approval is required for implementation at lower levels.

The best way to understand the tools that the government has or will have at its disposal is to consider a hypothetical disruption when U.S. stockpiles are inadequate. Assume that 5 million barrels per day of Persian Gulf oil production is terminated. The U.S. share of this shortage would be approximately one-third of the total. Because of the protracted transportation system, the first effects of the cutback would not be felt by end users until two or three months after production ceased.

During this early period, when there is little knowledge about the duration of the interruption, voluntary consumer and untried state conservation plans would be called into use. The President would exhort drivers to observe the 55 mile per hour speed limit and homeowners to lower thermostat settings. The expectations for the energy savings should be modest.

When it becomes apparent that stronger measures are necessary, the government would resort to its allocation authority to distribute available supplies of price-controlled gasoline. The allocation formula would have to be based on some ad hoc modification of historical gasoline usage which may or may not be close to the demand patterns of this particular emergency.

As the supply interruption continues, gasoline lines would lengthen and tempers would flare. Odd-even and minimum purchase requirements on the distribution of gasoline would temporarily reduce lines; but considering the size of the hypothetical interruption, efforts to lessen panic buying would only have a temporary effect. The government would then be forced to take more drastic action. It could either eliminate price controls to allow the marketplace to allocate supplies, or it could impose gasoline rationing. Lifting price controls would result in large temporary profit increases for oil companies and retail gasoline outlets. Consequently, the government will probably select gasoline rationing as the only acceptable political option.

At first consideration, gasoline rationing does not seem to be an unsatisfactory solution unless one is an ardent free market enthusiast. Rationing seems to provide an equitable way to distribute supplies, and many people remember it to have worked during World War II.

The rationing plan proposed to Congress begins with the federal government mailing out coupon entitlement books to owners of the nation's 150 million registered automobiles, trucks, and busses (DOE 1980c). The Department of Energy estimates that 90 percent of the coupons will reach their proper destination.[12] Yet the best-kept state registration records are only 80 percent accurate, and one-third of the vehicle fleet turns over each year. Even if the optimistic assessment by DOE is correct, 10 percent of the available gasoline would not be available for use until bureaucrats connect those motorists with their rationing books. Once a motorist receives a rationing book, he or she can go to the bank or another designated place and redeem it for rationing coupons. It is not hard to imagine gasoline lines being replaced by long lines at redemption centers.

The magnitude of the management challenge to the federal government is only part of the problem. Rationing would require the creation of an entirely new currency in the period of a few months. Over 20 billion coupons would be used during the first year, two-and-one-half times the units of paper money in circulation. Billions of dollars of the new currency would provide an enticing opportunity for counterfeiting. Exceptions and special allocations will require a new bureaucracy at the federal and local level to deal with a myriad of

---

12. Testimony of Douglas Robinson before the Subcommittee on Energy Regulation, Senate Committee on Energy and Natural Resources, June 2, 1980.

special circumstances and the entreaties of special interest groups. Since rationing coupons will be allocated on the basis of registered vehicles, there would be an incentive for motorists to buy junk cars to increase their allotment of this new currency.

There is no guarantee that available gasoline supplies in each locale will match coupon usage. Since gasoline prices will be controlled, no incentives will exist to shift around supplies as demand inevitably shifts, probably away from rural areas. At worst, motorists would have rationing tickets that could not be used.

With enough time and resources, gasoline rationing could be made to work at a respectable level. The only problem is that in an emergency there is no time. A functioning gasoline rationing program would not likely be available for much, if not all, of the period of those disruptions with the highest probability of occurrence.

The perceived advantage of rationing to the public is equity. Each car owner would be guaranteed a certain allotment of gasoline. The rationing plan also creates a white market system that would allow coupons to be bought and sold. If a motorist had sufficient money and valued driving heavily, he or she could buy more tickets at a white market center. Those who valued other goods or services more highly, or did not have need for all the coupons issued, could sell them at the center. Provided that they own cars and do not drive much, this approach would be a financial help for the poor and elderly who could trade in their gasoline coupons for necessities.

The value of coupons, along with the controlled price of gasoline, would represent the true market value of gasoline. For example, if the controlled price of gasoline were $1.50, and if rationing coupons were worth approximately $2.00, as estimated for a 20 percent gasoline shortfall,[13] then the market value of gasoline would actually be $3.50. Under a white market rationing system, citizens selling tickets would capture the temporary windfalls rather than the oil companies and retail gasoline dealers.

There are, however, ways to achieve identical equity benefits while allowing the marketplace to allocate supplies. The first step is to decontrol gasoline prices, which would eliminate gasoline lines by

---

13. In its "Standby Gasoline Rationing Plan," p. 41361, the U.S. Department of Energy projects the price of a ration coupon for a hypothetical 20 percent shortfall of gasoline. The Department assumed −0.2 for the short-term price elasticity of gasoline demand. Price elasticity is defined as the percentage change in demand in response to a percentage change in price.

bringing supply and demand into balance during and after the interruption. This action would avoid the need for government management of the supply system. An emergency windfall tax could then be imposed in either one of two ways. First, the Internal Revenue Service could collect up to 90 percent of any final price increase not associated with crude oil costs. The tax would be levied on increases over the base markups for refiners, wholesalers, and retailers of gasoline, and would supplement the existing Windfall Profits Tax on crude oil. The size of the tax would fluctuate according to market conditions, automatically disappearing if the price dropped to the base price. By retaining 10 percent of the windfall, the oil industry would have an incentive to allocate supplies to the neediest areas.

Alternatively, a variable emergency tax could be imposed at the retail level, again capturing most of the windfall that would arise from the shortage. For this proposal to work, the President would need authority to establish and vary a tax rate that represented roughly the difference between the pre-interruption price and the current market price. Although this proposal requires greater analytical prescience and political will at the time of an interruption, since the President must establish a tax rate as compared to the marketplace, it would be simpler to administer.

The taxes collected under either proposal should be rebated directly to the public. Proceeds could be returned to the registered owners of automobiles and be as fair as the proposed gasoline rationing scheme. Better yet, rebates could instead be given to all households using a distribution mechanism that passed the House of Representatives in 1977 in connection with the proposed Crude Oil Equalization Tax. Since the poor spend less for energy than the affluent, a per capita or per household rebate would be substantially more progressive than any system conferring economic benefits only on vehicle owners. To prevent inequities and "fiscal drag," tax withholding rates could be automatically adjusted during the course of a supply interruption. Under the current legislated definition, the Consumer Price Index would increase with a tax-rebate scheme but not with a white market-rationing system. However, new legislation could correct this artificial difference by allowing the rebates to offset higher gasoline prices in the index.

Any scheme that requires establishing, collecting, and rebating taxes to the public is bound to be extremely complex. In fact, with a little imagination, such a proposal can be made to sound as complicated as gasoline rationing. But there are fundamental differences. First, all the administrative problems of gasoline rationing will directly disrupt lives of millions of Americans. Most of the administrative problems of a tax and rebate scheme, on the other hand, will be borne by government and the oil industry. No doubt, audits five years in the future will indicate that some companies underpaid taxes, used the wrong base for calculation, or committed some other bureaucratic misdemeanor. But these problems would not result in hour-long lines at distribution centers, lost rationing coupons, counterfeiting, a whole new bureaucracy, and a number of other problems that are unique to rationing.

Considering the high probability of supply interruptions in the near future, the predictable administrative problems that would ensue from rationing, and the availability of equally fair allocation schemes, high priority should be given to preparing a market alternative to rationing. By waiting until a crisis occurs, the United States may find itself slipping inexorably into a rationing program that can only result in chaos and a strengthening of the perception that government is no longer capable of competent and effective action.

CONCLUSIONS: USE OF RESPONSE MEASURES

The size, duration, and cause of a supply interruption are all unpredictable. The causes could range from politically inspired embargoes to chaotic political events such as war, revolution, or terrorism. Although each case will be different, there are common elements in dealing with all interruptions at the early stage. No matter what the circumstances, the initial actions in all cases should be the following:

1. Immediately after a disruption occurs, the United States should announce a schedule of stockpile withdrawals from the strategic reserve and a pricing policy for the released oil. That action would be designed to counter panic and hoarding by oil companies, foreign governments, and the American public. It would also reduce upward price pressures on the spot price of oil. A lesson can be learned from the banking industry, which, in the face of panic, will move to restore certainty by "keeping the windows open."

2. The United States should immediately institute a standby emergency tax on gasoline to reduce demand soon after a supply interruption occurs and prior to the sixty or ninety days before shortfalls

actually appear in the marketplace. The experience of the Iranian cutbacks clearly demonstrates that the United States could probably have avoided gasoline lines in the summer of 1979 if such an emergency tax had been in effect early that year.

3. The United States should implement a market allocation system that uses decontrol of gasoline prices, together with a windfall tax and rebate to the consumer. When shortfalls begin to appear, the temporary flat gasoline tax could be dropped and the windfall tax and rebate system put into effect.

4. The government should initiate conservation and supply measures that were effective in past crises, such as temporary switching to natural gas and wheeling of electricity produced from coal and nuclear facilities.

With an aggressive domestic program to help reduce price pressures on the world oil market, the United States could work with its allies on cooperative measures. Specifically, the United States should encourage reasonable draw-downs of allied stockpiles, advocate demand restraint measures, and pursue an orderly oil purchasing policy as a "quid pro quo" for American stockpile releases. Although the United States would have less leverage on producing countries, efforts should at least be made to encourage price moderation and greater production from spare capacity.

As the depth and duration of the interruption become more apparent, the United States would have to adjust policies to fit the situation. If production were quickly restored, then the use of the strategic reserve along with the temporary gasoline tax and market allocation system would be adequate. If, however, the interruption were to persist, additional supply and conservation measures would be needed.

Predictable immediate actions seem to run against the instinct to "keep one's options open." Unfortunately, by keeping our options open, the United States is likely to drive other consuming nations into price bidding and competition over supplies, and oil companies into building up stocks. If the United States does take resolute and immediate action at the beginning of an emergency, it may be able to forestall the panic that leads to the upward spiralling of prices. But in order to do so, the United States needs to develop expeditiously the necessary tools—an adequate strategic petroleum reserve and a sensible standby domestic allocation program.

REFERENCES

American Gas Association. 1980. "Potential Substitution of Oil with Gas and Coal in Non-Transportation Uses." *Energy Analysis*, Policy Evaluation and Analysis Group (August 28).

Exxon Company, U.S.A. 1979. *Energy Outlook, 1980-2000*. December.

Mork, Knut Anton, and Robert E. Hall. 1980. "Energy Prices and the U.S. Economy in 1979-81." *The Energy Journal* 1, no. 2 (April).

Neville, Tom; Jerry Blankenskip; Mike Barron; and Bill Lane. 1980. "The Energy Problem: Costs and Policy Options." Office of Gas and Integrated Analysis, Policy and Evaluation, U.S. Department of Energy. Staff Working Paper, draft, March 5.

Office of Oil Policy. 1980. "An Analysis of Acquisition and Drawdown Strategies for the Strategic Petroleum Reserve." Policy and Evaluation, U.S. Department of Energy. Staff Working Paper, draft.

Parisi, Anthony J. 1980. "Oil Refining Upgrading Urged." *New York Times* (August 27): D1.

U.S. Department of Energy. 1979. *Response Plan: Reducing U.S. Impact on the World Oil Market*. DOE/IR-0048. Washington, D.C.: Government Printing Office, April.

_____. 1980a. *Excerpt from Secretary's Annual Report to Congress*. DOE/S-0010 (80). Washington, D.C.: Government Printing Office, January.

_____. 1980b. "Standby Federal Conservation Plan." *Federal Register*. Part II (February 1).

_____. 1980c. "Standby Gasoline Rationing Plan." *Federal Register*. Part VI (June 18) Economic Regulatory Administration.

_____. 1980d. *Final Report to the President on Oil Supply Shortages During 1979*. DOE/S-0011. Washington, D.C.: Government Printing Office, July.

_____. 1980e. *Weekly Petroleum Status Report*. DOE/EIA-0208 (80-29). Washington, D.C.: Government Printing Office, September 19.

U.S. Department of Justice. 1980. *Report of the Department of Justice to the President Concerning the Gasoline Shortage of 1979*. Washington, D.C.: Government Printing Office, July 1.

11 FINANCIAL IMPLICATIONS OF PETROLEUM DISRUPTIONS

Philip K. Verleger, Jr.

A major disruption of international oil markets could, if accompanied by substantial increases in oil prices, threaten the stability of international financial markets by causing large increases in the balance of payments deficits of oil-importing countries. While some countries could finance the increase out of export earnings or foreign exchange reserves, others would be forced to seek loans from commercial or international financial institutions. Should such loans be denied, the borrowing country could be forced to default on existing loans, which, in turn, could cause the failure of one or more major banks and possibly spread through the international banking system.

While the countries most likely to be forced to increase borrowings from international financial centers are the oil-importing underdeveloped countries and the developing countries (such as Brazil), the lending institutions would be located in the developed nations. Thus, default by the poorer nations could precipitate a worldwide financial crisis similar to the U.S. banking crisis during the Great Depression.

Although this dire scenario did not materialize after the 1973–74 Arab embargo or the 1979 Iranian crisis (two interruptions that were accompanied by price increases), many authorities still believe that a future oil crisis could topple the world financial system. To prevent such a calamity, some have recommended that an international financial organization such as the International Monetary Fund (IMF) replace private banks as the financier of oil deficits. Others have argued that such intervention would only make it easier for OPEC to engage in pricing mischief.

In our view these arguments confuse cause and effect. We believe the threat to financial markets is a result of increases in balance of payments deficits triggered by sudden increases in oil prices. To reduce this threat efforts should be made to prevent sudden surges in oil prices. This can be accomplished by developing strategic petroleum inventories, adopting standby plans to curtail oil consumption, and preventing or discouraging the panic buying that has induced sudden surges in oil prices in the past two crises. However, it is possible that even these measures would not stabilize oil prices during a major crisis. Therefore, as a second contingency measure, we suggest that emergency financing facilities in existing international monetary institutions (preferably the IMF) be developed to provide automatically short-term financing of the increased balance of payments debt incurred by oil importing countries as a result of sudden increases in oil prices. This facility would not replace private lending to oil-importing countries, but only provide interim, one- to three-year, financing for the increased cost of oil imports that resulted from the price increase. These two suggestions emerge from our analysis of the 1973−74 and 1979 crises.

FINANCIAL ASSESSMENT OF THE OIL CRISES OF THE 1970s

Concern for the viability of the world financial market was voiced after both the 1973−74 and 1979 disruptions. In June 1974 *The Wall Street Journal* quoted a pessimistic David Rockefeller: "My own view is that the process of recycling through the banking system may already be close to the end for some countries, and in general it is doubtful this technique can bridge the (payments) gap for more than a year or at the most 18 months." Six years later, still pessimistic in spite of the fact that the banking system had muddled through, Rockefeller projected more gloom from the 1979 oil price increase. According to the *Journal*, he forecast "treacherous economic seas and gale-force financial winds, strong enough to capsize even the most successful developing countries" (1980).

Rockefeller was not alone. After the 1973–74 episode five distinguished bankers and academics argued that

over the five years 1975 through 1979, the oil-importing countries of the world will pay these OPEC countries a total of at least $600 billion (in 1974 dollars) subject to four conditions:

1. that the importing countries individually can find the needed means of payment;
2. that their average annual economic growth continues close to the estimated global rate of about four percent for the next five years, or about two percent per capita;
3. that there are no major changes in the structure or stability of international political relations;
4. that the price of Middle East oil remains near the $10 level.

Whether or not any of these conditions can be fulfilled is, to say the least, problematical (Farmanfarmaian et al. 1975: 201).[1]

The authors then argued that the scale of the OPEC transfer problem was huge—so huge that "it is simply not conceivable that most of the importing countries can find matching inflows of funds, from OPEC countries at least, that would enable them to meet their oil deficit needs for very long." They suggested:

A looming problem is the ability of the major banks to continue to accept such a large volume of funds in the form of short term deposits. In all likelihood, unless further approaches to cooperative action are made within the next few months, some oil-importing countries will have run out of goods to sell, or markets to reach, or capacity to borrow to cover their deficits and a number may become unable to meet the servicing on the enlarged debts. Whether that would result in currency devaluations, in defaults by banking and business firms in those countries, in national debt moratoria, or in political revolution and debt repudiation, the entire structure of world payments and of trade and financial relationships would certainly be fractured (Farmanfarmaian et al. 1975: 204).

In the ensuing five years the cooperation called for by Farmanfarmaian et al. in world financial organizations was extremely lim-

1. The five authors of the article, Khodadad Farmanfarmaian, Armin Gutowski, Saburo Okita, Robert V. Roosa, and Carroll L. Wilson, were, at the time it was published, respectively, chairman of the Development Industrial Bank of Iran, professor of Economics and Development at the University of Frankfurt, president of the Overseas Economic Cooperation Fund and chairman of the Japan Economic Research Center, partner in Brown Brothers Hariman (and formerly Undersecretary for Monetary Affairs at the U.S. Treasury from 1961 to 1964), and professor at the Massachusetts Institute of Technology.

ited. An oil facility was created in the IMF and World Bank lending was increased, but in general the transfer of OPEC surplus funds to deficit countries was accomplished by private banks. The apparent success of this approach did not forestall new predictions of dire financial consequences after the 1979 price increases. For instance, the governor of the Bank of England, Gordon Richardson, and the president of the West German Bundesbank, Karl Otto Pohl, are reported by *The New York Times* to have warned that the recycling problems of the eighties will be worse than those of the seventies because deficits in the oil-importing countries will become more persistent.

The same view was expressed by Otmar Emminger, former president of the Deutsch Bundesbank, in a recent American Enterprise Institute pamphlet. According to Dr. Emminger,

> There are several differences between the present and the previous oil shock. The major one may turn out to be that this time the global payments imbalance between the oil-exporting and oil-importing countries is not likely to be reduced so quickly as after 1974, as oil prices are more likely to continue rising, while oil-exporting countries are unlikely to increase their imports as fast as after the first oil shock. Should this scenario turn out to be true, the financing of the deficits may require some new approaches, including a greater role of the IMF and more direct lending by the OPEC countries to the deficit countries (1980: 15).

The pessimistic view has been opposed by many economists who have argued that the international financial system is more resilient than the critics suggest. They argue further that the international payments problem is a zero sum game—that is, that in aggregate the surpluses exactly equal the deficits. Foremost among economists expressing this view has been C. Fred Bergsten (presently assistant secretary of the U.S. Treasury for International Economic Affairs). In 1974 Bergsten argued that "The prophets of doom confuse the balance of trade and the balance of payments. They ignore the simple but central fact that the oil exporters must invest in the industrial world any of their increased earnings that they do not spend. The Arabs will not bury the money in the ground. Thus there can be no deficit in the balance of payments of the industrialized world as a whole." He continued by arguing that the Eurocurrency capital markets could "handle the vast bulk of the money on their own, and are in fact doing so even as the full amount of the higher oil earnings is being invested."

This view was also supported by John Williamson of the University of Warwick. In 1975 he argued that the higher oil prices experienced after the Arab embargo would not bankrupt any oil-importing countries. Nor did he believe that any country would be forced into a state of "illiquidity"—that is, a situation where it could not obtain needed funds. Williamson defined bankruptcy as occurring,

> If an oil importing country were only able to finance the oil imports required for the maintenance of a full capacity level of output by borrowing and were only able to service that borrowing by further borrowing, so that it gradually surrendered an ever-increasing share of its assets to foreign control. If such a situation should develop, the country's net worth would tend in the course of time to approach zero in that the whole of its capital stock would ultimately be owned by foreigners, via the direct sale of assets or indirectly, through the contraction of an equivalent amount of debt (1976: 200).

Illiquidity of an oil importer could occur if, "some oil-importing countries would be unable to meet their contractual obligations to the outside world, or, more generally, would be faced with an acute liquidity problem. This is a problem that cannot arise for the oil importers in the aggregate, since all of the important methods by which the members of OPEC receive payment involve their acquisition of some form of claim on one or more oil-importing countries" (Williamson 1976: 202).

Williamson's analysis of the 1973 oil price shock suggests that the first problem, insolvency, was not relevant to either developed or undeveloped countries (1976). While he was less sanguine about the illiquidity problem, he argued that the problems seemed manageable. "Oil payments are made almost entirely by countries drawing on foreign exchange reserves and transferring foreign exchange to the members of OPEC" (1976: 203). Williamson further explained that "the principal recycling mechanism has been the Eurocurrency market. If an oil importer draws on reserves held in a reserve center while the OPEC member places its new reserves in the Euromarket, the Euro bank acquires additional funds which can be lent to the oil importer. . . . No liquidity problem will arise so long as this process continues" (1976: 204).

Williamson then discussed a number of actions that might be taken either by oil-exporting countries or by central banks in the developed countries, which might interfere with the process. He concluded that there was little reason to worry as long as the central banks remained willing to support the Euro market and stem any run, in which case global liquidity would be adequate. Further, he suggested that few individual countries would face liquidity problems if bankers adopted "appropriate criteria for evaluation," including "a clear prospect that indebtedness will not grow faster than debt-servicing capacity, which is to say that a country remains solvent" (1976: 207–208).

Williamson then noted that the prospects of all oil-importing countries remaining solvent would be greatly enhanced if each refrained from engaging in competitive trade policies such as those used in the 1930s. To avoid deflationary pressures that would lead to higher unemployment, he noted that oil-importing countries would have to compensate for increases in oil payments (which represent increased saving by OPEC countries) by reducing savings rates or increasing investments. He argued that maximizing the productivity of investments is the best route to long-run world growth.

The Williamson prescription was followed from 1974 to 1979. Thus, as Deese notes in Chapter 8, debt payments to foreign sources in certain developing countries have risen both in absolute terms and as a proportion of exports. This increase need not be viewed with alarm because the evidence suggests that investment has expanded rapidly. However, the debtor countries have leveraged themselves in a fashion that makes them more vulnerable to external economic forces, because, as with a corporation that increases its outstanding debt, the debt holders have a claim on a fixed amount of each year's sales. In the event of a decrease in sales or an increase in costs, the debt holders' claims must still be met. As the size of the debt increases relative to sales, the risk that creditors will not be satisfied in the event of a future shock increases.

This reasoning leads me to offer the following distinction between the pessimists such as Rockefeller and the optimists such as Williamson and Bergsten. In the view of the pessimists the increased borrowing of smaller LDCs was evidence that these countries were no longer creditworthy. The optimists viewed the loans as part of the necessary recycling process needed to support worldwide economic growth, without which most countries would be unable to meet their debt payments and pay their oil bills. However, neither the optimists nor the pessimists envisioned a world in which further oil price shocks would require additional increases in outstanding debt to maintain the status quo. Yet, as we have seen in the earlier chapters of this book, such shocks are quite possible, and, as Deese noted, these shocks will impose added balance of payments burdens on many countries that may have already stretched their outstanding debt to the limit. It is clear that further credit for these countries will be absolutely necessary should further price shocks occur.

CREDIT NEEDS RESULTING FROM SHARP INCREASES IN OIL PRICES

The credit problems that would face many oil-importing countries in the event of a sharp increase in oil prices can best be illustrated by studying the effect of higher prices on the trade deficits of these countries during 1973 and 1979. These deficits are summarized in Table 11–1 where the merchandise trade deficits of a selected set of less developed oil-importing countries are shown by region of the world. As the table shows, the aggregate deficit more than triples between 1973 and 1975, increasing from $10 billion to $38 billion. The $15 billion increase in the first year can be traced directly to the increase in oil prices, while the $13 billion increase in the second year resulted from both higher oil prices and the oil price induced recession in developed countries that reduced exports of the less developed countries. In 1977 and 1978 the deficits shrank back to the $25 billion level as the effects of the recession wore off.

The effects of the 1979 oil price increase appear less pronounced than those in 1974. In fact, deficits increased by only $6 billion from $41 billion in 1978 to $47.4 billion in 1979. The improvement is partly an illusion, however, because the 1979 oil price increase was smaller on an annual basis than the 1973 increase in that it was spread out over a period of six months. Thus, while the full effect of the earlier increase in oil prices was in place by January 1, 1974, the second peak was not reached until July 1979. Only in 1980 will the full impact on trade balances be apparent.

The impact of higher oil prices on the trade and services components of the balance of payments in some of these countries was equally striking. The data for five of the countries that are typical of this group show a large increase in deficits between 1973 and 1974 and again between 1978 and 1979 (see Table 11–2).[2] The data also

---

2. Due to time and reporting limitations data are shown for only six countries. These are the oil-importing countries: Pakistan, Brazil, Singapore, Korea, and the Philippines, and, for contrast, Mexico. At the time this chapter was written these were the only large countries from the Third World block that had reported complete data on their 1979 balance of payments performance.

Table 11–1. Merchandise trade deficits of selected oil-importing less developed countries[a] by region of the world (*billions $ U.S.*).

Region	1973	1974	1975	1976	1977	1978	1979
Africa	-0.16	-0.61	-4.26	-2.81	-4.15	-7.37	-5.30
Asia	-3.61	-8.93	-13.60	-6.76	-7.56	-14.40	-20.19
Middle East	-4.23	-6.66	-8.29	-6.51	-7.94	-10.45	-8.33
Western Hemisphere	-2.11	-9.34	-12.16	-9.15	-5.62	-8.87	-13.61
Total	-10.11	-25.54	-38.31	-25.23	-25.27	-41.09	-47.43

Source: International Monetary Fund (1976, 1980).

a. The countries are:

Africa: Cameroon, Ethiopia, Gabon, Ghana, Ivory Coast, Kenya, Madagescar, Mauritias, Morocco, Sudan, Tanzania, Tunisia, Zaire, Zambia.

Asia: India, Korea, Malaysia, Pakistan, Philippines, Singapore, Sri Lanka, Thailand.

Middle East: Bahrain, Egypt, Israel, Syria, Arab Republic.

Western Hemisphere: Argentina, Bahamas, Brazil, Chile, Colombia, Dominican Republic, Ecuador, El Salvador, Guatemala, Jamaica, Netherlands Antilles, Peru, Trinidad, Tobago.

Table 11–2.   Trends in trade and payments statistics for selected countries (billions $ U.S.).

Country	1973	1974	1975	1976	1977	1978	1979
Brazil:							
Merchandise and Services[a]	-2.2	-7.5	-7.0	-6.6	-5.1	-7.1	-10.5
Financial Flows[b]	4.5	6.5	5.8	9.1	5.8	11.7	7.3
Net	2.3	-1.0	-1.2	2.5	0.6	4.6	-3.2
Korea:							
Merchandise and Services	-0.4	-1.9	-1.9	-0.3	0.4	-1.1	-4.2
Financial Flows	0.8	1.8	2.3	1.6	0.9	1.8	5.1
Net	0.4	-0.1	0.4	-1.3	1.3	0.7	0.9
Pakistan:							
Merchandise and Services	0.0	-0.9	-1.0	-0.8	-0.4	-0.7	-1.2
Financial Flows	0.2	0.8	0.8	0.8	0.4	0.7	1.1
Net	0.2	-0.1	-0.2	0.0	0.0	0.0	-0.1
Philippines:							
Merchandise and Services	0.5	-0.2	-0.9	-1.1	-0.8	-0.7	-1.6
Financial Flows	0.2	0.8	0.9	1.0	0.8	1.6	2.0
Net	0.7	0.6	0.0	-0.1	0.0	0.9	0.4
Singapore:							
Merchandise and Services	-0.6	-1.1	-0.6	-0.6	-0.4	-0.7	-1.1
Financial Flows	1.1	1.6	0.8	1.0	0.9	2.1	1.7
Net	0.5	0.5	0.2	0.4	0.5	1.4	0.6
Mexico:							
Merchandise and Services	-1.5	-3.0	-3.1	-3.5	-2.0	-2.8	-4.8
Financial Flows	1.6	3.0	3.3	2.9	2.4	3.3	5.2
Net	0.1	0.0	-0.2	-0.6	0.4	0.5	0.4

Source: International Monetary Fund (1980).

a; Includes the net of merchandise exports less imports plus the net of income from services plus the sum of private and public unrequested transfers.

b. Includes all other balance of payments items, including direct investment, long- and short-term capital not included elsewhere, net errors and omissions, and counterpart items.

Table 11−3.   Ratios of deficits in merchandise and service accounts
to the income from exports of merchandise and services.

Country	1973	1974	1975	1976	1977	1978	1979
Brazil	33.4%	80.3%	70.4%	58.2%	37.9%	49.0%	58.3%
Korea	15.3	42.0	36.0	7.0	NR	9.1	23.9
Pakistan	5.1	60.6	59.9	38.8	14.1	21.5	28.5
Philippines	NR	5.4	26.6	30.2	18.8	13.7	24.0
Singapore	11.3	13.6	7.0	6.8	4.0	5.2	6.5
Mexico	30.8	47.6	44.8	49.5	24.6	24.0	29.5

Source: International Monetary Fund (1980).

Note: NR = Not relevant because a country's balance of payments was in surplus.

show that these countries were generally able to finance the increase
in trade deficits by increases in offsetting external financing. For
instance, offsetting sources of funds were available to Korea, the
Philippines, and Singapore through most of the period. However,
Brazil appears to have experienced difficulty (as frequently reported
in the financial press).

But oil prices were not the sole explanation for the difficulties.
Rather, as Table 11−3 illustrates, the problems can be traced to the
general trade imbalance that existed prior to the first oil price increase. Brazil's current account deficit amounted to 33 percent of
exports in 1973. It increased to 80 percent in 1974. (A ratio of 100
percent would imply that a country's imports of goods and payments for services were twice as high as its exports of goods and earnings from services.) By comparison, the deficits in the other countries
represented a much smaller percentage of export earnings after the
price increase.

Table 11−3 shows that these ratios improved between 1974 and
1978 in each of the five countries, implying that export earnings
were gradually catching up with imports. The 1979 oil price increase
set this process back, although not as far as in 1973. In other words,
Williamson and Bergsten appear to have been proven correct.[3]

3. The performance of the Mexican economy during the same period makes an interesting contrast to that of Brazil, Korea, and the other countries included in the table. As can be
noted from Tables 11−2 and 11−3, Mexico was able to finance its current accounts deficit
by a steady flow in offsetting external financial support, in spite of the fact that export

However, it must be noted that some bankers observe the same phenomenon with alarm. Recently, Zombanakis argued:

> The initial price increase by the Organization of Petroleum Exporting Countries in 1973 touched off a massive transfer of balances to countries that had no way of spending them on goods and services. So the balances had to be recycled as financial assets. As time went on, strong economies, such as Germany, Switzerland, and Japan, were able to sell enough goods in international markets to cover their oil payments and run a surplus in their balance of payments substantially higher than the OPEC surplus. Less aggressive exporters — including the U.S. — and most Third World countries continued to pile up deficits. In effect, they bought their oil on credit, and the credit was supplied mostly by the banks, which extended loans on their own account and recycled the petrodollars deposited with them by the oil-producing countries.
>
> The further increase in oil prices in the past year makes it impossible to keep this comfortable arrangement going. The price of oil more than doubled between the end of 1978 and the end of 1979. In 1980 the banks will have to provide not less than $150 billion to allow the debtor countries to service their existing obligations and finance new deficits. This compares with the $100 billion supplied in 1979, a record year (1980: 18).

In spite of this pessimism we would summarize this section by noting the following. First, the major developing nations have been able to adjust to the higher costs of oil imports in the past within a span of three to four years. While they still need to increase their debts to the developed world, their export earnings appear to increase at a rate that will support this increased debt. Second, the countries that appeared to be in the worst shape after the increase in oil prices (at least according to the financial press) were probably facing difficulties before the increase. In other words, oil represents a problem for international monetary markets, but by no means the only problem.

This does not necessarily imply that financial markets will be able to cope with future oil market interruptions. It is possible to imagine a very large interruption that would cause the price of oil to increase so rapidly that even the most solvent developing country would find itself unable to obtain the necessary credit to finance its oil imports for a transitional period. It is to this issue that we now turn.

---

earnings did not cover the cost of imports (as measured by the ratio of the current account deficit to the value of export earnings from merchandise trade and earnings from services). Of course Mexico succeeded where other countries, such as Brazil, failed because it has large deposits of oil and gas.

COPING WITH OIL MARKET DISRUPTIONS

Two steps can be taken to avoid the disorderly financial markets that result from loan defaults caused by chaotic oil markets. The first is to prevent an oil market disruption from causing an increase in the price of oil. If consuming countries quickly reduce their demand for oil to the supply level available after the disruption, large price increases will be less likely. If price increases are avoided then the problem remains essentially in the energy market with only modest implications for financial markets. However, it may not be possible to avoid a substantial price increase altogether. Thus, as a second step, measures to protect the viability of financial markets are required.

The need for standby programs to reduce consumption was vividly illustrated during both the 1973–74 embargo and the 1979 Iranian interruption. The uncertain circumstances surrounding the Iranian interruption caused consumers to bid up product prices on the Rotterdam and other petroleum markets after the middle of November 1978. The increases were modest, however, until the end of January 1979 when Saudi Arabia announced that it would reduce production by 1 million barrels per day, retroactive to the beginning of 1979. Spot prices on the Rotterdam market immediately increased 30 to 60 percent (see Table 11–4).

The increase on the Rotterdam market caused the value of an incremental barrel of Saudi Arabian crude oil to increase from $14.94 in December 1978 to $22.44 in March 1979. By July, continued anxiety about the stability of supplies had driven the value of the incremental barrel of crude to $35 (see Table 11–5). Postings in exporting countries were increased during 1979 to bring the prices of most crudes in line with these values.

Standby programs to reduce demand in oil-importing countries, such as the plans developed by each of the member countries in the IEA, may reduce the increase in the ultimate equilibrium price by preventing or slowing the increase in product prices on spot markets. To be effective, however, the plans must be triggered quickly.

To achieve this end, a workable program for reducing consumption, preferably by market mechanisms such as those suggested by Alm, and an adequate strategic petroleum stockpile, must be developed. The centerpiece of an ideal program would be the imposition

Table 11−4. Prices of principal petroleum products on Rotterdam market ($/bbl).

Date	Gasoline (Regular)	Gasoil (#2 Fuel Oil)	Residual Fuel Oil (1% Sulfur)
October 1, 1978	21.42	18.48	12.42
November 1, 1978	23.94	21.00	15.70
December 1, 1978	24.78	21.42	14.35
December 15, 1978	23.94	20.58	14.04
January 1, 1979	23.10	24.36	16.01
January 15, 1979	25.20	26.46	17.52
February 1, 1979	26.88	34.02	18.12
February 15, 1979	35.70	42.84	21.29
March 1, 1979	40.74	42.00	20.99
March 15, 1979	32.34	34.02	18.57
April 1, 1979	32.34	34.86	18.27
April 15, 1979	35.70	37.38	19.33
May 1, 1979	37.80	37.80	20.84
May 15, 1979	40.74	39.06	21.29
June 1, 1979	48.72	54.18	25.07
June 15, 1979	45.36	51.24	25.67

Source: *Platt's Oil Price Service* (1978 and 1979, various issues).

by all OECD nations of mandatory import quotas to reduce import demand to the available supply. To be effective, these quotas must be accompanied by taxes on petroleum products, rationing, or other measures to reduce consumption, together with fuel substitution programs and use of available inventories. Once such programs are in existence, the risks of future price surges on spot markets due to disruptions will be reduced.[4]

The logical intent of the standby programs would be to prevent increases in spot market prices that could trigger increases by OPEC.

---

4. We must realize that such programs could not prevent a surge in prices resulting from production cutbacks by all OPEC countries acting together: strategic inventories and standby programs can only provide protection against emergency disruptions. However, consuming countries have another weapon against the exercise of monopoly power. As Adelman (1980: 52) noted in "The Clumsy Cartel," the cartel would put itself in real danger if it ever raised the price to the point where it was near the true monopoly price, because at that point consuming countries could impose ad valorem tariffs that would reduce the cartel revenues.

Table 11−5.   Value of an incremental barrel of Saudi Arabian
marker crude netted back to Ras Tanura ($/bbl).

Date	Value	Official Sales Price
1978		
July	12.72	12.70
August	13.05	12.70
September	12.94	12.70
October	13.55	12.70
November	17.10	12.70
December	14.94	12.70
1979		
January	17.47	13.34
February	24.69	13.34
March	22.44	13.34
April	24.09	14.55
May	26.31	14.55
June	34.22	14.69
July	32.90	18.00
August	30.69	18.00
September	30.35	18.00
October	32.18	18.00
November	34.74	24.00
December	36.28	24.00

Source: Petroleum Intelligence Weekly (1978–1980, various issues).

However, even the best contingency plan may fail, leaving higher oil prices, enlarged trade deficits in oil-importing countries and consequent pressures on financial markets. As noted above, failure to offer the needed financing could precipitate a crisis that could cause the failure of some banks. Thus some type of program is needed to support financial markets during a disruption.

MAINTAINING FINANCIAL INSTITUTIONS IN THE ABSENCE OF A DISRUPTION

Experts have debated the role of the IMF and private banks in international financial markets—discussing who should finance the deficits of oil-importing countries, and the perceived risk to private banking institutions of failure by the IMF or other international financial bodies to absorb these deficits. But they have not directly addressed the problems that might arise in the event of a disruption. It is important to review this debate before adding the element of disruption.

In the section above we described the views of Rockefeller, Zombanakis, and Farmanfarmaian et al., who believe that private banks will shortly stop providing credit to many Third World countries and urge immediate IMF intervention. Opposed to this interventionist view are many economists, such as Houthakker, who argue that it is the role of the private banks to accept risk and that, given appropriate information, the interest rates will adjust to bring about an optimal distribution of loans by maturity. Some also argue that increased intervention by international financial institutions will make it easier for OPEC countries to raise prices. They suggest that the apparently precarious condition of the world monetary system acts as a brake on OPEC. Therefore, they conclude, the maintenance of a judicious tension in the monetary system will lead to a moderation in oil prices.

While discouraging substitution of the IMF for private institutions, some have argued for strengthening the structure of the international financial system. For instance, Stem noted in 1976, "Much has been written about the multinational character of Eurodollar banking precluding it from having a lender of last resort, with the additional contribution to confidence which such a lender would give the system." He goes on to note that some have called for the Federal Reserve to assume, "and presumably announce, such a role" (1976: 324). But Stem argues that such a role for the Federal Reserve is unnecessary. Instead, banks lending in the Eurodollar market in other countries can and should rely on the central banks in their home countries to act as lenders of last resort. These arrangements would provide a more appropriate means of protecting the system while leaving the supervision of banks to national authorities capable of distinguishing the insurance of confidence from the preservation of incompetence.

THE IMPACT OF AN OIL MARKET DISRUPTION
ON FINANCIAL MARKETS

Whichever argument one accepts in the debate over the role of public and private banking institutions in financing the trade deficits of oil-importing countries, assuring the safety of the banks, and achieving financial stability, a large-scale oil disruption presents a separate problem that has been overlooked. Sudden surges in oil prices increase the credit needs of oil-importing countries, perhaps to the point of undermining an otherwise stable financial market. To address this problem we would propose to let the IMF or some other international financial institution provide transitional loans to the oil importers for a period of one to three years. The point of such loans would be to defray temporarily part of the increased cost from large increases in the cost of oil (say, over 25 percent) and thus provide some means of protection against internal economic disorder. This financing should cover part of the initial plunge in the merchandise trade account; it would therefore provide a means of adjusting internal energy use and exports to the new, higher, oil price.

Credit arrangements of this type should be different from the traditional IMF loans, which are conditional. The conditions imposed by the IMF make many nations reluctant to borrow from the fund. It would be better policy in this case for the IMF to allow member countries to apply for standby lines of credit (really a line of credit), which could be used only in the event of oil price increases in excess of a predetermined percentage. Further, any loans actually made should not be counted against a country's existing IMF credit tranche. Otherwise the credit would be useless to those countries needing it most.

The purpose of the credits would be to cover a decreasing fraction of the increased cost of oil in the first three years after a disruption, allowing oil importers time to adjust to the higher prices. Funds for the loans would be borrowed from member countries—either the petroleum exporters or the international money markets.

This arrangement would have the advantage of leaving the job of determining the applicants' creditability to the private banks since each country seeking to avail itself of the facility would, presumably, have to meet the obligations it incurred before the price increase in accordance with usual rules. If a country had been relying on credit to cover its imports, then it would have met the conditions imposed by the bankers. And, if private sector bankers appraise risk correctly, oil-importing countries would have to maintain sound policies over the long run. In return, they would have a formalized insurance policy to meet the exigencies caused by higher oil prices.

It may be argued that this proposal would make it easier for OPEC to raise prices. However, this argument is specious. In the first place, large price increases seem to accompany accidents, wars, or acts of God, so it is unlikely that the absence of an international mechanism reduces the probability of such accidents occurring. Second, as noted above, other policies can be used to reduce the likelihood that the cartel will push for the monopoly price. Furthermore, even if OPEC did decide to follow such a strategy, the recycling mechanism described here would bring the oil-exporting countries into the recycling process and increase the chances that they would be hurt by their own actions.

It could also be argued that this proposal would encourage importing countries to postpone actions to reduce their imports. This point of view is also incorrect since the recycling arrangement would require them to satisfy bankers before any crisis developed and would provide only a fixed sum. The mechanism is like disaster insurance, not a dole.

CONCLUSION

Some commentators have argued that there are risks to the international financial markets from sudden sharp increases in the price of oil because private institutions could not recycle petrodollars. In 1973 these forecasts were incorrect. They may also appear incorrect today. So far, private banking institutions have managed to handle the increased credit demands. In the case of future disruptions, it is likely that they will continue to be able to make the adjustment. However, a small risk persists that a disruption in oil markets will kick off a disruption in financial markets. The probability of such a disruption can be reduced in two ways: (a) by preparing standby energy programs to moderate the increase in prices; and (b) by developing standby lines of credit within international institutions to provide a portion of the incremental funds that would be required by oil-importing countries to adjust to higher oil prices.

Standby energy programs are the most important policies that can be taken in preparation for an interruption because stockpiles, fuel substitutes, and conservation will dampen price increases on the spot markets at the onset of the interruption. Since panic-inspired spot price increases were the cause of higher overall prices in the last two oil crises, it stands to reason that preventing spot market panic is vital.

The development of standby credit lines will eliminate the risk of sudden surges of borrowing demand from developing countries trying to deal with a large oil price increase. Providing these countries with a known, assured, source of credit will lessen concern in the financial community about their financial stability and, thus, lessen concern about the stability of the international monetary markets.

REFERENCES

Adelman, Morris. 1980. "The Clumsy Cartel." *The Energy Journal* 1, no. 1 (January).

Bergsten, C. Fred. 1974. "Oil and the Cash Flow." *The New York Times* (June 4).

Emminger, Otmar. 1980. "The International Monetary System Under Stress, What Can We Learn From the Past?" American Enterprise Institute Reprint No. 112. Washington, D.C.: The American Enterprise Institute.

Farmanfarmaian, Khodadad; Armin Gutowski; Saburo Okita; Robert V. Roosa; and Carroll L. Wilson. 1975. "How Can the World Afford OPEC Oil?" *Foreign Affairs* 53, no. 2 (January): 201.

International Monetary Fund. 1976. *International Financial Statistics* (December).

_____. 1980. *International Financial Statistics* (August).

Petroleum Intelligence Weekly. 1978–1980. Various issues.

Platt's Oil Price Service. 1978 and 1979. New York: McGraw-Hill. Various issues.

Stem, Carl H. 1976. "Some Eurocurrency Problems: Credit Expansion, the Regulatory Framework, Liquidity, and Petrodollars." In *Eurocurrencies and the International Monetary System*, edited by Stem, Makin, and Logue. Washington, D.C.: The American Enterprise Institute.

The Wall Street Journal. 1974. (June 6) "Mideast Oil Money Proves Burdensome to Eurodollar Banks."

_____. 1980. (February 2): 1.

Williamson, John. 1976. "The International Financial System." In *Higher Oil Prices and the World Economy*, edited by Charles L. Schutze and Edward C. Fried. Washington, D.C.: The Brookings Institution.

Zombanakis, Minos A. 1980. "How to Handle the Payments Deficits." *Business Week* (April 7).

12 MILITARY FORCE AND MIDDLE EAST OIL

Geoffrey Kemp

Access to Middle East oil will remain in our vital interest for at least the next ten years, and probably longer. Policies to ensure access run the gamut from political and economic appeasement of Middle East oil producing countries, to the military seizure of the major oil fields. Although American strategy to ensure access to oil must include diplomatic, economic, and military components, this chapter devotes itself only to the military issue. Various military threats to Western interests will first be posited, followed by consideration of some of the ways in which certain military policies could be used to meet these threats. Particular attention will be paid to the relation between the use of military force in the Middle East and the well-being of the Western alliance.

It should be stressed at the outset that military options be carefully examined against a complicated and ever-changing political and economic environment. What may appear from a technical perspective to be a straightforward military issue can be counterproductive within the broader political context. It can be argued, for instance, that using the U.S. rapid deployment force to cope with many of the "lesser" contingencies that could arise in the Gulf would create more problems than it would solve because the issue of American military power arouses political traumas in the Gulf region. At the other extreme, in a major military crisis the political sensitivities of local countries—although still present—would become less of a constraint on military options because the stakes would be higher and the ground rules changed. Consider, for example, that the U.S. Navy does not now use South Africa's port facilities for fear of offending domestic and foreign, especially African, opinion. But in the event of a serious military crisis in the Indian Ocean, such restraints would no doubt be waived.

MILITARY THREATS TO OIL ACCESS

We confront dozens of possible situations involving military force and Persian Gulf oil supplies in the years ahead. They include a coup d'etat in Saudi Arabia, increased terrorism and guerrilla warfare along the Arabian littoral, a new Arab–Israeli war, a Soviet occupation of Iran, war between Iraq and Iran or Iraq and Kuwait, and, in the worse case, a Soviet attack on Gulf oil facilities. Obviously, the most suitable military responses to these threats will vary. Internal threats and border clashes among the regional powers may be contained by indirect Western support of local regimes through arms sales, training, and advice. Direct military intervention to support local regimes would carry great political risks even though it might, under certain circumstances, be desirable. Whether we like it or not, threats involving the Soviet Union and its surrogates may indeed require direct military responses.

When NATO was founded thirty years ago, the primary military threat to the West was posed by the forward deployment of the Soviet army in Eastern Europe. Between 1949 and 1979, the Soviet military threat changed radically. Now, as NATO faces its second thirty years, Soviet strategic and theater nuclear forces in Europe and the Far East are the primary threat. A second echelon of threats is posed by Soviet conventional ground and tactical air forces in Europe and the Far East. The Soviet maritime threat has also grown, especially in the last ten years, to the point where Soviet naval forces are now capable of challenging traditional Western maritime supremacy in certain vital sea areas of the world, such as the Eastern Mediterranean. Finally, Soviet ability to project power and to support surrogates in South and East Asia, the Middle East, and Africa has markedly improved.

The stark reality is that the Soviet invasion of Afghanistan in 1979 climaxed a momentous decade of growth in Soviet military power and the relative decline in American military power. For the first time since World War II, Soviet armed forces intervened en masse and orchestrated a coup d'etat in a non-Bloc country to install a regime under direct Soviet control. The invasion involved the airlift of thousands of Soviet airborne troops into key Afghani airports, followed by the rapid deployment by road of motorized rifle divisions, and the introduction of several well-equipped tactical air combat squadrons.

The strategic implications of the Soviet invasion, together with other crises in the region, represent the most serious threat to the security and unity of the Western alliance since 1945. Within a span of twelve months, the strategic balance throughout the northern Persian Gulf region had shifted decisively in favor of the Soviet Union. Iran, which under the Shah was a pro-Western bastion along the Soviet Union's southern frontier, was the beginning. One year before, in 1978, the Shah was still technically in power, and the Soviet Union had no forces in Afghanistan. But the fall of the Shah and the increasing anti-American stance of the Khomeini regime were soon followed by the systematic dismemberment of the Iranian armed forces, growing signs of anarchy and rebellion, and the hostage crisis, which has already led to the use of U.S. military force in Iran.

By early 1980, it had become increasingly difficult to separate the region's own internal conflicts from the broader questions of U.S.- Soviet military rivalry. Concern over the shifting military balance in the Middle East and the Persian Gulf is related to overall unease about the global military balance between the superpowers. Our underlying fear is that the Soviet Union either directly or covertly, will use force, or the threat of force, to increase its political control over Middle East oil at a time when Western dependency is still dangerously high and the Soviets face a potential future energy shortage.

U.S. MILITARY OBJECTIVES

The Soviet military challenge in the Middle East has to be met globally as well as locally. At the global level, greater investment in strategic nuclear forces is required to balance the growth of Soviet nuclear weapons. We should also build up Western maritime forces, to keep our superiority at sea, and retain a strong posture in Central Europe. In regional areas, the West must be able to deter local conflict and, in the last resort, fight Soviet and Soviet-supported forces.

U.S. military objectives in the Persian Gulf cover the spectrum of options from assisting local regimes against terrorism and insurgency to fighting a major Soviet invasion force. Our ability to meet these objectives is a function of three interrelated factors: the composition, size, and preparedness of Western forces available for deployment to the Gulf; the military reaction of local regimes; the military threats to Western interests in other strategic theaters, such as Europe and the Far East. Also important is the time frame in which U.S. capabilities are to be assessed against objectives. In this regard, there are significant constraints upon current U.S. capabilities that could probably not be overcome quickly, even if top priority and greater funds were assigned to Gulf contingencies. However, by between 1985 and 1990 there is a great deal that the United States could do to improve its current deficiencies, especially if its actions were matched by local countries and members of the Western alliance.

Presence and Peacekeeping Missions

The situation in the Persian Gulf today calls for U.S. presence and peacekeeping capabilities. Given the great sensitivities of Middle East states to charges of either imperialist or communist influence, it is unlikely that the United States or the Soviet Union would be able to build up a strong military presence in any such country under "normal" circumstances. Yet it is appreciated by the local powers, especially those with a pro-Western leaning, that some American military commitment and presence nearby may be desirable even on a day-to-day basis. For this reason, among others, a maritime presence in the Indian Ocean region was the only practical U.S. option following the hostage crisis and the invasion of Afghanistan. The United States does have the ability to deploy limited air and amphibious forces against local adversaries and, in times of major conflict involving the Soviet Union, might be able to establish a bridgehead and protect critical facilities until U.S. ground and tactical air forces arrived.

To build a greater maritime presence in the Indian Ocean, the United States needs facilities for land-based maritime air operations, for without good airborne surveillance, the effectiveness of any fleet operations is greatly diminished. Although P-3 reconnaissance aircraft can use Diego Garcia (a small island in the northern part of the Indian Ocean) on a limited basis and could even fly off a carrier in a crisis, access to a land base on the Arabian peninsula such as Masirah, an island off the coast of Oman, is a virtual necessity. In terms of offensive air capabilities, there is the possibility of rotating B-52s out of Diego Garcia, although this will not be possible until the runway has been widened in 1981 or 1982.

The buildup of U.S. maritime forces in the Indian Ocean as a result of the hostage crisis is the first test of "presence" operations. However, the new task force, which at one point included three attack carrier groups, was achieved at the expense of deployments in the Pacific and Mediterranean and poses great burdens on the support "tail" and crew readiness. Furthermore, since the invasion of Afghanistan the Soviet Union has had the ability to fly attack missions into the northwestern corners of the Indian Ocean with fighter cover. Prior to the invasion, Soviet fighters could not reach the Indian Ocean to protect the slow vulnerable bombers that now make up the bulk of the Soviet long-range air attack capability. Thus Afghanistan directly affected the U.S.–Soviet maritime balance in the northwest quadrant of the Indian Ocean and demonstrated how shifts in the balance of land power can influence the naval situation.

Peacekeeping operations involving U.S. forces could involve any number of activities: joint constabulary patrols with local powers; the protection from terrorists of oil fields, loading facilities, and transportation routes; and internal security operations in pro-Western countries such as Saudi Arabia and Oman. U.S. forces might also be called on to participate in peacekeeping operations between Israel, Syria, and Jordan. The physical and technical requirements of these operations would obviously vary with the contingency: protecting oil fields requires different forces and technical skills than policing the Golan Heights or the West Bank. However, on the assumption that such operations are only conceivable with the support of local powers, the military problems are primarily logistic in nature.

The Protection of Oil Facilities and Transit Routes

Threats to the oil flow come from many sources other than terrorists. Oil from the Middle East can be interdicted at various points between the wellhead and the ports of Europe, North America, and Japan. The oil wells themselves are obvious targets, so are the collecting systems, which pump oil through pipes from the fields to local terminal facilities. The local terminal facilities, containing gas–oil separation plants, local refineries, storage tanks, and loading facilities, could also be potential targets. And the pipelines and tankers carrying oil to destinations beyond the Gulf are no less vulnerable.

The most likely military threats are sabotage or air attack against land facilities and the interdiction of tankers by air or sea power. The land facilities can be defended either by ground forces and surface-to-air missiles or by air-defense fighters. However, as mentioned earlier, the invasion of Afghanistan has compounded the already difficult task of air defense by improving the Soviet Union's ability to attack targets in the Persian Gulf.

Attack at sea is most likely within the Gulf itself; once tankers have proceeded beyond the Straits of Hormuz, the threats diminish rapidly. Although the Soviet Union, or any power for that matter, could sink a few tankers in the early days of a conflict, only very large forces could sink enough to disrupt Western supplies seriously. At present, neither the Soviet Union nor the littoral states have the staying power to do this with ships and submarines, and tankers escape the range of Soviet naval aircraft soon after they leave the Gulf. Thus, protection of the sea lanes outside the Gulf is a feasible mission for the Western powers, provided that the Soviet Union has no major base outside its own borders. However, if the Soviet Union were able to establish and protect facilities in Southern Africa, Western Africa, or the Horn, it would pose a much greater threat in the future. The West would have to earmark major naval forces to liquidate these bases in the event of a general war.

U.S. MILITARY ASSETS

Assessments of the U.S. ability to counter direct Soviet military involvement in the Persian Gulf region are very sensitive to assumptions made about when the action might take place; the cooperation of local countries on such military issues as overflying, base rights, and direct military participation; and the geographical location of the confrontation. For instance, a united Western military effort including Turkey, Israel, Egypt, Saudi Arabia, Oman, and other friendly local forces could be formidable, considering the forward bases and logistical support that these countries could provide. Whether it could prevent the Soviet Union from using military power would depend on what area in the Middle East was being contested. The defense of northern Iran from Soviet attack would be much more difficult to mount than the defense of North Yemen.

Another determinant relates to the purpose of the Western military force. If its purpose were to *deter* Soviet military activity, then it would merely have to convince the Soviet Union that the costs of achieving victory would be unacceptably high. If, however, the force's purpose were literally to stop a Soviet offensive before it reached the major oil fields, would different capabilities be necessary? Some critics of Carter Administration policy would argue that unless we are prepared to fight Soviet forces with a reasonable expectation of victory, it is foolish and dangerous to announce that the United States will use force to meet further Soviet aggression—the Soviet Union's tactical nuclear capability in the area is superior to our own, and we do not have the conventional force necessary for a major regional war.

How do the capabilities of the proposed rapid deployment force relate to these problems? Deploying a force that is able to deter and fight well-armed adversaries is much more difficult than maintaining a maritime presence. The United States is currently ill-prepared to undertake this task, even in local wars not involving the Soviet Union, because some local countries—especially Iraq—have large inventories of heavy weapons.

Table 12–1 shows the approximate time required to deploy various U.S. units to the Gulf. A token force could be air dropped in 12 to 36 hours. The 82nd Airborne Division and the 101st Air Assault Division could be deployed to, say, Saudi Arabia in fifteen and twenty days. However, these forces are very "light"—that is to say, they carry only small caliber weapons and have little in the way of protection from heavily armored units except for antitank helicopters and portable antitank missiles. This force would probably be no match for the heavy armor the Iraqis could bring to the front,

Table 12-1. U.S. military force projection capabilities in the Persian Gulf.

Type of Force	Days to Deploy to Gulf	Support Requirements
Air drop or Marine Heliborn Token Force	12–36 hours	Significant U.S. strategic airlift or locally deployed marine amphibious units on U.S. ships
Division strength Ground Force, a. 82nd Airborne b. 101st Air Assault (from CONUS)	15 days 20 further days	Most of U.S. strategic airlift can do with C–130, C–141, but fewer a/c required if C–5 employed[a] Enroute refueling and overflight rights
Substantial Ground Force, e.g., 2 "light" Divisions (Infantry), 2 "heavy" Divisions (Armor or Mechanized) (from CONUS)[b]	90–150 alone, 45–60 alone, 90–120	Entire U.S. strategic airlift. Must have all C–5s, including CRAF. Inflight refueling Overflight and landing rights Most of Military Sealift Command (MSC), includes civilian shipping Forward base established
Marine Amphibious Forces, e.g., Marine Amphibious Brigade (MAB) (from CONUS)	7–21	Amphibious assault, transport, logistics ship Underway replenishment Embarked air for close-air support and assault (V/STOL, helos and Navy fighter/attack support)
Tactical Fighter Wings, e.g., 3 Wings (from Korea or Philippines)	1–3	Overflight rights Depending on distance, tankers for inflight refueling Forward base established
Carrier Task Forces[c], e.g., 2 Carrier Battle Groups (CVBG) (from Seventh Fleet, Pacific)	1–21	Underway replenishment Cruiser/destroyer/frigate escorts Embarked air wing configured for attack/fighter roles (F–14, F/A–18)

a. C–5 carries all outsize equipment, e.g., heavy tanks, self-propelled howitzers. C–141 can carry APCs, light tanks. C–130 can carry jeeps, trucks, no tanks or APCs.

b. Army units must come from CONUS, due to strategic airlift requirements. Major ground forces must rely on sealift as well, significantly increasing deployment times. MPS

Notes to Table 12—1. continued

(Maritime Prepositioning Ships) reduces slightly the lift requirements, since brigade-size equipment will be predeployed on MPS.
  c. Some Marine and most Navy forces are forward deployed, which reduces their transit times and logistics requirements.
  Sources: *Jane's Fighting Ships, 1979–1980.* U.S. Army Armor Reference Data, U.S. Army Armor School; Binkin, Martin and Jeffrey Record, *Where Does the Marine Corps Go From Here?*, Brookings Institution, 1976; Brown, Harold. *Department of Defense Annual Report, Fiscal Year 1981.*

unless the U.S. force were protected by tactical fighters with air superiority. If Soviet units were to engage these units, they would probably be mauled.

Marine units could also deploy quickly to the Gulf, but with heavier equipment, if their ships were already in the Indian Ocean. With more warning time, it would be possible to bring in a larger and heavier ground force in two or three months, but the support requirements would be horrendous if the force had to be carried all the way from the United States in ships and planes. Such an operation would also seriously interfere with current plans for reinforcing NATO's Central Front. Thus, in event of a simultaneous Gulf and NATO crisis, the airlift problem poses currently insurmountable barriers. The only quick solution would be to deploy stocks of heavy equipment in Turkey, Israel, or Egypt and hope that light forces and Marine units could hold their own until reinforcements arrived. Tactical air and attack carrier forces could be deployed more quickly, but support requirements in the event of a shooting war almost certainly require access to a major port for resupply.

On the other hand, the odds for U.S. success improve in areas more distant from the Soviet landmass, such as Ethiopia or Yemen. Even so, reports of major Soviet weapons stockpiles in South Yemen, Ethiopia, and Libya suggest that they may currently have much better forward-deployed heavy inventory than the United States and its allies. Plans in the fiscal year 1981 U.S. defense budget to increase the number of ships carrying heavy equipment for marines and infantry forces could begin to offset this deficiency, but only if the United States can negotiate access rights with countries in the Gulf, along the Arabian peninsula, and on the east coast of Africa. Without a reliable forward-based infrastructure, no operations but presence missions could be seriously undertaken. Administration plans to build rapid deployment capability are a step in the right direction. It is useful, for instance, to provide the Joint Chiefs with greater flexibility and control in planning limited contingencies—a step the new integrated command structure permits. The proposed plans for using forward-based logistics ships to equip marine units are also important, as is work to develop a host of specialized skills pertaining to oil field operations and desert warfare. More training in counter-terrorism and securing oil fields will also add punch to local forces.

Even so, without more money, much greater cooperation from our allies, and the granting of base rights by local countries, the prospects for seriously improving the rapid deployment force's fighting abilities in any major contingency are poor over the next five years. It could be argued that the rapid deployment force is significant not for its military potential but because it reflects a new American determination that will be recognized by the Soviet Union, which cannot be too smug about unfolding events in Afghanistan. Nevertheless, an overly belligerent American posture that is not backed by a strong military capability could tempt the Soviet Union to exploit its current strategic advantage in the Persian Gulf before we can effectively counter it.

Although the effectiveness of the rapid deployment force should not be exaggerated, it is irresponsible and fainthearted to argue that the military situation is hopeless. Given the problems the Soviet Union would face introducing major forces beyond northern Iran, and given the inherent weaknesses of the local countries, an imaginative U.S. defense posture could do a great deal to offset the current imbalance of power. However, experts such as Steven Canby point out the proposed U.S. rapid deployment force is an amalgam reflecting traditional U.S. force structures, which tend to emphasize large, extensively equipped units backed up by a vast supply line of sophisticated and heavy support packages. If the Army, Marine Corps, and tactical air forces were restructured to meet the unique condition of the Gulf, we could probably field a more effective, "rapidly deployable" force at considerably less cost (Canby 1980).

MILITARY CAPABILITIES OF LOCAL STATES

What of the possible contribution of local countries to the defense efforts?

Under the Shah, Iran had certain potential military advantages other countries in the region do not yet possess, including large oil revenues, a large population, and very close military ties with the

United States. But even so, the problems Iran faced as it attempted to rapidly build up its military forces were legion: bottlenecks in distribution systems, a nearly nonexistent logistics infrastructure, an acute shortage of skilled manpower, and corruption. It is unlikely that the more spectacular military programs the Shah embarked on would ever have amounted to anything more than showpieces developed at the expense of less glamorous but probably more relevant military capabilities.

Today the remaining "pro-Western" Gulf countries face similar, if not more severe, problems. Saudi Arabia, North Yemen, Oman, Kuwait, and the United Arab Emirates all have access to arms either by direct purchase or through military aid programs. But they all face severe manpower shortages, especially in the technical skills necessary to maintain modern military forces. Furthermore, since their total populations are small to begin with, there are strict limits to their military potential, regardless of their technical skills. Thus it is not realistic to expect any of these countries to contribute anything more to military operations than token combat support and access to their airfields and ports. It is even doubtful whether they are all capable in the near term of protecting themselves against local threats.

With regard to "anti-Western" or "radical" regimes, the picture is, unfortunately, somewhat different. Both Iraq and the People's Democratic Republic of Yemen (PDRY) have better military capabilities than their Gulf neighbors. Iraq has the largest, most experienced, and best equipped forces in the region; and although the Iraqi's military performance against Israel has been of questionable merit, their present forces could defeat those of Kuwait, Saudi Arabia, and possibly Iran. The PDRY forces have been equipped, trained, and supervised by the Soviet Union, and there is a considerable number of Cuban military in the country. If the PDRY were to become directly involved in a conflict with neighboring Oman, no doubt the latter would need a major contribution from external powers to survive.

Beyond the immediate area of the Gulf, the situation is much more favorable from the Western standpoint. Egypt, Israel, Turkey, and Pakistan, which at this time can be considered "pro-Western" have among them the largest, most experienced armed forces in the Middle East. Leaving aside Turkey and Pakistan as peripheral to the Gulf and oil supplies, Egypt and Israel alone have many military assets that could contribute greatly to regional security. For instance, in terms of quality and quantity, Israel's air force is the fourth largest in the world after those of the United States, the Soviet Union, and China. And if one discounts the large number of old aircraft in China's inventory, Israel's air force may in fact be eclipsed only by those of the superpowers. The Soviet Union could not ignore this potent force when considering a large-scale military intervention in the Middle East—we must assume Soviet planners also engage in "worse case" analysis. For their part, Western military planners must realize that even though the armed forces of Egypt and Israel could be employed outside their borders and that their infrastructure and basin networks would be invaluable in the event of intervention by the U.S. rapid deployment force, political factors make it unlikely that we could use them in any but the most serious of crises. Yet that these assets exist as a resource of the last resort is cause for satisfaction, not scorn.

THE MAJOR MILITARY CONTINGENCIES

In light of these considerations, what of the more specific contingencies the United States may have to consider in the future? Three have particular relevance: intervention in local interstate and civil wars with no direct Soviet involvement; the defense of Iran; and the defense of Saudi Arabia against major threats, including a Soviet attack.

U.S. Intervention in Local Interstate and Civil Wars

The United States will soon have the capability to intervene in several of the interstate and civil wars that could someday break out in the Middle East. Assuming no direct Soviet involvement, and U.S. access to local facilities, there is no reason why U.S. forces could not be effective against most of the local powers. The key to U.S. superiority over these powers would be established air supremacy, which should not be too difficult to achieve in the absence of Soviet forces. However, air superiority would only be the precondition for successful intervention. Ultimately, well-chosen ground forces with appropriate training would have to be introduced. And without a strong logistics support system, no ground force could survive for very long, especially against well-equipped local forces. In terms of actual contingencies, the United States could probably apply force effectively in conflicts between Ethiopia and Somalia; North and South Yemen; Oman and South Yemen; Saudi Arabia and any of its Arab neighbors, including Iraq; and in civil wars involving the United Arab Emirates, Bahrain, and Kuwait.

Whether U.S. military intervention in any of these conflicts would be sensible politically is another matter. In nearly all of these cases, the political risks to broader U.S. interests in the Gulf would probably outweigh the benefits of intervention. For one thing, the Soviet Union and its friends would almost certainly exploit American interference, seizing it as an excuse for further Soviet encroachment. Military intervention could also lead to another oil embargo and, perhaps most serious, could further widen the gap between West Europe and the United States concerning the overall direction of Middle East policy. So although the technical problems of military intervention in these types of contingencies are solvable, the political costs of carrying out military operations might be an overriding deterrent.

The Defense of Iran

Iran is central to both land and sea power in the Persian Gulf because of its borders with the Soviet Union and its strategic dominance of Gulf waters. If the Soviet Union were to invade and occupy Iran, its new access to Iranian ports and airfields at the head of the Gulf and at Bandar Abbas and Chah Bahar would radically alter the balance of power in the region. The Soviet Union's lack of infrastructure and support facilities in the Indian Ocean would be eased and its ability to project land-based maritime power against U.S. forces would be greatly improved.

In view of the supposed ease with which the Soviet Union could invade Iran, a brief sketch of modern military operations in the area has interesting lessons for us today. The Nazi–Soviet Pact of 1939 included a secret protocol that, in effect, promised the Soviet Union a free hand in the Persian Gulf region in the event of a German victory in the West. The German invasion of Russia in June 1941 radically altered the situation and led to a Soviet military agreement with Britain. In August 1941, British and Russian units invaded Iran on the pretext of enforcing its neutrality, which was jeopardized by German fifth columnists and the generally pro–German attitude of

Reza Shah. In reality, the attack was designed to do three things: first, to protect oil fields in Iraq and Iran; second, to secure a line of communication to protect the Gulf in case the German army broke through the Caucasus; and third, to establish a southern supply route to Russia. The Soviet government's legal pretext for invasion was the peace treaty it had signed with Iran in 1921. This treaty permitted it to place troops temporarily in Iranian territory for the purpose of self defense.

As General William Slim later referred to it, the invasion of Iran was *opera bouffe*. In less than a week, Russian forces that had entered Iran at five points dispersed along the entire northern border, routed the resistance, occupied Tabriz and Mashhad, and entered Tehran with the British. The Russian attack was well coordinated; the ground force invasion was accompanied by air strikes against airfields of the major northern cities. The performance of the Iranian forces was very, very poor, in spite of their modern German arms. Desertions were widespread, especially in the northeastern province of Khorasan.

Several elements of the Soviet attack have relevance today. Britain had consulted with the Soviet Union prior to the invasion and agreed that the Soviets should send a primary column from Tiflis to Tabriz and another column down the west coast of the Caspian to Banda Pahlavi. However, the Soviet attack also included the three other incursions into Khorasan Province that some sources claim were planned without the approval of the British government. The invasion of Khorasan was a masterpiece of deception and surprise. It overran the province in less than a week.[1]

With Iran secure but with the German armies threatening Allied positions in Egypt and the Caucasus, in May 1942 the commander-in-chief of the British Middle East Forces, General Sir Claude Auchinleck, made plans in event of a German attack through Iran from the Caucasus. Auchinleck stated that his objective was to ensure the security of bases, ports, oil supplies, and refineries in Iraq and Iran, all of which were located in the center and south of the region, by stopping the Germans as far north as possible. His belief was that if the Germans succeeded in breaking through the northern provinces

---

1. For more details, see Sir Clarmont Skrine, *World War in Iran*, (1962: 78, 103-107). The British forces invaded from bases in Iraq. One force under General Slim advanced from Baghdad through the Pai Tak pass to Kermanshah; the other force under General Harvey moved from bases at Basra to secure the oil facilities at Abadan and capture the port of Khorramshah. They achieved control over Southern and Western Iran in a few days.

of Iran it would be much more difficult to prevent them from eventually launching a two-pronged attack on the Gulf through Iran and Iraq.[2]

A similar strategic situation pertains today; in theory, the best place to confront Soviet forces is as far north as possible—provided the United States and its allies have access to the bases that Auchinleck held. Since we don't hold those bases any longer, our strategic ability to defend the Gulf against a Soviet attack is weak.

Even under the Shah, when Iran's armed forces were more disciplined than they are today, local defense efforts could only have been a series of holding actions because most of the country's military power was deployed along the Iraqi border and in the center and southwest regions. Yet a plausible defense of Iran might be possible if the Iranian forces were reconfigured, re-equipped, and retrained, and if an infrastructure for deploying American forces were established. Leaving aside the political feasibility of these measures at this time, it should be noted that the formidable terrain of northern Iran could be exploited to slow down a Soviet advance and create a logistics nightmare for armored forces fighting their way to the south. This defensive strategy would require troops well trained in mountain warfare and the sabotage of vulnerable communication lines, a conventionally equipped rear zone capable of rapid mobility to prevent Soviet outflanking maneuvers, and more airfields and better early warning systems to strengthen Iran's northern air defenses. Except for some advanced aircraft, surface-to-air missiles, and radar systems, the equipment employed in such operations need not be the high technology systems the Shah was so fond of. The basic need is not for tanks, fourth generation jets, and long-range warships but for an army that is prepared to fight in the early days of a war. If a combination of Iranian and U.S. forces could be mustered to resist any southward advance, a prudent Soviet military planner would have to think very carefully before attempting a major offensive toward the Gulf.

There is also the possibility that the United States would deploy forces south of the Zagros mountains if the Soviet Union invaded across Iran's northern border. This southern zone contains all the major oil fields and the ports on the Persian Gulf and Gulf of Oman.

2. Dispatch submitted to the Secretary of State for War on 27 January 1943 by General Sir Claude Auchinleck, "Operations in the Middle East from 1st November 1941–1st August 1942" (*London Gazette* 1948).

To make this option militarily feasible, however, U.S. forces would have to enter the region at the same time that the Soviet forces were crossing the northern border. It is very doubtful whether the United States could mount such an operation in the foreseeable future unless it had already positioned forces and equipment in Saudi Arabia. In the event that the two forces did deploy simultaneously, the geographical advantages would favor the Soviet Union in the long run, though the willingness of the United States to fight so far forward might be sufficient to deter Soviet intervention in the first place. The danger would be that the Soviet Union might call our bluff. We would then face a sort of Cuban missile crisis in reverse; that is to say, the options would be to fight a conventional war and lose, or threaten escalation to nuclear war at a time when the nuclear balance was shifting in the Soviets' favor.

The Defense of Saudi Arabia

Since the fall of the Shah there has been considerable speculation about the defense of Saudi Arabia, which is considered vital to U.S. and Western interests. How protectable is Saudi Arabia? And, is there any difference between defending a regime and protecting its oil? Again geography, local capabilities, and infrastructure are the three most important factors determining the effectiveness of any attacking or defending force. Geographically, Saudi Arabia is vulnerable on account of its large size, small population, and potentially hostile neighbors. Although Oman, Kuwait, and the United Arab Emirates have relatively stable pro–Saudi governments, at present long-range political predictions about the Gulf are hazardous. In view of the potential vulnerability of the Saudi regime, American planners should realize that any military threat to the integrity of Saudi Arabia could have major political significance for the future of the Saudi regime.

Unless the Saudi armed forces can deter and, if necessary, fight incursions by such powers as South Yemen, the credibility of the regime will be seriously weakened. In this regard, it is more important for the armed forces to be able to respond quickly and decisively to incursions than to fly F-15 jets. Against stronger enemies, the Saudis would have little chance fighting alone. In event of an Iraqi attack, they would be hard pressed without active American–

and conceivably Jordanian—assistance because their army and air forces are neither configured nor deployed to counter a concerted attack from that direction. And for the foreseeable future, there is little they could do against sophisticated opposition such as the Soviet Union except raise the costs of admission.

If the United States had time to deploy its own forces into Saudi Arabia with the support of the regime it would probably be sufficient in terms of an immediate response to send token ground forces, several tactical air wings, and some specialized forces for the protection and repair of oil fields. However, if the United States had to fight its way into Saudi Arabia against an established hostile force equipped with heavy armor, the proposed rapid deployment force would almost certainly fail unless help from local countries such as Israel and Egypt was forthcoming. This analysis demonstrates that the speed with which a force can deploy may be as important as its overall military capabilities.

A further problem relates to the composition and likely effectiveness of Saudi forces. Saudi Arabia is developing two very separate military organizations, the regular armed forces and the Saudi National Guard. Each organization has separate command structures, training programs, facilities, and communications. There is, in effect, a true "separation of powers" with the Army deployed far away from the major cities and the most modern National Guard units located outside Riyadh and Jedda. The reasons for this are clear: The Saudi royal family is not prepared to allow any one institution to gain a disproportionate share of raw power at the expense of the others. Most experts believe that it will be a long time before the Saudi armed forces could contribute importantly to any military operation in spite of the massive influx of new equipment and the vast sums of money spent on training and support facilities.

THE POSSIBILITY OF ESCALATION

A conflict with the Soviet Union in the Persian Gulf could spread to another theater or involve the use of nuclear weapons. In either case, a third world war might be the result.

Nuclear Options

Nuclear weapons give the United States and the Soviet Union over-whelming power to influence outcomes in any Middle East war. With nuclear weapons the Soviet Union could, in one blow, destroy the Middle East oil fields, close the Straits of Hormuz, eliminate local military adversaries, and pose a very serious, if not decisive, threat to U.S. maritime forces in the Indian Ocean and Eastern Mediterranean. In theory, U.S. nuclear weapons could be used to attack the Soviet Union's southern military bases and its overseas posts in South Yemen and Ethiopia; to block Soviet access to the Persian Gulf by sea and by land, including the Northern Iranian mountain passes; to eliminate Soviet surrogate forces in Iraq; to destroy all Soviet surface and submarine naval forces in the Indian Ocean and Eastern Mediter-ranean; and to attack important targets in the southern Soviet Union, including the Caucasus oil facilities.

These options may seem wildly improbable, but they demand con-sideration because the Soviet Union is now better prepared to under-take a nuclear war in the Middle East than the United States. The United States does maintain nuclear weapons in its Eastern Mediter-ranean and Indian Ocean fleets and could deliver more bases in Turkey and other forward countries, but these airfields and our giant aircraft carriers are more vulnerable to preemptive attack than Soviet nuclear weapons, which could be dispersed to dozens of separate bases along its southern border. The United States could reduce this disadvantage by redeploying more nuclear weapons to the area and by installing nuclear cruise missiles on ships other than aircraft carriers.

Any use of nuclear weapons in the Middle East would heighten the chances of drastic nuclear exchange. Both sides therefore have great incentives to avoid any such development. Yet if either side found itself confronted with a conventional military disaster, the temptation to at least threaten further expansion of the conflict would be high. For this reason, there is some justification for West-ern suggestions to the Soviet Union that an attack on vital Western interests in the Gulf would be tantamount to World War III—pro-vided, of course, that the Soviet Union regards such a response as unacceptable.

Conflicts Outside the Gulf

Some analysts have suggested that, in the event of a Soviet threat to the Gulf, the West could respond by threatening Soviet interests in other regions. Unfortunately, an analysis of our ability to apply persuasive counterpressures gives little cause for comfort. In fact, the Soviet Union can use this strategy to much greater effect than the West. If, for example, Soviet forces in Central Europe were placed on alert just as an attack on the Gulf commenced, the Allies would be hard pressed to determine priorities. No American president could ignore the threat to NATO, yet reinforcing the Central Front and putting the strategic nuclear forces on alert would divert forces from the Middle East. The truth is that the most vulnerable "hostage" targets are either those which are not as important as the Persian Gulf—the Soviet merchant fleet, Cuba or Vietnam—or which are so important that any Western attack on them would be the equivalent of an attack on the Soviet heartland—the Kola peninsula is an example. In short, there is no substitute for Western military capabilities in the Gulf itself.

THE ROLE OF ARMS TRANSFERS AND MILITARY TRAINING

The leaders of Gulf countries, no matter what their political persuasion, have a very traditional outlook on the role of military power: They respect it. Their concern with Soviet, American, and Israeli military power reflects their certainty that these three countries could in the last resort impose their will on others. Their perception does not discount the political and economic power of oil wealth. But oil power, as used by OPEC, is peacetime power. Arab leaders realize that if major war were to occur in the Gulf, the ultimate arbiters of victory would be tanks, warships, and combat airplanes—not oil prices. No wonder, then, that all Middle East leaders but Khomeini continue to place great importance on military purchases from the West and the Soviet Union. Their oil wealth, it seems, has made them feel less sanguine about their ultimate security.

Both the Soviet Union and the Western countries have made extensive use of arms transfers and military training in pursuit of their foreign policy objectives in the Middle East. Notable examples include Soviet military aid to Egypt between 1955 and 1975; current Soviet sales to Ethiopia, South Yemen, and Iraq; French arms sales to Israel through 1967; British aid and training to the smaller Gulf states during the 1970s; the U.S. relationship with Iran under the Shah; current American support of Saudi Arabia and Israel; and the abrupt shifts in U.S. and Soviet arms transfers to South Yemen, Ethiopia, and Somalia. So extensive and important have these arms transfers been that we could argue that they have been the cornerstone of relations between the external powers and the most important Middle East countries since the end of World War II.

The benefits and costs that have accrued to the suppliers and the recipients in these relationships are more difficult to assess. In some cases, arms transfers have been directly related to actual military conflicts; the results of these infusions are relatively easy to evaluate. But in other cases, the contribution of military aid to the security and stability of the region has been the source of considerable controversy. For example, U.S. military sales to Iran under the Shah were viewed by successive administrations as a cornerstone of U.S. security policy, but the contribution these sales made to Iranian fighting capacity is moot. Some observers go further and assert that in retrospect, the Shah's investment in advanced arms may have contributed to his eventual downfall.[3]

The Iranian case is an important one to examine because the United States is now embarked on an equally expensive, though less comprehensive, military sales program in Saudi Arabia. Do the arms transfer programs currently being funded by the Saudis *really* contribute to the stability of the regimes of the region? Or could it be that the rapid modernization of their armed forces will create the conditions for threatening political change? There is no way of being precise about these questions. But they do highlight the need for caution in predicting the longer term effects of military modernization on developing countries. We can at least say that a more carefully thought out arms sales policy within the Western Alliance is desirable regardless of Soviet behavior; it would remove some of the competitive "bidding" that currently bedevils arms transfer procedures in the Middle East.

3. Chubin writes "vast military acquisitions that principally benefited Western suppliers aggravated the Shah's latent legitimacy problem."

ASSIGNING WESTERN RESPONSIBILITIES
FOR THE DEFENSE OF THE MIDDLE EAST

In view of the extreme difficulties the United States would face in fighting a war by itself in the Persian Gulf region, should NATO "redraw" its boundaries beyond the Tropic of Cancer? In strategic terms, the answer should be "yes." In political terms, it is very difficult to imagine this redefinition occurring before a major crisis. Nevertheless, the Western industrial powers should formally recognize that the ability of the Soviet Union to divide the Alliance politically on oil access is the Achilles heel of the Alliance and that Middle East oil dependency is closely linked to the Allies' overall military posture.

Because of the geographical proximity of Greece and Turkey to the Middle East–Gulf, it makes sense to think of this region as part of the Soviet Union's Southern Front, which stretches from the Adriatic to Pakistan. Within this catchment area lie many of the most potentially explosive issues that may involve NATO and Soviet military power: Yugoslavia's succession, Cyprus and Greek–Turkish animosity, the Arab–Israeli conflict, unrest in Iran and Afghanistan, the future of Pakistan, instability in the Gulf itself, and the problems of the Horn of Africa. Formal recognition by NATO's political leadership of the linkages between these "local conflicts" and overall Western strategic interests would go a long way to ending the dangerous assumption that NATO's wartime responsibilities stop at Turkey's eastern border.

Beyond seeking consensus on these issues, several new strategic initiatives by the United States are necessary. First, it seems unrealistic at this time to expect more explicit extra–NATO military cooperation among the Allies, except on a bilateral basis. The major effort in this direction will therefore have to remain an American initiative. However, greater military cooperation between individual NATO members such as France and Britain, both of which have military assets relevant to Gulf contingencies is needed. Joint training exercises and planning make sense, as would cooperation in such activities as covert operations.

The other industrial Allies should accept that U.S. preparations for Middle East contingencies serve the overall interests of the Alliance and that adjustments in their own contributions to regional security will be required. If the United States guards the Gulf, then

Europe should contribute more to its own defense and Japan should spend more on East Asian security.

Highly probable low-level conflicts involving indirect Soviet initiatives pose, in many ways, relatively easy military problems. Unfortunately, at the same time, they pose complicated political difficulties, especially within the context of Alliance politics. In this regard, a much more concerted effort within the Alliance to launch political, economic, and covert operations against Soviet-sponsored governments and organizations in the Middle East would be desirable. Similarly, every effort should be made to prevent countries such as Iraq and Iran from falling under Soviet domination, even if doing so requires an extra measure of patience in dealing with Iran.

Special attention must be paid to the dire position of Turkey. This nation's role in the defense of the Middle East is vital, and yet it is in need of economic and military assistance. West Germany's agreement in June 1980 to provide such aid is a most healthy and useful beginning. The Allies, including Japan, should provide most of the economic aid, but the U.S. Administration should continue to press Congress for much greater military assistance.

Arms sales and training can help to bolster the defense capabilities and thereby enhance the stability of local regimes in the short run. Unfortunately, there is little cooperation among Western Allies on arms sales, and the present Administration's arms transfer policies do not do enough for the security of friends and allies. Greater cooperation on Western arms sales would be desirable, as would the abandonment of those restrictive qualitative clauses in U.S. arms transfer policy—especially those that prohibit the modification of advanced weapons systems solely for export. Current U.S. arms transfer policy tends to encourage local countries to buy weapons that are often too sophisticated for their own needs.

Western responses to Gulf crises should be considered in two time frames: correctives, which can be implemented over the coming few years; and longer term priorities requiring five or more years. The immediate priorities are to build up the rapid deployment capabilities of U.S. forces, preferably with greater funding; tie down firm commitments from local countries on base rights and access to facilities; expand the facilities at Diego Garcia; improve intra-Alliance cooperation in military aid and sales; strengthen the capabilities of countries such as Saudi Arabia and Oman to fight terrorism and low-level insurgency; and apply political and economic pressure to pro-

Soviet or Soviet-leaning regimes to reject further Soviet or Cuban presence in their territories.

Over the long haul, the military establishment should begin taking steps now so that it can make a much more powerful military commitment to the Middle East by the late 1980s. Beyond a major net increase in all Allied defense budgets, this preparation should include plans to reconfigure and re-equip air, ground, and maritime forces for rapid deployment. New fighting vehicles—light-weight tanks and armored personnel carriers—need to be designed and manufactured, and air and sealift forces must be assembled. Given the importance of the Alliance cornerstone and the need for a "two-way street" in Alliance weapons procurement, it might make good political sense for the United States to shop around Europe for some of the new equipment that it needs, especially in the areas of light armor and infantry weapons.

The crux of the problem is determining how to rapidly enhance U.S. military and political capabilities for quick, decisive action. The long-run capacity of the Western powers to stand up to Soviet pressures in the Gulf is good, especially if one counts the West's economic as well as military assets. Yet to mobilize these formidable resources may require a political commitment as far reaching as the creation of NATO. Because of the current divisiveness in Western policies, consensus on any proposed plan of action is elusive and the opportunities for Soviet interference are numerous.

REFERENCES

Canby, Steven. 1980. "General Purpose Forces." *International Security Review* (Fall).

Chubin, Shahram. 1979. *Foreign Policy.* (Spring).

London Gazette. 1948. "Operations in the Middle East from 1st November 1941–1st August 1942." Supplement, June 13.

Skrine, Sir Clarmont. 1962. *World War in Iran.* London: Constable & Company.

IV CONCLUSIONS

13 CONCLUSION
A U.S. Strategy for Energy Security

Joseph S. Nye
David A. Deese
Alvin L. Alm

Looking at America's energy policies over the past three decades, one is struck by two ironies. At the time when Middle Eastern supplies were secure to the West, we purposely cut them off with an oil import quota in 1959 and unnecessarily drained our own reserves in the 1960s. By protecting U.S. producers in the name of national security, we misused invaluable resources. Once it became impossible for us to live without increasing imports, we ended the quota and clamped on price controls. This subsidized imports of foreign oil just as if funds had been appropriated from the Treasury, increased demand for oil, and stifled production at home. In the 1970s, our preoccupation with the equity of prices and profits undercut our vital longer term energy, economic, and security interests. In essence, we failed to use Middle Eastern oil when it made sense to do so, and then encouraged its use after we were already heavily dependent on imports.

Americans failed to grasp fundamental economic and political change in the world oil market. Energy policy and foreign policy proceeded along different tracks, uncoordinated rather than molded together into an effective strategy for energy security. We failed to define and respond to three basic threats: the physical disruption of oil supplies, economic and political damage from rapid increases in oil prices, and the foreign policy consequences of our energy vulnerability.

PAST POLICIES AND ENERGY SECURITY

Ostensibly, the United States has considered energy a security problem for at least the past three decades. In reality, however, American policies have tended to address price and economic effects more than energy security. During the two decades before 1973, the main preoccupation of American energy policy was the glut of inexpensive oil on world markets: Persian Gulf oil was a threat to higher priced American oil.

Faced with rising demand for foreign oil, President Eisenhower instituted mandatory import quotas in 1959 to limit oil imports to roughly 12 percent of total consumption (Cabinet Task Force 1970). Although the import quota program had an explicit national security goal, its real political roots were in trade protectionism. The program was a failure as a security measure because it stimulated production levels that eroded domestic reserves rather than creating stockpiles and spare capacity.

In 1970, a Cabinet Task Force recommended the gradual elimination of the quotas on the grounds that they were costly to U.S. consumers and did little for national security; but the group did not urge a national stockpile policy. Ironically, this recommendation came at the same time that U.S. consumption was increasing rapidly and domestic oil production was peaking at 11.2 million barrels per day. U.S. spare capacity of 4 million barrels per day in 1960 had represented 44 percent of U.S. demand and 21 percent of free world demand (DOE March 12, 1980). By 1973, imports had risen to 30 percent of oil consumption.

The United States was ill-prepared for the 1973 Arab oil embargo. Although the government had attempted to play a conciliating role between OPEC nations and the major oil companies early in the 1970s, it had done little to prepare effectively for an embargo. When it came, the U.S. government encouraged oil companies to spread the burden equally among all consuming countries; it accelerated diplomatic efforts toward a Middle East peace settlement; and it took the lead in organizing the International Energy Agency (IEA). Domestically, the newly created Federal Energy Administration (FEA) administered oil price controls and allocated oil among refiners. These domestic activities actually aggravated the situation. The general public lacked real understanding of the U.S. energy security situation and tended to blame the Nixon Administration and the oil companies for the crisis (McKie 1975).

Between 1973 and 1979, the official objective of U.S. energy policy was to reduce dependence on imported oil. In 1973, President Nixon's "Project Independence" set the unrealistic goal of eliminating imports by 1980. One year later, the FEA realized the need for a strategic petroleum reserve along with their efforts to reduce import levels (which could be reduced painfully by stopping economic growth). But little changed in practice. In 1975, Congress passed an Energy Policy and Conservation Act which provided for the Strategic Petroleum Reserve; but American vulnerability continued to increase. Filling of the Strategic Reserve was delayed and domestic price controls continued to encourage oil imports to rise to a peak of 47 percent of oil consumption by 1977.

After a period of coordinated creativity marked by the formation of the IEA, U.S. policymakers kept energy policy and overall political-military strategy largely separate in the mid–1970s (Nau 1978). They expected the enormous 1973 price increase to stimulate exploration for new energy supplies, restrain demand, and eventually reduce the real price of imports. It was widely believed that the price of $10 per barrel would create a glut in the market and dissolve OPEC. At one point, ironic in retrospect, U.S. diplomacy in the IEA was focused on establishing a $7 floor price so that cheaper oil would not destroy incentives for investing in long-term energy alternatives. Preoccupied with price, the United States paid insufficient attention to the international political determinants of oil supply.

To an extent, the strategy worked despite the price controls imposed in the United States. Energy efficiency in American industry improved 10 percent from 1973 to 1977. Europe and Japan—which did better at passing oil price increases through to consumers—curtailed the rate of growth in their energy use, even after adjusting for recession. From 1975 to 1979, the real dollar price of oil dropped slightly, and even more in yen and deutschmarks. But these price decreases encouraged oil consumption and left Western nations even less prepared for the consequences of the Iranian revolution in 1979. Lower prices had perverse effects on governments' ability to take necessary actions and consumers' willingness to restrain demand.

The emphasis on current prices rather than on the danger of interruptions contributed to the divisive nature of the energy debate in the United States. In April 1977, President Carter announced his first energy plan, which eventually led to relaxing natural gas regulation and to increasing incentives for conservation. But the general public did not believe his statement that our energy situation was the "moral equivalent of war." The oil glut of 1978 did nothing for the nation's sense of urgency. With few exceptions, expert projections saw OPEC production approaching 40 million barrels per day (Missner 1979). It was widely expected that Saudi Arabia could be persuaded to increase production to 16 million barrels per day and that market tightness would not be a problem in the early 1980s. In 1979, just before the Iranian Revolution, the Strategic Petroleum Reserve contained only 92 million barrels—about twelve days' imports.

At least the events in Iran dramatized the fragility of the political assumptions behind previous American energy policy. Reliance on economic forces and gentle pressure on unstable Persian Gulf governments for ever-increasing production might mitigate price increases in the near term, but it increased vulnerability over the longer run. The most important resulting policy change was the April 1979 decision to decontrol oil prices by September 1981. This move was quickly followed at the Tokyo Summit by the U.S. agreement to hold future oil imports under 8.5 million barrels per day as part of a collective import ceiling of 24.6 million barrels per day by 1985. Subsequently, the President set a goal of cutting U.S. oil imports in half by 1990 while maintaining a growing economy.[1] The 1980 Venice Summit set a goal of doubling coal use and reducing oil from 53 to 40 percent of the Summit countries' energy use in 1990. Other domestic responses to the reduction in Iranian exports included passage of a major synthetic fuels program, enactment of additional conservation and solar energy subsidies, and proposed subsidies for the conservation of oil-fired facilities to coal and other fuel sources. Congress rejected efforts to create an Energy Mobilization Board and to impose an oil import fee that would have the effect of a $.10 increase in the tax on gasoline.

Despite the merits of these actions, they do little to solve our immediate energy security problems. Nor in the next five years will these initiatives or increased domestic production greatly reduce our vulnerability to an interruption in oil supply.

---

1. The U.S. oil import ceiling for 1980 was set at 8.2 million barrels per day.

Table 13−1.   U.S. targets for change in energy supply.

| | Percentage of Total Energy Supply | | |
	1978	1985	1990
Oil	50	40−43	33−38
Gas	25	23−24	21−22
Coal	17	23−24	28−31
Nuclear	4	7−8	8−9
Other	4	3	4−5

Source: DOE, Submission to the IEA, March 1980.

Table 13−1 presents the U.S. Department of Energy's projection of America's energy sources for the next decade. These estimates are highly optimistic. Even so, they make it clear that oil will remain our major energy source for at least the next decade. What is not certain is how much of our consumption will have to come from imports. DOE expects U.S. oil production to remain near current levels of 9 to 10 million barrels per day, and it assumes that depletion of conventional production in the lower forty-eight states will be offset by new production from Alaska, shale oil, and enhanced recovery methods. CIA and oil industry sources are more skeptical. For example, Exxon projects a dip to 7.1 million barrels per day of conventional and synthetic oil in 1990 before levels of 11 million barrels per day are achieved again by 2000 (Exxon 1979). The difference is significant: DOE expects our imports to fall to 4 million barrels per day by 1990, while Exxon projects an increase to over 9 million barrels per day.

In addition, DOE projects a decline of gas production from 9 to 8 million barrels per day of oil equivalent by 1990. Officials expect coal production to continue its growth from the record 775 million tons (approximately 8.4 million barrels per day of oil equivalent) in 1978 to from 13 to 15 million barrels per day of oil equivalent by 1990. But massive investments, many with decade-long lead times, will be required, and difficult environmental and infrastructure problems will have to be overcome. Government officials project nuclear generating capacity to increase from the current 50 gigawatts to 150 to 200 gigawatts by 2000−half the level projected three years ago− but major political obstacles may block the use of this technology.

The contribution of renewable energy sources is expected to increase from 1.5 to 2 million barrels per day of oil equivalent by 1990 (Duncan 1980). Although none of these projections should be taken too seriously, they do indicate the long lead times and uncertainties involved in relying on alternative domestic supplies to reduce our oil import dependence.

Demand restraint also plays a role in U.S. energy strategy. Rising prices already seem to have had a beneficial effect. Despite a 2.3 percent GNP growth, total U.S. energy consumption in 1979 did not grow, and gasoline consumption declined 5 percent. In comparison, U.S. energy consumption increased 1 percent per year between 1973 and 1978, while oil consumption increased 1.6 percent per year (DOE March 1980). Industry sources estimate that U.S. energy consumption in 1980 will be 6 million barrels per day less than it would have been on the basis of pre–1973 price and consumption patterns. These savings could come to an additional 10 million barrels per day by 1990. In addition to price effects, the government plans to spend $1 billion on conservation research and development, and grants to state and local governments. It also expects to extend significant conservation tax credits.

These measures to increase supply and reduce demand are steps in the right direction, but they do not constitute an adequate policy for energy security. We must aim to do much more than just reduce annual imports by allowing prices to rise. A truly effective strategy for energy security requires international as well as domestic action that is in harmony with our overall foreign policy and national security objectives.

FUTURE POLICY CHOICES

There is no quick fix or single solution to our energy security problem. A successful strategy must alleviate the short-term problem while reducing our vulnerability over the next decade by making use of a wide variety of domestic and foreign policy instruments. Table 13–2 lists some of these options according to their relevance to different threats which are generally classified as either bargained extortions or chaotic interruptions. Extortions include large price increases, subtle pressures to adopt foreign policies favorable to producers' positions, and the political use of threats to cut back or

Table 13–2. Inventory of policy instruments, by situation.

	I. Bargained Extortions		II. Chaotic Interruptions	
	Domestic Policy	Foreign Policy	Domestic Policy	Foreign Policy
Deter and prevent actions	Demand restraint Strategic reserves Private stocks	Military posture Diplomacy Diversification of Sources Import restraints		Military posture Diplomacy
Defend flows				Intelligence Military assistance Intervention
Restore flows		Foreign policy concessions Intervention	Stock surplus equipment	Repair capacity Airlift capacity
Alleviate effects	Strategic reserves Private stocks Emergency procedures Disruption tariff or taxes Surge production	IEA sharing plan Coordinated stocks Coordinated demand restraint	Strategic reserves Private stocks Emergency procedures Disruption tariff or taxes Surge production	IEA sharing plan Coordinated stocks Coordinated demand restraint

withhold oil entirely; they imply a bargaining relation with rational actors. Chaotic interruptions may arise from war, revolution, accident, or sabotage — actions generally beyond the control of producer governments.

No matter what the threats, we must design a strategy to deter or prevent unfriendly actions, defend the flow of oil, restore it, and alleviate the effects of disruptions on our domestic and foreign policies. Strategies must be both resilient and flexible since, during any crisis, information will be scarce and confusion high. The mixture of policy responses will also vary according to the size of the interruption. Although the domestic and international aspects of the problem are often inseparable in practice, in some cases domestic or foreign policy instruments will be most effective for particular purposes. The table's construction suggests the importance of integrating domestic and foreign policy instruments. It also reveals that, in some situations, we have few instruments to defend ourselves.

Domestic Measures

The highest priority must be placed on putting U.S. energy affairs in order. Misguided domestic energy policies have helped make the United States extremely vulnerable. By demonstrating leadership at home, we can reduce this vulnerability and profoundly improve our international position and our relations with allies, with producer countries, with developing nations, and even with the Soviet Union. It is important to continue demand reduction and supply enhancement measures to reduce our dependence over time. The decontrol of oil and gas prices provides signals for energy efficiency throughout the economy as well as incentives for increased production. Legislated efficiency standards for automobiles and buildings, and subsidies to encourage conservation and develop new alternatives to oil, can also help stimulate appropriate investment decisions. But, as noted earlier, such measures contribute only modestly to solving the vulnerability problem that looms so large over the next five years. It is this problem that requires our attention now.

The United States has no significant Strategic Petroleum Reserve, no effective way to allocate shortages, no meaningful and workable emergency conservation program, and no policy to guide its responses to energy emergencies. On the other hand, we are spending billions of dollars on fusion, advanced nuclear concepts, synthetic fuels, and renewable technologies that will not have an appreciable effect on our security until the 1990s or beyond. We should place at least equal priority on the more immediate, and potentially devastating, problem of supply interruptions, including at least some degree of centralization of emergency planning and operational responsibilities, perhaps at the level of a presidential appointee in the DOE.

Plans to deal with supply interruptions should address three separate problems: the direct disruption of supplies, economic shocks arising from sharp price increases and panic stockpiling, and the disruption of our alliances and foreign policy. These plans must be flexible enough to deal with a range of unpredictable emergencies— from a small shortfall to complete termination of Persian Gulf imports. The measures we select should allow us to respond to politically inspired embargoes (bargained extortions) and reductions arising from wars, revolution, and other forms of political turbulence (chaotic interruptions). We must also allow ourselves time to assess the extent of the interruption and to implement longer term policies. Our energy plans must go into effect almost automatically to avoid placing untenable political demands on the President and Congress that could lead to rash decisions and prevent adequate treatment of strategic, nonenergy concerns. Finally, they should be applied quickly and resolutely to overcome uncertainties that lead to panic.

The United States has three policy instruments to help weather supply interruptions. Withdrawing oil from stockpiles could reduce world price pressures, help meet IEA sharing requirements, and dampen domestic dislocations. Allocating shortages through higher prices or regulations could minimize dislocations and inequities. And reducing demand for petroleum through price emergency curtailment actions or supply enhancement would reduce the amount of oil subject to any allocation system. In essence, substantial withdrawals from stockpiles could minimize the damages from interruptions, while allocations and emergency curtailment and supply measures could generally only make interruptions somewhat more bearable.

The Strategic Petroleum Reserve. To say that the Strategic Petroleum Reserve is behind schedule is to be guilty of gross understatement. The stockpile now contains about 20 percent of the 500 million barrels contemplated by 1980, a mere thirteen days' supply of imports. Faster filling of the reserve is hampered by limits to the rate at which it can be filled and to our ability to increase its storage capacity. The reserve's current capacity is 250 million barrels, and it is projected to increase to 400 million barrels in 1985 and 540 million barrels in 1986. If funding is granted soon to proceed with design and the purchase of land, the reserve capacity could be increased to 750 million barrels in 1989 and perhaps 1 billion barrels in 1991. Compare this bleak prognosis to the goal set in President Carter's 1977 National Energy Plan: 1 billion barrels of fill by 1985.

We started filling the reserve in 1977. New purchases for the reserve stopped in 1979 because of administration fears of adding further pressures to a tight world oil market. Due to congressional prodding, the government has begun filling the Strategic Petroleum Reserve again. But Congress mandated a fill rate of only 100,000 barrels per day, a third of the fill rate prior to the Iranian revolution. If the Department of Energy fills at this minimum rate, it would take over twenty years to reach even the 750 million barrel level and almost twenty-eight years to stockpile 1 billion barrels. If reserve fill proceeds at the earlier rate of 300,000 barrels per day, storage capacity would be limited by 1983. At that point, the rate of fill would have to be decreased until new storage facilities were made available. Achieving even a semblance of the original 1 billion barrel goal by the mid-1980s is blocked by both the fill rate and storage capacity.

This picture is discouraging enough, yet recent analyses of the potential damages of interruptions suggest that a strategic reserve of 3 to 4 billion barrels could be justified (DOE 1980). At current rates, it would be far into the next century before such a reserve could be stockpiled.

The Strategic Petroleum Reserve could help us preserve a healthy economy during interruptions, nurture cohesion in the alliance, and gain leverage over producers. In Chapter 10 it was suggested that the occurrence of an interruption half again as large as the Iranian oil crisis has more than a 75 percent probability of occurring sometime in this decade. The probability of much larger interruptions, although less likely, is also high enough to be a real concern. Given this impending threat, the low priority accorded the Strategic Petroleum Reserve is amazing. The United States spends about $150 billion annually for national defense to be prepared for the widest range of potential threats, many of which are considerably less menacing.

The United States needs to seize the initiative immediately by developing new storage facilities and filling the Strategic Petroleum Reserve at a minimum rate of 300 thousand barrels of oil a day, the same level as before the Iranian revolution. U.S. imports are about

1.5 million barrels a day lower than in 1977. Savings from new federal initiatives—phased decontrol of crude oil, reducing oil use in utility boilers, greater production of heavy oil, conservation initiatives—will be greater than strategic reserve purchases in the future. Unless the Iran–Iraq war escalates or continues for months, the world oil market will not be affected significantly by the small withdrawals contemplated to fill the U.S. SPR. It is vitally important to get the fill rate up to a reasonable plateau quickly. Once at such a level, continued fill of the reserve should not pose any serious political issue with producers or our allies; no one objected to the previous fill rate of 300 thousand barrels of oil a day in the summer of 1978. Timidity today may lead a future generation to wonder why we were so short-sighted to national security interests.

Private Stockpiles. Ironically, private stockpiles are larger now than those in the Strategic Petroleum Reserve. The total private stock of oil and products in the United States was about 1.36 billion barrels, or 194 days of imports, in mid-1980. However, most of this supply is required to run the petroleum production and distribution system. Private stocks were about 260 million barrels above the minimum level required for normal operations. Thus, private stockpiles could replace all imports for thirty-seven days.[2] This surprising bit of good news is generally unrecognized. Yet without federal support, these stockpiles could be frittered away.

The United States should alter its policy toward private stockpiles. Not only do they constitute much of the small protection we currently have, but they also have special advantages. There is more flexibility in having numerous sources of reserve supply. Purchases of private stocks do not create the political problems that attend government purchases for a strategic stockpile. And private stocks seem particularly suitable for dealing with a small crisis that might only entangle government reserves in confusion and policy conflict.

Three policy options to increase industrial petroleum reserves should be carefully assessed. First, the government could provide incentives for private stockpiles and guarantees that subsequent regulations will not allocate stocks to other less efficient refineries. If

---

2. This calculation is based on imports of 7 million barrels per day, roughly the level of gross imports for 1980. Imports may increase with U.S. economic recovery in 1981.

additional incentives are needed, consideration should be given to tax breaks or other forms of subsidy to induce industry to build and hold larger stockpiles. Economic incentives minimize government involvement, but they allow uncertainty about resulting stockpile levels and how they would be managed during an emergency.

Direct government regulation of private stockpiles overcomes these uncertainties, albeit at a bureaucratic cost. The government could follow the example of West European nations and require minimum stockpile levels—for example, based on average refinery production. To lower physical storage costs, the government might, at least temporarily, lease space in the strategic reserve. To encourage draw-downs during an emergency, the government could be given regulatory authority to require use of the stocks in specified amounts or it could simply increase the price of the leased storage.

Creation of a public–private corporation similar to the one established by the Federal Republic of Germany may also make sense. The corporation could undertake filling a public–private reserve, relieving refineries from raising capital and storing oil. Stockpile purchases could be funded by per-barrel assessments on refineries.

All of these options have drawbacks. Just relying on market incentives has the positive feature of less government involvement. But government coordination of stock withdrawals is inconsistent with a policy of nonintervention. And if the government cannot intervene, the oil companies have strong incentives to hold back stockpile use until the price rises, precisely what the government is trying to prevent. Government regulation of both stockpiles and their use circumvents this problem. But it politicizes stockpile use during an emergency. Moreover, the option confronts oil companies with a new regulatory requirement and consumers with slightly higher prices from the cost of maintaining stocks in private storage. A public–private corporation might have been a good idea at the inception of the strategic reserve program. But injecting a new institution and method of financing at this late date may just delay the program for a few more critical years unless steps are taken simultaneously to assure that its momentum is sustained.

The Management of Stockpiles. Historically, government stockpiles of strategic materials have been hoarded during emergencies rather than used. Similarly, the oil companies built up their stocks during the last two supply interruptions and so encouraged explosive price increases. If, therefore, the United States does not have a workable management and pricing plan for its strategic reserve and all the various private stockpiles, the consequences could be serious.

To discourage panic stockpiling, the government should amend the Strategic Petroleum Reserve plan with a schedule of stockpile releases that would be triggered automatically by supply interruptions of various magnitudes. Oil withdrawn from the reserve should be sold to the highest bidder at market prices. Selling stockpiled oil at less than market prices would only reduce the supplies available during the shortage, encourage the hoarding of private stocks, force the unnecessarily fast depletion of the reserve, prolong difficulties in managing the shortage, and allow higher prices later.

Emergency Conservation and Supply Measures. During the Iranian crisis, the Department of Energy issued a response plan describing the demand-curtailment and fuel-switching steps being taken to mitigate shortages. Besides voluntary conservation and programs already underway to increase supply, such as accelerated production at the Elk Hills Naval Petroleum Reserve, the plan called for the following: greater use of the increased supplies of natural gas resulting from the Natural Gas Policy Act of 1978; increased redistribution of electricity from utilities with coal and nuclear power to those heavily dependent on oil-fired generation; mandatory controls on building temperatures; and reductions in federal use of oil. Although the emergency response measures reduced oil use somewhat, the savings did not approach the projected 1.2 million barrels per day for the summer of 1979, and what savings there were came in residual fuel oil which was in surplus throughout the emergency. The measures in the Response Plan were certainly not adequate to minimize, in any substantial way, the dislocations resulting from the shortage.

There are other ways to cut consumption further, as described in Chapter 10, but they are not particularly promising by themselves. Although the savings may be small, such steps could help prevent panic and, in combination with other measures, help relieve pressure on demand. An employer-based commuter plan issued by the federal or state government could require employers of 100 or more persons to develop emergency transportation programs for their employees. Although the goal of enabling the work force to get to jobs during an interruption is laudatory, the energy savings estimated by DOE are small, only 50,000 barrels per day. Furthermore, the plan fails to assure affected employers of additional allocations of fuel to put the ridesharing into operation.

A so-called sticker plan would ban private vehicles from the roads for one, two, or three days per week. Although DOE estimates potential energy savings of up to 345,000 barrels per day for the one-day plan, 730,000 barrels per day for the two-day plan, and 1,350,000 barrels per day for the three-day plan, the estimates depend on very optimistic assumptions about compliance and enforcement. Moreover, this proposal would be inequitable to suburban or rural residents who might not be able to get to work or who would be stranded for entire weekends. Enforcing this unpopular program would fall on local police. The sticker plan is less flexible and more inequitable than gasoline rationing, although it could be implemented more quickly and with less government cost.

Most emergency supply or fuel switching measures are not much more promising. Less potential may exist now for switching oil users to natural gas because the gas surplus existing at the time of the Iranian crisis is being used up. Although some speedup in production at existing gas wells and small draw-downs from storage are possible, their potential contributions are unknown at this time. The one possibility for a substantial emergency source of supply would be excess Canadian natural gas, perhaps the equivalent of 500 barrels of oil a day. For this source to be dependable in an emergency, we would need to reach an agreement beforehand with Canadian officials.

Our capacity to transport electricity generated by coal and nuclear energy to oil-dependent regions is limited. The intertie systems that can ship coal and nuclear energy over transmission lines are approaching their capacity. Without expensive new interconnections, we cannot take advantage of current excess capacity in some regions, which could be even larger in the future.

Despite these limitations, greater attention should be given to fuel switching and emergency supply enhancement. Considering the dramatic price increases that would result from large interruptions, the possibilities for tapping additional supplies may be greater than first appear. For current planning purposes, however, one should assume that emergency curtailment, fuel-switching, and supply enhancement measures, will, at most, only slightly reduce the amount of petroleum that will have to be allocated.

We must carefully assess how the capacity of the refinery industry to use oils of various weights and sulfur content will affect our ability to respond to future disruptions. Due to the high use of gasoline in the United States and tighter environmental standards, American refineries tend to use lighter and lower sulfur oil than the average in the world oil market. During a supply interruption, it is quite possible that heavier and higher sulfur crude oil will be more abundant. This has been a problem during past disruptions and it promises to be more serious as the world oil market shifts toward heavier crudes. This fact not only makes it more difficult to attain the supplies appropriate to our refineries, but can also result in refinery production of more of the heavy products such as residual oil, which are less in demand in the United States. The refinery industry is currently making investments to convert 550,000 to 800,000 barrels per day of capacity to use heavier and higher sulfur crude. Although these changes will take many years, they also respond to the shift in world markets toward heavier crudes and to the need to reduce U.S. oil imports through more efficient production of gasoline and lighter distillates.

The Allocation of Shortfalls. The allocation of gasoline has been the backbone of America's emergency shortage management during the last two supply cutoffs. As Chapter 10 shows, this blunt and cumbersome instrument led to serious regional inequities and nerve-wracking gasoline lines during the Iranian crisis. Nevertheless, if an interruption occurred tomorrow, gasoline allocation would again be the only major tool the government could use to distribute shortfalls.

Gasoline allocations to dealers is an adequate method for handling small shortfalls without large gasoline lines. As shortfalls exceed 10 percent, however, gasoline lines would likely spread around the block throughout the country. The odd–even and minimum purchase limitations that were imposed by a number of states during the Arab oil embargo and the Iranian cutback apparently had some success in reducing panic hoarding and gasoline lines. But they did not really save much energy. A larger interruption creating actual shortages, rather than just panic, would doubtless show the limits of their utility.

Since the passage of the Energy Policy and Conservation Act (EPCA) of 1975, Congress has assumed that gasoline rationing would be needed for large interruptions. That legislation mandated the Federal Energy Administration (now DOE) to prepare a standby rationing plan. The plan submitted to Congress in June 1980, five years after passage of EPCA, will not be in place as a standby measure until late 1981. Even then, the rationing plan will require at least ninety days to be put into operation.

Congress cautiously limited the President's authority to impose gasoline rationing. Without prior congressional approval, the President can only initiate rationing when shortfalls are expected to be 20 percent or greater—three times the gasoline shortfalls during the Iranian crisis. During shortages of 10 to 20 percent, unbearable gasoline lines and political pressure to take other actions could build while Congress debated the wisdom of imposing rationing.

Even when the authority to impose rationing is clear, the bureaucratic and management obstacles are formidable. As Chapter 10 shows, rationing requires no less than the creation of a duplicate currency within a few months, provides enticements to counterfeiting, leads to mismatches between coupons and consumers, and creates a myriad of other bureaucratic complications. A gasoline-rationing program could not be put into place quickly enough for the most probable interruptions and would not be likely to be worth its expense and confusion during a sustained interruption.

The argument for gasoline rationing is that it is the fairest way to distribute the pain of shortfalls. But this argument is highly debatable in theory, and in fact the standby plan agreed to by Congress is little more than a complicated market allocation system. White market coupons, which could be bought and sold on the open market, would be worth money. The value of these coupons, on top of the controlled price of gasoline, would be the same as the market price of gasoline. There is no reason why the government could not just as fairly send consumers money and achieve the same equity benefits without all the expensive red tape.

The first step in such an alternative to gasoline rationing during an emergency is to decontrol gasoline prices, eliminating gasoline lines by bringing supply and demand into balance. An emergency windfall tax could then be imposed to prevent windfall profits to oil companies, ensure that consumers are treated fairly, prevent losses in consumer income, and avoid adverse macroeconomic effects. Such a tax could be imposed in two ways. First, the Internal Revenue Service could collect up to 90 percent of any final price increase not associated with crude oil costs. The tax would be levied on increases over the base markups for refiners, wholesalers, and retailers of gasoline and would supplement the Windfall Profits Tax on crude oil.

The second method would be to impose a variable emergency tax at the retail level, again capturing most of the windfalls that would arise from the shortage. For this proposal to work, the President would need authority to establish and vary a tax rate that represented roughly the difference between the pre-interruption price and the current market price. Although this proposal requires greater analytical prescience and political will at the time of an interruption, it would be simpler to administer.

The taxes collected under either proposal would be rebated directly to the public. Proceeds could be returned to the registered owners of automobiles; that would certainly be as fair as the proposed gasoline-rationing scheme. Better yet, rebates could instead be given to all households using a distribution mechanism that passed the House of Representatives in 1977 in connection with the proposed Crude Oil Equalization Tax. Since the poor spend less for energy than the affluent, a per capita or per household rebate would be substantially more progressive than any system conferring economic benefits only on vehicle owners. To prevent inequities and "fiscal drag," tax withholding rates could be automatically adjusted during the course of a supply interruption. Under the current legislated definition, the Consumer Price Index would increase with a tax-rebate scheme but not with a white market rationing system. However, new legislation could correct this artificial difference by allowing the rebates to offset higher gasoline prices in the Index.

There are two compelling reasons to create a market allocation system. First, this method could be employed to reduce gasoline lines during shortages of less than 20 percent. And second, it could substitute for rationing as a tool for distributing larger shortages. Now is the time to establish this alternative. By waiting until a crisis occurs, the United States may find itself inexorably slipping into a rationing program that will unnecessarily inconvenience millions and strengthen the perception that government is no longer capable of competent and effective action. As *The New York Times* (1980) editorialized on gasoline rationing alternatives: "Rarely is the sensible course for public policy so obvious."

The Use of Response Measures. The size, duration, and causes of a supply interruption are unpredictable. The causes could range from politically inspired embargoes to chaotic political events such as war, revolution, or terrorism. Although each case will be different, certain basic steps are essential to an effective response to the early stages of any interruption. No matter what the situation, our initial actions, as outlined in Chapter 10, should be the following:

First, immediately after a disruption occurs, the United States should announce a schedule of stockpile withdrawals and a pricing policy for the released oil. That action would counter panic and hoarding by oil companies, foreign governments, and the American public. It would also reduce upward price pressures on the spot price of oil. Energy policymakers can learn a lesson here from the banking industry; when depositors are in a panic, the best thing to do is "keep the windows open."

Second, the United States should quickly institute a standby emergency tax on gasoline to reduce demand immediately after a supply interruption and prior to the sixty-to-ninety-day period before shortfalls actually appear in the marketplace. The experience of the Iranian cutback clearly demonstrates that the United States could well have avoided gasoline lines in the summer of 1979 if such an emergency tax had been in effect early that year.

Third, the government should initiate conservation and supply measures that proved effective in past crises, such as temporary switching to natural gas and the redistribution of electricity produced from coal and nuclear facilities.

Fourth, with an aggressive domestic program that helped reduce price pressures on the world oil market, the United States could work with its allies on cooperative measures. Specifically, the United States could encourage reasonable draw-downs of allied stockpiles, advocate demand restraint measures, and establish an orderly purchasing policy as a quid pro quo for U.S. stockpile releases. Although the United States would have less leverage on producing countries, efforts should at least be made to moderate prices and to encourage greater production from spare capacity.

As the depth and duration of the interruption become more apparent, the United States would have to adjust its policies. If production were quickly restored, then the use of the strategic reserve along with a temporary gasoline tax and market allocation system would be adequate. If, however, the interruption were to persist, additional supply and conservation measures would be needed.

Predictable immediate actions seem to run against the instinct to keep one's options open. Unfortunately, by keeping our options open, the United States would be likely to drive other consuming nations into price bidding and competition while encouraging oil companies to build stocks. If the United States were to take resolute and immediate domestic action, it could forestall the panic that leads to upward spiralling of prices and lay a sound basis for pursuing international corrective measures.

Foreign Policy

A sound strategy for energy security must integrate the major foreign policy dimensions discussed earlier in this volume: our political-military posture vis-à-vis the Soviet Union and the Persian Gulf, leadership and cooperation among major consumers, relations with our neighbors, stable growth for the developing countries, and interdependence with OPEC producers. Although it is convenient to discuss each dimension separately, in practice the policies are highly interactive. If U.S. and West European policies differ on an important issue, for example, this is likely to affect all the other foreign policy dimensions.

Political and Military Posture toward the Soviet Union and the Persian Gulf. No longer can we afford to neglect our political–military posture in the Persian Gulf. Gone are the days of relying simply on a single head of state, such as the Shah of Iran, to protect our profound strategic interests in the region. Nor can we launch an arms control proposal, such as the demilitarization of the Indian Ocean, without regard to the impact on our energy security posture.

The United States, other oil-importing nations, and the major oil exporters face a complex set of threats to Middle East oil supplies. Ranked on a scale of descending likelihood of occurrence and ascending military response required, these threats are: (1) terrorist sabotage of key loading facilities; (2) civil or interstate wars that destroy production capacity; (3) takeover of a major producer state by Soviet proxies or allies; and (4) Soviet airborne and tank-led invasion. Thus, Soviet control of, or heavy influence over, our vital economic lifeline would have the most far-reaching effects on Western security; but the lower level threats pose the more imminent problem for stability in the Gulf. Since these threats are interactive, designing responses is a difficult task. If we concentrate on the most serious threat, the prominent military posture most effective in deterring further Soviet aggression may actually increase the probability of indigenous threats.

This situation calls for clear and consistent U.S. foreign policy and defense signals: signals to the allies that we will work closely on political–military measures in the Gulf; to the Soviets that any direct threat to, or actual attack on, oil supplies from the Gulf will elicit immediate military responses; and to key producers that military training, arms and equipment, and even direct military support are available for defense against external aggression. We can work to redress the military imbalance in the region while not building expectations that we can reverse the geographic reality of Soviet borders some 500 miles from the oil fields.

Not surprisingly, this mixture of threats and policy responses has led to local ambivalence about the U.S. military role. As the Saudis sometimes put it, they want a U.S. presence, but just over the horizon. Chapter 12 maintains that this requirement can best be met by combining a strong naval presence with equipment stockpiles in the region and the acquisition of significant basing rights closer to the oil fields (Wohlstetter 1980). A good military solution also involves the sharing of intelligence, development of rapid repair capacity, and technical assistance. In some instances, a division of labor with our allies makes political sense. West European nations can improve their rapid deployment capabilities, strengthen their military cooperation in the Indian Ocean (especially Britain and France), and, with Japan, carry more responsibilities for their own local and regional security. The military card must be played with neither too heavy nor too light a hand.

Also important is our role as intermediary in regional conflicts that could escalate into destructive wars. The most important of these conflicts is the Arab–Israeli dispute. Because the 1973 oil embargo was related to the Yom Kippur War, some people assume that resolution of this conflict will bring with it the solution of our energy security problem. But the Arab–Israeli conflict is not the sole source of instability in the Gulf, as Chapter 3 demonstrates. The loss of 6 million barrels per day of oil from Iran at the end of 1978 should have destroyed this myth. Nonetheless, a resolution would remove *one* of the important incentives to terrorism and extortion, *one* of the important inhibitions to more forward military basing in the Gulf, and *one* important source of friction in U.S.–Saudi relations.

Perhaps the greatest threats of disruption in the area are revolution and regional war. Although our ability to moderate certain conflicts, between Iran and Iraq, for example, is limited, we can help maintain a balance of power between regional rivals. Similarly, in cases of revolution or civil war in which oil facilities are threatened or actually destroyed, we and our allies can respond promptly to requests for assistance in protecting or restoring those facilities.

Given that 60 percent of Persian Gulf oil flows through three ports and eight critical pump sites, the prospects for terrorism and sabotage are great (Levy 1980). Terrorists could probably succeed in damaging some of these facilities, but we can reduce their chances of success by offering Gulf states assistance in intelligence and training. If and when terrorism or sabotage occurs, we should be prepared to reduce the length of the resulting supply interruptions by stocking replacement pumps and valves and by planning for their rapid transportation when emergency repairs are required.

Cooperation among Major Consumers.   Cooperation among the major consumers is often treated pessimistically. Yet there has been progress. Before 1973, officials met in the OECD. After 1974, the ministers of the Western consuming nations except France met in the context of the IEA. By 1979 and 1980, energy was the major topic of the annual summit meeting of heads of state and government of the major market economies. Still, this progress falls short of what is necessary. In particular, it has focused largely on the longer term problems of oil import reduction and the development of alternative energy supplies.

Given the condition of world oil markets described in Chapter 2, there is no way to isolate the effects of individual actions by the major consumer nations. The seven summit nations represent three-quarters of world oil consumption. Their agreements on import ceiling targets at Tokyo and Venice add to the effect of our domestic demand restraint. But although these ceilings are useful, they are not a sufficient international energy policy. Since key OPEC countries are producing more oil than their revenue needs require, they could cut production to match the ceilings and thus reduce the beneficial effects on price. Moreover, ceilings designed for normal conditions are irrelevant in a disruption. International emergency measures are therefore needed.

The basis for consumer cooperation in an emergency already exists in the IEA, established in the aftermath of the 1973 OAPEC oil embargo. (See appendix for description). Under the IEA emergency oil sharing plan, members agree to maintain reserves equivalent to 90 days of imports; to develop programs to reduce consumption in an emergency by 7 or 10 percent depending on the severity of the shortfall; and to allocate the remaining available oil by a predetermined formula designed to spread the shortfall relatively equitably. A shortfall must reach 7 percent of the group's consumption (or about 2.8 million barrels per day) before the plan takes effect. Alternatively, if a single country suffers a shortfall greater than 7 percent of its consumption, the sharing plan can be triggered, but that country alone must reduce its consumption by 7 percent before the others share oil with it.

How well does the IEA work? It has a number of flaws, the three most obvious being its lack of a major consumer (France), the unwieldiness of getting its twenty-one members to agree quickly, and its longstanding caution about any action appearing to force a confrontation between consumers and producers. Nonetheless, it has an able secretariat and has at times provided a useful forum when states have desired to act (Keohane 1978). But will it work in an emergency? The answer depends in part on the situation.

Earlier, we classified security threats as extortions and as chaotic interruptions. These basic categories can be divided for purposes of analyzing the IEA into three general levels of threat, which are set forth with appropriate responses in Table 13–3.

Large Price Increases. As stated in the Introduction and Chapter 8, large price increases can be a security threat, even if they are not accompanied by political threats or interruptions, because of their disruptive effects on consumer economies, political systems, and international financial stability. Consumer government cooperation on limiting demand and encouraging alternative sources can help promote price moderation insofar as market conditions determine price. Summit meetings have helped encourage such steps as import targets, the increased use of coal, and the development of synthetic

Table 13-3.   Energy security threats and consumer government responses.

I. Bargained Extortions	Domestic Measures	International Measures
1. Large price increases	Impose demand restraint, tariffs, quotas; use alternative supplies; maintain high stocks	Import ceilings (up to a point) Encourage extra capacity Encourage alternative supplies
2. Extraneous political pressures	Demand restraint High stocks	Consumer sharing if selective embargo Political–Military counterpressure
3. Embargo	Demand restraint High stocks	IEA Sharing Plan Political–Military counterpressure
II. Chaotic Interruptions		
4. Small (up to 2 million barrels per day)	Demand restraint by price or tax Modest SPR use	Encourage surge capacity use Repair/restore capacities Informal (below 7%) IEA plan: a. stock release b. informal sharing c. restraint in market
5. Large (up to 8 million barrels per day)	Demand restraint by price or tax Major SPR use	IEA Sharing Plan Coordinate SPR use and tariffs/taxes Repair/restore capacities
6. Huge (up to 20 million barrels per day)	Demand restraint by rationing Emergency marginal supplies Full SPR use	Emergency Summit and allocation plans Political–Military repair/ restore measures

fuels. The IEA has played a modest though useful role both in helping to set the agenda for summits and in working out the details of vague summit agreements in areas such as the encouragement of oil-to-coal conversion and the elaboration of "yardsticks" to judge future import behavior.

There are several intrinsic limits, however, to consumer government cooperation to prevent large price increases under normal circumstances. First, certain actions, like developing alternative supplies, bear fruit only over the long term. Second, ceilings may have only limited effects on price if those OPEC countries whose revenues exceed their needs reduce their production. Third and most important, there are limits to how far democracies can commit themselves and their successors to tight energy import ceilings that, in effect, allocate future patterns of economic growth. Neither the IEA nor other mechanisms for consumer cooperation are likely to eliminate the effects of large price increases. They can only help.

Extraneous Political Extortion. Producer governments may also exert extraneous political pressure that can prevent the achievement of societal or foreign policy goals set by consumers. Examples include an agreement in a 1980 Saudi–Danish oil contract that Denmark would not "defame" Saudi Arabia (compliance with which the Saudis have the sole right to judge); Libya's cutoff of oil to India in 1979 when the latter refused to share nuclear weapons technology; and Iraq's linkage of oil contracts to sympathetic European foreign policy behavior. Although such pressures are not dramatic or really much different from what others have done in the age-old game of international politics, consumer governments are understandably anxious to limit their effects. Various steps are possible. Some large consumers, for example, can exercise counterpressure by delaying arms sales, hinting that future aid will be diminished, and stepping up assistance to regional rivals. Consumer governments can also reinforce each other by agreeing to share oil informally or under IEA auspices if their countermeasures result in a selective embargo.

Embargo and Cutback. The most serious bargaining threats are the embargo and the production cutback. But since selective embargoes are easily defeated by switching a few oil destinations, only the cutback is really important. The classic case was the 1973 OAPEC embargo of governments that were too friendly to Israel, accompanied by a general 25 percent reduction in production. These provisions ensured that no country could avoid some pain, but they directed the most pressure at targeted nations. It was to avoid a repetition of this action that the IEA sharing plan was created. And the sharing plan, together with certain political and military pressures, is the appropriate consumer government response.

A number of questions have been raised about whether the sharing plan will work. One concern, the absence of French membership, is not a major problem since France is almost a de facto member by virtue of its quiet cooperation with the IEA and its participation in European Community sharing. Another concern is that the decline in the major companies' share of oil and the increase in destination controls has undercut the required flexibility of private distribution systems. Chapter 2 notes that although it is too early to be certain, the increased role of small firms with fewer vested interests may actually *increase* market flexibility. In any case, the majors can be expected to retain control of enough oil to permit reallocations sizeable enough to deal with modest cutbacks. Furthermore, OPEC solidarity on the political objectives at issue and the varying willingness of key members to sacrifice revenues for political goals both set some limits to the scale of embargoes and cutbacks, leaving a reasonable prospect that the sharing plan would work.

Fears that the sharing plan will not work center on shortsighted responses by consumer countries. One important concern is that the U.S. Congress does not fully comprehend the IEA plan and that it will therefore resist Secretariat efforts to redirect tankers serving American firms or destined for American ports. However, the U.S. ability to coerce the companies and tankers (many of which are not of U.S. registry) is in doubt.

European governments might also be shortsighted, of course. In another OAPEC embargo related to Israel, European governments might think that because of their government-to-government contracts and more pro–Arab posture they could do better outside the IEA. Ironically, this strategy is likely to be faulty since production cutbacks would cause a general shortage and competitive bidding for the remaining oil in international trade would raise prices, equalizing shortfalls for all consumers. This was the French experience in 1973 and, under different circumstances, in 1979. Either case of consumer shortsightedness is likely to produce the same result: roughly equal shortfall in imports, but at higher prices, and worse political conditions than under cooperation. Assuming national governments can make simple calculations of their own self-interest, the IEA plan may be expected to work under most foreseeable embargoes.

Small Chaotic Interruptions. The second broad category of energy security threat is the chaotic interruption. A small interruption of up to 2 million barrels per day could come from the loss of a producer such as Libya, Kuwait, Venezuela, or Nigeria. As Chapter 10 shows, the 1979 shortfall related to Iran was in this category. Consumer cooperation could have further alleviated much of the disruption and enormous price increases caused by the Iranian revolution.

Another reason for our difficulties was that the disruption was too small to trigger the IEA system. Sweden and Italy briefly reached the 7 percent trigger point, but both the Secretariat and the principal consuming countries preferred to deal with the special and temporary causes in each case by informally asking the majors to reschedule a few shipments. The Iran experience, in which a 4 percent maximum shortfall led to a 130 percent price increase, pointed out that the consumers need a procedure to deal with small chaotic interruptions.

Steps to create such a procedure have been taken, but the problem is not yet solved. In May 1980, the Energy ministers of the IEA countries agreed to meet quickly if the Secretariat determined that markets were disrupted. They would decide whether to transform the yardsticks of import performance agreed to in May 1980 into ceilings to restrain demand. But lower ceilings may be difficult to agree upon and are unlikely to be sufficient.

As soon as possible, consumers must take further steps to ensure restraint in disrupted markets. They should resolve to release stocks whenever a price spike threatens. They should also allow the Secretariat to work informally with the oil companies to arrange for the equalization of minor shortfalls among member countries. This measure would require some easing of U.S. and German antitrust restrictions. Both steps would be strengthened by bilateral guarantees for particularly vulnerable countries like Japan, and a useful precedent for such guarantees exists. In April 1980 the United States quietly assured Japan that it would not suffer disproportionately from the imposition of sanctions against Iran.

Large Chaotic Interruptions. Large chaotic interruptions might occur if, for example, there were fighting in Saudi Arabia or expansion of the destructive war between Iraq and Iran. Supply reductions would surely exceed the 7 percent trigger, and the sharing plan would come into effect. The prospects for the plan's success under these conditions should actually be greater than for smaller embargoes since political extortion, with its divisive effects on consumer cohesion and cumbersome destination controls, would be relatively less important. The use of strategic reserves, the imposition of emergency tariffs or taxes to limit the wealth transfers, and quicker and better information on market conditions and the location of cargoes would also be open to IEA members. Consumers could also encourage uninvolved producers to stretch any surge capacity to the utmost, and they could initiate political or military measures to help restore or repair oil capacities.

Huge Chaotic Interruptions. Finally, there is the threat of "Arabian nightmare," the loss of Persian Gulf production that could conceivably occur from widespread regional conflict or a Soviet invasion. A loss on this scale is probably beyond the capacity of the IEA sharing plan to repair.

As the size of interruptions increases, the sharing formula shifts from allocating supplies *on the basis of consumption* (the basis for sharing during the last two interruptions) *to allocating them by import shares.* To illustrate, the United States and Japan would share equally on the traditional basis of consumption at a petroleum cutback of 3 million barrels of oil per day. If there were a 10 million barrel per day interruption, however, the U.S. share would be 22 percent higher than it would be with a consumption allocation, and Japan's share would be 22 percent lower. Facing a 20 million barrel per day cutback, the United States would be 38 percent better off than with allocation by consumption, and Japan would be 30 percent worse off. Although this would help keep the United States within the IEA sharing arrangement, Japan and our European allies would have great trouble living with an allocation that favored the nation with the richest domestic energy resource base during the worst interruptions. In short, the incentives are strong to jettison the IEA agreement when huge interruptions occur.

More to the point, such a catastrophic event would probably change the parameters of action. By definition, one cannot be too precise about such situations. Domestic economies would probably be put on a wartime emergency footing. Political and military measures would probably overshadow energy measures, although strong emergency responses in all the major consuming nations would allow time to assess the situation carefully before taking more dramatic steps. Emergency summits of key consumer countries would probably be called, and representatives might agree to some special emergency mechanism to allocate remaining oil supplies. Rapid action would require the meeting and agreement of a small number of countries.

New Policy Measures. Our survey of various supply threats indicates that the IEA has a significant ability to defend consumer countries in most situations—but not in all. The IEA agreement legitimizes equalizing forces within the market and creates a presumption against government interference. More generally, it also provides a useful forum for the exchange of information and the coordination of policies, especially when coordination requires that the energy ministers of several nations press their colleagues back home to "do the right thing" and restrain domestic demand. The great weakness of the IEA is that it deals only with energy issues, narrowly defined, when a workable energy security strategy must incorporate nonenergy measures and be an integral part of the foreign and national security policies of all consuming nations.[3]

The first priority is to shore up the IEA. Consideration should be given to crafting supplementary agreements to remedy the flaws in the current sharing system. The main concern should be to loosen the requirements for triggering the agreement so as to deal with small chaotic interruptions. In relation to huge interruptions, we could investigate allocating supplies mainly, if not exclusively, on the basis of consumption. Finally we should find ways to describe the IEA plan in simpler terms for better public understanding and develop a domestic political basis for this "energy equivalent of NATO."

The second immediate priority must be the coordination of stockpiles. As we have seen, stockpiles are at historically high levels in Europe, Japan, and the United States. It is vital that the United States get its own programs in order and encourage other consuming countries to expand both government and private reserves. Although buying the oil for those foreign stockpiles will create short-term price pressures in the world market, all consuming countries stand to benefit substantially if that reserve oil is used to moderate prices during

---

3. The agreement is also technically opaque, hindering public understanding. Definitions of stockpiles are complex and unrelated to usable reserves for emergency conditions. The formula cannot be read and understood, but rather requires complicated calculations. It is probably fair to say that many usually knowledgeable people in Congress, the Executive branch, business, and the press do not understand this critically important agreement.

a disruption. Free world consuming nations could use the existing framework of the IEA to revise the required stockpile level from 90 to 120 days and to plan for coordinated releases in the early stages of an emergency. Eventually, such a coordinated emergency reserves policy might be molded into an effort to create an international strategic reserve.

A third priority is to forge agreements on controlling panic buying in disrupted markets. One step is better information exchange and limits in spot market purchases agreed upon in the IEA, but we might also consider a supplementary bilateral agreement between the United States and Japan since they alone account for 50 percent of world oil imports. Panic in even one of these major consuming nations could disrupt the entire market system. Any agreement to prevent such a panic will require creditable assurances that remaining supplies will be shared fairly. As we have seen, the IEA emergency sharing plan is an important assurance in some situations, but it is of no use for small disruptions unless the amended procedures suggested above are implemented, or credible bilateral assurances of sharing are extended.

Improved cooperation must begin within the current framework of the International Energy Agency sharing agreement, but it must not stop there. A fourth priority for consumer governments is to consider new bilateral and multilateral procedures to supplement and reinforce the IEA. It might be useful, for example, to create an energy security group at the ministerial level that would involve France, stimulate broader participation in Germany and Japan, include both energy and foreign policy officials, and focus on the broad aspects of the energy security issues that are not now addressed by the IEA.

One matter this group could raise is the development rate of North Sea oil, particularly the prospect of building European emergency surge and reserve capacity, as discussed in Chapter 6. Norway, and to a lesser extent Britain, want to husband their reserves and avoid the inflationary effects of overly rapid development, but as NATO members they also have an interest in European security that would be enhanced by the development of some surge capacity and emergency stockpiles. Again, the political bargaining over how to share the costs will be difficult, but it need not be impossible if the participants approach energy as a security issue.

A final step in improving consumer cooperation may take longer to achieve, but is worth discussion now. "Disruption tariffs" are potentially an effective way to reduce wealth transfers to OPEC during a supply interruption. Designed to raise prices to market-clearing levels during an interruption, disruption tariffs could take the form of an actual per-barrel tariff on imports or an internal tax on oil products. If the major consuming nations could all agree to establish emergency tariffs (or tax equivalents) high enough to bring demand and supply in balance during any interruption, then producers would find it more difficult or even impossible to raise prices to clear the market as they did during the Iranian disruption. The tariff would raise oil prices in every consuming country, but each government could rebate the revenues to prevent the loss of disposable income and to blunt the domestic wealth transfers and other economic losses arising from the interruption.

There are serious political barriers to the implementation of a disruption tariff. It would quickly fail if some countries refused to comply, choosing instead to reap the "free rider" benefits of lower world oil prices and the ability to sell many export commodities more cheaply than the countries that had imposed the tariff. Furthermore, the argument for a disruption tariff may be too sophisticated for the political discourse of the industrial democracies. It may at first appear to the voting public that its own government is adding to the problem. In Europe, other problems relating to jurisdictional disputes between the European Community and the member countries might crop up. It is also unclear whether OPEC members would take retaliatory action in oil production or pricing policies if the consuming countries instituted a disruption tariff. Despite these problems, analysis and discussion of disruption tariffs are worth pursuing not just with other governments but with the U.S. Congress and affected domestic interest groups.

Relations with Neighbors, Producers, and Innocent Bystanders. Although we and our major allies account for three-quarters of world oil imports, relations with our Western hemisphere neighbors are also important dimensions of our energy security problems. Among some observers, there is a recurring belief that Western hemisphere or a North American common market could assure us of a reliable source of energy imports. In the 1960s, special quotas were provided for "more secure" Western hemisphere oil, and the 1970 Cabinet Task Force had an optimistic view of the North American contribution to our security. Since then, conditions have changed. Both we and our allies import more oil.

Although increased Western hemisphere production will be important in the near future, North American oil will not save us from a serious disruption. And even if it could, we would remain vulnerable through our allies. As Chapter 5 describes, Canada itself is vulnerable to oil disruptions despite its net self-sufficiency. Efforts to lock up remaining Western hemisphere or North American oil for the United States would more than likely destroy consumer government cooperation and inter–American relations. Our North American neighbors have no interest in close energy relations with the United States. They already fear the extent of American influence over their economies and societies and are loathe to see it increase. A cardinal rule of politics in both countries is to keep the Yankees at arms' length. In the case of Mexico, in particular, pressure for rapid expansion of oil exports could create another type of security and foreign policy problem.

What we *can* do with Mexico and Canada is quietly discuss procedures for emergencies and help them develop their long-term production capacity. Both nations have an interest in the growth of the American economy and the stability of American policy. Mutually beneficial steps could be taken by Mexico to provide surge production capacity and by Canada to redistribute supplies or to produce more oil or gas in any emergency.

Our allies and neighbors are not the only countries about which we must be concerned. We have vital economic, foreign policy, security, and humanitarian concerns in developing countries all around the world. The eighty-five oil-importing developing countries (OIDCs) import only about 15 percent of internationally traded oil, but their oil import burden now poses a first-order problem to most of humanity. That burden disrupts their security and threatens ours. Their dependence will persist over the next decades; their severe vulnerability will almost certainly worsen. Of all the countries laboring under these strains, the OIDCs will remain the most threatened and the least able to define and solve the causes of their misfortune.

As Chapter 8 showed, these nations have very few options. They must manage better their own domestic economies and energy policies, especially foreign exchange rates, deficit financing, and the pricing of petroleum products. They should encourage carefully designed increases in foreign assistance and foreign private investment, conceive new lines of exports, and renew efforts to accelerate the export of traditional goods. Perhaps most important, they should strive to come to agreements with oil producers to assure themselves of supplies during disruptions and of lenient pricing policies under all conditions.

There are also several important steps that we can take to help these nations. First, we can avoid making their situation much worse by depressing our demand and closing our markets to their exports. Almost as important is controlling the inflation in Western economies, which drives up the prices of the goods they import from us. Third, we should use international channels to press OECD nations, OPEC, and international organizations to help them cope with oil price increases. Price concessions for the poorest countries would cost very little and could be the single most direct and effective response available. Fourth, as Chapter 11 suggested, we can support larger and less conditional IMF loans to back up the private banking system financing OIDC deficits. Finally, through bilateral assistance, the IBRD, the foundations, and many other private sources, we can encourage the development of conventional and new energy sources in those countries. Reviewing these proposals, Western readers will see that their own welfare also depends on taking the recommended steps to help developing countries.

The final international dimension of the U.S. energy security problem concerns our relations with the key producing countries. Although these relations have an adversarial dimension, they involve a certain amount of cooperation. However, as we showed in the Introduction, conditions are not propitious for successful collective bargaining. Even if the agenda of such a bargaining session were limited to energy, the prospects for creating a more satisfactory oil market structure will not be good until the consumer governments do more to get their individual and collective houses in order. But these facts do not prevent low-keyed bilateral and broader dialogue. International financial and foreign assistance issues—especially means to alleviate the economic effects of rapid oil price increases—should be discussed with producers in the IMF and IBRD. The special problems of the OIDCs could be dramatized by discussion in the United Nations and elsewhere. Bilateral talks and arrangements with producers could center on expanding their capacity, especially the use of surge capacity for emergencies, in return for transfer of technology, investments, and assistance with their development plans. In short, quiet and decentralized dialogues can establish the basis for longer term cooperation between consumers and producers.

The hard work of forging a realistic energy security strategy requires the resolution of difficult issues and the deft application of various economic, military, and diplomatic measures. The fate of many other nations' energy security rests on the effectiveness of America's response, but this nation needs to do a great deal at home before it can hope to lead and help others. Even as we work patiently for a more sustainable international oil market structure, we must assume a far greater sense of urgency with respect to our domestic affairs.

Our preparedness for oil interruptions has only minimally improved over the last decade. The strategic reserve is only a skeleton of what it should be, and a workable allocation program is nonexistent. Our historic emphasis on import reduction has diverted our intellectual and physical resources from our most pressing energy problem: vulnerability to a supply interruption. Our preoccupation with imports and prices has made us less, rather than more, secure.

Can we learn from the past and prepare for the future? If the United States can develop large public and private stockpiles, a market allocation system that gives it confidence in its ability to survive interruptions, and the foreign policy measures described above, then its renewed self-confidence and international credibility will provide the moral power of leadership. Only with leadership from the world's greatest consumer can we create a more stable world economic order, secure in its energy future.

REFERENCES

Cabinet Task Force on Oil Import Control. 1970. *The Oil Import Question.* Washington, D.C.: Government Printing Office, February.

Department of Energy. 1980. "The Energy Problem: Costs and Policy Options." Staff Working Paper, Draft, March 12.

_____ . 1980. "Submission to the I.E.A." March.

_____ . 1980. "An Analysis of Acquisition and Drawdown Strategies for the Strategic Petroleum Reserve." Staff Working Paper, Draft, Office of Oil Policy, Policy and Evaluation.

Duncan, Charles. 1980. "Posture Statement Before Committee on Science and Technology, House of Representatives." Washington, January 31.

Exxon Company, U.S.A. 1979. *Energy Outlook, 1980–2000.* December, p. 16.

Keohane, Robert. 1978. "The International Energy Agency." *International Organization* (Autumn): 929 ff.

Levy, Walter. 1980. "Oil and the Decline of the West." *Foreign Affairs* (Summer): 1010.

McKie, James. 1975. "The United States." *Daedalus* (Fall): 85.

Missner, Susan. 1979. "A Comparison of Energy Forecasts, 1977–79." Stanford University International Energy Program.

Nau, Henry. 1978. "Continuity and Change in U.S. Foreign Energy Policy." *Policy Studies Journal* (Autumn): 121–32.

New York Times. 1980. August 1.

Wohlstetter, Albert. 1980. "Half-Wars and Half-Policies in the Persian Gulf." In *From Weakness to Strength,* edited by W. Scott Thompson, p. 123 ff. San Francisco: Institution for Contemporary Studies.

APPENDIXES

THE INTERNATIONAL
ENERGY AGENCY

In response to the Arab oil embargo of 1973–1974, the United States proposed an International Energy Program (IEP) to coordinate the energy policies of the industrial oil-importing states. The IEP, signed by sixteen nations in November 1974, established the International Energy Agency (IEA) to carry out the program. This agency was designed to mitigate chaotic conditions in the world oil market that might accelerate price increases, to act as an oil-consumers' coalition against OPEC, and, in the U.S. view, to help reestablish U.S. leadership in the industrial world.

The IEA and its parent organization, the Organization of Economic Cooperation and Development (OECD), are located in Paris. The IEA is composed of four "Standing Groups" and a Committee on Energy Research and Development. A Governing Board consisting of ministers or their high-ranking representatives from each participating country exercises final authority. The Executive Director and his staff make up the Secretariat, which answers to the Standing Groups and the Governing Board. Votes in the IEA are weighted according to energy consumption, but voting procedures are so ordered that no one nation or region is able to force a decision on other members.

A brief description follows of the Standing Groups and committees:

- Standing Group on the Oil Market (SOM)—collects and maintains information on the international oil market and the policies of the oil companies. The IEA receives data on oil prices from the oil companies, but only through submissions to the companies' governments. The data are treated confidentially to protect the competitiveness of the industry.

- Standing Group on Relations with Producer and Other Consumer Countries (SPC)—coordinates relations with other nations, both producers and nonmember consumers. It monitors the relations among these nations, and reviews the international energy situation.

- Standing Group on Long-Term Cooperation (SLT)—promotes conservation, development of alternative sources of energy, and other measures designed to reduce long-term dependence on oil.

- Committee on Energy Research and Development (CERD)—performs most of the research and development functions formerly held by the SLT. One activity is oversight and promotion of collaborative projects in over thirty areas of research, ranging from coal and conservation to fusion and solar power.

The Standing Group on Emergency Questions (SEQ) develops, refines, and maintains the emergency energy program of the IEA. Member nations are required to build up reserve stocks of at least 90 days of oil imports. Each nation must also have in place an effective demand restraint program enabling it to cut consumption 7 percent in the face of a 7 percent reduction in oil supplies, and by 10 percent if the shortfall is greater than 12 percent.

The Office of Information and Emergency Systems Operations of the IEA Secretariat is responsible for testing and refining the emergency mechanism. Although the mechanism has been tested in three "dry runs," it has never been activated in a real emergency. Following the shortfalls resulting from the Iranian crisis in May 1979, Sweden and Italy requested activation of the emergency system, but the Secretariat and larger nations decided to respond informally by diverting a few tankers since the causes of their shortages were special and temporary.

If an oil interruption is greater than 7 percent, the Secretariat makes a "finding" and the emergency allocation system goes into action. The finding can be overturned by a special majority vote of the Governing Board; but because of the voting weights and procedures, there must be significant opposition or else the Secretariat's finding will hold. The affected nation must cut consumption by the required amount, and the other member nations will share the remaining shortfall over either the 7 or 10 percent trigger levels. Sharing by member nations is in proportion to each nation's pre-embargo consumption level, determined from a base period of consumption over the previous four quarters for which statistics are fully available.

The emergency allocation system is a complicated one, based on a sophisticated and increasingly complicated distribution system and the energy needs of many different nations. If the IEA members as a group suffer an aggregate reduction in the range of 7 to 12 percent, each must cut consumption by 7 percent and take part in the emergency system of sharing based on pre-embargo import levels. Through a complex formula based on consumption after application of demand restraint and on supply shortfall and reserve commitment, some nations are entitled to receive oil while other members are required to give some up. Remaining oil shipments are to be reallocated (hence the role of the oil companies) and each nation utilizes its emergency stockpiles. At higher levels of supply disruptions, the formula favors those nations with significant domestic oil production.

The IEA has been fairly effective in reviewing national progress on energy policy and commitments. These reviews have the effect of peer pressure on members, and may have produced some progress toward fulfillment of promises. Beyond the power of persuasion, the IEA has served as a mechanism for forming transnational coalitions among officials with similar interests. The IEA is constantly training officials of various governments, and much professional and informal contact takes place.

The IEA emergency system has focused almost exclusively on access to oil, leaving behind the severe problem of price escalations during an emergency. There is an interim, but not permanent, plan for the IEA to mediate price disputes. At their May 1980 meeting, ministers of the IEA member nations recognized the need for limiting short-term price disruptions, perhaps by using the 90-day stockpile reserves, but there has been no further concrete progress in this area.

Figure A–1.   International Energy Agency. Stock definitions and stock levels in "normal" and crisis markets.

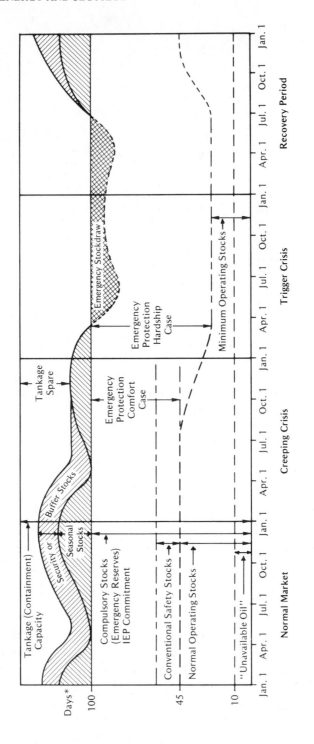

Note: Operating stocks for large indigenous oil producers may exceed IEA compulsory stocks.
*Days of Consumption (country without own oil prod.) Northern Hemisphere.

WORLDWIDE PRODUCTION AND USE OF CRUDE OIL

(Tables B-1 through B-4)

Table B-1. World crude oil production, excluding natural gas liquids.

	1973	1979
World	55,830	62,400
Noncommunist Countries	45,805	48,370
Western Hemisphere	16,135	15,270
United States	9,210	8,535
Argentina	420	465
Brazil	165	160
Canada	1,800	1,495
Colombia	200	125
Ecuador	210	215
Mexico	450	1,460
Peru	70	195
Trinidad and Tobago	165	215
Venezuela	3,365	2,355
Other	80	50
Eastern Hemisphere	29,670	33,100
Western Europe	385	2,265
Norway	30	405
United Kingdom	Negl.	1,570
West Germany	130	95
Other	225	195
Middle East	21,160	21,385
Bahrain	70	55
Iran	5,860	3,035
Iraq	2,020	3,435
Israel	90	35
Kuwait[a]	2,755	2,215
Neutral Zone[b]	525	565
Oman	295	295
Qatar	570	505
Saudi Arabia[a]	7,335	9,250
Syria	105	165
United Arab Emirates	1,535	1,835
Abu Dhabi	1,305	1,465
Dubai	230	355
Sharjah	—	15

Table B—1. continued

Noncommunist Countries *(cont'd.)*		
Eastern hemisphere *(cont'd.)*	*1973*	*1979*
Africa	5,900	6,595
Algeria	1,070	1,135
Angola/Cabinda	160	150
Congo	40	55
Egypt	165	525
Gabon	150	205
Libya	2,175	2,065
Nigeria	2,055	2,305
Tunisia	85	100
Other	Negl.	55
Asia–Pacific	2,225	2,855
Australia	370	440
India	150	245
Indonesia	1,340	1,590
Malaysia–Brunei	320	500
Other	45	80
Communist Countries	**10,025**	**14,030**
USSR	8,420	11,470
China	1,140	2,120
Rumania	300	260
Other	165	180

a. Excluding Neutral Zone production.

b. Production is shared about equally between Saudi Arabia and Kuwait.

Source: U.S. Central Intelligence Agency, *International Energy Statistical Review*, ER–IESR 80–012, (26 August 1980).

Table B–2. Petroleum consumption for major free world industrialized countries.[a]

	Canada	France[b]	Italy	Japan	United Kingdom	United States	West Germany	Other IEA[c]	Total IEA[d]
				Thousand Barrels per Day					
1973 Average	1,597	2,219	1,525	5,000	1,958	17,308	2,693	3,969	34,050
1974 Average	1,630	2,094	1,521	4,872	1,829	16,653	2,408	3,937	32,850
1975 Average	1,595	1,925	1,468	4,568	1,633	16,322	2,319	3,795	31,700
1976 Average	1,647	2,075	1,503	4,786	1,601	17,461	2,507	4,155	33,660
1977 Average	1,661	1,973	1,476	5,015	1,655	18,431	2,478	4,094	34,810
1978 Average	1,701	2,077	1,551	5,115	1,683	18,847	2,596	4,257	35,750
1979 Average	1,766	2,107	1,607	5,170	1,690	18,434	2,664	4,469	35,800
1980 January[e]	1,812	R2,465	R1,778	5,258	1,769	18,509	2,665	4,409	36,200
February[e]	1,946	R2,444	R1,864	5,721	1,620	18,721	2,393	4,635	36,900
March[e]	1,734	1,983	1,656	5,430	1,581	R17,279	2,405	4,315	34,400
April[e]	1,515	2,110	1,532	4,642	1,472	17,240	NA	NA	NA

United States geographic coverage: the 50 United States and District of Columbia.

a. These data represent inland consumption, i.e., sales of petroleum products excluding refinery fuel, refinery losses, and ocean bunkers except for the United States, where it represents domestic products supplied.

b. Not a member of the International Energy Agency (IEA).

c. Other is a calculated total derived from the difference between total IEA consumption and the nations represented above.

d. The 20 signatory nations of the International Energy Agency (IEA) are: Australia, Austria, Belgium, Canada, Denmark, West Germany, Greece, Ireland, Italy, Japan, Luxembourg, Netherlands, New Zealand, Norway, Spain, Sweden, Switzerland, Turkey, United Kingdom, and United States. In 1979 Australia joined IEA. In an effort to maintain comparability within this time series, consumption data for Australia have been incorporated into the IEA total for all years.

Notes to Table B–2. continued

e. Preliminary data.

R = Revised data.

NA = Not available.

Sources:

- U.S. Department of Energy, *Monthly Energy Review: August 1980*, DOE/EIA–0035 (80/08); U.S. Central Intelligence Agency, "International Energy Statistical Review," 30 July 1980 (except United States).
- IEA totals for most recent months are EIA estimates.
- 1973–1980 United States data obtained from:

1973 through 1976: Bureau of Mines *Mineral Industry Surveys*, "Petroleum Statement, Annual" (except unleaded gasoline) and "PAD Districts Supply/Demand, Annual."

Unleaded gasoline—Energy Information Administration (EIA) "Monthly Petroleum Statistics Report."

1977 and 1978: EIA *Energy Data Reports*, "Petroleum Statement, Annual" and "PAD Districts Supply/Demand, Annual."

January 1979 through March 1980: EIA *Energy Data Reports*, "Petroleum Statement, Monthly" and "PAD Districts Supply/Demand, Monthly."

Penultimate and preceding month: EIA "Monthly Petroleum Statistics Report" (except domestic production and exports).

Domestic production for the 3 most recent months are EIA estimates based on historical data from State Conservation Agencies.

Exports for penultimate and preceding month are preliminary data based on Form EIA–87 and the Bureau of the Census publications EM 522 and EM 594.

Data for the most recent month are estimates based on EIA weekly data.

Sources for the *Energy Data Reports* and the "Monthly Petroleum Statistics Report" are: EIA Forms EIA–64 (Natural Gas Liquids Operations Report), EIA–87 (Refinery Report), EIA–88 (Bulk Terminals Report), EIA–89 (Pipeline Report) and EIA–90 (Crude Oil Stock Report); Economic Regulatory Administration (ERA) Forms ERA–60 (Imports) and FEA P133 (Imports from Puerto Rico); Bureau of the Census publications IM 145 (Imports), EM 522 (Exports), and EM 594 (Exports); and State Conservation Agencies (Crude Production).

Table B-3.   Estimated imports of crude oil and refined products, 1979 (thousand b/d).

	U.S.[a]	Japan	Canada	Western Europe	West Germany	France	U.K.	Italy	Netherlands	Spain	Other Western Europe
Algeria	634	6	10	458	196	102	15	59	18	30	38
Bahrain	1	33	–	Negl.	–	–	Negl.	–	–	–	–
Egypt	55	–	7	67	8	–	59	–	–	–	–
Iraq	108	265	10	1,665	45	489	119	448	40	117	407
Kuwait	30	604	16	870	63	97	216	233	183	31	47
Libya	802	7	–	1,055	358	83	12	306	24	110	162
Qatar	37	140	–	209	10	76	6	23	25	28	41
Saudi Arabia	1,441	1,871	183	3,639	359	893	301	677	378	344	687
Syria	9	Negl.	–	60	17	43	–	–	–	–	–
United Arab Emirates	329	510	–	730	151	173	59	56	86	99	106
OAPEC	3,446	3,436	226	8,753	1,207	1,956	787	1,802	754	759	1,488
Ecuador	49	–	2	–	–	–	–	–	–	–	–
Gabon	48	–	–	68	18	29	–	2	10	8	–
Indonesia	423	764	–	13	9	2	–	1	1	–	1
Iran	440	520	40	932	233	140	66	47	112	89	245
Nigeria	1,134	2	–	936	294	193	10	60	263	4	112
Venezuela	942	8	209	322	32	84	31	50	15	44	66
OPEC[b]	6,417	4,697	470	10,897	1,768	2,361	835	1,962	1,155	904	1,912

Canada	532	—	—	13	4	—	1	1	6	1	—
Mexico	437	—	—	—	—	—	—	—	—	—	—
Other[c]	960	905	147	2,143[d]	1,175	358	576	472	591	137	1,888
Total	**8,411**	**5,635**	**624**	**13,180**[d]	**2,972**	**2,762**	**1,471**	**2,435**	**1,752**	**1,042**	**3,800**

a. Products traced to source of crude.

b. OAPEC members excluding Bahrain, Egypt, and Syria plus other countries shown.

c. Includes unknown.

d. Excluding intra–West European trade.

Source: U.S. CIA, *International Energy Statistical Review*, ER–IESR 80–012 (26 August 1980).

Table B–4.   Petroleum production in key OPEC nations outside the Persian Gulf *(thousand b/d)*.

	Peak Oil Production, 1973–1980[a]		Crude Oil Production as of June 1980[b]	Projected Production, 1985[c]
	Production	Year		
Algeria	1160	Dec. 1978	1000	900
Indonesia	1740	Mar. 1977	1545	1600
Libya	2210	Mar. 1977	1700	1600
Nigeria	2440	Jan. 1979	2110	1900
Venezuela	2950	June 1974	2050	1900

a. National Foreign Assessment Center, U.S. Central Intelligence Agency, *International Energy Statistical Review*, ER–IESR 80–012 (26 August 1980) p. 3.

b. Ibid., p. 1. These figures, which exclude natural gas liquids, are preliminary.

c. Fereidun, Fesharaki "Petroleum Sector Policy Plans and Options and the Major Oil–Exporting Nations in the 1980s," study prepared for inclusion in the *UN World Energy Balance in the 1980s* (January 1980). Production estimates are based on author's expectation of production cutbacks due to political, economic, and technical constraints.

THE MILITARY FORCES OF PERSIAN GULF NATIONS*

ABBREVIATIONS

<	under 100 tons	ATGW	anti-tank guided weapon(s)
—	indicates part of establishment is detached	ATK	anti-tank
		Aus	Australian
AA	anti-aircraft	AWACS	airborne warning and control system
AAM	air-to-air missile(s)		
AB	airborne	AWX	all-weather fighter(s)
ABM	anti-ballistic missile(s)		
ac	aircraft	bbr	bomber
AD	air defence	bde	brigade
AEW	airborne early warning	bn	battalion *or* billion(s)
AFV	armoured fighting vehicle(s)	Br	British
		bty	battery
ALBM	air-launched ballistic missile(s)		
		Can	Canadian
ALCM	air-launched cruise missile(s)	cav	cavalry
		cdo	commando
amph	amphibious	Ch	Chinese (PRC)
APC	armoured personnel carrier(s)	cmd	command
		COIN	counter-insurgency
Arg	Argentinian	comms	communications
armd	armoured	coy	company
arty	artillery		
ASM	air-to-surface missile(s)	det	detachment
ASW	anti-submarine warfare	div	division

*Reproduced with permission from International Institute for Strategic Studies, *The Military Balance 1980–1981* London, 1980.

ECM	electronic counter-measures
ELINT	electronic intelligence
engr	engineer
eqpt	equipment
EW	early warning
FAC(G)	fast attack craft (gun)
FAC(M)	fast attack craft (missile)
FAC(P)	fast attack craft (patrol)
FAC(T)	fast attack craft (torpedo)
FB	fighter-bomber(s)
fd	field
FGA	fighter(s), ground-attack
flt	flight
Fr	French
FRG	Federal Republic of Germany
GDP	gross domestic product
GDR	German Democratic Republic
Ger	German (West)
GLCM	ground-launched cruise missile(s)
GNP	gross national product
GP	general-purpose
gp	group
GW	guided weapon(s)
hel	helicopter(s)
how	howitzer(s)
hy	heavy
ICBM	inter-continental ballistic missile(s)
indep	independent
inf	infantry
IRBM	intermediate-range ballistic missile(s)
km	kilometres
KT	kiloton (1,000 tons TNT equivalent)
LCA	landing craft, assault
LCM	landing craft, medium/mechanized
LCT	landing craft, tank
LCU	landing craft, utility
LCVP	landing craft, vehicles and personnel

LHA	amphibious general assault ship(s)
log	logistic
LPD	landing platform(s), dock
LPH	landing platform(s), helicopter
LSD	landing ship(s), dock
LSM	landing ship(s), medium
LST	landing ship(s), tank
lt	light
m	million(s)
MARV	manoeuvrable re-entry vehicle(s)
MCM	mine counter-measures
mech	mechanized
med	medium
MICV	mechanized infantry combat vehicle(s)
MIRV	multiple independently-targetable re-entry vehicle(s)
mod	modified
mor	mortar(s)
mot	motorized
MR	maritime reconnaissance
MRBM	medium-range ballistic missile(s)
MRCA	multi-role combat aircraft
MRL	multiple rocket launcher(s)
MRV	multiple re-entry vehicle(s)
msl	missile
MT	megaton (1 million tons TNT equivalent)
n.a.	not available
Neth	Netherlands
nm	nautical miles
OCU	operational conversion unit(s)
para	parachute
pdr	pounder
Pol	Polish
Port	Portuguese

RCL	recoilless launcher(s)	TA	Territorial Army
recce	reconnaissance	tac	tactical
regt	regiment	tk	tank
RL	rocket launcher(s)	tp	troop
RV	re-entry vehicle(s)	tpt	transport
		trg	training
SAM	surface-to-air missile(s)		
SAR	search and rescue	UNDOF	United Nations Disengagement Observation Force
sig	signal		
SLBM	submarine-launched ballistic missile(s)		
		UNFICYP	United Nations Force in Cyprus
SLCM	sea-launched cruise missile(s)	UNIFIL	United Nations Interim Force in Lebanon
Sov	Soviet		
SP	self-propelled	UNTSO	United Nations Truce Supervisory Organization
spt	support		
sqn	squadron		
SRAM	short-range attack missile(s)	USGW	underwater-to-surface guided weapon
SRBM	short-range ballistic missile(s)		
SSBN	ballistic-missile submarine(s), nuclear	veh	vehicle(s)
		v(/s)TOL	vertical (/short) take-off and landing
SSM	surface-to-surface missile(s)		
SSN	submarine(s), nuclear		
sub	submarine	Yug	Yugoslav

BAHRAIN

Population: 373,000.
Estimated GNP 1977: $1.7 bn.
Total armed forces: 2,500.
Defence expenditure 1979: 37.5 m dinar ($98 m).
  $1 = 0.384 dinars (1979), 0.388 dinars (1978).

Army: 2,300.
1 inf bn.
1 armd car sqn.
8 *Saladin* armd, 8 *Ferret* scout cars; 93 *Panhard*
  M-3 APC; 6 81mm mor; 6 120mm RCL; RBS-70
  SAM.
(On order: 17 Panhard M-3 APC.)

Coastguard: 200.
2 TNC-45 FAC(M) with *Exocet* SSM.
2 Lürssen 38-metre FAC(G).
14 coastal patrol craft.
1 hovercraft.
2 landing craft: 1 *Loadmaster*, 1 60-ft.

Police: 2,500.
2 *Scout*, 3 BO-105, 2 Hughes 369D hel.

IRAN

Population: 38,250,000.
Military service: 18 months.
Total armed forces: 240,000.*
Estimated GNP 1978: $76.1 bn.
Defence expenditure 1980: 300 bn rials ($4.2 bn).
  $1 = 71.5 rials (1980). 70.45 rials (1978).

Army: 150,000.*
3 armd divs.
3 inf divs.

---

* Pre-1979 manpower and holdings shown. Present totals
are believed to be considerably less, and serviceability,
particularly of ships and aircraft, is low.

(Footnote refers to all Iran entries)

4 indep bdes (1 armd, 1 inf, 1 AB, 1 special force).
4 SAM bns with *HAWK*.
Army Aviation Command.
875 *Chieftain*, 400 M-47/-48, 460 M-60A1 med, 250 *Scorpion* lt tks; BMP MICV, about 325 M-113, 500 BTR-40/-50/-60/-152 APC; 1,000+ guns/how, incl 75mm pack, 330 M-101 105mm, 130mm, 112 M-114 155mm, 14 M-115 203mm towed, 440 M-109 155mm, 38 M-107 175mm, 14 M-110 203mm SP; 72 BM-21 122mm MRL; 106mm RCL; *ENTAC*, SS-11, SS-12, *Dragon*, *TOW* ATGW; 1,800 23mm, 35mm, 40mm, 57mm and 85mm towed, 100 ZSU-23-4 and ZSU-57-2 SP AA guns; *HAWK* SAM.
Ac incl 40 Cessna 185, 6 Cessna 310, 10 O-2A, 2 F-27, 5 *Shrike Commander*, 2 *Falcon*.
205 AH-1J, 295 Bell 214A, 50 AB-205A, 20 AB-206, 90 CH-47C hel.

RESERVES: 400,000.

Navy: 20,000, incl Naval Air.*
3 destroyers with *Standard* SSM: 1 ex-Br *Battle* with *Seacat* SAM, 2 ex-US *Sumner* with 1 hel.
4 *Saam* frigates with *Seakiller* SSM and *Seacat* SAM.
4 ex-US PF-103 corvettes.
9 *Kaman* FAC(M) with *Harpoon* SSM.
7 large patrol craft: 3 *Improved* PGM-71, 4 *Cape*.
3 ex-US coastal, 2 inshore minesweepers.
14 hovercraft: 8 SRN-6, 6 BH-7.
2 landing ships, 1 ex-US LCU.
1 replenishment, 2 fleet supply ships.
3 Marine bns.

Bases: Bandar Abbas, Booshehr, Kharg Island, Korramshar, Bandar-e-Enzli.

NAVAL AIR:*
1 MR sqn with 6 P-3F *Orion*.
1 assault hel sqn with 6 S-65A.
1 ASW hel sqn with 20 SH-3D.
1 MCM hel sqn with 6 RH-53D.
1 tpt sqn with 6 *Shrike Commander*, 4 F-27, 1 *Mystère* 20.
Hel incl 4 AB-205A, 14 AB-206, 6 AB-212.

Air Force: 70,000; 445 combat ac.*
10 FGA sqns with 188 F-4D/E.
8 FGA sqns with 166 F-5E/F.
4 interceptor/FGA sqns with 77 F-14A.
1 recce sqn with 14 RF-4E.
2 tanker/tpt sqns with 13 Boeing 707, 9 Boeing 747.
5 tpt sqns: 4 with 54 C-130E/H; 1 with 18 F-27,
    3 Aero *Commander* 690, 4 *Falcon* 20.
Hel: 10 HH-34F, 10 AB-206A, 5 AB-212, 39
    Bell 214C, 2 CH-47C, 16 *Super Frelon*, 2 S-61A4.
Trainers incl 45 F33A/C *Bonanza*, 9 T-33.
AAM: *Phoenix, Sidewinder, Sparrow.*
ASM: AS-12, *Maverick, Condor.*
5 SAM sqns with *Rapier*, 25 *Tigercat*.

Para-Military Forces: 75,000. Gendarmerie and
    Revolutionary Guards with Cessna 185/310
    lt ac, 32 AB-205/-206 hel, 32 patrol boats.

IRAQ

Population: 13,110,000.
Military service: 21–24 months.
Total armed forces: 242,250 (177,200 conscripts).
Estimated GNP 1979: $21.4 bn.
Defence expenditure 1979: 789.3 m dinars
    ($2.67 bn).
    $1 = 0.295 dinars (1979).

Army: 200,000 (150,000 conscripts).
3 corps HQ.
4 armd divs (each with 2 armd, 1 mech bdes).
4 mech divs.
4 mountain inf divs.
1 Republican Guard armd bde.
2 special forces bdes.
100 T-34, 2,500 T-54/-55/-62, 50 T-72, 100 AMX-30
    med, 100 PT-76 lt tks; about 2,500 AFV, incl
    200 BMP MICV, BTR-50/-60/-152, OT-62, VCR
    APC; 800 75mm, 85mm, 122mm, 130mm and
    152mm guns/how; 120 SU-100, 120 ISU-122 SP
    guns; 120mm, 160mm mor; BM-21 122mm MRL;

26 *FROG*-7, 12 *Scud* B SSM; *Sagger*, SS-11, *Milan*
ATGW; 1,200 23mm, 37mm, 57mm, 85mm,
100mm towed, ZSU-23-4 and ZSU-57-2 SP AA
guns; SA-7 SAM.
(On order: T-62, AMX-30 med tks; *Sucuri* SP ATK
guns; EE-9 *Cascavel, Jararaca* armd cars; Panhard, EE-11 *Urutu* APC; SP-74, SP-73 SP how;
Scud B SSM; SS-11, 360 *HOT* ATGW).

RESERVES: 250,000.

Navy: 4,250 (3,200 conscripts).
12 ex-Sov FAC(M) with *Styx* SSM: 4 *Osa*-I, 8 *Osa*-II.
5 ex-Sov large patrol craft: 3 SO-1, 2 *Poluchat*⟨.
12 ex-Sov P-6 FAC(T)⟨.
10 ex-Sov coastal patrol craft: 4 *Nyryat* II, 6⟨
    (2 PO-2, 4 *Zhuk*).
5 ex-Sov minesweepers: 2 T-43 ocean, 3 *Yevgenya*
    inshore.
4 ex-Sov *Polnocny* LCT.
(On order: 1 Yug, 4 *Lupo* frigates, 6 corvettes,
    1 spt ship.)

Bases: Basra, Umm Qasr.

Air Force: 38,000 (10,000 AD personnel); 332
    combat aircraft.
1 bbr sqn with 12 Tu-22.
1 lt bbr sqn with 10 Il-28.
12 FGA sqns: 4 with 80 MiG-23B, 3 with 40 Su-7B,
    4 with 60 Su-20, 1 with 15 *Hunter* FB-59/FR-10.
5 interceptor sqns with 115 MiG-21.
2 tpt sqns with 9 An-2, 8 An-12, 8 An-24, 2 An-26,
    12 Il-76 (6 civilian), 2 Tu-124, 13 Il-14, 2 *Heron*.
11 hel sqns with 35 Mi-4, 15 Mi-6, 78 Mi-8, 41
    Mi-24, 47 *Alouette* III, 10 *Super Frelon*, 40
    Gazelle, 3 *Puma*, 7 *Wessex* Mk 52.
Trainers incl MiG-15/-21/-23U, Su-7U, *Hunter*
    T-69, 10 Yak-11, 40 L-29, 50 L-39, 48 AS-
    202/18A, 16 *Flamingo*.
AAM: AA-2 *Atoll*. ASM: AS-11/-12, AM-39.
SAM: SA-2, SA-3, 25 SA-6.
(On order: 150 MiG-23/-25/-27, 60 *Mirage*
    F-1C/-1B fighters; C-160 tpts; 40 PC-7 *Turbo-*

Trainer; *Super Frelon, Gazelle, Lynx*, 36 *Puma*,
3 Mi-8, Mi-24, 6 AS-61TS, 8 AB-212 ASW hel;
Super 530 AAM.)

Para-Military Forces: 4,800 security troops,
75,000 People's Army.

KUWAIT

Population: 1,318,000.
Military service: 18 months.
Total armed forces: 12,400.
Estimated GNP 1977: $11.9 bn.
Defence expenditure 1979: 274 m dinars
   ($979 m).
   $1 = 0.277 dinars (1979), 0.275 dinars (1977).

Army: 10,000.
1 armd bde.
2 inf bdes.
1 SSM bn.
70 Vickers, 50 *Centurion*, 160 *Chieftain* med tks;
   100 *Saladin* armd, 20 *Ferret* scout cars; 130
   Saracen APC; 10 25-pdr guns; 80 AMX 155mm
   SP how; *FROG*-7 SSM; *HOT, TOW, Vigilant,
   Harpon* ATGW; SA-6/-7 SAM.
(On order: *Scorpion* lt tks, 175 M-113 APC, arty,
   TOW ATGW.)

Navy: 500 (coastguard).
43 coastal patrol craft‹.
3 88-ft landing craft.
(On order: 4–5 FAC(M).)

Air Force: 1,900,* 50 combat aircraft.
2 FB sqns with 30 A-4KU.
1 interceptor sqn with 18 *Mirage* F-1C, 2 F-1B.
Tpts: 2 DC-9, 2 L-100-20, 1 Boeing 737-200.
3 hel sqns with 24 SA-342K *Gazelle*, 10 *Puma*.
Trainers incl 2 *Hunter* T-67, 6 TA-4KU.

---

* Excluding expatriate personnel.

AAM: R-550 *Magic, Sidewinder.* ASM: *Super* 530.
SAM: 50 *Improved HAWK.*
(On order: *Improved HAWK*).

Para-Military Forces: 15,000 Police.

OMAN

Population: 930,000.
Military service: voluntary.
Total armed forces: 14,200.†
Estimated GNP 1977: $2.55 bn.
Defence expenditure 1980: 304 rial omani ($879 m).
   $1 = 0.346 rial (1980), 0.346 rial (1977).

Army: 11,500.
2 bde HQ.
8 inf bns.
1 Royal Guard regt.
3 arty regts (2 lt, 1 med).
1 sigs regt.
1 armd car sqn.
1 engr sqn.
1 para sqn.
Scorpion lt tks; 36 *Saladin* armd cars; 5 25-pdr, 36
   105mm guns; 81mm, 120mm mor; *TOW* ATGW;
   4 ZU-23-2 AA guns.

Navy: 900.
3 corvettes (1 Royal Yacht, 2 ex-Neth *Wildervank*).
6 Brooke Marine large patrol craft (2 with *Exocet*
   SSM).
4 75-ft coastal patrol craft (marine police).
1 log spt ship (amph).
3 *Loadmaster* landing craft, 2 LCU.
(On order: 3 *Skima*-12 hovercraft, 1 FAC(M).)

Bases: Muscat, Raysut.

Air Force: 1,800;† 38 combat aircraft.
1 FGA/recce sqn with 12 *Hunter* FGA-6, 4 T-7.

† Excluding expatriate personnel.

1 FGA sqn with 8 *Jaguar* S(O) Mk 1, 2 T-2.
1 COIN/trg sqn with 12 BAC-167.
3 tpt sqns: 1 with 3 BAC-111, 1 *Falcon*; 2 with 7 *Defender*, 14 *Skyvan*.
Royal flt with 1 *Gulfstream*, 1 VC-10 tpts, 2 AS-202 *Bravo* trainers, 1 AB-212 hel.
1 hel sqn with 16 AB-205, 2 AB-206, 5 AB-214B.
2 AD sqns with 28 *Rapier* SAM.
(On order: 2 DHC-5D tpts, 250 *Sidewinder* AAM).

Para-Military Forces: 3,300 tribal Home Guard (*Firqats*). Police Air Wing: 1 *Learjet*, 2 *Turbo-Porter*, 2 *Merlin* IVA ac; 4 AB-205, 2 AB-206 hel.

QATAR

Population: 220,000.
Total armed forces: 4,700.
Estimated GNP 1977: $1 bn.
Defence expenditure 1978: 238 m ryal ($61 m).
    $1 = 3.87 ryal (1979), 3.95 ryal (1977).

Army: 4,000.
2 armd car regts.
1 tk bn.
1 Guards inf bn.
2 inf bns.
2 arty bns.
24 AMX-30 med tks; 20 EE-9 *Cascavel* armd, 10 *Ferret* scout cars; 30 AMX-10P MICV, 8 *Saracen* APC; 4 25-pdr guns, 6 155mm how; 81mm mor.
(On order: *HAWK* SAM.)

Navy: 400, incl Marine Police.
6 Vosper Thorneycroft large patrol craft.
29 coastal patrol craft⟨ (2 75-ft, 2 45-ft, 25 *Spear*.)
Base: Doha.

Air Force: 300, 4 combat aircraft.
3 *Hunter* FGA-6, 1 T-79.

1 *Islander* tpt.
2 *Whirlwind*, 4 *Commando*, 2 *Gazelle*, 3 *Lynx* hel.
Tigercat SAM.
(On order: 6 *AlphaJet* trainers.)

SAUDI ARABIA

Population: 8,224,000.
Military service: conscription.
Total armed forces: 47,000.
Estimated GDP 1979: $94.6 bn.
Defence expenditure 1980–81: 68.9 bn Saudi riyals
   ($20.7 bn).
   $1 = 3.33 riyals (1980), 3.77 riyals (1979).

Army: 31,000.
1 armd bde (being increased to 2).
1 mech bde.
3 inf bdes.
1 Royal Guard Regt (3 bns).
3 arty bns.
2 para bns.
18 AA arty btys.
10 SAM btys with *HAWK*.
280 AMX-30, 100 M-60 med tks; 200 AML-60/-90
   armd, *Ferret*, 50 *Fox* scout cars; 150 AMX-10P
   MICV, 200 M-113, Panhard M-3 APC; 105mm
   pack, 105mm and 155mm SP how; 75mm RCL;
   TOW, *Dragon* ATGW; AMX-30 30mm, M-42
   40mm SP AA guns; *HAWK*, *Crotale* SAM.
(On order: 370 AMX-30, 150 M-60 med tks; 94
   V-150 *Commando*, AML-90 armd, 50 *Fox*
   scout cars; *Panhard* M-3, 200 AMX-10 APC;
   Dragon, 50 *TOW* ATGW; M-163 *Vulcan* 20mm,
   86 35mm SP AA guns; *Redeye*, *Shahine*, *Crotale*,
   6 btys *Improved HAWK* SAM.)

Navy: 1,500.
3 *Jaguar* FAC(T).
1 large patrol craft (ex-US coastguard cutter).
72 coastal patrol craft‹ (coastguard).
4 MSC-322 coastal minesweepers.
2 ex-US LCM, 4 ex-US LCU.

(On order: 4 corvettes with *Harpoon*; 9 FAC(M) with *Harpoon* SSM; *Exocet* SSM.)

Bases: Jiddah, Al Qatif/Jubail, Ras Tanura, Damman, Yanbo, Ras al Mishab.

Air Force: 14,500; 136 combat aircraft.
3 FB sqns with 65 F-5E.
1 interceptor sqn with 15 *Lightning* F-53, 2 T-55.
3 OCU with 24 F-5F, 16 F-5B, 12 *Lightning* F-53, 2 T-55.
2 tpt sqns with 34 C-130E, 25 C-130H, 6 KC-130H, 2 *Jetstar*, CASA C-212.
2 hel sqns with 12 AB-206, 12 AB-205, 10 AB-212.
Other ac incl 1 Boeing 707, 2 *Falcon* 20 tpts, 2 *Alouette* III, 1 AB-206, 1 Bell 212, 2 AS-61A, KV-107 hel.
Trainers: 39 BAC-167, 12 Cessna 172G/H/L.
AAM: *Red Top, Firestreak, Sidewinder*, R-530, R-550 *Magic*. ASM: *Maverick*.
(On order: 45 F-15 fighters; 15 TF-15 trainers; 1 Boeing 747, 20 CASA C-212-200 tpts; 660 *Sidewinder* AAM; 916 *Maverick* ASM.)

Para-Military Forces: 20,000 National Guard in 20 regular and semi-regular bns; 150 V-150 *Commando* APC. 6,500 Frontier Force and Coastguard; 70 small patrol boats, 8 SRN-6 hovercraft. General Civil Defence Administration units.

UNITED ARAB EMIRATES (UAE)

Population: 920,000.
Military service: conscription.
Total armed forces: 25,150.*
Estimated GDP 1978: $12.0 bn.

---

* The Union Defence Force and the armed forces of the United Arab Emirates (Abu Dhabi, Dubai, Ras Al Khaimah and Sharjah) were formally merged in May 1976.

Defence expenditure 1979: 2.88 bn dirhams
  ($750 m).
  $1 = 3.84 dirhams (1979), 3.88 dirhams (1978).

Army: 23,500.
1 Royal Guard 'bde'.
4 armd/armd car bns.
7 inf bns.
3 arty bns.
3 AD bns.
45 *Scorpion* lt tks; 6 *Shorland*, 150 AML-90 armd
  cars; AMX VCI, Panhard M-3 APC; 22 25-pdr,
  105mm guns; 6–10 AMX 155mm SP how;
  81mm mor; 120mm RCL; *Vigilant* ATGW;
  Rapier, Crotale, RBS-70 SAM.
(In store: 70 *Saladin* armd, 60 *Ferret* scout cars,
  12 *Saracen* APC.)
(On order: 20 *Lion* med, 35 *Scorpion* lt tks.)

Navy: 900.
6 *Jaguar* FAC(G).
6 Vosper Thorneycroft large patrol craft.
3 Keith Nelson coastal patrol craft⟨.
(On order: 10 P-1200 FAC.)

Base: Abu Dhabi.

Air Force: 750; 52 combat aircraft.
2 interceptor sqns with 26 *Mirage* 5AD, 3 5RAD,
  3 5DAD.
1 FGA sqn with 7 *Hunter* FGA-76, 2 T-77.
1 COIN sqn with 10 MB-326KD/LD, 1 SF-260WD.
Tpts incl 2 C-130H, 1 Boeing 720-023B, 1 G-222,
  4 *Islander*, 1 *Falcon*, 3 DHC-4, 4 DHC-5D, 1
  Cessna 182.
Hel incl 4 AB-205, 6 AB-206, 3 AB-212, 7 *Alouette*
  III, 9 *Puma*.
AAM: R-550 *Magic*.
ASM: AS-11/-12.
(On order: 1 G-222 tpt, *Lynx* hel.)

Para-Military Forces: Marine Police; 20 coastal
  patrol boats.

MEMORANDUM FOR THE SECRETARY OF ENERGY
Preparing for an Energy Emergency

SUBJECT: PREPARING FOR AN ENERGY EMERGENCY

There is a fair chance that a significant interruption of international oil supply will occur during your term in office. A sustained interruption of oil imports could devastate the world economy, create havoc in financial markets, and, possibly, lead to armed conflict. This vulnerability of the world to sudden supply curtailment is far more serious than the parallel problem of the continuing economic drain of high oil import payments. Yet, few of our long-term policies such as price decontrol, conservation subsidies and standards, fuel conversions, and synthetic fuel programs will significantly reduce our near-term vulnerability. And, the danger is imminent.

The precise sequence of events leading to a sudden oil supply curtailment cannot be predicted with confidence. Any one of a number of possible scenarios could unfold and it is unlikely that the details would match those envisioned in planned contingency plans. Any real crisis will be clouded by uncertain and incomplete information. It is not profitable, therefore, to develop precise plans for managing the crisis. There are two good ways, however, to prepare the potential crisis managers to deal with the emergency when it comes. First, crisis precipitating events can be imagined and we can speculate on the questions that will be asked, the information that will be sought, and the early decisions that must be made. This "gaming" conveys the flavor of the crisis decision problem and suggests the information and capabilities that will be needed. This leads, secondly, to creating a "Crisis Checklist" of current studies and actions that you may someday wish someone had done.

Crisis: The First Hours

Imagine you are awakened at 4:00 a.m. with reports of a possible interruption of Persian Gulf Oil, e.g., a coup in Kuwait or mines in the Straits of Hormuz. The reports will almost certainly be sketchy. You don't know "who dunnit" or how big an interruption there may be. You run the risk that the actions you recommend can cause panic in domestic or foreign financial and oil markets and thus create a first-order crisis out of what otherwise might turn out to be a minor event.

Your major problem in the first hours will be information — getting it and giving it. Giving out information may be the more urgent problem. If the government speaks with many ill-informed and contradictory voices, the risk of panic increases. When the AP reports a ridiculous statement by some Deputy Assistant Secretary, you will probably wish for a prior Presidential Directive (known to the press) that in the event of a possible energy emergency, all statements will come from the Secretary of Energy as Chairman of the Energy Coordinating Committee (or his designee), or from the White House Press Secretary; and that contraveners will be disciplined. Having a known command and control structure visibly in place in advance will be critical. You should also establish how you are going to inform and involve a few key congressional figures in these early stages.

After activating your command and control structure, what should the Energy Coordinating Committee do first? Most actions will focus on getting and giving out better information; but on one subject, you should act even in the absence of adequate information. Financial markets can react extremely quickly. If you wait to act here, the President may spend the first day trying to cope with a monetary crisis on top of an oil crisis. The ECC (or you) should discuss whether the Secretary of the Treasury and/or the Chairman of the Federal Reserve Board should call their counterparts in a few key countries to arrange joint announcement of special pre-arranged "energy-emergency swaps" designed to prevent panic switching of currencies. (If the situation is clearly severe, it may be necessary to take further financial market measures.)

Your other actions in the early hours will probably focus on what information you should get out to the domestic public; key allies; producer states; the USSR; and perhaps others (e.g., Israel and Egypt?). What should be said in the first official statement? When should the President speak? It would be useful to have key allies designate in advance the points of contact for communication in an energy emergency. Perhaps liaison officials should be flown to Washington. Depending on what we know about the nature of the problem and threats, you will have to decide whether any early messages should be sent to warn about protection of facilities; or to indicate the strength of our interest to the USSR.

Crisis: The First Day

As the first day unfolds, you will be trying to get a better feeling for the possible length and depth of the interruption, and to determine what you can do to limit or repair the damage. It may be several days before it is clear whether you are dealing with a single terrorist event or more complex plans. This period will require coordinating critical input from CIA and other intelligence agencies, State, DOD, DOE, and Treasury. Following are some of the questions you will probably ask them (and which they should start now to be prepared to answer):

Intelligence: Are we dealing with a single act or a series of events? Who are the perpetrators? What evidence exists of Soviet involvement? Have the Soviets changed the status of their military forces or other significant behavior? Will the crisis spread? Is there any sign of participants in another conflict (e.g., Israelis–Palestinians) taking advantage of our distraction to launch a separate crisis? How severe is the disruption of oil supplies likely to be? Do we have a good intelligence on loading facilities? Are other vulnerable spots protected? What are the obstacles to restoring supply or repairing facilities? Is the tanker pipeline on the sea undisturbed? (Have intelligence resources been allocated ahead of the crisis so that the Agency will be able to answer such questions?)

State: What cables have we received from our embassies and other governments? Where do we want to get in with our message first? What are the political costs and benefits of various strategies for restoration and repair? Should there be a high or low U.S. government profile? If repair efforts encountered force, what are the bilateral and multilateral diplomatic steps that should be taken? Are our allies in accord with our early actions? What can they do to help?

Defense: If repairs are necessary, what airlift capacity do we have in place? Has there been adequate advance coordination with DOE and corporations so that key parts and personnel are identified and available? Have the preparations been made for their protection? If mine-sweeping (or some similar specialized military task) can remove the problem, is it readily deployable? What other kinds of military action should be considered?

Energy: What disruptions have occurred in oil markets at home and abroad? What can we do to prevent hoarding? Do we have authority to encourage draw-down of private stocks? How, if at all, should we prepare to use the SPR? What should we do in the IEA? Have there been any significant changes in tanker loadings and movements? What should we ask of the oil companies? What are they likely to ask and how should we reply? Is there anything we have to do to-day from a domestic political point of view? How long will it take for shortages to hit the U.S.? How will we handle domestic political pressures and Congress? Who is helping us from the Hill?

Treasury: What is the condition of the money markets? Are additional steps necessary?

OMB: What extraordinary budgetary authority can be called upon, if necessary, to respond to the crisis?

Crisis: The First Week

As the crisis unfolds, information and surprises multiply. There are too many contingencies for pre-planned scenarios to handle realistically. However, "gaming" or working through some possible surprise scenarios by top officials can be useful forms of preparation.

One question that may be missed deserves attention during the first and following weeks. How would you like things to be at the end of the crisis? Crises are often opportunities for significant change. Do you merely want to restore the status quo ante, or can you take advantage of the situation to bring about improvements in the international oil system or in regional political balances? Some "end-state" planning should be done now, and someone should be adjusting it and looking for opportunities to employ it during the first week. Your end-state planning can affect your choice among tactics.

Preparations and Studies: "Crisis Checklist"

The imagined unfolding of a crisis indicates a number of preparations and studies including constant updating of this "Crisis Checklist."

1. *Establish the command and control structure.* Exercise the structure for energy emergencies. If the group hasn't worked together in advance, it may not work efficiently in the crisis. Discuss procedures and contingencies. Make sure emergency communications channels (and backups) are understood.

2. *Plan congressional involvement.* Identify which Senators and Congressmen (just the leadership?) will be involved early. Discuss procedure and plans for crisis with them now. Plan how other Congressmen will be kept informed.

3. *Establish emergency procedures with allies.* Designate points of contact. Ensure that communications will be rapid. Investigate the possibility of having liaison officers flown to Washington in the early stages. Examine when and how (through the Director? an emergency meeting?) to involve the IEA.

4. *Establish procedures to reassure money markets.* Have the Group of Five quietly discuss procedures for an emergency, including the possibility of announcing special swaps early in the crisis. Study possible further monetary measures.

5. *Examine intelligence tasking under current and emergency conditions.* Insure that resources are being allocated in a manner that will maximize the possibility of getting good answers to the key questions identified above early in a crisis. See if data can be improved to provide early alert of a crisis.

6. *Develop repair capabilities.* Identify custom-built parts and key personnel here and abroad. Discretely arrange for their availability or for appropriate substitutes in time of emergency so that the interruption time is minimized. Ascertain company plans and capabilities. Plan with DOD to assure relevant military capabilities are coordinated with repair capabilities.

7. *Develop plans for handling the oil market.* Have procedures and legal authorization to affect stocks in place. Develop a strategy for using the SPR. Develop a plan for price rises (and tax rebates) as an alternative to rationing. Study when it would be best to use them. Make sure IEA can produce short-term information under emergency conditions. Study what measures can be taken by the U.S. and other countries to diminish panic behavior in the spot market. Study possible uses of the IEA.

8. *Plan for public education about oil threats and crises.* What information would be usefully disseminated in advance? To Congress? To the press? For example, should we be explaining IEA now as an "energy equivalent of NATO?"

9. *Begin "End-State" planning.* Develop plans for where you would want to see the international oil system ending up if an emergency catalyzes a major change.

10. *Develop flexible DOE emergency preparations.* Keep planning flexible. Try exercises that involve top officials and identify the need for further studies or preparations. Try to identify factors that will determine the length and depth of interruptions (e.g., the nature of the threat, repair capabilities, consumer cooperation).

Continually refine this Crisis Checklist!

ABBREVIATIONS
AND ACRONYMS

bbl	barrel
bd	barrels per day
BEPS	Building Energy Performance Standards
Btu	British thermal unit(s)
CAA	Clean Air Act
CIA	U.S. Central Intelligence Agency
CMEA	Council of Mutual Economic Assistance (also known as COMECON)
CPI	Consumer Price Index
DOE	U.S. Department of Energy
EC	European Community
ECPA	Energy Conservation and Production Act of 1976
EEC	European Economic Community
EMR	Ministry of Energy, Mines and Resources, Canadian government
EPCA	Energy Policy and Conservation Act of 1975
ERDA	U.S. Energy Research and Development Administration
EURATOM	European Atomic Energy Community
FEA	U.S. Federal Energy Administration

GDP	gross domestic product
GNP	gross national product
GWe	gigawatt(s) (electric) = 1,000 MWe
ICC	U.S. Interstate Commerce Commission
IEA	International Energy Agency
IMF	International Monetary Fund
kw	kilowatt(s)
kWe or kwe	kilowatt(s) (electric)
kwh	kilowatt-hour(s)
LDC	less-developed country
LNG	liquified natural gas
mbd	million barrels per day
Mcf	thousand cubic feet
MER	maximum efficient rate of recovery
MITI	Ministry of International Trade and Industry, Japanese government
mtoe	million tonnes of oil equivalent
MW	megawatt(s) = 1,000 kw
NATO	North Atlantic Treaty Organization
OECD	Organization for Economic Cooperation and Development
OIDC	oil-importing developing country
OPEC	Organization of Petroleum Exporting Countries
PEMEX	Petroleos Mexicanos
quad	one quadrillion (10^{15}) Btu(s)
RDF	rapid deployment force
R&D	research and development
RD&D	research, development, and demonstration
RDD&D	research, development, demonstration, and deployment
SDR	Special Drawing Rights
SELA	Latin American Economic System
SIP	State Implementation Plan

tcf	one trillion (10^{12}) cubic feet
TPE	total primary energy consumption
UNDP	United Nations Development Program

GLOSSARY

Coal Conversion: Now most commonly used to denote coal gasification and liquefaction. But strictly speaking, any process that transforms coal into a different form of energy (e.g., electricity).

Coal Gas: Low, intermediate, or high Btu content gases produced from coals.

Coal Liquefaction: The conversion of coal into liquid hydrocarbons and related compounds by the addition of hydrogen.

Cogeneration: The generation of electricity with direct use of the residual heat for industrial process heat or for space heating.

Competitive Price: Price of a product or service established in a competitive market.

Constant Dollars: Dollar estimates from which the effects of changes in the general price level have been removed, reported in terms of a base year value.

Creditworthiness: A measure of a country's ability to obtain external financing of its trade deficit, in this case caused by increases in oil prices.

Crude Oil: Mixture of hydrocarbons in liquid phase in natural underground reservoirs which remains liquid after passing through surface-separating facilities. The quality of crude varies from light, which is more easily refined into gasoline and light fuel oils, to the heavier crudes, which are refined into residual fuel oil, bunker oil, sludge, and pitch.

Current Account: In matters of foreign trade, the value of goods and services entering imports and/or exports; excludes capital transactions.

Current Dollars: Dollar values that have not been corrected for changes in the general price level.

Decontrol: Removal of price controls so that supply and demand determine the price of a product. For example, domestic crude oil prices in the United States will be decontrolled in late 1981.

Deficit: A situation when government spending exceeds income so that the capital and current accounts of a country are out of balance.

Dependence: Reliance on imported sources of energy and related technologies and services.

Devaluation: An exchange rate policy to improve the international competitive position of a country that reduces the worth of a country's currency so that imports cost more and exports cost less.

Disruption Tariff: An emergency tariff imposed by an oil-consuming country designed to raise oil prices at the beginning of an interruption; in principle, a way to reduce wealth transfers to OPEC.

Downstream: That part of the petroleum industry that involves refinery, transportation, and marketing operations as contrasted with upstream operations of exploration, development, and production.

Electrical Grid: A net or system that connects a number of power-generating stations and users of electricity (load centers) to permit interchanges and more economical utilization of participating facilities.

Enhanced Oil Recovery: Technology for lifting oil from wells beyond the amount recovered through natural reservoir pressure. Commonly defined to exclude simple methods such as injecting water as a driving force.

Entitlement: A device for allocating the higher cost of imported oil among refiners so that every refiner pays the price for crude he would pay if he purchased it in the proportion between domestic and imported oil that prevails for the industry as a whole.

Ethanol: A colorless, volatile, flammable liquid of the chemical formula C_2H_5OH, which is found in fermented and distilled liquors; also made from petroleum hydrocarbons.

Eurocurrency (Xenocurrency): A balance expressed in a currency held in a bank outside the territory of the nation issuing the currency: originally applied to deposits held in European banks, but now widely used in the generic sense.

Federal Pre-emption: The right granted to the federal government by the Constitution to supersede state or local laws that are in conflict with federal laws or regulations.

Gasohol: Refers either to alcohol derived from an organic material (grain, sugar, waste, etc.) or to a mixture of such alcohol with gasoline, both intended as motor fuel.

Gross Domestic Product: Equals Gross National Product, diminished by net factor income originating in foreign enterprises and investment.

Gross National Product: Aggregate value of goods and services produced in a national economy.

Heavy Oil: Crude oil of such low viscosity (usually 15 percent or less) that it does not flow freely enough to be lifted from a reservoir reached by the drill.

Illiquidity: The situation where a country does not have sufficient funds, in this case to finance oil.

Infrastructure: The underlying or associated foundation or basic framework required to utilize a given product or service (as of a system or organization).

Interties: The connecting links among major electric power grids.

Kola Peninsula: Russian territory located near the Arctic Circle which is vital to Soviet strategic interests. The port of Murmansk is on the Kola Peninsula.

Lignite: The lowest rank coal with low heat content and fixed carbon and with high percentage of volatile matter and moisture; an early stage in the formation of coal.

Load: The amount of energy or electric power required of an energy system during any specified period of time and at any specified location or locations.

Load Factor: The annual average output of a utility system divided by its maximum potential output.

Majors: Generally, the vertically integrated, international oil companies—Standard of California (SOCAL), Mobil, Texaco, Exxon (the four partners in Aramco, the producer of Saudi Arabia's oil), Gulf, British Petroleum, and Royal Dutch Shell. Often the term "majors" includes a number of large domestic U.S.-based companies such as Occidental Petroleum or European companies such as France's Elf Acquitaine.

Marginal Cost Pricing: Charging users for all units consumed at that rate that corresponds to the cost of the final unit that needs to be supplied to meet demand. Sometimes referred to as "incremental" pricing.

Megawatt: The unit by which the capacity of production of electricity is usually measured. A megawatt is a million watts or a thousand kilowatts.

Oil Premium: The opportunity costs and benefits adjusted to reflect the likelihood of a supply interruption, which indicate the difference between the true costs of oil imports and the price on the world oil market.

Oil Shale: Rock containing organic matter (kerogen) that, upon being heated to 800 to 1,000° F, yields commercially useful oil and/or gas.

Oil Stocks: These may be grouped into five categories:

Operating Stocks (also called working or commercial stocks): crude oil product required for the operation of the oil industry from the wellhead to the customer in order to maintain the continuous flow of crude to the refineries, to guarantee the uninterrupted processing of crude, and to maintain the product distribution network.

Strategic Stocks (also called obligatory or compulsory stocks): intended to provide a security element in the case of major supply disruptions. Government regulations may require that minimum stock levels be held by industry or by the government in government-owned stockpiles such as the U.S. Strategic Petroleum Reserve located in salt domes in Louisiana and Texas.

Seasonal Stocks: required for oil products with a demand that varies throughout the year.

Consumer Stocks (also called tertiary stocks):   range from gasoline in car tanks and heating oil in storage tanks to the quantities held by industry and utilities.

Stocks at Sea and Stocks in Bonded Areas: in transit on either land or water that have not yet cleared customs.

Primary Energy: Energy before processing or conversion into different or more refined form.

Quota: A trade barrier that physically limits the quantity of a product entering a country.

Reprocessing: The chemical and mechanical processes by which plutonium–239 and the unused uranium–235 are recovered from spent reactor fuel.

Reserves: Resources well identified as to location and size and commercially producible at current prices and with current technology.

Salt Dome: A subterranean geologic formation frequently associated with the occurrence of oil and/or gas; after original hydrocarbon material has been withdrawn, it can be used for storage of oil or gas.

Saudi Marker Crude: A quality of light crude oil, with 34° viscosity, used as the basic reference material for determining differential prices for other types of oil.

Spot Price: Price formed in a market for one-time (usually quick) delivery of a specific cargo and destination. In times of stringency, spot market prices can greatly exceed prices for identical products sold under long-term contracts.

Surge Production Capacity: Excess oil production capacity that can be put into operation to meet emergency demands. For example, Saudi Arabia's surge capacity made up for the loss of Iranian production in 1979.

Surrogates: Clients of a major power which, armed by that power, represent it in armed conflicts in a third country. For example, Cuban soldiers stood for the Soviet Union in Angola.

Synthetic Fuels: A term now commonly reserved for liquid and gaseous fuels that are the product of a conversion process rather than mining or drilling; most frequently applied to cover liquids or gases derived from coal, shale, tar sands, waste, biomass.

Tar Sands: Also known as bituminous sands; unconsolidated sands permeated with bitumen, subject to surface mining and refining, and produced in commercial-sized installations in Canada.

Term Oil: Oil sold under contract at the official price plus a premium.

Terms of Trade: A measure of change over time in the ratio of export prices to import prices; used to judge changing advantage in foreign trade.

Val: A Soviet planning term where efficiency is measured in terms of gross output. This approach has been replaced by a system of net normative output, where premiums are based on "value added" to production.

Vulnerability: The expected damage from a supply interruption which has economic, political, and foreign policy implications.

Wellhead Tax: A tax imposed on oil (or gas) at the top of the production well.

Wheeling: A form of fuel switching to electricity generated by coal and nuclear plants to displace oil.

Windfall Profits Tax: A tax imposed so that the government rather than the oil companies receives some of rent realized from a rise in oil prices.

INDEX

ABOUT THE EDITORS

David A. Deese is a Research Fellow and Assistant to the Director at the Center for Science and International Affairs. He also directs the Energy and Security Research Project and teaches in the John F. Kennedy School of Government. After serving four years as a naval officer, including two years with the U.S. Sixth Fleet and with NATO, he took his M.A. (1975), M.A.L.D. (1976) and Ph.D. (1977) at the Fletcher School of Law and Diplomacy at Tufts University. His early articles and first books, *Nuclear Power and Radioactive Waste* and *Nuclear Nonproliferation: The Spent Fuel Problem* (co-edited with Frederick C. Williams) probed the response of international politics and institutions to problems posed by science and technology. His research and teaching focus on international political economy, U.S. and international security, and U.S. foreign policy. He has been an expert advisor to the Institute of International Studies at the University of California, Berkeley; MIT; the U.S. Arms Control and Disarmament Agency; the U.S. Congress, Office of Technology Assessment; and International Energy Associates, Limited.

Joseph S. Nye is Professor of Government at the John F. Kennedy School of Government and the Center for International Affairs (CFIA) and an Associate Member of the Center for Science and

International Affairs. From January 1977 to January 1979, he was Deputy to the Under Secretary of State for Security Assistance, Science and Technology, and chaired the National Security Council Group on Non-Proliferation of Nuclear Weapons. Upon his departure, Secretary Cyrus Vance awarded him the highest Department of State commendation, the Distinguished Honor Award. Mr. Nye is a member of the Commission on International Relations of the National Academy of Sciences, and has served as Chairman of the Research Advisory Committee for Economic Development. He was a member of the Ford Foundation's Nuclear Energy Policy Study. A member of the editorial boards of *Foreign Policy* and *International Organization*, he is the author of many articles in professional journals. His most recent book is *Power and Interdependence* (co-authored with Robert Keohane).

ABOUT THE CONTRIBUTORS

Alvin L. Alm is a Research Fellow of the Energy and Environmental Policy Center, a participant in the Energy and Security Research Project, and Program Director at the Aspen Institute for Humanistic Studies, Committee on Energy. He maintains a key interest in the development of new policy capabilities and policy responses for meeting the problems of energy emergencies. Mr. Alm's professional experience includes positions as the Assistant Secretary for Policy and Evaluation of the Department of Energy, Assistant Administrator for Planning and Management of the Environmental Protection Agency, and Staff Director of the Council on Environmental Quality.

E. William Colglazier is a former research physicist who now works on public policy issues connected with science and technology. He is a Research Fellow at the Center for Science and International Affairs at Harvard University and Associate Director of the Aspen Institute Program in Science, Technology and Humanism. He received his Ph.D. from the California Institute of Technology and has worked at the Stanford Linear Acceleration Center and the Institute for Advanced Study in Princeton. In 1976–77, he was a Congressional Science Fellow sponsored by the American Association for the Advancement of Science.

Marshall I. Goldman is Associate Director of the Russian Research Center, Harvard University and Professor of Economics at Wellesley College. He is the author of *The Enigma of Soviet Petroleum: Half Empty or Half Full* (1980), and *Detente and Dollars: Doing Business with the Soviets* (1975).

Fen Hampson is a doctoral candidate in the Department of Government, Harvard University. He is a graduate of the University of Toronto and the London School of Economics. His current interests are energy policies in Canada and Mexico.

William W. Hogan is a Professor of Political Economy and Director of the Energy and Environmental Policy Center at Harvard University's John F. Kennedy School of Government. Prior to joining the John F. Kennedy School in 1978, he was a member of the Departments of Engineering-Economic Systems and Operations Research at Stanford University. While at Stanford, he founded the Energy Modeling Forum and served as its first Executive Director, coordinating comparative analyses of the use of energy models as applied to policy analysis in the Federal Energy Administration, first as the Director of the Office of Quantitative Methods and subsequently as the Deputy Assistant Administrator for Data and Analysis (1974–1976). He is the Energy/Environment editor of *Operations Research*, and is involved in various research activities in the development and application of energy and environmental policy models.

Barbara Kates-Garnick is a researcher at the Center for Science and International Affairs at Harvard University and a Ph.D. candidate at the Fletcher School of Law and Diplomacy at Tufts University. Her recent work examines the prospects for a future international energy regime from the perspective of the industrial oil-consuming nations. She has served in local government and has been a consultant to the Department of Energy and several state energy offices.

Geoffrey Kemp is an Associate Professor of International Politics at the Fletcher School of Law and Diplomacy at Tufts University. He was born in England and was educated at Oxford University. He received his Ph.D. in Political Science from the Massachusetts Institute of Technology. He has written extensively on arms transfers, defense policy, and strategy for the newly industrialized countries, and on Middle East military affairs.

Linda B. Miller is Professor of Political Science at Wellesley College and Adjunct Research Fellow, Center for Science and International Affairs, Harvard University. She is the author of *World Order and Total Disorder* (1967) and *Dynamics of World Politics* (1968) and has written extensively on American foreign policy, European politics, international organization, and energy problems for a variety of U.S., British, and European journals. She has taught and done research at Harvard, Princeton, and Columbia University and held fellowships at the Council on Foreign Relations and the Rockefeller Foundation.

Kevin J. Middlebrook is an associate of the Center for International Affairs at Harvard University. In January 1981, he will join the Department of Political Science, Indiana University–Bloomington. His research interests include the domestic and foreign policies of Mexico and other Latin American nations.

Thomas L. Neff is Principal Research Scientist and Manager of the International Energy Studies Program at MIT's Energy Laboratory. His primary research interests are in the economic and political dimensions of international energy trade—with special emphasis on oil and nuclear fuels—and in the financial and institutional impacts of the massive wealth transfers associated with energy trade. He has served as an expert advisor to the State Department, the Arms Control and Disarmament Agency, and the Office of Science and Technology Policy.

Gary Samore is an associate of the Center for Science and International Affairs at Harvard University, where he analyzes internal, regional, and international threats to Persian Gulf oil and appropriate American responses to these threats. He is also a Teaching Fellow and Ph.D. candidate in the Department of Government at Harvard University. His recent work examines the changing patterns of American interests and strategies in the Persian Gulf.

Philip K. Verleger is a senior research scholar at the School of Management, Yale University. He has served as a senior staff economist on the President's Council of Economic Advisers and in the capacity of Special Assistant for Energy Matters at the U.S. Treasury.